D1592634

# GERMAN STRATEGY
# AGAINST RUSSIA
## 1939–1941

# GERMAN STRATEGY
# AGAINST RUSSIA
## 1939-1941

---

BARRY A. LEACH

OXFORD
AT THE CLARENDON PRESS
1973

*Oxford University Press, Ely House, London W. 1*

GLASGOW  NEW YORK  TORONTO  MELBOURNE  WELLINGTON
CAPE TOWN  IBADAN  NAIROBI  DAR ES SALAAM  LUSAKA  ADDIS ABABA
DELHI  BOMBAY  CALCUTTA  MADRAS  KARACHI  LAHORE  DACCA
KUALA LUMPUR  SINGAPORE  HONG KONG  TOKYO

*Printed in Great Britain*
*at the University Press, Oxford*
*by Vivian Ridler*
*Printer to the University*

*To Laurence*
*who encouraged*
*and to Dorothea*
*who sustained*
*this study*

# PREFACE

THIS work owes much to many people to whom I wish to express my sincere thanks. It began in 1953 when Colonel H. C. Slessor of the British Army encouraged me to use the results of my correspondence with Field-Marshal von Rundstedt and discussions with many former officers and men of the Wehrmacht as an operational study of the German campaign in Russia for use at the Staff College, Camberley. In 1962 Professor John S. Conway of the University of British Columbia suggested that this study might form the basis of an analysis of German leadership in the Second World War with particular reference to the relationship between Hitler's policies and German strategy in the East. Generous grants from the Department of History, the University of British Columbia, and the Canada Council made it possible for me to take up this suggestion.

Throughout the period of research and writing, Professors Robert C. Walton and L. E. Hill have, by their advice and guidance, encouraged a critical assessment of the mass of material on this subject which has become available since the war. Though I have not always agreed with their interpretation of events, Field-Marshal Erich von Manstein, Colonel-General Franz Halder, General of Panzer Troops Freiherr Geyr von Schweppenburg, General of Artillery Walter Warlimont, Lieutenant-General Curt Siewert, Lieutenant-General Burckhart Müller-Hillebrand, and Major-General Alfred Philippi have in discussions and correspondence provided great stimulus to this study and valuable insights into the methods and attitudes of the German officer corps. I am also indebted to Professor Dr. Hans-Adolf Jacobsen of the University of Bonn, Professor Dr. Andreas Hillgruber of the University of Freiburg, and Professor Charles Burdick of San José State College, California, for their kindness in giving me their advice and hospitality during my research.

I wish to express my appreciation to Mr. George E. Blau of the Special Studies Division, Office of the Chief of Military History, United States Army, Heidelberg, Dr. A. Hoch of the *Institut für Zeitgeschichte*, Munich, Colonel Forwick of the *Bundesarchiv-Militärarchiv*, Freiburg, Lieutenant-Colonel Elbele of the *Militär-geschichtliches Forschungsamt*, Freiburg, Professor E. M. Robertson of the University of Edinburgh, Mr. Lev Besymenski of Moscow, and Mr. Hans Burndorfer of the Library of the University of British Columbia, who have helped me to obtain much of the essential source material for this study. My thanks are also due to my wife for her constant aid in translating and typing.

*Institute of International Studies*                    BARRY LEACH
*Douglas College*
*British Columbia*
*1972*

# CONTENTS

# LIST OF PLATES

(between pp. 168 and 169)

(Photographs by courtesy of General Curt Siewert and International Video Applications)

# LIST OF MAPS

# NOTE ON ABBREVIATIONS, TITLES, AND GERMAN WORDS USED IN THE TEXT

OKW    *Oberkommando der Wehrmacht,*
High Command of the Armed Forces.

OKH    *Oberkommando des Heeres,*
High Command of the Army.

OKM    *Oberkommando der Kriegsmarine,*
High Command of the Navy.

OKL    *Oberkommando der Luftwaffe,*
High Command of the Air Force.

The phrase 'the Army leaders' refers to the Commander-in-Chief and the Chief of the General Staff.

The various ranks between Major-General and Colonel-General are abbreviated to 'General'.

Formation titles are capitalized and given in the following form in the text:

| *Army* | *Air Force* |
|---|---|
| Army Group 'North' | Air Fleet 2 |
| 18th Army | |
| Panzer Group 4 | |
| XXXVIII Army Corps | VIII Air Corps |
| 4th Infantry Division | |

German words are used where there is no exact English equivalent (e.g. *Oberquartiermeister*) or where they carry a greater significance than their literal translation (e.g. *Lebensraum*). Where a German appointment has a British counterpart involving similar duties (e.g. *Generalquartiermeister*, Quartermaster-General) the English term is used.

# ABBREVIATIONS USED IN THE FOOTNOTES

| | |
|---|---|
| *DGFP*(D) | *Documents on German Foreign Policy, 1918–1945, from the Archives of the German Foreign Ministry*, Series D (13 vols.; Washington, 1949). |
| FCNA | 'Fuehrer Conferences on Naval Affairs, 1939–1945', *Brassey's Naval Annual* (London/New York, 1948), pp. 25–496. |
| *FNC* | *Fuehrer Conferences on Matters Dealing with the German Navy, 1939 to 1945.* Translated and issued by the U.S. Navy Department (9 vols.; Washington, 1946–7). |
| *Halder KTB* | Hans-Adolf Jacobsen (ed.), *Generaloberst Halder: Kriegstagebuch* (3 vols.; Stuttgart, 1963). |
| *IMT* | *Trial of the Major War Criminals before the International Military Tribunal* (42 vols.; Nuremberg, 1947). |
| *KTB OKW* i | Hans-Adolf Jacobsen (ed.), *Kriegstagebuch des Oberkommandos der Wehrmacht* (*Wehrmachtführungsstab*), *1. August 1940–31. Dezember 1941*, Vol. I of *Kriegstagebuch des Oberkommandos der Wehrmacht* (*Wehrmachtführungsstab*), *1940–1945*, General editor, Percy Ernst Schramm (4 vols.; Frankfurt a. M., 1961–5). |
| *MK* | Adolf Hitler, *Mein Kampf*, trans. James Murphy (London, 1939). |
| *NCA* | *Nazi Conspiracy and Aggression* (10 vols.; Washington, 1946). |
| *NSR* | Raymond J. Sontag and James S. Beddie (eds.), *Nazi-Soviet Relations 1939–1941, from the Archives of the German Foreign Office* (Washington, 1948). |
| U.S.N.A. | United States National Archives and Records Service and American Historical Association Committee for the Study of War Documents, Microcopies of German Documents. |
| *VfZ* | *Vierteljahrshefte für Zeitgeschichte.* |
| *WR* | *Wehrwissenschaftliche Rundschau.* |
| *ZfG* | *Zeitschrift für Geschichtswissenschaft.* |

# INTRODUCTION

IN this study of German strategic planning for the eastern campaign
I have endeavoured to answer four questions. Did Hitler follow a
great preconceived plan? Why did he decide to invade Russia before
ending the war against Britain? What role did the German military
leaders play in planning the invasion of Russia? Why did the *Blitzkrieg* fail in Russia?

The best-known debate among British historians on Hitler's aims
and plans focused mainly upon the events leading up to the Second
World War. A. J. P. Taylor and E. M. Robertson asserted that the
policy statements made by Hitler in *Mein Kampf* had little relevance
to his foreign policy in practice.[1] This view was challenged by Hugh
R. Trevor-Roper who saw in Hitler's early writings 'a programme of
Eastern Colonisation entailing a war of conquest against Russia'.[2]
The views of British and American historians have been similarly
divided over Hitler's wartime policy. One group has regarded the
decision to attack Russia as the act of an opportunist recoiling from
failure in the West.[3] The other has described it as part of a policy of

[1] See A. J. P. Taylor, *Origins of the Second World War* (London, 1964), p. 98.
In Taylor's opinion 'Statesmen are too absorbed by events to follow a preconceived plan . . . [Hitler's] systems were day-dreams . . . the generalisations of
a powerful, but uninstructed, intellect.' See also E. M. Robertson, *Hitler's Pre-
War Policy and Military Plans: 1933–1939* (London, 1963), pp. x, 1–4. Robertson
asserted that 'Hitler seldom looked more than one move ahead; and the view
that he had tried to put into operation a programme, carefully formulated in
advance, is quite untenable . . .' (p. 1). See also E. M. Robertson (ed.), *The Origins
of the Second World War* (London, 1971), in which the major critical articles
provoked by Taylor's work are brought together. In editing this collection
Robertson modifies his own interpretation of Hitler's policy.

[2] Hugh R. Trevor-Roper, 'A. J. P. Taylor, Hitler and the War', *Encounter*, 17
(July, 1961), 91. Also reprinted in John L. Snell (ed.), *Outbreak of the Second
World War: Design or Blunder?* (Boston, 1962), pp. 88–97. T. W. Mason, 'Some
Origins of the Second World War', *Past and Present*, 29 (1964), 67–87, also
criticizes Taylor's work on the grounds that it 'is not informed by any con-
ception of the distinctive character and role of National Socialism. . .' (p. 68).

[3] John Strawson, *Hitler as Military Commander* (London, 1971), pp. 114, 119,
131 ff. See also F. H. Hinsley, *Hitler's Strategy* (Cambridge, 1961), p. 124 ff.;
Gerald Reitlinger, *The House Built on Sand, Conflicts of German Policy in Russia,
1939–1945* (London, 1960), pp. 10–11. Reitlinger's view that the chaos and improvisations of the German administration in Russia were hardly compatible
with a great preconceived plan was welcomed by A. J. P. Taylor, who stated

B

eastern expansion 'from which Hitler had never wavered since he wrote *Mein Kampf*'.[1]

A similar division of opinion between historians of East and West Germany has been sharpened by its relevance to the Cold War and to the origins of the situation in which the Germans have found themselves since the war. This historiographical battle was opened by the German generals who in testimonies, interviews, histories, and memoirs claimed that though Hitler dominated the higher direction of the war, he lacked the strategic training and ability to develop and follow a consistent war plan.[2] Many of them viewed the invasion of Russia as a preventive war by which Hitler sought with one blow to avert the consequences of the political and military mistakes made in 1939 when he encouraged Soviet expansion westward and involved Germany in a war with Great Britain which she was unable to conclude.[3] They also blamed Hitler's bungling interference for the subsequent failure of the campaign in Russia.[4]

East German historians and their Soviet colleagues strongly condemned these interpretations as a blatant attempt by the 'Fascist' generals to revive militarism in West Germany by freeing their caste from responsibility for the crimes and failures of Nazi aggression.[5]

that 'Hitler, it seems clear, had no defined aim when he attacked Russia except victory for its own sake. He simply wanted to win another war.' Review of *The House Built on Sand* by Gerald Reitlinger in the *Observer*, 13 Mar., 1960. See also Taylor, *Origins*, p. 24.

[1] Alan Bullock, *Hitler: A Study in Tyranny* (London, 1962), p. 594; see also pp. 574, 597–8, 622. Hugh R. Trevor-Roper, Introduction, *Hitler's War Directives, 1939–1945* (London, 1964), pp. xii–xvii; Albert Seaton, *The Russo-German War, 1941–45* (London, 1971), p. 24; Alexander Dallin, *The German Rule in Russia* (London, 1957), pp. 7 ff.; John R. Bengtson, *Nazi War Aims:The Plans for the Thousand Year Reich* (Augustana, 1962), pp. 11–12, 16 ff.; Ihor Kamenetsky, *Secret Nazi Plans for Eastern Europe, A Study of Lebensraumpolitik* (New York, 1961), pp. 32, 33–5; William L. Shirer, *The Rise and Fall of the Third Reich* (New York, 1962), p. 1044. All of these works link Hitler's decision to attack Russia with his statements on foreign policy in *Mein Kampf*.

[2] Erich von Manstein, *Lost Victories*, trans. Antony G. Powell (London, 1958), pp. 154, 169; Franz Halder, *Hitler as Warlord*, trans. Paul Findlay (London, 1950), pp. 17, 22 ff.; Peter Bor, *Gespräche mit Halder* (Wiesbaden, 1950), p. 199; B. H. Liddell Hart, *On the Other Side of the Hill* (London, 1951), pp. 468–9.

[3] See Bor, p. 195; Walter Görlitz (ed.), *Keitel, Verbrecher oder Offizier?* (Göttingen, 1961), p. 245; Manstein, pp. 181–2.

[4] See Kurt Dittmar, Introduction to Karlheinrich Rieker, *Ein Mann verliert einen Weltkrieg* (Frankfurt a. M., 1955), pp. 5, 8.

[5] See Andreas Hillgruber and Hans-Adolf Jacobsen, Introduction to Boris S. Telpuchowski, *Die sowjetische Geschichte des Großen Vaterländischen Krieges, 1941–1945*, trans. Robert Frhr. von Freytag-Loringhoven *et al.* (Frankfurt a. M., 1961), pp. 51E, 54–5E. See also P. A. Nikolaev, 'Versuche zur Rehabilitierung des

They countered with works which depicted the German attack as
the ultimate step in an aggressive, expansionist plan conceived, not
by Hitler alone, but by the 'monopoly capitalists and militarists'
behind him.[1] They pointed out that the decision to strike eastwards
was made immediately after the fall of France, and that German
operations against Britain across the Channel and in the Mediterranean were mere side-shows.[2] Furthermore, they attributed the
failure of the campaign in Russia not to Hitler's interference nor
to the material weaknesses in the Wehrmacht but to the political,
social, and economic solidarity of the Soviet people and the inevitable
triumph of Socialism.[3]

In 1965 a Soviet historian Aleksandr Nekrich attempted to depart
from the established interpretation of the origins and initial phase
of the Great Patriotic War.[4] He refused to belittle the diplomatic
and military mistakes made by Stalin in 1941 merely because the
Soviet Union was ultimately victorious. To do so, he warned, would
be a disservice to the State suggesting 'incorrect conclusions from
the lessons taught us by history'.[5] This new approach caused such
concern in Russia that the Department for the History of the Great
Fatherland War of the Marxist-Leninist Institute called a meeting
in Moscow on 6 February 1966 to discuss it.[6] Although there were

deutschen Militarismus in der modernen bürgerlichen Historiographie', *ZfG* 10
(1962), 50.

[1] Telpuchowski, pp. 64–5E. See also Hans Höhn (ed.), *Auf antisowjetischem
Kriegskurs. Studien zur militärischen Vorbereitung des deutschen Imperialismus auf
die Aggression gegen die UdSSR (1933–1941)* (Berlin, 1970); Johannes Zuckertort,
'Der deutsche Militarismus und die Legende vom Präventivkrieg Hitler deutsch-
lands gegen die Sowjetunion', *Der deutsche Imperialismus und der Zweite Weltkrieg.
Materialien der Wissenschaftlichen Konferenz der Historiker der DDR und der
UdSSR, 14.–19. Dezember 1959 in Berlin* (Berlin, 1960–3), I. 145 ff.; Gerhard Hass,
'Hans-Adolf Jacobsens Konzeption einer Geschichte des Zweiten Weltkrieges',
*ZfG* 12 (1965), 1163; P. Zhilin, 'Military History and Modern Times', *Soviet
Military Review*, 10 (1966), 37–8; Lev Besymenski, *Sonderakte Barbarossa* (Stutt-
gart, 1968).

[2] V. Ryabov, 'Reflections on the Past War', *Soviet Military Review*, 6 (1966),
35. See also Gerhard Förster, Olaf Groehler, Günther Paulus, 'Zum Verhältnis
von Kriegszielen und Kriegsplanung des faschistischen deutschen Imperialismus'
*ZfG* 22 (1964), 943–5.

[3] See Zhilin, pp. 36–8; Hass, pp. 1158–9; Besymenski, pp. 270–1.

[4] Alekandr M. Nekrich, *1941, 22 iyunya* (Moscow, 1965). See also the English
translation in Vladimir Petrov, *June 22, 1941: Soviet Historians and the German
Invasion* (Columbia, S.C., 1968), pp. 33–245.

[5] Ibid., p. 4. See also Daniel R. Brower, 'The Soviet Union and the German
Invasion of 1941: A New Soviet View', *The Journal of Modern History*, 40, 3
(1969), 327–34.                          [6] See Petrov, pp. 250–61.

heated arguments in the course of the meeting, none of the speakers was willing to oppose the publication of Nekritch's book. Nevertheless, attacks on Stalin have diminished since then, and in the study *Sonderakte Barbarossa*, published in 1968, Lev Besymenski devoted much effort to justify Stalin's policies in the period 1939–41.

It was significant that special efforts were made to have Besymenski's book published in West Germany for it was there that a school of military historians had worked throughout the 1960s to resolve some of the conflicts between the extremes of the Communist and German apologist interpretations.[1] They rejected the 'legend of preventive war' and agreed that the German motive was aggressive expansionism.[2] But they did not accept completely the idea that the decision to attack Russia was the result of a preconceived plan. They presented it rather as a desperate strategic expedient by which Hitler attempted to cut the 'Gordian knot' of the military, political, and economic problems resulting from the inconclusive nature of the campaign in the West and the *ad hoc* strategy followed between August and November 1940.[3]

Much of the disagreement between these various schools on the question of whether Hitler followed long-term plans can be reduced to differences of opinion on what constitutes a plan. A. J. P. Taylor, for instance, regards a plan as 'something which is prepared and worked out in detail'.[4] He rejects most of Hitler's writings and statements as 'daydreams . . . the generalisations of a powerful but uninstructed intellect'.[5] Similarly, many of the former German officers and the archivists of the Wehrmacht who now occupy an influential place in the West German school of military history tend to regard Hitler's rambling writings and speeches about *Lebensraum* as too vague and fantastic to be accepted as the basis of a war plan or a grand strategy.[6]

[1] The leading historians of this school were Percy Ernst Schramm, Hans-Adolf Jacobsen, Andreas Hillgruber, and Walter Hubatsch. Their approach to the historiography of the Second World War was indicated in Hans-Adolf Jacobsen, 'The Second World War as a Problem in Historical Research', *World Politics*, 16 (July 1964), 620–41. See also 'Die amtliche militärgeschichtliche Forschung in Westdeutschland', *ZfG* 10 (1962), 1669–71.

[2] Jacobsen, 'The Second World War . . .', p. 631. See also Görlitz, *Keitel*, p. 245; Andreas Hillgruber, *Hitlers Strategie, Politik und Kriegsführung, 1940–1941* (Frankfurt a. M., 1965), p. 533.

[3] *Halder KTB* ii, p. viii; *KTB OKW* i. 67E. See also Walter Hubatsch and Percy E. Schramm, *Die deutsche militärische Führung in der Kriegswende* (Cologne/Opladen, 1964), pp. 73–5.     [4] Taylor, *Origins*, p. 24.     [5] Ibid., p. 98.

[6] See *KTB OKW* i. 42E; Manstein, p. 154; Rudolf Bogatsch, 'Politische und

However, the most important consideration is not whether the soldiers or post-war historians consider the ideas of *Mein Kampf* to constitute a plan, but whether Hitler did so himself. His attitude on this subject was clear. In *Mein Kampf* he criticized the foreign policies of the Kaiser's Empire and of the German Republic for their lack of any planned approach to the problems confronting the nation.[1] In his second book he was even more emphatic and warned that if Germany failed to define a clear foreign policy, 'aimlessness on a large scale will cause planlessness in particulars. This planlessness will gradually turn us into a second Poland in Europe.'[2] The pursuit of a fixed political goal which he advocated in the subsequent pages was intended to prevent such a fate, and thus was evidently regarded by Hitler as a plan.

He was not without justification. For planning does not need to conform to rigid procedures, nor does it have to involve detail. Indeed, planning in the realm of long-term policy and strategy can seldom include detail since flexibility is essential to deal with unforeseeable opportunities.[3] Hitler sought to combine such flexibility with clarity of purpose, to use opportunist methods for the attainment of a fixed goal. He regarded this as a revival of Bismarck's techniques, which he described as

. . . a mastery of specific momentary situations with an eye on a visualized political aim . . .

In pursuit of this aim Bismarck utilized every opportunity and worked through the diplomatic art as long as it promised success; he threw the sword into the scales if force alone was in a position to bring about a decision.[4]

militärische Probleme nach dem Frankreichfeldzug', *Vollmacht des Gewissens* (2 vols.; Frankfurt a. M./Berlin, 1965), ii. 28 ff.

[1] *MK*, pp. 521-2. See also Werner Maser, *Hitlers Mein Kampf* (Munich, 1966), p. 177.

[2] Adolf Hitler, *Hitler's Secret Book*, trans. Salvator Attanasio (New York, 1961), p. 143.

[3] See Maurice Matloff and Edwin M. Snell, *Strategic Planning for Coalition Warfare, 1941-1942* (Washington, 1953), p. ix. 'National planning in this field [of strategy] extends from the simple statement of risks and choices to the full analysis of an immense undertaking. Strategic decisions are rarely made and military operations are rarely conducted precisely in the terms worked out by the planning staffs . . .' See also George A. Morgan, 'Planning in Foreign Affairs: The State of the Art', *Foreign Affairs*, 39, 2 (Jan. 1961), p. 271, 'Planning is thinking ahead with a view to action.'

[4] Hitler, *Secret Book*, p. 53. See also *MK*, p. 558; Alan Bullock, 'Hitler and the Origins of the Second World War', in Robertson (ed.), *The Origins of the Second World War*, p. 193.

On 20 July 1937 he stated in a public speech

I don't need to assure you that a man who has succeeded in rising from
an unknown soldier of the World War to be Führer of the nation will also
succeed in solving the coming problems. No one may doubt my determination also to realize, by one means or another [so oder so] my preconceived
plans.[1]

The last sentence again implied the combination of preconception
of aim, with flexibility of method. But Hitler's flexibility was reduced
as he came nearer to the achievement of his major aims. He then
had cause to regret the clarity with which they had been expressed in
Mein Kampf. In spite of the pragmatism and opportunism of his
methods, his enemies' prior knowledge of his Lebensraumpolitik
threatened to deprive him of the element of surprise so essential
to his policy. He attempted to draw a veil of deception across his
actions. He stated that large parts of Mein Kampf were 'no longer
valid', and admitted that 'he should not have let himself be pinned
down to definite statements so early.'[2] Nazi policy releases were
deliberately vague and special stress was laid on avoiding a definition
of aims which 'immediately brings us enemies and increases the
opposition'.[3] But in spite of the confusion which Hitler's vagueness
and deceptions have since caused among historians, they could not
completely conceal his intentions. As he lost the psychological
advantage gained from the uncertainty, disunity, and material weakness of his opponents his choice of methods became more restricted.
The aims and the rigidity that characterized them, came more and
more to determine the choice of action. Obstacles, which could no
longer be evaded by bluff and deception, were to be overcome by
efforts of will. Thus planning became unbalanced and unrealistic.

In this study the process of planning is regarded as comprising
three stages: the critical analysis of the situation; the definition of
aims; and the selection and organization of the means by which the
aims are attained. Since the executors do not require the first stage,
the final plan embodies the last two stages. The last stage may not be
fully completed until circumstances present a favourable opportunity
or demand for the implementation of the plan.

[1] Max Domarus, Hitler, Reden und Proklamationen, 1932–1945 (2 vols.;
Würzburg, 1962), i. 42.
[2] Albert Speer, Inside the Third Reich, trans. Richard and Clara Winston (New
York, 1970), p. 122.
[3] Hans-Adolf Jacobsen, Der Zweite Weltkrieg, Grundzüge der Politik und
Strategie in Dokumenten (Frankfurt a. M., 1965), p. 181. See also KTB OKW i. 90E.

Strategic planning cannot be restricted to purely military terms, because it is conducted at two levels, grand strategic and military strategic. Grand strategy, which the Germans called *Wehrpolitik* or military policy, is the co-ordination and direction of 'all resources of a nation, or band of nations towards the attainment of the political object of the war—the goal defined by national policy'.[1] Thus grand strategy comprises political and economic considerations as well as military ones. Pure or military strategy, which was known in the Wehrmacht as *Kriegsführung*—'war direction' or 'military leadership', is 'the art of distributing and applying military means to fulfil the ends of policy'.[2] But even here ideas which fail to conform to procedures and jargon of military institutions should not be excluded. In the 1930s Hitler showed far greater understanding of many of the psychological and technological factors influencing military strategy than most of the professional soldiers who, he complained, had made war 'into a secret science . . . surrounded with momentous solemnity'.[3] Nevertheless, he admitted the need for an officer corps to conduct the mechanical task of converting military strategic thought into systems and procedures,[4] plans and orders culminating in military action: operations, or the deployment and movement of forces; and tactics, or the employment of weapons in fighting.

To trace the development of German planning for the eastern campaign from its political origin through the levels of grand and military strategy I have first re-examined the policy statements on this topic made by Hitler in *Mein Kampf*, in his second book which was published only after the war, in his conversations as recorded by Hermann Rauschning and Martin Bormann,[5] and in his speeches,

[1] Basil H. Liddell Hart, *Strategy* (New York, 1954), pp. 335–6.
[2] Ibid., p. 335.
[3] Hermann Rauschning, *Hitler Speaks* (London, 1939), p. 16.
[4] The usual stages of German military planning were: (1) the memorandum (*Denkschrift*), (2) the operational study (*Operationsstudie*), (3) the draft plan (*Operationsentwurf*), (4) the command exercise or war game (*Kriegsspiel*), (5) the deployment directive or plan (*Aufmarschanweisung*).
[5] The authenticity of Rauschning's work is confirmed by comparison between his account of Hitler's conversations between 1932 and 1934 and statements made by Hitler after the publication of Rauschning's book. Ideas, sentences, and phrases are frequently repeated in almost identical form in Hitler's secret speeches and in his later conversations. See Hugh R. Trevor-Roper, 'The Mind of Adolf Hitler', Introduction, *Hitler's Secret Conversations*, trans. Norman Cameron and R. H. Stevens (New York, 1961), p. x. This collection of notes is translated from the *Bormann-Vermerke* in the possession of François Genoud of Switzerland.

especially those given to restricted audiences of military leaders
between 1933 and 1941. The war directives which Hitler issued to
the three services[1] and to the war industry[2] give a valuable outline
of his grand strategy in practice, especially if they are related to the
records of Hitler's military conferences and verbal orders described
in the War Diaries of the Armed Forces High Command and of
Field-Marshal von Bock and Colonel-General Franz Halder, the
Chief of the General Staff between 1938 and 1942.[3] These War
Diaries also reveal the progress of the military strategic planning for
the attack on Russia. However, it must be pointed out that General
Halder's volumes were not written as diaries but were books of notes
summarizing each day's work and recording matters requiring
further attention. These entries are abbreviated, often tantalizingly
vague, and occasionally misleading. Even when opinions of situations
are recorded it is sometimes difficult to make out whether they are
those of Halder or of someone else. Dr. Hans-Adolf Jacobsen, the
editor of the published version, has endeavoured, with General
Halder's help, to clarify such entries. But his footnotes sometimes
tend to given an interpretation more favourable to the reputation
of the General Staff and its former chief than is justified by the entries
themselves or by evidence from other sources. Nevertheless, Halder's
daily notes constitute one of the most important documents available
to historians of the Second World War.[4] They are especially useful
if related to the documents on the campaign in Russia contained in
the files of the German military staffs microfilmed by the American
Historical Association and General Services Administration, and
the files and records held by the *Bundesarchiv-Militärarchiv* in Freiburg and by the *Institut für Zeitgeschichte* in Munich. Thanks to the
kindness of Mr. George Blau, Director of the Special Studies Division, Office of the Chief of Military History, the United States Army,

[1] Walter Hubatsch (ed.), *Hitlers Weisungen für die Kriegführung, 1939–1945,
Dokumente des Oberkommando der Wehrmacht* (Munich, 1965).
[2] Georg Thomas, *Geschichte der deutschen Wehr -und Rüstungswirtschaft (1918–
1943/45), Schriften des Bundesarchivs*, ed. Wolfgang Birkenfeld (Boppard am
Rhein, 1966), pp. 402 ff.
[3] Fedor von Bock, *Tagebuchnotizen* (Bundesarchiv-Militärarchiv N22/7).
Percy Ernst Schramm (ed.), *Kriegstagebuch des Oberkommandos der Wehrmacht
(Wehrmachtführungsstab), 1940–1945* (4 vols.; Frankfurt a. M., 1961–5). Hans-
Adolf Jacobsen (ed.), *Generaloberst Halder: Kriegstagebuch* (3 vols.; Stuttgart,
1963).
[4] See Hans-Adolf Jacobsen, 'Das Halder-Tagebuch als historische Quelle',
*Festschrift Percy Ernst Schramm zu seinem siebzigsten Geburtstag von Schülern
und Freunden zugeeignet*, ii (Wiesbaden, 1964), 251–68.

I was able also to use the manuscript memoranda and strategic studies written by German officers shortly after the war. To these were added the personal comments and letters that I received from many of these officers.

After a careful examination of this material I have concluded that Hitler followed a broad plan, albeit an ill-conceived and erroneous one. It had as its main aim the winning of *Lebensraum*, 'living space' for settlement and exploitation in the East, by means of political opportunism and the concept of *Blitzkrieg*, short wars waged against an isolated opponent 'with surprise effects and . . . superior technical weapons'.[1] Although Hitler gambled that he would avoid it, the outbreak of a general European war in 1939 was the result of his determination to adhere to the aims of his great plan even though the conditions for their successful achievement had not been fulfilled. Until 1938 Hitler had hoped that it would not be necessary to fight Great Britain in order to win freedom to expand in central and eastern Europe. Thus when the Western Powers declared war in 1939 Germany was ill prepared for warfare directed against the British Isles on the sea or even in the air. In the summer of 1940 Hitler knew he could defeat the British only if their nerve had been so cracked by the fall of France that they would succumb to a further demonstration of force. An analysis of German strategic planning in the second half of 1940 will show that he was willing to commit the Wehrmacht to such a demonstration only because he then had time and forces available. But in 1941 he was not prepared to postpone his great task of conquering Russia in order to complete first the defeat of Britain.

The contemporary documents related to the German planning in 1940 and 1941 indicate that although the German military leaders played a subordinate role they were neither so ill informed of Hitler's aggressive intentions in the East nor so critical of the decision to strike or the methods to be used there as their post-war accounts assert. The swift victory over France caused them to swing from pessimism and grudging acceptance of the *Blitzkrieg* doctrine to a mood of surprisingly excessive optimism. It will be shown, too, that persistence of this mood throughout the period of detailed planning for the campaign in the East accounts to a great degree for the failure of the *Blitzkrieg* in Russia.

[1] Thomas, p. 8.

# CHAPTER I

# The Bases of Hitler's Strategy—
## *Lebensraumpolitik* and *Blitzkrieg*

### Lebensraumpolitik *and* Blitzkrieg *in Theory and Practice*

HITLER's early policy statements all indicate that he had a set of aims and methods which he regarded as a grand strategic plan. Furthermore, in the early 1930s he began to express definite ideas on the role and form of military strategy to be employed by Germany under his leadership. His grand strategy was designed for the conquest of *Lebensraum* in the East. His military strategic ideas contributed to the development of the *Blitzkrieg*.

In practice both Hitler's *Lebensraumpolitik* and his *Blitzkrieg* failed through the flaws contained in his original concept. He misjudged the attitude of the British towards Germany, he underestimated the strength of the Soviet State, and he wrongly assessed what could be achieved by military means with the resources and leadership available to him. Thus the conditions he envisaged for the attainment of his aims were not fulfilled. Nevertheless, Hitler refused to abandon them, and his foreign policy and strategy were shaped by his attempts to adhere to the aims of his preconceived plans, even though the means left to him were grossly inadequate. His career is remarkable for the fact that by efforts of will, by bluff, and risk-taking he came very close to the successful conquest of *Lebensraum* to which he had aspired as an almost unknown political prisoner in 1924.

### *The Concept of* Lebensraum

Although *Lebensraum* can be literally translated as 'living space', it had for Hitler's Germany a far more complex significance. It provided the progaganda of the Nazi Party with a myth capable of evoking in the masses 'a devotion which . . . inspired them, often a kind of hysteria which . . . urged them to action'.[1] In contrast to the restricted and mundane policies of the Weimar Republic, *Lebensraum* summoned up romantic visions of the 'Germanic crusade', 'the road formerly trodden by the Teutonic Knights',[2] and the *Drang nach Osten*. For those who sought a more tangible goal, *Lebensraum* offered 'soil for the German plough',[2] a cure for the economic ills of the day and for the worse problems of overpopulation predicted for the future. A vast audience at the Nuremberg Rally in 1936 was told by Hitler: 'If we had at our disposal the incalculable wealth and stores of raw material of the Ural Mountains and the unending fertile plains of the Ukraine to be exploited under National Socialist leadership . . . our German people would swim in plenty.'[3] To the military leaders of Germany such gains offered not only autarky but also the re-establishment of the buffer states which Ludendorff had fleetingly obtained by the Treaty of Brest Litovsk in 1918. To Hitler *Lebensraum* offered even more. It was a means of satisfying his lust for struggle and power which expressed itself in his urge to exterminate the Jews and his desire to seize and defend a great Germanic Empire. In 1932 he explained his eastern policy to a small circle of Party comrades as follows:

I do not follow General Ludendorff nor anyone else, . . . I am not thinking in the first instance of economical matters. Certainly we need the wheat, oil and the ores . . . But our true object is to set up our rule for all time, and to anchor it so firmly that it will stand for a thousand years.[4]

Thus the concept of *Lebensraum* was a panacea. Its acquisition was to restore World Power status to the German race by assuring it of sufficient territory, foodstuffs, and raw materials to make it economically self-supporting and so militarily and politically impregnable.[5] But Hitler's *Lebensraumpolitik* had no sound economic or agronomic foundations. Its economic goals, geographical limits, and military objectives were expressed only in vague terms. Dr. Goebbels

---

[1] *MK*, p. 294. (The abbreviations used in the footnotes are as listed on p. xv.) See also Rauschning, pp. 229–30; Bullock, p. 339. Cf. Georges Sorel, *Reflections on Violence*, trans. T. E. Hulme (Glencoe, Illinois, 1950), p. 145. Sorel pointed out that every great social movement finds its driving force in 'a body of images' or a myth.

[2] *MK*, p. 132.

[3] Max Domarus, *Hitler: Reden und Proklamationen, 1932–1945*, i. 642–3.

[4] Rauschning, pp. 47–8. For further indications of Hitler's dream of empire see Speer, pp. 75, 135, and 152.

[5] *MK*, p. 548; see also pp. 124, 520. See also Hitler, *Secret Book*, pp. 145, 195, 209–10; *DGFP*(D) i. 31–2; *IMT*, xxvi, 789–PS, 329–30; Bengtson, pp. 18–20.

remarked cryptically in April 1940: 'Today we say "Lebensraum".
Each can make of that what he likes. What we want we shall know
when the time is right.'[1] Hitler had no wish to set limits to his aims,
nor to define the difficulties involved in their attainment. The
imagination of the masses was to be fired by racial, geopolitical, and
romantic myths, not repelled by the realities of war that *Lebensraumpolitik* clearly involved in both its preparatory and final stages.[2] In
the second paragraph of *Mein Kampf* Hitler stated that 'the tears
of war will produce the daily bread for the generations to come',[3]
but he usually preferred to use romantic phrases like 'the German
sword' or the euphemisms 'struggle' or 'conflict' instead of the plain
term 'war'.[4]

A war of conquest against Russia was for Hitler the main means of
fulfilling his desire for *Lebensraum*. Not only was she the possessor
of vast territories rich in resources, but she was also the centre of
Bolshevism, which Hitler regarded as a Jewish plot for world
domination.[5] Thus the defeat of Russia offered him the opportunity
to achieve simultaneously both his economic and ideological aims.
Furthermore, Bolshevism, Hitler considered, had so weakened the
internal structure of Russia and deprived her of external allies that
she was 'ripe for dissolution'.[6] Thus eastern expansion could be
achieved without the long and ghastly battles or fatal coalition warfare that had resulted from the Kaiser's simultaneous conflicts with
Russia, France, and the British Empire. A 'continental policy' of
expansion into adjacent territory over land, was not only better suited
to Germany's military experience as a land power, but would also
enable her to avoid a further conflict with Great Britain.[7] Indeed,
Hitler asserted in *Mein Kampf*, the British should even welcome a
revival of German strength if it were used to counter the threat of
Bolshevism and to check the further growth of French influence.[8]
'A last decisive struggle with France', he stated, was necessary to
'make it possible for our people finally to expand in another quarter.'[9]

[1] Hillgruber, *Strategie*, p. 22; Jacobsen, *Der Zweite Weltkrieg, Grundzüge der Politik und Strategie in Dokumenten*, p. 181. Cf. *KTB OKW*, i. 89E (*IMT*, 221-L).
[2] See *MK*, pp. 557, 570–1; Hitler, *Secret Book*, pp. 83, 145, 195, 209–10; *IMT* xxvi, 789-PS, p. 330.      [3] *MK*, p. 11.
[4] Ibid., pp. 132, 557.      [5] Ibid., p. 562.      [6] Ibid., p. 557.
[7] Ibid., pp. 126 ff. See also Trevor-Roper, *Hitler's Secret Conversations*, pp. xvi-xvii, 206. Hitler was convinced that the British would prefer to devote their strength to keeping their Empire intact than to become again involved in European quarrels.
[8] *MK*, p. 526.      [9] Ibid., p. 570–1; see also p. 564.

Before the preliminary war against France or the conquest of territory in the East could begin, the internal consolidation of the Reich had to be completed.[1] This involved the winning of power in Germany, the psychological and material rearmament and unification of Greater Germany, including Austria and adjacent areas occupied by German-speaking people. Then Germany would be capable of making the alliances with Italy and Great Britain, which would enable her to destroy French political and military power.[2] These alliances would also lead to the collapse of the Little Entente and expose Czechoslovakia, Rumania, Poland, and the Baltic States to German domination. The way would then be open for the advance into Russia.

## *The Concept of* Blitzkrieg

This sequence of events was the basis of Hitler's grand strategic plan. It depended for its success upon the avoidance of a great coalition war. There was no doubt that wars would have to be fought, probably against France, perhaps against some of the eastern states if they refused to become vassals, and ultimately against the Soviet Union. Thus Hitler's grand strategy was based upon a series of local wars, each to win an easily attainable objective in a short, swift, decisive campaign.[3] This concept, which Hitler described in the early thirties, was developed into what became known as the *Blitzkrieg*.

To Hitler the *Blitzkrieg* was not just a military concept, a tactical application of mechanical equipment to avoid the futilities of positional warfare. It was designed to avoid a repetition of the political, economic, and psychological strains of the First World War. Unlike Ludendorff whose concept of total war was a co-ordination of all aspects of national life primarily for an enormous *military* effort,[4] Hitler believed that Germany would 'never be able to proceed against the forces now mobilized in Europe by relying only on military means'.[5] 'Why', he asked,

should I demoralise the enemy by military means if I can do so better and more cheaply in other ways? . . . The place of artillery preparation for

[1] Ibid., pp. 11, 552–3.
[2] Ibid., pp. 132, 524–32, 536, 542–5, 564.
[3] Rauschning, pp. 17 ff.
[4] Erich Ludendorff, *Der totale Krieg* (Munich, 1935), p. 10. See also Liddell Hart, *Strategy*, pp. 226–7; Chapter IV, p. 95 n. 3 below; Speer, p. 214.
[5] Hitler, *Secret Book*, p. 128.

frontal attack by the infantry in trench warfare will in future be taken by revolutionary propaganda, to break down the enemy psychologically before the armies begin to function at all.[1]

When diplomatic pressure, subversion, and propaganda had reduced the enemy's will to resist he would launch a swift overwhelming blow by the 'largest air fleet' and by 'mass armies' spearheaded by 'highly qualified special formations'.[2] Such a war, he predicted, would be 'unbelievably bloody and grim', but at the same time it would be 'the kindest, because it will be the shortest'. Much would depend upon the timing of the attack and this decision Hitler was determined to reserve for himself. 'There is only one most favourable moment,' he told his party comrades; 'I shall not miss it. I shall bend all my energies towards bringing it about. That is my mission.'[3]

It was also important to control the duration of the war. For what Hitler was seeking was the achievement of Clausewitz's classical definition of war as 'the continuation of policy by other means'. Even Bismarck had not been completely successful in preventing the military leaders from losing sight of policy aims and deluding the people into a pursuit of military glory and victory for its own sake. To avert a repetition of the foolish 'hurrah patriotism' which he had himself shared in the First World War, Hitler decided that it must be the mission of National Socialism

to develop in our people that political mentality which will enable them to realize that the aim which they must set themselves for the fulfilment of the future must not be some intoxicating Alexandrian campaign, but industrious labour with the German plough, for which the sword has only to give the soil.[4]

In other words, war must be limited to the ruthless achievement of the main political aim, the conquest of *Lebensraum*.

### The Leadership of the Wehrmacht

Hitler regarded his own personal, direct leadership as a key to future military success. He rejected the concept of a committee of political, economic, and military planners to develop grand strategy. Such

[1] Rauschning, pp. 17, 19.
[2] Ibid., pp. 17, 158. Since Hitler envisaged expansion over land he did not require large naval forces. See *MK*, p. 132; Hitler, *Secret Book*, p. 145.
[3] Rauschning, p. 21.                                        [4] *MK*, p. 557.

methods, he stated in his Leadership Principle, reduced the leader
to 'the executor of the will and opinion of others'.[1] The role of
committees and military staffs, like that of all 'intermediary organi-
sations' in the Nazi State, was 'to transmit a certain idea which
originated in the brain of one individual to a multitude of people
and to supervise the manner in which this idea is being put into
practice'.[2] Hitler acknowledged his need for the officer corps to
provide the Wehrmacht with superior 'military qualities',[3] but the
expertise of the generals made them incapable of exercising imaginative leadership on the highest level. They were, he said, 'sterile . . .
imprisoned in the coils of their technical knowledge'.[4] He, on the
other hand, was a 'creative genius . . . outside the circle of experts'
with 'the gift of reducing all problems to their simplest foundations'.[4]
As such, he predicted in 1932, he would not allow himself 'to be
ordered about by "commanders-in-chief" '.[5]

During the early 1930s Hitler made efforts to ensure that the
German military leaders were fully informed of his plans and of
their role in them. On 4 December 1932 he wrote a letter to Walther
von Reichenau, then a Colonel and Chief of Staff of the 1st Military
District, East Prussia, outlining the initial, internal phase of his
plan.[6] His first policy statement to the senior commanders of the
Army and Navy, on 3 February 1933, was couched in similar terms,
but extended to the question of how Germany's renewed political
and military power was to be used. 'Perhaps', he suggested, 'the
winning of new export possibilities, and—much better—the conquest
of new living space in the East and its ruthless Germanization.'[7]
A year later, on 28 February 1934, Hitler confirmed further elements
of the plan proposed in *Mein Kampf* when he told the leaders of the
Army, the S.A., and the S.S. that the Wehrmacht should be ready for
defensive war in five years and offensive war within eight years.
It would be necessary, he warned, to deliver 'short decisive blows
first in the West and then in the East'.[8]

---

[1] Ibid., p. 300.   [2] Ibid., p. 301.
[3] Hitler, *Secret Book*, p. 85.   [4] Rauschning, p. 16.
[5] Ibid., p. 20.
[6] Robertson, *Hitler's Pre-War Policy . . .*, p. 4. See also Thilo Vogelsang,
'Hitlers Brief an Reichenau vom 4. Dez. 1933', *VfZ*, 4 (1959).
[7] Walter Hofer, *Der Nationalsozialismus. Dokumente, 1933–1945* (Frankfurt
a. M., 1957), p. 180. See also Gerhard L. Weinberg, *The Foreign Policy of Hitler's
Germany: Diplomatic Revolution in Europe 1933–36* (Chicago and London, 1970),
pp. 26–7.
[8] Robert J. O'Neill, *The German Army and the Nazi Party, 1933–1939* (London,

## Lebensraumpolitik *in Practice, 1933–1939*

The fact that events turned out differently from what Hitler suggested in his writings and speeches was due not to any weakening of his determination to carry out his plan, but rather to the fallacies on which his plan was based. From the start Hitler's *Lebensraumpolitik* contained two errors of judgement which limited his chance of success; first, the conviction that Britain would be prepared to abandon her traditional 'Balance of Power' policy and tolerate a German hegemony in Europe; second, the belief that for racial and political reasons the Soviet Union was a rotten structure on the point of collapse. These two errors persistently marred Hitler's attempts to adhere to his preconceived plans and were ultimately major reasons for his failure and defeat. Nevertheless, there was enough crude logic in his judgement to enable him to follow his 'grim erroneous system'[1] with remarkable consistency and success between 1928 and 1937.

Hitler's first foreign policy success, the Non-Aggression Pact with Poland, reduced the danger of outside interference at 'the most dangerous time . . . during the build-up of the Wehrmacht'.[2] It also brought about an improvement in German-Polish relations which enabled the Nazi leaders to suggest the possibility of a 'concerted march against Russia' which would fulfil Polish aspirations for an outlet to the Black Sea.[3] Meanwhile, throughout the mid 1930s the Soviet state showed encouraging signs of the 'ferment of decomposition' which Hitler had predicted in *Mein Kampf*[4] as Stalin conducted purges of staggering size and ruthlessness. According to the accounts given by former members of the German intelligence services, Reinhard Heydrich, then head of the *Sicherheitsdienst*, helped to extend the purges into the Red Army by sending into Stalin's hands forged documents revealing that Marshal Tukhachevsky and other Soviet generals were plotting to overthrow Stalin's regime with the help

1966), pp. 39–41, 127–8. See also Karl Dietrich Bracher, Wolfgang Sauer, Gerhaud Schulz, *Die nationalsozialistische Machtergreifung* (Cologne, 1960), p. 749; Erich von Manstein, *Aus einem Soldatenleben, 1887–1939* (Bonn, 1958), p. 185.

[1] Trevor-Roper, *Hitler's Secret Conversations*, p. xxvi.     [2] Hofer, p. 180.
[3] Poland, Ministry of Foreign Affairs, *Official Documents concerning Polish-German and Polish-Soviet Relations, 1933–1939* (Polish White Book) (London, 1940), pp. 23–7. See also Hans Roos, *Polen und Europa, Studien zur polnischen Außenpolitik, 1931–1939* (Tübingen, 1957), p. 209.
[4] *MK*, p. 557.

of the German General Staff. By committing this intrigue without Hitler's knowledge Heydrich presumably sought not only to provoke a crisis in the Soviet High Command but also to undermine the Führer's trust in his own generals. However, it was not until the Army's attempt on his life on 20 July 1944 that Hitler admitted that 'He still had no more evidence than before (of the reasons for the Tukhachevsky purge) . . . but he could no longer exclude the possibility of treasonous collaboration between the Russian and German general staffs.'[1] The other effects of Heydrich's work were more immediate. The execution of Tukhachevsky and hundreds of senior Red Army officers helped to convince Hitler that Stalin had seriously impaired his own military power and would ultimately give Germany the opportunity for eastward expansion by destroying his regime from within.

Hitler's policies in the West also developed well at first. In 1935 he laid the foundations for an improvement in relations with Great Britain by sending von Ribbentrop to London to sign the Anglo-German Naval Agreement. This limited the German fleet to 35 per cent of that of Britain as a demonstration of German determination not to repeat the Kaiser's error of challenging the British Empire. In *Mein Kampf* Hitler had envisaged both Britain and Italy as allies of Germany, but after Mussolini's aggression in Ethiopia in the autumn of 1935 he had to make a choice. Albert Speer described his anguished Führer admitting:

It is a terribly difficult decision. I would by far prefer to join the English. But how often in history the English have proved perfidious. If I go with them, then all is over between Italy and us. Afterwards the English will drop me, and we'll sit between two stools.[2]

The choice of Italy had favourable short-term results. Hitler was able to follow Mussolini's example and support General Franco in Spain to the discomfort of France. Meanwhile, in 1936 he had militarized the Rhineland and two years later achieved *Anschluß* with Austria without provoking a violent reaction from London. But neither Hitler's naval gesture nor the sympathy he had won in the West with his anti-Bolshevist policy was enough to persuade the British to acquiesce in further revision of the territorial boundaries

[1] Speer, p. 390. See also Walter Schellenberg, *The Schellenberg Memoirs*, trans. Louis Hagen (London, 1956), pp. 46 ff.; Wilhelm Hoettl, *The Secret Front*, trans. R. H. Stevens (London, 1953), pp. 79 ff.
[2] Speer, p. 71.

of Central and Eastern Europe without negotiation. Their policy helped to frustrate Hitler's hopes of bringing Bohemia, Moravia, and Poland under German domination 'in one campaign'.[1] Instead, much to his subsequent regret, he was forced to settle for the Sudetenland and to postpone the seizure of the rest of Bohemia and Moravia until the following spring. Furthermore, the attitude of the British during the Munich crisis strengthened Hitler's growing conviction that they would not dissociate themselves from France. War with Britain was neither desirable nor inevitable but the danger of it was great enough to justify major changes. Thus on 27 January 1939 he finally abandoned the naval policy that he had advocated and followed since the 1920s and gave the expansion of the German fleet top economic priority.[2] Admiral Raeder's great construction programme which Hitler approved in February 1939 was based upon the assumption that war with Britain would not take place 'before about 1944'.[3]

In the meantime, Hitler was determined to complete the 'nucleus' in Central Europe which, he had stated in 1932, 'will not only make us invincible, but will assure us once and for all time the decisive ascendency over all the European nations'.[4] It was a difficult task, for it involved the extension of his domination over the rest of Czechoslovakia, part of Poland and the Baltic States without provoking a general war.[5] Nevertheless, he was again initially successful. In March 1939 the frightened and ailing President Hacha delivered Bohemia and Moravia into his hands, Slovakia accepted the status of a vassal state, and Lithuania ceded the city of Memel to Germany. Throughout the winter of 1938–9 Hitler exerted diplomatic pressure in Warsaw in order to convert Poland into a German satellite for a future war against Russia. Since Munich he had seen that he might also need 'to establish an acceptable relationship with Poland in order to fight first against the West'.[6] But the Polish leaders refused

---

[1] *IMT* xxvi. 789–PS, 329. See also François Genoud (ed.), *The Testament of Adolf Hitler: The Hitler–Bormann Documents, February–April 1945*, trans. R. H. Stevens (London, 1961), pp. 58, 84.

[2] *IMT* xxxv. 855–D, 597. See also Erich Raeder, *My Life* (U.S. Naval Institute, Annapolis, 1960), p. 158; Anthony Martienssen, *Hitler and his Admirals* (London, 1948), pp. 12–14; Rolf Benzel, *Die deutsche Flottenpolitik von 1933 bis 1939. Beiheft 3 der Marine-Rundschau* (Berlin and Frankfurt a. M., 1958), p. 53.

[3] Martienssen, p. 19.                                          [4] Rauschning, p. 46.

[5] Ibid. Cf. *IMT* xxvi. 789–PS, 328: 'The next step was Bohemia, Moravia and Poland.'

[6] Ibid. p. 339.

to make territorial concessions or to accede to the Anti-Comintern Pact. In doing so they gained the support of Britain and France, and 'the Polish problem' became 'inseparable from the conflict with the West'.[1] This necessitated a major change in Hitler's grand strategy because, as he warned his military leaders on 23 May 1939, Poland saw 'danger in a German victory in the West' and would 'attempt to rob us of our victory'.[2] He, therefore, decided 'to attack Poland at the first suitable opportunity'[2] in the hope of destroying her before the Western Powers' rearmament programmes had given them the strength to intervene. He knew that it would be a gamble and that Germany might be confronted by an alliance between France, Britain, and Russia. But in such a case, he asserted confidently, he 'would be constrained to attack Britain and France with a few annihilating blows'.[3] He attempted to set the generals an example in resolution by telling them that 'The principle whereby one evades solving the problem by adapting oneself to circumstances, is inadmissable. Circumstances must rather be adapted to aims.'[4] Thus he had no intention of abandoning the aims of his *Lebensraumpolitik* and in this address he returned repeatedly to this old familiar theme.

The adaptation of circumstances to aims involved on this occasion the isolation of Poland. This Hitler said would be 'decisive' and he gave a hint of the radical changes in foreign policy it might involve when he explained that 'Economic relations with Russia are possible only if political relations have improved. A cautious trend is appearing in [Soviet] press comment. It is not impossible that Russia will show herself to be disinterested in the destruction of Poland.'[5] Nevertheless, the political, ideological, and strategic effects of establishing

---

[1] Ibid. xxxvii. 079–L, 549; Leonidas Hill, 'Three Crises, 1938–39', *Journal of Contemporary History*, 3, 1 (1968), p. 126, points out that there are a number of interpretations of Hitler's statements in April and May 1939. Walter Hofer, *Die Entfesselung des Zweiten Weltkrieges* (Frankfurt a. M., 1964), pp. 428–9, 440, considers that Hitler wanted war. Taylor, *Origins*, p. 304, states that Hitler's speech on 23 May, was intended only to impress and frighten his generals. This is an exaggeration. Hitler presented them with the worst possibilities because war is the business of generals and they should be prepared for the worst. In fact, they failed to react to his warnings and were caught unprepared for the conflict in the West. The most balanced assessment is that of Bullock, pp. 510–11, who accepts the explanation Hitler gave his generals. He wanted a localized war with Poland, because it served his 'continental expansion eastwards' and the needs of a possible future war with Britain. But he also wanted 'to keep and exploit his freedom of diplomatic manoeuvre during the summer'.

[2] *IMT* xxxvii. 079–L, 549.          [3] Ibid., p. 550.
[4] Ibid., p. 548.                          [5] Op. cit.

a *rapprochement* with the Soviet Union were a bitter pill to swallow. Hoping desperately for some other means of isolating Poland from the West, Hitler delayed taking this step until the eleventh hour, and then rushed von Ribbentrop to Moscow with unconcealed haste. The price of Soviet co-operation was accordingly high. Hitler was forced to give his arch-enemy, Stalin, the prestige of regaining territories lost since the Civil and Polish Wars. Furthermore, the acquisition of bases and the shortening of the Soviet western frontier greatly strengthened the defences of the Soviet Union against a future German attack. To make matters worse, the new pact with Russia did not prevent Britain and France from declaring war when Germany invaded Poland.

Recalling these events in 1944, Hitler stated that 'the disastrous thing about this war is the fact that for Germany it began too soon and too late.'[1] He was not fully prepared for the struggle in the West in 1939, and he regretted that he had not consolidated his position in Eastern Europe by invading Czechoslovakia in 1938. Instead at Munich he had lost 'a unique opportunity of easily and swiftly winning a war that was in any case inevitable'[2] while the Western Powers were still hesitant.

Nevertheless, Hitler did not allow the declaration of war by Britain and France to deter him from his course. Though he could not completely avoid the disadvantages of his self-imposed weakness at sea, he determined to make the maximum use of his land and air forces to destroy his enemies in the West as a prelude to expansion in the East. He was encouraged in this decision by the success of the *Blitzkrieg* in Poland. But this doctrine, like his *Lebensraumpolitik*, contained deep-seated flaws which ultimately contributed to his defeat.

### The Development of the Blitzkrieg, 1933–1939

Like his foreign policy, Hitler's rearmament policy in practice also fell short of his plans. His errors in this case were a misjudgement of his Army leaders and an underestimation of the economic difficulties involved in his concept of warfare. Thus the doctrine of *Blitzkrieg* which formed the basis of German military strategy in the first three years of the Second World War was not the fully preconceived and carefully prepared system that the propaganda of

---

[1] *Testament of Adolf Hitler*, p. 58.                              [2] Ibid., p. 84.

both Germany and her opponents depicted.[1] The Wehrmacht in 1939 had neither the material strength nor the unanimity of leadership that Hitler had expected, and he never forgave the Army leaders for their part in causing these deficiencies.[2] In fact much of the blame lay with Hitler himself and was due to his blind disregard for the fiscal and economic difficulties involved in his policies.

Hitler's original concept of a new form of warfare was designed to avoid a repetition not only of the tactical and psychological blunders but also the economic mistakes of the First World War.[3] In practice his superficial grasp of economics merely replaced the old problems with new ones. After coming to power he began to develop the Nazi party institutions for maintaining morale at home and for exerting pressures through diplomacy, propaganda, and subversion on his enemies abroad. Together with the rearmament of a Wehrmacht capable of launching a 'gigantic, all-destroying blow'[4] these preparations amounted to a 'total mobilisation' of the national resources. Yet the actual military striking power produced was low in relation to the over-all effort and cost, because in addition to rearmament Hitler demanded simultaneously the maximum production of consumer goods and exports, the construction of highways, public buildings, and monuments, and the expansion of the Nazi party's subsidiary organizations.[5] As a result the leaders of the Wehrmacht became involved in a highly competitive struggle for economic resources with the Nazi Party, the Labour Front, industrial and commercial interests and the departments of state. In 1936 Hitler

[1] Alan S. Milward in *The German Economy at War* (London, 1965), p. 11, gives the impression that the *Blitzkrieg* was developed as 'a whole idea and system'. But the contributing factors which he describes formed part of an evolutionary process rather than a planned development. See Mason, p. 86: 'the *Blitzkrieg* strategy was perhaps as much a product of . . . problems, as *the* consideration which determined the level of rearmament . . .'

[2] Op. cit., p. 59. See also Hitler's final message to the German Armed Forces, quoted by Hugh R. Trevor-Roper, *The Last Days of Hitler* (London, 1952), p. 195; *Hitler's Secret Conversations*, pp. 589–90: '. . . in 1939 we had nothing. I cannot tell you with what fury and anger I had to work in order to get what I wanted.' See also Heinz Guderian, *Panzer Leader*, trans. Constantine Fitz-Gibbon (London, 1952), pp. 87–8; O. E. Moll, *Die deutschen Generalfeldmarschälle, 1935–1945* (Rastatt, 1961), p. 19.

[3] Ibid., p. 80; Rauschning, pp. 13, 207–8; *MK*, p. 162; *Hitler's Secret Book*, pp. 8–9; Milward, p. 7.

[4] Rauschning, p. 20.

[5] See *Hitler's Secret Conversations*, pp. 409, 433–4, 589–90; Peter de Mendelssohn, *The Nuremberg Documents, Some Aspects of German War Policy, 1939–45* (London, 1946), pp. 89–90.

realized that the Armed Forces were faring badly in this struggle and he intervened to establish the Four Year Plan under the direction of Hermann Göring.

The new economic chief was no better qualified than Hitler to handle the complex financial and management problems that confronted him. Göring sought to instil a sense of urgency in his subordinates by reading to them an economic memorandum written by Hitler in the summer of 1936. He introduced it with the warning that 'it starts from the basic thought that a showdown with Russia is inevitable.'[1] Nevertheless, economic factors, especially limited supplies of raw material and oil, continued to influence the quantity and types of equipment and thus the tactics and strategy of the Wehrmacht. In spite of Hitler's early expression of enthusiasm for the development of armoured forces,[2] General Ludwig Beck, Chief of the General Staff between 1934 and 1938, rejected the establishment of 'a short-term and hastily created offensive instrument without consideration for the financial and industrial means available'.[3] Even in Göring's Luftwaffe the plans for a fleet of long-range four-engined 'Ural' bombers were abandoned on economic grounds. Since cheaper, lighter aircraft lacked the carrying capacity for area bombing, dive bombing was introduced to give accuracy instead of weight.[4]

In 1938 when the War Minister, von Blomberg, and the Army Commander-in-Chief, von Fritsch, were forced to resign, Hitler took over personal direction of the Wehrmacht and became fully aware for the first time of the inadequacy of the rearmament measures and strategic and tactical thinking of his generals.[5] For the Army it was a year of crisis, change, and improvisation. Several of the more conservative generals were pushed aside to make way for men whom

[1] Mendelssohn, p. 18; *IMT*, Doc. EC-416.
[2] Guderian, p. 30.
[3] Statement by General Otto Stapf, quoted by W. Förster, *Generaloberst Beck, sein Kampf gegen den Krieg* (Munich, 1953), pp. 35-7. See also Guderian, pp. 32-3; Manstein, *Soldatenleben*, p. 240 ff.
[4] *The Rise and Fall of the German Air Force, 1933-1945*, Air Ministry Publication (London, 1947), p. 43; Hermann Plocher, *The German Air Force versus Russia, 1941*, U.S.A.F. Historical Study No. 153 (Aerospace Studies Institute, 1965), pp. 43-4; Werner Baumbach, *The Life and Death of the Luftwaffe*, trans. Frederick Holt (New York, 1960), pp. 23, 321; Telford Taylor, *The Breaking Wave* (New York, 1967), p. 104; Höhn, pp. 394-8.
[5] See especially Hitler's criticisms of the Army's plans for operations against Czechoslovakia in 1938; *IMT* xxv. 338-PS, 429-32, 441-5, 463-4, 466-9. See also O'Neill, pp. 124, 162 ff.

Hitler thought he could trust to carry out his wishes. The armoured and motorized forces were hastily increased and the construction of defences in the East and West speeded up.[1] Similar hurried expansion and changes in tactics that took place in the Luftwaffe in 1938 and 1939 were reflected in the loss of no less than 572 aircraft in flying accidents including an entire squadron of thirteen dive bombers which plunged through low cloud into the ground.[2] To mask the defects and deficiencies massed parades of armour and motorized troops and displays of large formations of aircraft were staged at State and Party occasions.[3] The success of these measures was demonstrated by the exaggerated estimates of German military strength which prevailed in the rest of Europe.[4] As a result of the skilful use of propaganda the tactical doctrines of *Blitzkrieg* were described and analysed in the popular press before they were fully accepted in the Wehrmacht.[5] Later even Hitler admitted that 'the expression *Blitzkrieg* is an Italian invention, we picked it up from the newspapers.'[6]

In spite of the success of his propaganda abroad Hitler's greatest difficulty was to convince his own officer corps that psychological factors outweighed the deficiencies in material and training of which they were well aware, and that the statesman '. . . cannot wait until the *Wehrmacht* is ready in every respect . . .'[7] Memories of the First

[1] See Guderian, p. 62; Burckhart Müller-Hillebrand, *Das Heer, 1933–1945; Entwicklung des organisatorischen Aufbaus*, i. 39–43; Goerlitz, *Keitel*, pp. 185, 196–7.

[2] See C. Bekker, *The Luftwaffe War Diaries*, trans. F. Ziegler (New York, 1969), pp. 38–40; Manstein, *Lost Victories*, p. 27.

[3] See Ernest K. Bramsted, *Goebbels and National Socialist Propaganda* (Michigan, 1965), pp. 214–18; Fritz Terveen, 'Der Filmbericht über Hitlers 50. Geburtstag. Ein Beispiel nationalsozialistischer Selbstdarstellung und Propaganda', *VfZ*, 7 (1 Jan. 1959), 75–84.

[4] French estimates of German strength in 1940 varied from 3,700 to 8,000 tanks, and from 14,865 to 15,700 aircraft. See Theodore Draper, *The Six Weeks War* (London, 1946), pp. 42–3. The official German figures showed that 2,574 tanks and 3,530 combat aircraft, 475 transport aircraft, and 45 gliders were employed in the West on 10 May 1940. See Guderian, p. 472; *The Rise and Fall of the German Air Force*, p. 66. See also A. Goutard, *The Battle of France, 1940*, trans. A. R. P. Burgess (New York, 1959), pp. 23 ff. R. H. S. Stolfi, 'Equipment for Victory in France in 1940', *History*, 55 (1970), 1–20.

[5] See Brigadier-General Reilley, Report on the Spanish Civil War, *Illustrated London News*, 19 Aug. 1939.

[6] See *Hitler's Secret Conversations*, p. 182; see also F. O. Miksche, *Atomic Weapons and Armies* (London, 1955), p. 61.

[7] U.S.N.A. Microfilm, Guide No. 18, Serial T77-775, Frames 5500629-30. See also Speer, p. 163.

World War caused many of the generals to reject the view 'that just
the efficiency of modern weapons will be the guarantee of a
short "lightning war" '.[1] Their fears of a repetition of the defeat of
1918 also made them critical of the increasing risks that Hitler was
prepared to take in order to adhere to his policy of expansion in
1938 and 1939. But their past collaboration with Nazism, their
isolation in German society, and the divisions in their own ranks
prevented them from effectively resisting Hitler's foreign policy.[2]
The conflicts of 1938 deepened those divisions but they also resulted
in the retirement of the most outspokenly critical military leaders,
leaving Hitler free to reorganize the high command and establish
methods of issuing orders and conducting planning that gave him
sole control of grand strategy and the power to intervene in military
strategy.

### The Strategic Direction of the Wehrmacht

Neither in tradition nor training were the German Army leaders in
a strong position to challenge the right of the Head of State to
exercise sole control of grand strategy. In the First World War,
the Supreme Command had obtained great powers over the political,
social, and economic life of the nation. But it failed to use those
powers to formulate a viable grand strategy which ensured that
military strategy and operations served realistic policy aims.[3] After
the war this problem remained unsolved. German strategic thought
was restricted by the small size of the Reichswehr which made the
planning of major operations impossible. Most of its officers were
preoccupied with internal security tasks, and with the improvisation

---

[1] Hermann Foertsch, *The Art of Modern War* (New York, 1940), p. 123; see
also pp. 137 and 160. Critical views on the effect of modern weapons on tactics
and operations were provoked in the military journals. See General Ernst Busch,
'Ist die Schlacht entscheidende Rolle der Infanterie zu Ende?', *Jahrbuch für
Wehrpolitik und Wehrwissenschaften* (Berlin, 1937–8), pp. 11–27; General
Hermann Geyer, Über die Zeitdauer von Angriffsgefechten', *Militärwissenschaftliche Rundschau*, IV (1939), 178–86. The naval leaders shared the generals'
scepticism towards the ability of the tank and aeroplane to overcome the effects
of firepower. See Carl Axel Gemzell, *Raeder, Hitler und Skandinavien. Der Kampf
um einen maritimen Operationsplan* (Lund, 1965), p. 50.

[2] Gordon A. Craig, *War, Politics and Diplomacy* (London, 1966), pp. 132–5.

[3] Corelli Barnet, *The Sword Bearers* (London, 1966), p. 306. The failure of the
German Supreme Command to develop an effective grand strategy was criticized
by Hans Delbrück, *Krieg und Politik* (Berlin, 1918–19), ii. 95, 187; iii. 123.

of tactical means of defending the nation's borders with inadequate strength.[1]

In the early 1920s grand strategic planning was confined to a small select group headed by General Hans von Seeckt in the secret General Staff, the *Truppenamt*. In 1915 von Seeckt had defined an eastern policy similar to Hitler's in later years: 'Separate peace with France and Belgium, on basis of *status quo*. Then all land forces against Russia. Conquest [of] ten thousand [square] miles expelling the population, except of course Germans . . .'[2] But faced with the cold realities of 1920 von Seeckt adopted the view that 'Only in firm co-operation with a Great Russia does Germany have a chance of regaining her position as a world power.'[3] The main purpose of his new eastern policy was to bring about the disappearance of Poland and regain the frontiers of 1914.[4] The military and economic agreements that resulted from von Seeckt's policy encouraged among the leaders of the Reichswehr hopes of a 'War of Liberation' against Poland. But these never had any substance. In 1921, when the Russians would have welcomed German support for attack on Poland, von Seeckt was not prepared to risk provoking the intervention of France and Czechoslovakia. Later the Russians became cautious and, while they apparently valued German assistance in training the Red Army, they had no serious intention of developing this co-operation into a military alliance. In spite of some irresponsible statements by General von Seeckt and members of the *Truppenamt*,[5] the benefits derived from the military training centres and armaments works in Russia were quite insufficient to make the Reichswehr capable of waging even a limited war against Poland.[6]

The election of Field-Marshal von Hindenburg as President brought into the political arena a figure capable of countering von Seeckt's political influence. Hindenburg favoured Stresemann's

[1] General Franz Halder, letter to author, 22 Apr. 1966.

[2] Gustav Hilger and Alfred Meyer, *The Incompatible Allies* (New York, 1953), pp. 191–2.

[3] *Nachlaß Seeckt*, box 15, no. 212, quoted by F. L. Carsten, 'The Reichswehr and the Red Army, 1920–1933', *Survey*, 44/5, 1962. See also G. W. F. Hallgarten, 'General Hans von Seeckt and Russia, 1920–1922', *The Journal of Modern History*, 21 (1949), 29–30.

[4] Carsten, p. 116.

[5] John Erickson, *The Soviet High Command* (London, 1962), p. 156. See also John Wheeler-Bennett, *Nemesis of Power* (London, 1964), pp. 133–8; Gordon Craig, *The Politics of the Prussian Army, 1640–1945* (Oxford, 1964), p. 413, n. 1; Bracher, Sauer, and Schultz, p. 774.

[6] Carsten, p. 119.

'western' foreign policy, and in 1926 von Seeckt ineptly gave the President and his other critics an opportunity to force him to resign. Nevertheless, the idea of a localized war with Poland, which von Seeckt had favoured, remained in the minds of many German soldiers. Since the acquiescence of Russia was essential to this concept, the German Army did not allow expansionist ambitions or the anti-Bolshevik feelings of the conservative officer corps to influence its official attitudes towards the Soviet Union. In this respect it differed from the Navy, which in the mid twenties regarded Russia as 'the greatest enemy of Germany because Bolshevism was the greatest enemy of western culture . . .'.[1] Of course, the Army could claim that it had more to gain than the Navy from co-operation with Russia. Very few officers and men of the Reichswehr were trained in Soviet military installations.[2] Nevertheless, they were able to experiment in the fields of mechanization, chemical and air warfare to meet the needs of a small but very mobile, hard-hitting army.

The doctrine of offensive action by troops trained to use initiative and flexibility in the attack was fostered by General von Seeckt. This was partly the result of his experiences on the eastern and south-eastern fronts in the First World War. But it was also inevitable that the Reichswehr, restricted to 100,000 men on long terms of service, should become an élite force and should seek to compensate for its lack of size by means of speed and striking power. However, this offensive doctrine did not meet any strategic need defined by the policies of the Weimar Republic. As a result under von Seeckt's successors, Heye and von Hammerstein, questions of strategy tended to be ignored by the Reichswehr. Instead the soldiers waited for the emergence of a political leader whose foreign policy suited their tactical doctrine. In 1933 such a man became Chancellor.

However, even after Hitler had removed the restrictions of the Treaty of Versailles, reintroduced conscription, and authorized re-armament, interest and understanding for grand and military strategic questions failed to grow in porportion to the size and capability of the armed forces. The German officer corps became engrossed in applying the tactical and technical ideas developed in the Reichswehr to the new formations of the expanding Wehrmacht. The small groups of experts and enthusiasts were broken up and dispersed among the training cadres for the large numbers of new formations. Their influence was reduced by the demands of routine basic training

[1] Carsten, p. 128.    [2] Ibid., p. 124.

and administrative duties. But they persisted, and throughout the various arms and services of the Wehrmacht individuals and new groups fostered the tactical doctrines which were later brought together as the characteristics of the *Blitzkrieg*. The names of Lutz, Guderian, Nehring, and von Thoma were associated with the development of Panzer formations. Self-propelled armoured assault artillery was the brain-child of von Manstein. Rommel defined the tactics of infantry in the attack. Udet and Jeschonnek urged the development of fast medium bombers, and Freiherr von Richthofen experimented in Spain with their use in support of ground forces. Osterkamp, Galland, and Mölders gained experience in the use of interceptor fighters. Kurt Student built up the Luftwaffe's paratroop force. The contributions of these men to the evolution of the doctrines and tactics of *Blitzkrieg* have been described in their memoirs and numerous other works.[1] Most of them were of middle rank, colonel or major-general, during the years of the expansion of the Wehrmacht. They were concerned with the tactics of their new formations and apparently gave little thought to the grand strategic purpose to be served by the armed forces as a whole. Nor did their superiors.

The senior generals of the Reichswehr were men whose lives had been dominated by the disillusionment and humiliation of defeat.

---

[1] The best short study is Robert J. O'Neill, 'Doctrine and Training in the German Army, 1919–1939', *The Theory and Practice of War. Essays for Captain B. H. Liddell Hart*, ed. Michael Howard (London, 1965). The memoirs of Guderian, von Manstein, Kesselring, and Galland also contain valuable material. See also Hans Höhn (ed.), *Auf antisowjetischem Kriegskurs. Studien zur militärischen Vorbereitung des deutschen Imperialismus auf die Aggression gegen die UdSSR (1933–1941)* (Berlin, 1970), which gives detailed accounts of the build-up of the Wehrmacht. However, it is a tendentious work, crediting Hitler with the achievement of a much greater co-ordination of the economic and military resources of Nazi Germany than the evidence suggests. Predictably, it omits reference to the technical and tactical advantages gained from the co-operation between the Reichswehr and the Red Army. This is described in John Erikson, *The Soviet High Command*; Hans W. Gatzke, 'Russo-German Military Collaboration during the Weimar Republic', *American Historical Review*, 63 (1958); F. L. Carsten, 'The Reichswehr and the Red Army, 1920–1933', *Survey*, 44/5 (1962). For further details of the early development of the Luftwaffe see Karl-Heinz Völker, *Die Entwicklung der militärischen Luftfahrt in Deutschland 1920–1933* (Stuttgart, 1961). Later tactical doctrines are described by Paul Deichmann, *German Air Force Operations in Support of the Army*, U.S.A.F. Historical Studies No. 154 (New York, 1966); and in Cajus Bekker, *The Luftwaffe War Diaries*, trans. and ed. Frank Ziegler (New York, 1969). For the development of the Panzer formations see K. J. Macksey, *Panzer Division—the Mailed Fist* (New York, 1968); H. Scheibert and C. Wagner, *Die deutsche Panzertruppe, 1939–1945* (Bad Nauheim, 1966); Herbert Rosinski, *The German Army* (New York, 1966).

Traditionally conservative, they had become cautious and often sceptical in outlook. When the new Chancellor expressed his enthusiasm for certain areas of development, such as the armoured and motorized troops, the senior generals did not feel obliged to allow the opinions of a former corporal to influence or hurry their professional judgements.

The older generals were even less prepared to develop strategies to meet the needs of Hitler's foreign policy statements. Their experience in the Reichswehr had given them little scope for far-reaching strategic planning. Thus these men to whom self-restraint and caution had become second nature, were not inclined to hurl themselves with enthusiasm into plans for wars of aggression at the behest of an obvious fanatic.

There were exceptions. Initially the most notable was Field-Marshal von Blomberg. But until his resignation in 1938 the War Minister's devotion to the Nazi cause tended only to hide from Hitler the fact that he had failed to win over the sceptics among his colleagues. The majority of the Army leaders regarded Hitler's references to the conquest of *Lebensraum* as the vague fantasy of a vulgar propagandist.[1] Perhaps their lifelong training in staff planning procedures and military security made it difficult for them to believe that the Head of State could seriously be following a plan discernible in a book available in any German bookstore or public library. They were of course not alone in this error. But having heard Hitler's secret policy statements between 1933 and 1939 the senior generals had less reason than others in Germany and Europe to believe that Hitler in office would settle for something more limited than the aims of Hitler the political agitator. Nevertheless, the OKH refrained from revealing any sign of agreement with Hitler's grand strategy. Indeed, until 1938 the only acknowledgement that it understood his long-term aims was given when the Army Commander-in-Chief, General von Fritsch, used them to support the Army's case for directing the operations of the entire Wehrmacht in war. In a memorandum submitted to von Blomberg, in August 1937, he stated: 'As long as the objective of a German victory can lie only in eastern conquests then only the Army can bring about a final decision

[1] Sauer, *Machtergreifung*, pp. 749, 764–5; Karl Otmar Frhr. von Aretin, 'Die deutsche Generale und Hitlers Kriegspolitik', *Politische Studien*, 10 (1959), p. 570; Hugh R. Trevor-Roper, 'Why didn't they invade?', *Sunday Times Magazine*, 16 May 1965, p. 32; O'Neill, pp. 125 ff.

by conquest in the East and defence in the West, because no eastern
state can be fatally struck from the air or sea.'[1] In spite of this statement, no methodical preparation in the form of studies and plans
was undertaken by the Army for operations against France until
1939 or against Russia until 1940.

In contrast, studies and war games conducted by the Navy between
1936 and 1939 were based upon the idea of a conflict with Russia
and France.[2] In a study written for the major war game conducted
by the Baltic Fleet Station early in 1939, Admiral Albrecht stated:

> The great objective of German policy is seen as securing Europe from the
> western border of Germany as far as, and including, European Russia
> under the military and economic leadership of the Axis Powers. . . . (This
> means) basically defence in the West and attack towards the East . . .
> either from the south-east over Rumania and the Ukraine or across the
> Baltic States into northern Russia.[3]

Admiral Fricke, Chief of Naval Operations, tried to restrain such
open aggressiveness and suggested that before planning supporting
operations for a Baltic offensive 'we will wait and see what "political
objective" the Führer gives us'. Nevertheless, the attitude of the
Naval Staff towards Hitler's strategic plans was obviously very
different from that of the Army.

Similarly, the leaders of the Luftwaffe, with their close ties with
the Nazi Party, had no hesitation in accepting Hitler's grand strategic
aims. In a study entitled 'Thoughts on the Air Situation in Europe
in the spring of 1939' the Luftwaffe Staff stated that owing to the
internal crisis 'Russia would participate in a European war only if
the risk of losses was low.'[4] Nevertheless, the idea of an attack on
the Soviet Union was not ruled out, and echoing the view expressed
by Hitler in *Mein Kampf*, the writers expected that 'Stalin's regime
would collapse under strong pressure from the outside.' However,
since the Luftwaffe was mainly concerned with the technical and
tactical problems of air defence and giving close support to the field
army its staff played little part in grand or even military strategic
planning.

---

[1] Görlitz, *Keitel*, p. 128.

[2] C. A. Gemzell, *Raeder, Hitler und Skandinavien. Der Kampf um einen
maritimen Operationsplan* (Lund, 1965), p. 45. See also Höhn, pp. 428–43.

[3] Gemzell, pp. 68–9.

[4] *Europäischer Beitrag zur Geschichte des Weltkrieges II, 1939–45. Die deutsche
Luftwaffe im Krieg gegen Rußland, 1941–45*, Institut für Zeitgeschichte, Munich,
MA 54 (I).

The creation of the Luftwaffe as an independent service with strong Nazi attitudes caused new problems and rivalries within the German High Command which further discouraged the development of a staff capable of giving advice and direction in grand strategy. Hitler's War Minister, Field-Marshal von Blomberg, and later, the Chief of the OKW, General Keitel, both attempted to extend the responsibilities of their offices to embrace the co-ordination of the economy, the national propaganda, and the three services in wartime.[1] Their efforts were frustrated, not only by Hitler's wish to exercise direct leadership of the Wehrmacht, but also by the attitude of the OKH, which preferred to take orders directly from the Führer rather than see the War Ministry or the OKW become a supreme staff for the direction of the entire Wehrmacht. However, Hitler's failure to make the OKW responsible for directing grand strategy did not raise the status of the OKH; it merely gave Hitler direct control over the three services and their strategic planning.[2]

During 1938 Hitler developed the procedure by which he exercised this control throughout the following three years. First he presented his political and grand strategic decisions verbally to the Commanders-in-Chief of the Army, Navy, and Air Force. They and their senior staff officers worked out a military strategy and an operational plan to meet the needs of those decisions. The draft plan was then submitted to the Führer by the Army Commander-in-Chief. If approved it was passed to the OKW which prepared a directive encompassing the proposals of the three services and any amendments made by Hitler. A similar procedure was used for the co-ordination of the war economy with the needs of policy and strategy. Hitler gave commands to the Reich Defence Council, presided over by Göring as Head of the Four Year Plan Organization,[3] and to the War Economy and Armament Office of the OKW. Their detailed plans were then incorporated into a directive by the *Wehrmachtführungsamt*[4] of the OKW and issued to the relevant civil and military departments.

[1] Keitel's memorandum on the role of the OKW is presented in Görlitz, *Keitel*, pp. 154 ff.

[2] Ibid., p. 168. See Chart I.

[3] Field-Marshal von Blomberg had hoped that the *Reichsverteidigungsrat* might be the means by which the military would obtain supervision of the war economy. But instead Göring, Fritz Todt and, later, Albert Speer gained control of economic planning. See Craig, p. 133; see also Milward, pp. 19 ff.

[4] The *Wehrmachtführungsamt* was the operational planning staff of the OKW. See *KTB OKW* i, pp. 132E ff. and Trevor-Roper, *Hitler's War Directives*, pp. xix ff. for details of its organization and function.

Thus the OKW was usually no more than a centre for confirming decisions made by Hitler and the operational plans made by the three services.[1] In the view of General Warlimont, who served in the *Wehrmachtführungsamt*, 'When the Second World War broke out no established headquarters existed capable of undertaking the over-all direction of the German war effort. . . .'[2]

Not merely the direction, but also the co-ordination of the three services lay in the hands of Hitler alone. Unlike the British and American Chiefs of Staff, who met in committee almost daily during the Second World War, the heads of the German Army, Navy, and Air Force only came together when they attended a Führer Conference to receive their orders, or at State or Party functions. The broad outline of their co-operation was indicated by Hitler verbally or in the War Directives issued on his authority by the OKW. The details were arranged by liaison officers of each service on the main staffs, or occasionally, by visits of senior staff officers, though these were infrequent as the service staffs were often in widely dispersed locations.[3]

The lack of co-operation and consultation between the leaders of the three services was not, however, entirely a product of Hitler's influence. He merely took advantage of the sort of narrow specialization already prevalent in the German officer corps. This was reflected in the words of Colonel Hermann Foertsch, later Commandant of the War Academy, who stated in a book on the art of war that 'it would not be proper for . . . an officer of the Army, to consider also questions of naval and aerial warfare . . .'.[4]

The readiness of the Army leaders to accept the role of narrow specialists and to eschew even an advisory role in the field of grand strategy did not prevent Hitler from interfering in their remaining fields of military strategy, operations, and even tactics to ensure that the *Blitzkrieg* methods which he favoured were put into practice. This habit helped to maintain the resentment and hostility with which he was regarded by some of the generals. But only one of them, General Adam, was prepared to follow the example of General Beck, whose protests at Hitler's readiness to invade Czechoslovakia

[1] See Walther Warlimont, *Inside Hitler's Headquarters*, trans. R. H. Barry (London, 1964), pp. 18, 20.

[2] Ibid., p. 3.

[3] See *KTB OKW* i. 169E–174E; see also Ronald Wheatley, *Operation Sea Lion, German Plans for the Invasion of England, 1939–1942* (Oxford, 1958), p. 147.

[4] Foertsch, p. 12, n. 1.

led to his resignation from the post of Chief of the General Staff in August 1938.

The man on whom Beck had most relied for support, the Commander-in-Chief of the Army, General von Brauchitsch, had limited his independence by accepting Hitler's assistance in obtaining a divorce in order to marry a woman who was an enthusiastic Nazi. Frequently torn between his military judgement, the influence of his second wife, and his loyalty to Hitler, he became vacillating and ineffectual.[1] To make matters worse von Brauchitsch was a man of aristocratic bearing and outlook. He had an extremely reserved manner and in the presence of Hitler, whose coarse style of speech offended and bewildered him, he became completely inhibited. Unable to cope with Hitler's arguments, he spoke seldom. When he did force himself to overcome his constraint, he argued in a curt and sometimes impetuous tone which Hitler resented.[2] On the outbreak of war, when Beck's successor, General Franz Halder, insisted that he as Chief of the General Staff should direct the operations of the Army, the office of Commander-in-Chief deteriorated into one of comparative unimportance.[3]

General Halder's attitude and conduct was more equivocal. Since the war he has been depicted as an active member of the military opposition group working against Hitler.[4] But after November 1939 Halder's acts of opposition were conducted without arousing the disapproval of von Brauchitsch and without sabotaging or affecting the needs of the fighting troops.[4] Thus they can hardly have amounted to more than the maintenance of critical attitudes towards Hitler and an avoidance of initiating new aggressive plans until Hitler's orders made further delay impossible.[5] It also appears from his diary and from the testimony of others that Halder's ability to conduct even this type of resistance effectively was further reduced by the professional satisfaction that he evidently derived from his work.[6]

[1] See O'Neill, pp. 68, 146–8, 172. Von Brauchitsch succeeded von Fritsch on 4 Feb. 1938.

[2] Author's conversations with General Halder, 23 June 1969, General Philippi, 30 May 1969, and General Siewert, former First Staff Officer to von Brauchitsch, 8 July 1969.

[3] See *KTB OKW* i. 135E–136E. See Chart II. 246.

[4] Kurt Sendtner, 'Die deutsche Militäropposition im ersten Kriegsjahr' *Vollmacht des Gewissens*, pp. 393 ff.

[5] Ibid., p. 403.

[6] Ulrich von Hassell, *The von Hassell Diaries, 1938–1944* (London, 1948), pp. 88–9, 121–2, 158; Elizabeth Wagner (ed.), *Der Generalquartiermeister. Briefe*

In many ways he was the old-fashioned, Protestant bureaucrat his appearance suggested, with his pince-nez, clipped moustache, short-cropped hair and rather impatient manner. Utterly devoted to duty, he lived by the General Staff motto 'Achieve much, appear little', and demanded the same of his subordinates. He told the assembled chiefs of staff of the army groups and armies:

As long as I am the 'Guardian of the Grail' we shall not depart by one hair's breadth from this spirit of the German General Staff. I expect you to educate the German General Staff in this manner. He to whom the mantle of honour has no more meaning than a badge of rank or an increase in pay lives on a different plane to that on which the Prussian General Staff was founded and has grown great.[1]

In attempting to uphold such principles while working for a political leader for whom he felt neither loyalty nor trust Halder set himself an impossible task. Thus an atmosphere of unreality pervades the accounts of his relations with Hitler, and it is still open to question whether the deterioration of German military strategic planning into a series of individual responses to the demands of the Führer was due to deliberate 'passive' resistance of the General Staff or merely a paralysis resulting from the pessimism, bordering on defeatism, that seems to have prevailed in the German Army in 1938 and 1939.

Nevertheless, the General Staff contained a small, isolated group of officers whose resistance to Hitler was based not merely upon the fear that he was leading Germany to defeat but upon moral objections to his aims and methods. They included some of Halder's closest associates, General Karl-Heinrich von Stülpnagel, the Deputy-Chief of the General Staff, General Wagner, the Quartermaster-General, General Fellgiebel, Inspector-General of Signals, and Colonel von Tresckow, the Staff Officer Ia of the Operations Department of the General Staff. In 1944 these men paid with their lives for their resistance. Also in this group were several officers of the OKW including Admiral Canaris, Chief of the *Abwehr*, and General Oster, one of his department heads. General Thomas, Head of the War Economy and Armament Office, was also an opponent of Hitler, but like Halder, he abandoned hope of a military *coup d'état* late in 1939 and

*und Tagebuchaufzeichnungen des Generalquartiermeisters des Heeres General der Artillerie Eduard Wagner* (Munich and Vienna, 1963), p. 183. See also Jacobsen, 'Das Halder-Tagebuch als historische Quelle', pp. 260, 264–5.

[1] Jacobsen, 'Das Halder-Tagebuch als historische Quelle', p. 265.

thenceforth confined his opposition to professional criticism of Hitler's decisions.

In the OKW the members of the resistance were a small minority. At the top, General Wilhelm Keitel was the most notorious sycophant. In retrospect Albert Speer stated that 'perhaps Keitel embodied most precisely the type of person Hitler needed in his entourage'.[1] He combined enthusiasm for Nazism, diligence in military administration, and an impressive stature and bearing with a complete lack of talent. His selection ensured that the OKW would never be more than a military secretariat. Keitel repaid his Führer for the unexpected honour of his appointment with such devotion that even Hitler described him as 'loyal as a dog'.

Keitel was ever at Hitler's elbow. He attended party functions, diplomatic meetings, and military conferences. But he was there for his appearance, not for his advice. Hitler's closest military adviser was General Alfred Jodl, the Chief of the *Wehrmachtführungsamt*. Jodl was an intelligent but taciturn man, who was so reserved that even his closest subordinate, General Warlimont, had difficulty in obtaining information or guidance from him. This characteristic increased his estrangement from his Army colleagues. His open admiration for Hitler had already set him apart. Furthermore, his office, which appeared to challenge the General Staff's control of planning, aroused resentment in the officer corps. Yet his isolation made him all the more acceptable to Hitler. To the suspicious dictator a lone adviser was more welcome than the representative of a clique. Jodl's laconic manner was also to his advantage in his personal relations with Hitler. In Speer's words, he 'rarely contradicted Hitler openly. He proceeded diplomatically. Usually he did not express his thoughts at once, thus skirting difficult situations. Later, he would persuade Hitler to yield or even to reverse decisions already taken.'[2] Nevertheless, Jodl did not always attempt to dissuade Hitler from decisions with which he disagreed. He probably recognized the hopelessness of disputing certain basic elements of Hitler's policy. Furthermore, both Jodl and Keitel limited their criticism in an attempt to set an example in loyalty to the Führer before the rest of the generals.

The majority of the German generals preferred the example set by their Commander-in-Chief, von Brauchitsch. They suppressed

---

[1] Speer, p. 244; see also Warlimont, p. 13.
[2] Speer, p. 244. See also Seaton, pp. 28–9.

their doubts and, out of a sense of duty, for the sake of ambition, or merely to escape an 'insoluble dilemma',[1] obeyed Hitler's orders. This group included the senior army group commanders, von Bock, a soldier who combined a guardsman's discipline with a driving ambition, and von Rundstedt, who viewed with scepticism the value of attempts to resist Hitler as long as he had the support of the troops and the people.[2]

While most of the field commanders shared such views, some were clearly impressed by Hitler's abilities. Without necessarily simulating the servility of Wilhelm Keitel, or the enthusiasm for 'the genius of the Führer'[3] expressed by Alfred Jodl, they admired his remarkable insight into the technical and psychological factors of modern war and served him with loyalty. The leading personalities in this group at the start of the war were von Reichenau and his gifted Chief of Staff, Paulus, and also Busch, Fromm, and Guderian. Although such men constituted only a small minority, their presence was enough to encourage Hitler in the hope that the Army would meet the needs of his policy and, together with the Luftwaffe, provide the military instrument for the *Blitzkrieg*. This hope was further fostered by Hitler's senior military adjutant, Colonel Rudolf Schmundt, a highly competent staff officer who regarded him with uncritical devotion and made constant attempts to develop greater understanding and contact between the Führer and the OKH. But in fact Hitler did not enjoy the company of the older, conservative generals. He was more at ease among younger men with new ideas which seemed to coincide with his own. Typical of these was Colonel Erwin Rommel, the author of *Infanterie greift an*, a book advocating vigorous, offensive infantry tactics. In 1938 when Hitler accompanied the troops occupying the Sudetenland, he appointed Rommel to command his field headquarters and escort battalion. During this operation, instead of joining the Commander-in-Chief, Hitler chose to eat his meals at the headquarters of the most junior corps commander in the Army, General Heinz Guderian, the Panzer general who, like Rommel, had won Hitler's attention through his writings. In *Achtung Panzer!* and other works Guderian had urged the development of armoured formations as the instrument for the sort of

---

[1] Manstein, *Lost Victories*, p. 80.
[2] Moll, p. 223. See also Jacobsen, 'Das Halder-Tagebuch als historische Quelle', p. 259.
[3] Jodl's Diary, 10 Aug. 1938, quoted by Warlimont, p. 14.

mobile offensive operations that Hitler needed to follow up the blows struck by the Air Force.[1]

The leaders of the Luftwaffe, selected and led by Göring, were loyal to the Nazi regime. So too were the German admirals, though they had ample grounds to be critical of the situation in which Hitler's policies had placed them. Having been assured in February 1939 that there would be no war with Britain for another five or six years, Admiral Raeder wrote on 3 September that the German surface forces could 'do no more than show that they know how to die gallantly . . .'.[2] But since Hitler depended mainly upon the Army for the fulfilment of the aims of his *Lebensraumpolitik*, it was of the utmost importance that he should instil confidence in the leaders of the OKH and General Staff, and overcome their unwillingness to develop their military planning on the basis of his grand strategy. This, however, he was unable to do.

Like the admirals, the generals were disappointed at the failure of Hitler's foreign policy to prevent Britain and France from declaring war in September 1939. Although the victory over Poland was a welcome solution to a problem which had rankled them since 1919, it did not encourage them to challenge the French Army in battle. The German operations had been satisfactory, but the strategic and material weaknesses of the Poles made the outcome inevitable. The Luftwaffe had given an impressive display of its ability to support the ground operations. In spite of a number of incidents in which German troops were bombed in error, it was clear that the ideas developed in peacetime and tried out on a small scale by Generals Sperrle and von Richthofen with the 'Condor Legion' in Spain had been vindicated. So too had the theories of Heinz Guderian. Even though the Mark I and II tanks had proved too light for combat use, the Panzer divisions had fully exploited the vulnerable flanks of the Polish Army. The significance of their successes was partly hidden by the fluidity of the campaign in which rapid movement was achieved by the whole field army. There were complaints that the Panzer divisions had left the infantry behind by advancing too fast, but several generals, including von Brauchitsch and von Bock, were critical of the infantry for being over cautious,

---

[1] Guderian's other works included: 'Die Panzertruppen und ihr Zusammenwirken mit anderen Waffen', *Militärwissenschaftliche Rundschau*, v (1936), 607–26; 'Kraftfahrkampftruppen', *MR* i (1936), 52–77; 'Schnelle Truppen einst und jetzt', *MR* iv (1939), 229–43.

[2] Martienssen, p. 21.

and too often waiting for artillery support. After a conference with von Brauchitsch on 29 September, Halder noted that the form of attack used in Poland would not provide 'a recipe for the West against a well-knit army'. So, while the press of both Germany and her enemies gave glaring prominence to the triumph of the *Blitzkrieg*, the leaders of the German Army underrated it and began to seek 'new methods' such as gas or super-heavy tanks which might be ready to assault the French defences by 1941 or 1942.[1] But there was no real conviction behind these suggestions. Several of the senior generals saw a negotiated peace as the best course. Thus Hitler's demand for an offensive in the West found them with neither enthusiasm nor plans.

[1] *Halder KTB* i. 29 Sept. 1939; see also R. M. Kennedy, *The German Campaign in Poland* (Washington, 1956), pp. 130–5.

# CHAPTER II

# The War in the West and its Results
## October 1939–July 1940

### *The Reluctant Warriors*

IT has been asserted that in 1939 Hitler had no war plan, 'no all-embracing strategic conception in which the political purpose, means, and military objectives were meaningfully related'.[1] The evidence of Hitler's secret speeches and directives does not support this assertion. It is true that his 'war plan' was not set down in writing.[2] It is also true that there were discrepancies between his aims and means, especially since it had become necessary to fight Great Britain as well as France, but he was not prepared to admit this. The basis of his plan for the conquest of *Lebensraum* remained unchanged; having consolidated his hold over central Europe he would strike in the West and then in the East. The outbreak of a general war in September 1939 had come as a disappointment; it was momentarily disconcerting, but not entirely unexpected. On 23 May he had warned his service chiefs that it might be necessary 'to attack Britain and France with a few annihilating blows',[3] and even suggested, on the basis of a critical analysis of the errors of the First World War, that a 'wheeling movement towards the Channel ports'[4] and the cutting of Britain's food supply routes might be the decisive actions of a war in the West. But the Army leaders failed to respond to these hints. They could no longer regard Hitler's strategic ideas as mere fantasies, but out of short-sightedness, mere pessimism, or, in the case of a very few, moral indignation, they still ignored them. As a result it was they, not Hitler, who were caught totally without a plan in September when Britain and France declared war.

---

[1] *KTB OKW* i. 42E. See also Manstein, *Lost Victories*, pp. 154, 169; Craig, p. 136; *Vollmacht des Gewissens*, ii. 28 ff. Albert Kesselring 'Der Krieg im Mittelmeerraum', *Bilanz des Zweiten Weltkrieges* (Oldenburg/Hamburg, 1953), p. 152.
[2] See Hermann Hoth, *Panzer Operationen* (Heidelberg, 1956), p. 25.
[3] *IMT* xxxvii, 079–L, 550.　　　　　　　　　　　　　　[4] Ibid., p. 554.

By means of verbal orders on 27 September, a written directive and a memorandum on 10 October, and a long speech on 23 November, Hitler managed to convince the Army leaders of the seriousness, if not the wisdom, of his decision to strike as soon as possible in the West.[1] They then produced 'an imitation of the famous Schlieffen Plan of 1914',[2] a response that provoked humiliation and despair among some of their more imaginative subordinates.[3] Most of the senior generals argued that the operation should be postponed. General von Stülpnagel advised that it should not be attempted until 1942, and even Hitler's most ardent supporter among the field commanders, General von Reichenau, urged him to delay it until the spring.[4] Some considered that it should not be attempted at all. The commander of the army group facing the Maginot Line, General Ritter von Leeb, suggested to von Brauchitsch that Hitler should seek a negotiated peace and set aside his 'far-reaching plans'.[5] He even proposed that much of the *Lebensraum* conquered so far should be restored to the Czechs and Poles.[5] General von Rundstedt also wrote to von Brauchitsch on the same day, 31 October, warning him that 'once Germany's offensive strength has been used up in the West . . . anything may happen in the East.'[6] However, the Army leaders were far too preoccupied with problems in the West to give consideration to the East where they relied upon the pact with Russia and a mere nine divisions to hold the frontier. Before September they had concentrated upon preparations for the Polish campaign and ignored the possibility of an attack on France in 1939. Now they focused their gaze on the campaign in the West, albeit reluctantly, and ignored all indications that a victory there would be but a prelude to an attack on Russia.

Such indications were not hard to find. In the memorandum that

---

[1] *Halder KTB* i. 86 ff., 27 Sept. 1939; Hubatsch, pp. 37–8; Hans-Adolf Jacobsen, *Dokumente zur Vorgeschichte des Westfeldzuges, 1939–1940* (Berlin/Frankfurt a. M., 1956), pp. 4 ff.; *IMT* xxvi, 789–PS, 327 ff.; ibid. xxxvi. 052–L, 467 ff.

[2] Manstein, *Lost Victories*, p. 98.

[3] Ibid.; see also Guderian, p. 89.

[4] Ibid., p. 82; see also Hans-Adolf Jacobsen. *Fall Gelb, der Kampf um den deutschen Operationsplan zur Westoffensive, 1940* (Wiesbaden, 1957), p. 10.

[5] Moll, p. 102. See also Nuremberg Document NOKW–3433, quoted by Shirer, p. 855.

[6] Nuremberg Document NOKW–511, quoted by G. L. Weinberg, *Germany and the Soviet Union, 1939–1941* (Leiden, 1954), p. 98. See also Heinrich Uhlig, 'Das Einwirken Hitlers auf Planung und Führung des Ostfeldzuges', *Aus Politik und Zeitgeschichte, Beilage zur Wochenzeitung Das Parlament* (16 Mar. 1960), p. 164.

he read to von Brauchitsch and Halder on 10 October, Hitler stated that the German war aim was to deprive the Western Powers of the ability to oppose 'the state consolidation and further development of the German people in Europe'.[1] A week later he gave a clear indication of where this 'further development' lay when he ordered General Keitel and the Quartermaster-General of the Army, General Wagner, to ensure that the roads, railways, and lines of communication in eastern Poland were to be kept in order because 'the territory is important to us from a military point of view as an advanced jumping off point and can be used for the strategic concentration of troops.'[2]

On 23 November Hitler sought to quell the doubts and criticisms of his military leaders by explaining the grand strategy behind his decision to attack in the West to a wider audience of generals. His speech made it quite clear that his goal was still 'to create a rational relation between the number of people and the space for them to live in'.[3] Although he did not wish to provoke further pessimism by over-stressing his determination to attack Russia, he did not attempt to conceal the possibility of a future conflict in the East. He pointed out that Germany should make full use of her opportunity to fight on only one front, because Russia would keep the pact that made this possible 'only as long as she considers it to be to her advantage'.[4] He warned 'we can oppose Russia only when we are free in the West.'[5] The cause of the conflict would, he suggested, be future Soviet expansion because, in addition to strengthening her position in the Baltic, Russia was 'striving to increase her influence in the Balkans and towards the Persian Gulf'.[4] He also stated that 'at the present time the Red Army is of little worth. For the next year or two the present situation will remain.'[4] But it was clear that this gave him only the minimum time necessary to win the war in the West and prepare the German forces for the conflict in the East. This was probably one of the reasons for his impatience to start the campaign against France as soon as possible and for his open criticism of those generals, particularly von Brauchitsch, who counselled caution on the grounds that the German troops were not yet equal to the task in the West.

---

[1] *KTB OKW* i. 50E. See also Shirer, p. 853.
[2] *IMT* xxvi. 864–PS, 379. See also *Halder KTB* i. 107, 18 Oct. 1939.
[3] *IMT* xxvi. 789–PS, 329.                    [4] Ibid., p. 331.
[5] Op. cit.

General von Brauchitsch was mortified at the criticism of the Army leadership in Hitler's speech. Anxious to avoid a repetition of this humiliating experience, he suggested to Halder that the General Staff should perhaps conduct studies of the operational possibilities in the Balkans, the Middle East, and Scandinavia[1] which Hitler had mentioned. Halder, however, declined to take up these proposals on the grounds that 'the clear, political objectives for such studies were lacking, because Hitler had only made vague suggestions'.[2]

The least 'vague' of Hitler's suggestions was that the campaign in the West would be followed by a conflict with Russia. Yet this was not even mentioned as the topic for a General Staff study by von Brauchitsch. Quite apart from Hitler's statements, the changes in the strategic situation in the Baltic area, Finland, and Eastern Europe resulting from the secret protocol to the Russo-German Pact would alone have justified more than the routine observations of the Foreign Armies East Branch of the General Staff. Yet until mid-summer 1940 neither the OKH nor the OKW conducted any major study of the military situation in the East.[3]

Preoccupation with the immediate problem in the West was no reason for the military staffs to ignore the East altogether. Furthermore, the alacrity with which the OKH turned to the question of Russia after the defeat of France rules out the possibility that the Army leaders were restrained by an aversion for planning aggressive war. It seems more likely that the same tendency to avoid problems of grand strategy, the narrow outlook, and rigid, bureaucratic working methods that had characterized the General Staff in the past was still limiting its initiative. But above all, it appears that the Army leaders had so little hope of winning a decisive victory in the West that they regarded long-term planning for a war in the East as futile.

### German Operational Planning, 1939–1940

In spite of the remarkable success achieved by German arms in 1940 the German operational planning conducted between October 1939

---

[1] Hitler had described Scandinavia as 'hostile to us because of Marxist influences'. Ibid.
[2] *Halder KTB* i. 132–3, n. I, 25 Nov. 1939.
[3] Warlimont, pp. 55–6.

and April 1940 was mainly the product of pessimism. Until the spring of 1940 even Hitler expected the offensive in the West to win only 'territory in Holland, Belgium and Northern France as a base favourable for waging extensive air and sea warfare against Britain and as a wide protective belt before the essential Ruhr area'.[1] The final victory was to be won by knocking Britain out of the war, but no one expected a quick success. Before the war Hitler had toyed with the idea of a swift surprise attack directed against the Royal Navy.[2] However, once Britain had declared war the slender chance of successfully crippling the British fleet with one blow dissolved.[3] Instead Hitler placed his trust in a blockade conducted by his Navy and the Luftwaffe, especially the U-boat fleet and the new magnetic mines laid by aircraft. On 23 November he told his military leaders that 'the permanent sowing of mines along the English coasts will bring Britain to her knees.'[4] Neither Admiral Raeder nor General von Brauchitsch were convinced by this show of confidence.[5] They both sought more orthodox means of striking at the British Isles and conducted studies for an invasion of England. But these proved no more encouraging and in January 1940 the Army, confronted by the difficulties predicted by the Navy and Air Force, abandoned further planning.[6]

Meanwhile, the Naval Staff had turned to an alternative. Sceptical of the Army's chance of winning the Channel ports in the West, Admiral Raeder attempted to interest Hitler in the possibility of obtaining bases in Norway from which to conduct a vigorous siege of Great Britain.[7] Though in 1934 Hitler had envisaged the possibility of 'a daring, but interesting' operation in Scandinavia 'protected by the fleet, and with the co-operation of the air force',[8] he was anxious to avoid diverting forces from the coming offensive

---

[1] Hubatsch, p. 37; *KTB OKW* i. 56E.

[2] *IMT* xxxvii. 079–L. 552.

[3] The sinking of H.M.S. *Royal Oak* and damaging of H.M.S. *Repulse* in Scapa Flow by U-boat 47 in October 1939 showed that Hitler's hopes of surprise attack on the Royal Navy were not entirely impracticable. On 13 Dec. 1941 he told the Japanese Ambassador in Berlin, General Oshima, that the attack on Pearl Harbour had been 'the right declaration of war!'. Andreas Hillgruber (ed.), *Staatsmänner und Diplomaten bei Hitler* (Frankfurt a. M., 1967), p. 683.

[4] *IMT* xxvi. 789–PS, 335.

[5] A German Naval Staff memorandum stated in January 1940 that 'the effect of mining all the ports of the island cannot yet be foreseen.' Wheatley, pp. 10–11.

[6] See ibid., pp. 7–8; see also Taylor, *Breaking Wave*, pp. 202–3.

[7] *IMT* xxxiv. 122–C, 423–4.

[8] Rauschning, p. 143.

in the West. He agreed to do so only when persuaded that the British might land there first.[1] The operation that resulted was a further demonstration of the tactical skill of the Wehrmacht. Nevertheless, the German fleet suffered heavy losses which seriously impaired its ability to support an invasion of England four months later. Furthermore, the fact that Hitler was forced to divert part of his forces and keep them in Norway was an ominous indication of the advantages of sea power with which Britain could foil his attempts to limit the war to *Blitzkrieg* campaigns at a time and place of his choosing.[2] The Norwegian campaign was the first of several operations that led to delays and diversions of German forces to counter threats on the periphery of Europe, especially in the Balkans.

The Germans' concern for the security of their interests in the Balkans, especially the vital Rumanian oilfields began to develop in December 1939. The first step was taken by Admiral Canaris, Chief of the *Abwehr*, who arranged co-operation with the Rumanian security forces.[3] Early in January, after a meeting between Generals Keitel and Halder, the Army General Staff began an operational study of measures to safeguard the oil-fields.[4] Meanwhile General Jodl, Chief of the Operations Staff of the OKW, produced a strategic study in which he echoed the view expressed by Hitler that Germany should divert the Russians from the Balkans by encouraging them to expand into the Middle East where they would also threaten the bases of the Western Allies.[5] This idea was repeated in a further memorandum written by Jodl, dated 21 March 1940.[6] In it he made the additional suggestion that a Soviet force advancing from the Caucasus might be reinforced by German units and leadership. However, Jodl hastened to add that such an operation would only

[1] See Earle K. Ziemke, *The German Northern Theatre of Operations, 1940–1945.* Department of the Army Pamphlet no. 20–271 (Washington, 1959), pp. 7–10; Christopher Buckley, *Norway, the Commandos, Dieppe* (London, 1951), p. 4; Hinsley, p. 51; Gemzell, pp. 289–90.
[2] See *KTB OKW* i. 135E; Buckley, p. 4.
[3] Andreas Hillgruber, *Hitler, König Carol und Marschall Antonescu: die deutsch-rumänischen Beziehungen, 1938–1944* (Wiesbaden, 1954), p. 67.
[4] *Halder KTB*, i. 151, 2 Jan. 1940.
[5] *DGFP*(D) viii. 514. Hitler is reported as saying on 23 Nov. 1939 that 'Russia is striving to increase her influence in the Balkans and towards the Persian Gulf. That is also the goal of our foreign policy' (*IMT* xxvi. 789–PS, p. 331). Two days later Admiral Raeder interpreted Hitler's remark to mean that 'the expansion of Russian interests towards the Persian Gulf is supported by Germany' (Mendelssohn, p. 246).
[6] U.S.N.A. Guide No. 18, Serial 177–775, Frame 5500651 ff.

be thinkable once the Western Powers were considerably weakened in the European theatre.

By the spring of 1940 improvements in the operational plan and better equipment, preparations, and intelligence about the capabilities of their opponents had encouraged the German leaders to view the prospects of the offensive in the West with more optimism.[1] Nevertheless, the OKW made no attempt to question the need for an attack on Norway in view of the probable capture of the Low Countries and Flanders. The possible effects of Italy's entry into the war, the problem of defeating Britain and the results of Soviet expansion were still ignored. Nor was there any attempt to co-ordinate the strategic planning of the three services and the OKW Operations Staff within the framework of aims that Hitler had repeatedly expressed. General Warlimont, Jodl's senior department head, later admitted that in contrast to the Chiefs of Staff Committee in Britain or the Joint Chiefs of Staff in the United States there was nothing but a 'disastrous vacuum' at this level of strategic planning in Germany.[2] But without the support of detailed studies, prepared and co-ordinated by the military staffs, Hitler's broad grand strategic ideas proved inadequate to meet the demands of the changing situation. Thus it was mainly as a result of the omissions resulting from their pessimism that the German military leaders were caught unprepared for the consequences of the swift collapse of France.

## The Effects of Victory in the West

On 31 January 1940 the Chief of the General Staff expressed the opinion that after a success in the West the Army will be strong enough to assert itself at home (*im Innern*) 'also with regard to the S.S.'.[3] But although by June that success had been won, the idea of the Army intervening in the political arena had been quietly forgotten. The concept was not realistic in the first place, for resistance to the regime was hardly to be fostered by Nazi successes. On the

---

[1] General Fromm, Chief of the Reserve Army, told von Hassell on 25 Apr. 1940: 'We will push through Holland and Belgium at one blow, and then finish off France in fourteen days; the French will run like the Poles. France will then make peace, England will fight on alone for a while but will finally give up too. Then the Führer will make a very moderate, statesmanlike peace.' Hassell, p. 127. See also *KTB OKW* i. 56E.

[2] Warlimont, p. 54.

[3] Jacobsen, 'Das Halder-Tagebuch als historische Quelle', p. 265.

18 June 1940 von Hassell, one of the leaders of the German opposition movement, noted that 'on the domestic front we are all agreed
that at the moment there is nothing we can do'.[1] In fact, the victory
in the West was far more of a triumph for Hitler than for the generals
and the General Staff. It was the Führer who was greeted as a
returning hero by the Berliners strewing flowers before his car. It
was the genius of Hitler, the new *Feldherr*, that had made possible
the dazzling successes of the operations in the West. Unfortunately
there was sufficient truth in the propaganda image to force the Army
leaders to realize that they were weakened rather than strengthened
by the military defeat inflicted on France.

Not only had the OKH failed to acquire political status, it had,
during the course of the planning and conduct of the spring campaigns in Scandinavia and the West, lost the control over military
strategy and operations that it had exercised in Poland. The planning
for Operation 'Weser Exercise', the invasion of Norway, was carried
out by the OKW and a special staff drawn from the Navy and
General von Falkenhorst's XXI Army Corps. Ostensibly the exclusion
of the OKH was intended to confine planning to the minimum
number of personnel for the sake of secrecy. It also enabled the
OKH to concentrate upon planning Operation 'Yellow', the offensive
in the West. But even here the OKH was not given freedom of
action. The attempts by the OKH and most of the senior field commanders to dissuade Hitler from mounting a winter offensive in the
West only resulted in drawing him into detailed discussion of the
strategic, operational, and tactical factors to be considered. The
Commander-in-Chief, von Brauchitsch, seriously undermined Hitler's
confidence in him when he expressed the opinion that the troops
were too slack and insubordinate to undertake an attack against
strong defences.[2]

The unimaginative replica of the Schlieffen plan produced by the
OKH prompted Hitler to press his own operational ideas. He was
further encouraged by the fact that von Manstein, a staff officer
with an outstanding reputation, independently produced an alternative plan based on concepts similar to his own.[3]

[1] Hassell, p. 133.

[2] *Halder KTB* i. 120, 5 Nov. 1939. See also Harold C. Deutsch, *The Conspiracy
against Hitler in the Twilight War* (Minnesota, 1968), pp. 226–31.

[3] See Hans-Adolf Jacobsen, *Fall Gelb, der Kampf um den deutschen Operationsplan zur Westoffensive, 1940* (Wiesbaden, 1957); Telford Taylor, *March of
Conquest*, pp. 41–64, 155–86; Guderian, pp. 84 ff.; Manstein, pp. 67 ff.

The events of the winter of 1939–40 reduced Hitler's respect for the General Staff and added to his conviction that but for his will and determination the offensive would never have been attempted, and without his strategic perception and judgement it would have been based upon a second-rate plan. As a result Hitler was no longer content, as in Poland, to visit the front and give words of encouragement to the troops. He set up a field headquarters from which he exercised personal direction over the conduct of operations. His nervous interference caused anger and frustration at OKH which marred the satisfaction derived from the success of the offensive. His personal endorsement of the decision of General von Rundstedt to halt the Panzer Groups at Dunkirk significantly reduced the success of the envelopment achieved by Manstein's plan. These events also caused a deterioration in the relations between von Brauchitsch and Halder. As the German armies converged on Dunkirk Halder hoped that the Commander-in-Chief would follow the 'logical and manly' course and take personal command of the operation. He was appalled by the failure of von Brauchitsch to do so, and noted caustically that he seemed 'glad to let someone else take the responsibility'. 'But with that', added Halder, 'he also forgoes the honours of victory.'[1] The strains of the campaign added to the jealous rivalry between the OKH and OKW, and the staffs of all three services became more isolated from one another. Thus the German victory in the summer of 1940 was tempered by bitterness.

After the campaign there were all the outward trappings of military success and the congratulations of a grateful Führer. But these were directed mainly to the troops and their field commanders. The Commander-in-Chief, von Brauchitsch, was awarded the baton of a field-marshal. But so too were all the senior army group, army and air fleet commanders. Göring had the rank of *Reichsmarschall* especially created for him. Wilhelm Keitel and Erhard Milch, Under-Secretary of State for the Luftwaffe, also won batons, though their administrative roles hardly seemed to qualify them for the distinction. Halder's meticulous staff work in co-ordinating the complex movements in each phase of the campaign had done much to ensure its success. Yet he was merely promoted to Colonel-General. Hitler's Reichstag speech in which these promotions were announced omitted any real acknowledgement of the contribution of the General Staff. Instead Hitler himself claimed credit for all the significant

[1] *Halder KTB*, i. 317, 23 May 1940.

strategic decisions of the campaign. The American newspaper corre-
spondent William Shirer, who was present, thought that Halder
appeared to be the 'saddest figure' in the Kroll Opera House that
night.[1]

The deterioration in the political and military status of the OKH
was clear enough to von Brauchitsch and Halder. But for most of
the generals and the rank and file of the German Army the spring
and summer of 1940 was a period of unbelievable success. In days,
or even hours, they had crossed battlefields on which the Imperial
Army had been locked in ghastly struggle for four long years. As
they drove or marched in dusty columns through the villages and
towns of Flanders they felt that they had revived the 'classical' warfare of manœuvre and thrust in the tradition of Frederick, Clausewitz, and Moltke. So intoxicated were they by their great triumph
that for a time they forgot that it was not complete.

### The Strategic Problem of Britain

The German victory in the West caused a wave of optimism among
the German leaders which had far-reaching effects on their subsequent
conduct of the war. The first result, towards the end of May, was
the growing belief that the defeat inflicted upon the armies of the
Western Allies would cause not only the collapse of France but also
that of Great Britain. Even though this hope proved unfounded,
the continued resistance of Britain was regarded as likely to be
ineffectual. Thus neither Hitler nor his Army leaders were discouraged
from turning in July to preparations for an attack on Russia.

The assumption that Hitler had no 'war plan', or had abandoned,
or at least postponed, his aims of further expansion in the East has
encouraged the view among Western historians that an invasion of
Britain was the next logical step after the defeat of France.[2] But his
failure to prepare plans for a Channel crossing at the time of planning
the campaign in the West, his half-hearted attitude towards the
belated attempts to repair this omission, and the badly planned and
ill-co-ordinated efforts of the Luftwaffe in August and September

[1] William L. Shirer, *Berlin Diary* (New York, 1941), p. 454. See also Telford
Taylor, *The March of Conquest*, pp. 345–50; Manstein, *Lost Victories*, p. 150.
[2] See Peter Fleming, *Operation Sea Lion* (New York, 1957), p. 240; Wheatley,
pp. 28, 38, 133; Karl Klee, *Das Unternehmen 'Seelöwe'. Die geplante deutsche
Landung in England, 1940* (Göttingen, 1958), p. 244; Mendelssohn, pp. 209–11,
215.

1940 all suggested that Hitler's main interest after June 1940 lay in the East.[1]

Here too the influence of the victory in the West unbalanced the judgements of Hitler and his Army leaders. Doubts about the efficiency of the *Blitzkrieg* were now completely dispelled, and the attitude of the General Staff swung from pessimistic truculence to over-confident zeal. Naturally, the most extreme effects of the exhilarating experiences of the campaign in the West wore off when the problems confronting the Wehrmacht on the sea and in the air were more soberly assessed. Nevertheless, enough of the aura of invincibility on land remained to give the German leaders an inflated image of what could be achieved with the forces at their disposal and a correspondingly low opinion of their opponents in the East and West.

Hitler's ambivalent attitude towards the British combined the anger of frustration with the lingering conviction that his assessment of them could not have been completely wrong. Though he desired victory over Great Britain, he claimed that he had no wish to destroy her or her empire.[2] He clung to the hope that a serious set-back would 'bring the British to their knees', and that they would then be ready to reach an agreement with Germany as he had always predicted.[3] In May and June 1940 Hitler thought that the defeat inflicted on the Western Allies in the Low Countries and France was sufficient for this purpose. On 20 May, hearing that the Panzer thrust from the Ardennes had reached the Channel, he told General Jodl that 'the British can get a separate peace at any time'.[4] When the British Expeditionary Force was surrounded at Dunkirk he exclaimed to General von Rundstedt and his Chief of Staff, von Sodenstern, that he expected that Britain would come to a 'sensible peace arrangement' and that he would at last have his hands free 'for his real major task, the conflict with Bolshevism'.[5]

In the first half of June, while optimism about the favourable outcome of the war in the West still flourished, Hitler began to

---

[1] See Trevor-Roper, 'Why didn't they invade?', pp. 28 ff.

[2] See *Halder KTB* ii. 21, 13 July 1940; Schellenberg, p. 107.

[3] Ibid.

[4] *IMT* xxviii. 1809-PS, 431. See also *Halder KTB* i. 308, 21 May 1940.

[5] Klee, p. 189. The cryptic remark that he added: 'The only problem is how shall I break it to my child?', probably referred to the German public. Hitler's concern at 'having to call the German people to arms once more in the years to come' was mentioned later by Jodl (Warlimont, p. 112).

plan new production priorities to meet the future needs of the Wehrmacht.[1] On 7 June he told von Brauchitsch that with the collapse of France 'the task of the Army in this war would be essentially ful-filled.'[2] The phrase 'in this war', meaning the war in the West, was later omitted by Halder in a diary entry on this subject.[3] This, together with his persistent use of the term 'peacetime Army'[4] to describe the new organization, has fostered the impression that Hitler ordered a reduction of his Army because he had abandoned or postponed his intention of attacking Russia.[5] This was not so. A year earlier, in accordance with his determination to avoid warfare of the 1914–18 style, Hitler had stated that once 'the Army . . . has taken the most important positions [in the West], industrial produc-tion will cease to flow into the bottomless pit of the Army's battles and can be diverted to the benefit of the Air Force and Navy'.[6] As Milward has pointed out, Hitler's *Blitzkrieg* war economy gave him the flexibility to do this.[7] Nevertheless, the Army was not excluded from the new economic programme. On the contrary, it was to be transformed into a more mobile, harder-hitting force of 120 combat divisions fully equipped in the light of the experience gained in mobile warfare. The Panzer divisions the main *Blitzkrieg* striking power, were to be increased in number from ten to twenty and equipped with heavier tanks. The six motorized divisions were to be increased to ten. The age of the fighting troops was to be kept if possible below thirty.[8] The reduction of the Army involved the dis-bandment of twenty-two under-equipped infantry divisions, nine *Landwehr* divisions, and four fortress divisions.[9]

These improvements in the Army were not made for the war against Britain. At the time when they were ordered Hitler still did not consider that an invasion of Britain would be necessary, and even when he did decide to plan a landing he lacked the ships to carry

---

[1] Tentative planning began late in May. See *Halder KTB* i. 324, 28 May 1940. But written directives were not issued until June. See also Müller-Hillebrand, *Das Heer*, ii. 62; *KTB OKW* i. 968–9; Milward, p. 37; Warlimont, p. 104.

[2] Thomas, p. 406.

[3] *Halder KTB* i. 357, 15 June 1940.

[4] Ibid., p. 324, 28 May; 357, 15 June 1940.

[5] See Taylor, *Breaking Wave*, pp. 21, 50; Fabry, p. 231; Greiner, p. 289; Mendelssohn, p. 210; Wheatley, p. 18, n. 6, p. 141, n. 3; Weinberg, *Germany and the Soviet Union*, p. 104.

[6] *IMT* xxxvii. 079-L, 554.　　　　　　　　　　　[7] Milward, pp. 25, 37–8.

[8] Thomas, p. 406.

[9] Müller-Hillebrand, ii. 62–3.

all the armoured formations already available across the Channel.[1]
Clearly the reorganization of the Army was conducted with a
different purpose in mind, and on 5 July Dr. Fritz Todt, the Minister
of Armaments and Munitions, gave an indication of the nature of
that purpose. Speaking at a conference, he stated that the conversion
of the Army would not mean any easing of the pressure on the war
economy, but merely 'a transfer of effort from munitions to equipment, above all for the mobile troops'.[2] He acknowledged that every
effort must be made to complete the victory over Britain, but 'the
aims of the Führer' he defined as 'to expand the Army until it equals
the sum of the enemy armies, and . . . to complete the cultural and
social build-up of Germany'.[2] The 'enemy armies' could only have
been those of Britain and Russia, because they alone could equal
the proposed German total of 120 divisions. Thus the armament
programme instituted in June, to which Dr. Todt was referring, was
designed to meet the short-term needs of exerting pressure on Britain
from the air and sea to force her to come to terms. But it also met
the long-term needs of a great mobile campaign in the East. This was
confirmed on 18 July when a meeting of the Reich Defence Council
placed the expansion of the mobile forces, the railway rolling stock
and locomotive programme, road transport, and synthetic rubber
tyre programmes, in 'Priority Level No. 1', together with the Junker
88 (bomber) programme and the U-boat programme.[3]

Until the middle of July Hitler's strategy remained based upon the
hope that Britain would abandon the struggle that summer. This
would leave almost a year in which to complete the Army reorganization and re-equipping programme, because, once Britain came to
terms, interference in European affairs by the United States would
become most unlikely. Furthermore, Hitler did not think that Russia
would abandon her Non-Aggression Pact with Germany until the
spring of 1941, by which time the Wehrmacht would be ready to
attack in the East.[4]

The situation was changed when Hitler realized that Britain would

[1] The Army Order of Battle for Operation 'Sea Lion' on 26 July included in
the second wave six out of the ten available Panzer divisions. But the Navy lacked
the ships to carry them, and in September this number was reduced to four. See
Wheatley, pp. 186–7.

[2] *KTB OKW* i. 74E.

[3] See Thomas, pp. 413–16. Cf. Hitler's remarks to Mussolini on 4 Oct. 1940;
Hillgruber, *Staatsmänner*, p. 108.

[4] See *IMT* xxvi. 789–PS, 331.

not give up easily. On 13 July he accepted the recommendations of the Army operational study for a cross-Channel invasion,[1] and three days later issued Directive No. 16, 'Preparations for a Landing Operation against England'.[2] As a result, on 26 July, the Reich Defence Council was forced to amend its plans for an air and sea war against Britain and until 31 August the preparations for a landing, Operation 'Sea Lion', were placed above 'Priority No. 1' of the Economic Directive issued on 18 July.[3]

In spite of the confidence with which the OKH presented its first plans for a landing, Hitler was never enthusiastic about the operation.[4] He recognized the risks of a cross-Channel attack and the adverse effect a failure would have upon the aura of invincibility surrounding the Wehrmacht, and he was not eager to make the attempt before turning his triumphant armies upon Russia. He agreed with Admiral Raeder that it should be a last resort, carried out against an enemy already broken by blockade and air attacks.[5] But Hitler knew that his U-boat force was too weak to achieve swift results and he had already expressed doubt about the possibility of defeating Britain quickly from the air.[6] An air and sea war might drag on for many months especially if the United States increased her economic and political support to Britain or entered the war. Furthermore, Russia might abandon the Non-Aggression Pact during this period, for she had already strained it by claiming Bukhovina from Rumania. It therefore seems likely that from mid July onwards Hitler was never fully convinced that it would be possible to finish the war in the West before attacking Russia.

Hitler's growing doubts about the willingness of the British to give up or the ability of the Wehrmacht to make them do so quickly caused him to reconsider the size of the land forces he would require in 1941. On 13 July he told General Halder that of the thirty-five divisions earmarked for disbandment twenty should merely be sent on prolonged leave to enable the men to return to industry and yet have them ready for a quick recall.[7] The only apparent reason

[1] See Wheatley, pp. 32, 35. This study was the result of data that Halder had been hastily collecting since the beginning of the month.
[2] See Hubatsch, pp. 71–5; Wheatley, pp. 36–8.
[3] Thomas, p. 417.                                          [4] Wheatley, p. 35.
[5] Ibid., p. 34.
[6] See *IMT* xxxvii. 079-L, 552. See also *Halder KTB* ii. 49, 31 July 1940: 'U-boat warfare and air attacks can win the war but they will take 1 to 2 years.'
[7] Ibid., p. 20, 13 July 1940; Müller-Hillebrand, ii. 63–4.

for this change was Hitler's growing conviction that Britain 'will not take the path to peace'.[1] By the end of the month he had decided that in addition to the 120 divisions required for Russia, the number planned in June, he would require a further sixty divisions to garrison Scandinavia and the West.[2] Thus, the modifications in Hitler's plans for the war economy and reorganization of the Army were due to the British determination to fight on, and not to changes in his intentions towards Russia. They had remained constant. Nevertheless, the German military leaders were made increasingly uneasy at the prospect of attacking Russia while Britain still fought on in the West, and their nagging doubts later weakened the confidence and enthusiasm with which, in July 1940, they approached the task of invading Russia.

### The OKH and the Initial Planning for the East

The victory in the West not only dispelled most of the scepticism that the senior Army leaders had shown towards the *Blitzkrieg*, it also removed their main objection to Hitler's leadership. Hitherto most of them had based their criticism, not on any political or moral disagreement with his aims, but upon the irresponsible risks involved in his foreign policy and grand strategy. For the past two years they had dreaded a repetition of the defeat and humiliation of 1918. But when Hitler dictated the armistice terms to France at Compiègne their fears dissolved. The depth of the change is reflected in the enthusiastic letters that the Quartermaster-General, Eduard Wagner, sent to his sister in June 1940. 'And wherein lies the secret of this victory?' he wrote, 'Indeed in the enormous dynamism of the Führer . . . without his will it would never have come to pass.'[3] With this new respect for the Führer the German military leaders gained a new confidence in themselves. Not since Hannibal's victory at Cannae, boasted Wagner, has there been such a successful envelopment battle, except of course those of von Moltke at Sedan and Hindenburg at Tannenberg. 'You must have watched with bated breath' wrote Wagner to his sister,

We have got used to it now. Nothing surprises us any more. It should really be recorded for . . . world history how Halder sits at the map, measures off the distances [of the advance] with a meter rule, and already

---

[1] Müller-Hillebrand, ii. p. 21, 13 July 1940.
[2] Ibid., p. 50, 31 July 1940.          [3] E. Wagner, pp. 182–3.

deploys [forces] across the Loire. I doubt whether Seeckt's synthesis 'cool judgement and warm enthusiasm' has ever found such shining reality as in the General Staff during this campaign.[1]

For a short time there seemed no question about the ability of the German Army to overcome the tasks that obviously remained both in the West and in the East. But instead of new campaigns, the generals were confronted by a period of *große Politik*, 'of which', wrote Wagner, 'we understand nothing, and which the Führer conducts quite alone, without any assistance, even from Göring'.[2] As a result the senior commanders of the army groups and armies became 'unbearable through inactivity'.[3] When Army Group B was given the task of occupying the French coast between Brest and the Spanish border von Bock noted with derision that all he had to do was 'to watch out that the sea-shore wasn't carried away or the demarkation line stolen'.[4] These attitudes 'got on Halder's nerves' and the Chief of the General Staff no longer felt it possible to exercise restraint in planning new operations. Nor did von Brauchitsch see any divergence between Hitler's further aims and the interests of the Army. In contrast to their previous custom and to their postwar accounts of these events, the leaders of the Army and senior general staff officers, encouraged by a report that Hitler's attention had turned to the East, began in July 1940 to plan an attack on the Soviet Union, even before Hitler had given any direct orders to do so.[5]

General Halder's attitude towards Russia at this time was shaped by a number of factors. As a conservative and a staunch Protestant he was instinctively hostile towards Bolshevism. Like many South Germans he viewed the Slavs with a mixture of suspicion and contempt. Throughout the period since the Polish campaign he had been able to reduce the German forces on the new frontier with Russia only because he doubted the ability of the Soviet Union to undertake any major military adventure. This attitude seemed to be justified by the poor Russian performance in Finland. Nevertheless, Soviet expansion in the Baltic and Black Sea areas had lent substance to the anxieties that had been fostered throughout the winter by his predecessor General Ludwig Beck.

Since his retirement during the Czech crisis Beck had not been

[1] Ibid., p. 183. See also p. 187.      [2] Ibid., p. 195.
[3] Ibid., p. 194.      [4] Bock, *Tagebuch*, 28 June 1940.
[5] See *IMT* xx. 576–7.

idle. From his pen had flowed a series of memoranda criticizing Hitler's policy and grand strategy. These papers had been circulated anonymously among the senior members of the General Staff by Colonel Helmuth Groscurth. It may be presumed that Halder and all the senior department heads read them. General von Tippelskirch, *Oberquartiermeister IV*, was moved to write on one the comment 'Does this memorandum originate from an Englishman or a German? In the latter case he is over-ripe for a concentration camp.'[1] However, it is likely that Halder and Stülpnagel were well aware of the author's identity.

One of Beck's main themes was that Russia might become 'a serious or, under certain circumstances, a deadly danger'. In 'The Russian Question for Germany, a sketch' Beck argued that Russia's policy was to drive towards the sea, either in Europe or in Asia. After her defeat in the First World War and in the Polish War of 1920 she had turned towards Asia. But in 1939 she had been drawn back into Europe by Hitler's astonishing offer of a non-aggression pact. If Hitler draws Russia on to a common frontier over the corpse of Poland he will have 'exchanged Beelzebub for the Devil', warned Beck. Furthermore, he also predicted that 'Russia's next aims lie . . . in the Baltic States (Baltic Sea) and in Bessarabia (Black Sea).'[2]

A similar warning was sounded in a memorandum written by the Foreign Office Liaison Officer to the OKH, Dr. Hasso von Etzdorf. The Soviet Union, he stated,

will extend her power wherever there is the least risk, under certain circumstances also against Germany (plucking the corpse!).

She will thus build up a front against us with which in the long run, we will be unable to compete . . . either war economically . . . or psychologically.

The result will be a collapse of the military and home fronts—disintegration—Bolshevism . . .[3]

It can no longer be established with certainty whether the arguments of Beck and those who shared his views had much influence upon Halder's actions after the fall of France. However, it is note-

---

[1] Helmuth Groscurth, *Tagebücher eines Abwehroffiziers 1938–1940*, ed. Helmut Krausnick and Harold C. Deutsch (Stuttgart, 1970), p. 478.

[2] Ibid., pp. 490–2.

[3] Ibid., pp. 498–9. See also the even more outspoken memorandum written by Commander Franz Liedig in Dec. 1939 in which Hitler was accused of reversing the programme 'to save Europe from . . . the execrable Bolshevism of Russia', and of making Germany 'a Russian outpost in Europe' (pp. 509–14).

worthy that in the months that followed the fears of Soviet long-term intentions expressed by Halder all reflected those written in the memoranda of his former chief.[1] But if the purpose of Beck's memoranda was to widen the schism between the OKH and Hitler they must be judged, like so many of the general's acts of opposition, a tragic failure.[2] For as soon as it was clear that France was defeated Hitler's eyes turned eastward, and at the same time the General Staff began to seek means to counter the danger of Russia of which Beck and others had persistently warned throughout the winter. Thus, during the critical period of decision-making and planning for the invasion of Russia, opposition to Hitler's strategy among the military leaders was at its lowest ebb. Far from turning his former colleagues against their Führer, Beck unwittingly conditioned them for the next major task Hitler was to give them.

At the end of June 1940 General Halder returned to Berlin where Baron von Weizsäcker briefed him on Hitler's view of the political situation.[3] Attention was now focused on the East, the State Secretary explained. This was not due entirely to recent Soviet expansion. On the contrary, Hitler had been satisfied with Russia's readiness to limit her claim in North Bukhovina. The reason seemed to lie rather in Hitler's long-term plans, for he took the view that 'Britain will probably need a further demonstration of our military strength before giving up and leaving our rear free for the East.'[4] The prospect of further military effort was evidently not welcome to von Weizsäcker, and he prophetically warned Halder, 'the difficulties lie less in the present situation than in the future developments because the preservation of our success by military means must lead to over-exertion'.[5] But the Chief of the General Staff was in no mood to be deterred by the cheerless counsel of a diplomat. Without awaiting direct instructions from Hitler he proceeded to examine the military

[1] See for example Halder's comments on Russia to the senior staff officers, *Halder KTB* ii. 227–8, 13 Dec. 1940.

[2] Beck's resignation in 1938 had also proved quite ineffectual as a means of registering disapproval of Hitler's policy, but his most tragic failure was the abortive attempt on Hitler's life on 20 July 1944.

[3] *Halder KTB* i. 374, 30 June 1940. Halder had not conferred with Hitler since 8 June.

[4] Ibid., p. 375, 30 June 1940.

[5] Ibid. Hitler's view at this time was illustrated by the following snatch of conversation overheard by Speer at field headquarters: 'Now that we have shown what we are capable of . . . believe me, Keitel, a campaign against Russia would be like a child's game in a sand-box by comparison' (*Speer*, p. 173).

tasks which von Weizsäcker's statement had raised. Next day he visited the Chief of the Naval Staff, Admiral Schniewind, and discussed the possibility of undertaking an invasion of England.[1] He also conferred on the reorganization of the Army for its future tasks with General Fromm, Chief of the Reserve Army, who, he noticed, 'seemed unwilling to disband formations in the East'.[2] On arriving back at Fontainebleau he warned Colonel von Greiffenberg of the Operations Branch that there were two major problems still to be solved, the defeat of England, and the delivery of 'a military blow at Russia which will force her to recognise Germany's dominant role in Europe'.[3]

At this time the Deputy Chief of Staff, General von Stülpnagel, and his chief assistant, General Mieth, were both transferred to the Armistice Commission. This placed a heavy burden of work on Colonel von Greiffenberg, and Halder warned him that in order to cope with the strategic planning to be expected he should divide his Operations Branch into separate working groups.[4]

Next day Halder and Colonel Kinzel, Chief of the Foreign Armies East Branch, held a briefing conference with General von Küchler and his Chief of Staff, General Marcks.[5] A week before the end of the campaign in the West the General Staff had begun to plan the transfer of fifteen divisions to the East. On 25 June this number was increased to twenty-four, including six Panzer and three motorized divisions.[6] All formations in the East were now to be placed under von Küchler's command for 'special military tasks'. Halder told von Küchler and Marcks that for the time being their purpose in the East was 'to demonstrate (*dokumentieren*) the presence of the German Army'. However, it was stressed that they should not 'openly reveal a hostile attitude'. Their arrival in the East was to appear part of the normal redisposition of forces after the completion of a campaign. Thus one of von Küchler's first acts in his new command was to issue an order to his formation commanders designed to scotch rumours of a deterioration in Russo-German relations.[7] In fact, the

[1] *Halder KTB* ii. 3, 1 July 1940.

[2] Ibid., p. 4, 1 July 1940.

[3] Ibid., p. 6, 3 July 1940; see also ibid., p. 15, 9 July 1940: '*Rußland – England*.'

[4] Ibid., pp. 6–7, 3 July 1940.

[5] Ibid., p. 8, 4 July 1940; *AOK 18 Ia, 157/40gKdos Chefs KTB AOK 18*, Bundesarchiv-Militärarchiv.

[6] *Halder KTB* i. 358, 16 June and 372, 25 June 1940.

[7] ND NOKW–1531. See also G. L. Weinberg, 'Der deutsche Entschluß zum Angriff auf die Sowjetunion', *VfZ*, 1 (1953), 303.

transfer of German forces had been given extra impetus by the suspicion aroused in the German Army when the Soviet Union attempted to occupy not only Bessarabia, which lay within her 'sphere of influence', but also Bukhovina, which did not.[1] Subsequent changes in the General Staff's attitude towards Russia made the movement of forces to the East part of a continuous build-up of German might which culminated in the invasion of Russia in 1941.

Though Russia was not ignored in the plans and deployments of July 1940, the problem of England occupied most of the attention of the General Staff. The possibility that Britain was continuing the struggle in the hope of an alliance with Russia was discussed on 11 July by Halder and von Etzdorf, the representative of the Foreign Office with the General Staff.[2] Two days later Hitler repeated the same idea, but professed himself reluctant to expend German blood on the destruction of the British Empire, only to see it fall into the hands of 'Japan, America and others'.[3] The logical but as yet unspoken, conclusion to this line of argument seemed to be an attack on Russia to forestall an Anglo-Russian alliance, and so von Brauchitsch warned Halder to give further thought to the Russian problem so that 'the OKH shall not be caught unprepared'.[4]

This remark reflected another aspect of the attitude of the Army leaders to the possibility of a war with Russia. Pique at Hitler's failure to acknowledge the contribution of the General Staff to the recent victory over France and a humiliating awareness that their pessimistic warnings of French military power had proved unfounded had made the generals anxious to restore their status and prestige.[5] None was more eager in this endeavour than the Commander-in-Chief of the Army. Flushed with the victory and promotion won for him by more imaginative men, and impatient to prove that the Army could complete the establishment of a German hegemony over Europe,[6] Field-Marshal von Brauchitsch rushed with incautious zeal into the preparation of plans for an attack on Russia and for an invasion of England.

---

[1] See *NSR*, pp. 78, 155–6, 157 ff.; *Halder KTB* i. 358, 16 June 1940.

[2] Ibid., p. 18, 11 July 1940. See also Hassell, p. 134.

[3] Ibid., p. 21, 13 July 1940.                    [4] Klee, p. 191, n. 521.

[5] Op. cit., p. 7, 4 July 1940; see also p. 63, 13 August 1940.

[6] This intention clearly lies behind the discussion between von Brauchitsch and Halder on 30 July. See ibid., p. 46, 30 July 1940. Cf. Halder's discussion with von Greiffenberg, p. 6, 3 July 1940.

*The Conference on 21 July 1940*

When von Brauchitsch arrived for the Führer Conference on 21 July, Hitler was probably unaware that his Army Commander-in-Chief had discarded his customary attitudes of caution and pessimism.[1] Thus, he approached the subject of an attack on Russia guardedly, presenting it as a precautionary measure made necessary by Stalin's 'flirting' with Britain.[2] The response he received must have come as an agreeable surprise. For, according to Halder's account of the conference, a proposal was submitted to Hitler outlining the concentration, aims, and comparative strengths for an autumn campaign in Russia.[3] The punctuation as well as the form, normal staff sequence, and content of the proposal indicates that it was made by one speaker.[4] It was a proposal of extraordinary optimism. It suggested that using only 80 to 100 divisions Germany could defeat Russia in the autumn of 1940. Their concentration would take from four to six weeks. The military aims were loosely expressed as

the defeat of the Russian army or the capture of at least as much Russian territory as necessary to prevent enemy air attacks against Berlin and the Silesian industrial areas. It would be desirable to advance far enough to attack the most important Russian centres with our air force.[5]

The political aims were strongly reminiscent of the terms of the Treaty of Brest Litovsk which the Germans had imposed on Russia in 1918: the creation of a 'Ukrainian Empire' and a federation of Baltic States as a 'thorn in the flesh' of Russia. White Russia and Finland were merely named in Halder's notes, presumably they were to become part of a system of vassal buffer states from the White Sea and the Baltic to the Black Sea.[6] It was admitted that an eastern campaign in the autumn of 1940 would have the disadvantage of

---

[1] The last Führer Conference attended by von Brauchitsch was on 13 June 1940. See *KTB OKW* i. 158E.

[2] *Halder KTB* ii. 32, 22 July 1940.

[3] Ibid., pp. 32–3, 22 July 1940. The proposal comprises paragraphs 8 (*a*) to (*d*) inclusive. Paragraph (*e*) outlines the questions and discussion customary at the end of a presentation of this sort. The questions were probably posed by Hitler.

[4] The proposal conforms to the normal staff method and sequence for presenting a plan: (1) an indication of the basic idea; (2) aims; (3) method or allocation of force; (4) co-operation (omitted on this occasion); (5) logistics (also omitted); (6) questions. Cf. outline Plan 'Barbarossa', ibid., pp. 266 ff., 2 Feb. 1941.

[5] Ibid., p. 32, 22 July 1940.

[6] Ibid., p. 33, 22 July 1940.

relieving Britain from the pressure of air attacks, and would enable the United States to deliver supplies to both Great Britain and Russia.[1]

The only person present who could have made such a proposal was Field-Marshal von Brauchitsch. Generals Halder, Siewert, and Philippi all stated when questioned on this point that it would have been quite out of character for their former chief to act in this way.[2] Halder pointed out that a great schism existed between the aristocrat who had been a page to the last Empress and 'the man from the gutter'. But this attitude ignored the effect of the isolation in which von Brauchitsch found himself, an isolation to which Halder had also contributed by keeping the control of operations in his own hands. It also ignored the fact that in November 1939 von Brauchitsch had already shown himself capable of suddenly abandoning his normally withdrawn attitude in Hitler's presence and of making impetuous, ill-considered statements. General Siewert, who was Chief Staff Officer to von Brauchitsch in 1940, could not recall that he had any studies or plans for an attack on Russia at that time. Nevertheless, the evidence of Halder's diary indicates that such studies did exist in the General Staff and could have been in the Field-Marshal's brief-case for use if the occasion arose on 21 July. It is significant that General Warlimont, who, as a former member of the OKW, probably felt less personal loyalty to von Brautchitsch, thought that by the summer of 1940 he was desperately seeking ways to counter the growing influence of the OKW and to reassert himself as Commander-in-Chief of the Army.[3] Warlimont agreed that the proposal of a major land campaign would serve both these purposes.

The alternative explanation, that the entry in Halder's diary on 22 July 1940 records a dialogue between Hitler and someone else, seems unlikely, not only because it has the unity of form of a single report, but also because none of Hitler's economic or strategic directives gave any hint that he contemplated an attack in the East in 1940. Later he admitted that he was attracted by the idea, but his subsequent doubt about its feasibility suggests that it was not his.[4] Neither General Jeschonnek, Chief of Staff of the Luftwaffe, who represented Göring at the conference, nor Admiral Raeder would have presented an outline plan for a land campaign. Keitel and

[1] Ibid.
[2] Conversations with the author, June–July 1969.
[3] Conversation with the author, 27 June 1969.
[4] *Halder KTB* ii. 49–50, 31 July 1940.

Jodl never initiated proposals of this type at conferences attended by the chiefs of the other senior staffs. It is therefore most unlikely to have come from them, especially since they rejected it within a week of this conference.[1]

In contrast, the OKH had been discussing an operation against Russia since the beginning of July. Furthermore, the General Staff worked upon the proposal for a week after the conference on 21 July with every sign of approval. So, irrespective of whether the proposal stemmed from von Brauchitsch or not, the OKH undoubtedly accepted Hitler's first verbal orders for the preparation of plans for a war with Russia with neither surprise nor protest.

During the following week Halder discussed operational possibilities, comparative strengths, and road and rail communications in the East with various department heads of the General Staff.[2] On 29 July he sent for General Marcks, Chief of Staff of the 18th Army, and told him to delay his departure for the East in order to undertake a 'special task', the planning of the invasion of Russia.[3] But even as he briefed Marcks for his task Halder was plagued by uncertainties. On the following evening he reviewed the over-all situation with von Brauchitsch and reached the conclusion that an attack on Russia, as an alternative to the invasion of England in 1940, could be dangerous.[4] A number of factors could have contributed to their change of mind. The latest estimates from the Foreign Armies East Branch showed that the Soviet strength was much greater than the 50 to 75 good divisions reported on 21 July.[5] Furthermore, General Fellgiebel stated on 26 July that the simultaneous preparation of signals networks for 'Sea Lion' and the East was impossible.[6] On 28 July the Army leaders received from the Naval Staff a memorandum which seemed to upset all their previous ideas about a cross-Channel invasion.[7] The situation was further complicated by pessimistic reports about the forthcoming Italian operation in North Africa.[8]

The combined effect of these factors made von Brauchitsch and

[1] See *Halder KTB.* ii. 32, n. 9; Hillgruber, *Strategie*, p. 218, n. 52.

[2] *Halder KTB* ii. 35, 24 July; 37, 26 July; 39, 27 July; 40, 28 July 1940.

[3] Ibid., p. 41, 29 July 1940.

[4] Op. cit., pp. 45–6, 30 July 1940.

[5] John Erickson, *The Soviet High Command, A Military Political History 1918–1941* (London, 1962), p. 557, n. 125; *IMT*, vii. U.S.S.R. 228, 301.

[6] *Halder KTB* ii. 33, 22 July, 36, 26 July 1940.

[7] Ibid., p. 40, 28 July 1940.

[8] Ibid., p. 38, 27 July; p. 45, 30 July 1940.

Halder realize that it was essential, first of all, to knock Britain out of the war by means of an invasion. But if this could not take place in the autumn the greatest danger would be the loss of the strategic initiative in the West. They decided, therefore, that the Wehrmacht should not turn East but strike at Britain by conducting operations against Gibraltar, Palestine, and Suez, by supporting the Italians with Panzer formations and by encouraging Russian expansion towards the Persian Gulf. The possible value of Russian co-operation and the dispersion of the German forces in these widespread operations made an attack on the Soviet Union neither desirable nor practicable until Britain had been defeated. They felt that rather than start a war on two fronts it would be better to remain friendly with Russia. In contrast to the later assertions of the need for a preventive war, von Brauchitsch and Halder agreed that there were really no grounds for conflict over Soviet aspirations towards the Persian Gulf and the Straits, and in the Balkans, where Germany did have economic interests, the two countries could 'keep out of one another's way'.[1] Under these circumstances von Brauchitsch and Halder began to question the idea of an eastern campaign and decided that

we can decisively strike the British in the Mediterranean and push them away from Asia, assist the Italians to build up their Mediterranean Empire, and, with the help of Russia, build up our own empire in West and Northern Europe. We can then face with confidence a protracted war with Britain.[1]

Confronted by unexpected complications, the Army leaders were evidently reverting to their earlier caution. But some aspects of their discussion on 30 July were just as unrealistic as their earlier support for an autumn attack on Russia. Von Brauchitsch well knew that in advocating an operation in the East he was anticipating the wishes of the Führer, thus he must have been equally aware that Hitler would welcome neither the idea of limiting his *Lebensraum* to north or western Europe, nor of turning the Wehrmacht to the south, especially within days of having been assured of the feasibility of an autumn campaign in Russia. By revealing such vacillation von Brauchitsch would surely have revived all the contempt that Hitler had felt towards him in the autumn of 1939.[2] It was thus fortunate

[1] Ibid., p. 46, 30 July 1940.
[2] In November 1939 Hitler admitted to General Guderian, then a junior corps commander, that the only reason he had not sacked von Brauchitsch was that he lacked a suitable replacement. See Guderian, pp. 87–8. Later Hitler said of his

for the Army leaders that Hitler was not yet prepared to abandon Operation 'Sea Lion' and it was left to Admiral Raeder in September to become the chief advocate for the diversion of the major effort to the Mediterranean.

The naval records of the conference on 21 July do not mention the proposed attack on Russia. It seems probable that, as in the case of the conference on 31 July, Admiral Raeder left before this topic was discussed.[1] Nevertheless, awareness of Hitler's long-term aims[2] and doubts about the possibility of a short war in the West caused the Naval Staff also to examine the prospects in the East. In a study entitled 'Observations on Russia', dated 28 July 1940,[3] it urged the establishment of an impregnable continental base and an autarkic war industry, and suggested the conquest of Russia as a means to those ends. The defeat of the inferior Soviet forces and the occupation of an area extending to Lake Ladoga–Smolensk– Crimea was described as 'militarily feasible'. Displaying the same optimism as that of the OKH a week earlier, the Naval Staff stated that the operation in the East might be carried out in the autumn of 1940 if Britain could be held down with comparatively small air forces. Indeed, the whole concept had a marked similarity to the outline plan presented to Hitler on 21 July. However, unlike Field-Marshal von Brauchitsch, Admiral Raeder did not support the idea of an attack in the East before Britain was defeated, and there is no evidence that he ever revealed the contents of this study to Hitler.[4] Nor did Hitler consult him on the decision to turn East. Leaving both the Naval and Luftwaffe Staffs to conduct their planning for the war against Britain, Hitler relied upon his leading soldiers for advice upon this question.

Army Commander-in-Chief, 'He's no soldier, he's but a poor thing and a man of straw.' *Hitler's Secret Conversations*, p. 194.

---

[1] See Hillgruber, *Strategie*, p. 218, n. 53.     [2] See above p. 29.

[3] West Germany, Bundesarchiv Koblenz, K10–2/10, 75MS 'Betrachtungen über Rußland', quoted by Klee, pp. 191–2, and Hillgruber, *Strategie*, pp. 220–1. See also Horst Steigleder, 'Zur Rolle der Kriegsmarine bei der Vorbereitung des Überfalls des faschistischen Deutschlands auf die UdSSR', Hans Höhn (ed.), *Auf antisowjetischem Kriegskurs*, pp. 440–3.

[4] Steigleder describes the study as presenting the 'true attitude of the Naval Staff towards the attack on the U.S.S.R.' However, it probably represents the ideas of a certain group within the Naval Staff. The resemblance between this study and the proposal of 21 July could have resulted from the use of data supplied by the OKH liaison staff at Naval Headquarters. Raeder's subsequent attempts to dissuade Hitler from the decision to strike eastward make it most unlikely that he agreed with the contents of this document.

CHAPTER III

# Hitler's Grand Strategic Decisions
# July–November 1940

## The Decision to Attack Russia in 1941

PROFESSOR J. B. BURY once stated: 'When a war breaks out, there are two things to be explained which must be kept distinct: why the aggressors go to war at all, and why they go to war at the time they actually do.'[1] The reason why the Germans invaded Russia at all was that such an attack was an essential step in the policy of conquering *Lebensraum* which Hitler had followed throughout his career. His actions in the summer of 1940 confirm that this policy was still the driving force behind his grand strategy. The desire to attack Russia as soon as possible was the only compelling reason for his initial choice of a strategy of annihilation against Britain, the attempt to defeat her quickly by direct assaults on her homeland, in preference to a strategy of exhaustion, combining a major effort in the Mediterranean with a blockade by sea and air forces. The Mediterranean theatre in July 1940 offered ample opportunities for a series of swift *Blitzkrieg* campaigns of the type that appealed to Hitler's impatient mentality and need for spectacular action. But his desire for conquest, though far from limited, was too strongly oriented eastwards. He rejected any strategy that left uncertain the date of the attack of Russia. Thus the main decision was not whether to attack Russia but only when. How and when to defeat Britain depended in turn upon this decision.

The reason why Hitler decided to attack Russia in the spring of 1941 was that after consulting his closest military advisers, Keitel and Jodl, he felt that this was the earliest and also the latest date on which he could safely concentrate sufficient forces in the East for the attack. The contents of Hitler's economic directives suggest that in June 1940 he hoped for a period of peace, a recuperative pause,

[1] J. B. Bury, *The Ancient Greek Historians* (New York, 1958), pp. 93–4.

between the war in the West and the coming struggle in the East.[1]
In July he realized that it might not be possible to defeat Britain
quickly with the limited forces at his disposal. On the other hand,
Soviet pressure on Rumania made him acutely aware that the
Russians might not remain bound by their agreements with Germany
long enough for him to build up the necessary naval and air strength
in the West to defeat Britain by a strategy of exhaustion, and then
convert the Wehrmacht for war in the East. The vital question,
whether to attempt a swift blow in the East in the autumn of 1940
or to delay the eastern campaign and invade England first, was
openly raised at the conference on 21 July. At this time von Brauchitsch and Halder showed unbounded, if short-lived, confidence
in the ability of the Wehrmacht to conduct whichever of these
operations the Führer chose. Hitler, however, was not certain that
either operation could succeed. He viewed the situation far more
realistically than his Army leaders. On 21 July he described the
invasion of England as 'not just a river crossing, but the crossing
of a sea which is dominated by the enemy'.[2] Similarly, he greeted the
proposal for an autumn attack on Russia not with unrestrained
enthusiasm but with questions which reflected doubts about its
feasibility: 'What operational objectives can we set? What strength?
Time and place for preparation?'[3] He was evidently not convinced
by the answers he received from von Brauchitsch, and shortly after
the conference he asked Keitel and Jodl for their views. They replied
in a memorandum signed by Keitel and probably written by Jodl,
that the time, space, and weather factors rendered an autumn attack
on Russia 'totally impracticable'.[4] Hitler accepted their objections
and informed them that he had already decided to plan the operation
for the spring of 1941.

This decision was a compromise solution. It did not make a choice

[1] See Thomas, pp. 406–7. The general impression given by the directive of
14 June 1940 is one of a basic recuperation to be undertaken by all three services. See also Hillgruber, *Strategie*, p. 208.
[2] Naval War Staff Diary, 21 July 1940, quoted by Wheatley, p. 43. See also
*Halder KTB* ii. 31, 22 July 1940; E. Wagner, p. 194.
[3] Ibid., p. 33, 22 July 1940.
[4] Warlimont, p. 112. Keitel's post-war account was confused and inaccurate,
probably with the deliberate intention of underplaying his role in the decision
to invade Russia. He stated that he heard of the decision only in August and com-
posed a memorandum opposing the idea. However, this is evidently not the same
document as that seen by Warlimont in July. See Görlitz, *Keitel*, pp. 240, 242–5;
and *IMT* x. 425 ff.

between concentrating all efforts upon first defeating Britain and then attacking Russia or vice versa. It gave Germany almost a year in which to prepare for the war in the East. During this time a series of blows could be launched at Britain which, though they might not defeat her, would further reduce her ability to interfere on the Continent. Though some forces might have to remain in the West, the bulk of the Wehrmacht could be employed in the East for a full summer and autumn campaign. Thus there seemed to be a good chance of defeating Russia in a single *Blitzkrieg* campaign.[1] Since Britain was powerless to intervene Hitler regarded it as hardly legitimate to refer to a two-front war.

Hitler has been correctly criticized for his failure to appreciate the importance of naval power. Thus it is illogical to attribute to him an inordinate dread of a war on two fronts in 1940 when the shattered remnants of Britain's land forces were confined to their home islands or to distant outposts overseas. As on previous occasions her refusal to see 'logically' was a nuisance involving improvisations and delays, but it was not to be allowed to change the entire pattern or main aims of Hitler's grand strategic plans. He ordered the air attacks and preparations for an invasion of Britain in the hope of snatching an easy victory from his maimed and isolated opponent. Operation 'Sea Lion' was not a mere bluff prepared merely for its psychological effect, because if the British morale or economy had suffered a collapse it would have been launched.[2] Nevertheless, Hitler realized that the British might refuse to be cowed and that under these circumstances his decision to turn east might be subjected to some criticism. Thus, at conferences on this subject Hitler played the role of master strategist before his generals, justifying his aggressive designs with a series of political exaggerations and inconsistent strategic rationalizations. He countered Keitel's misgivings with a vague reference to the 'threatening danger' to be fended off in the East and stated that

he had already ordered von Brauchitsch to double the number of Panzer divisions . . . he had not built up this great mobile army just to let it be idle in wartime. The war wouldn't end itself and he could no longer attack the British with the Army in 1941; a landing in England would by then be impossible.[3]

---

[1] See *Halder KTB* ii. 49, 31 July 1940.
[2] Ibid., p. 48, 31 July 1940: 'If we get the impression that the British are collapsing, and that after a time the [desired] effect will follow, then attack [i.e. landing operation].'                [3] Görlitz, *Keitel*, p. 243.

A further indication of Hitler's thoughts on the East was given on 29 July when General Jodl informed Colonel Warlimont and his three section chiefs in the National Defence Department of the OKW of the decision to launch 'a surprise attack on Russia ... at the earliest possible moment, i.e. in May 1941'.[1] Although it conflicted with the ideas expressed in his earlier studies and memoranda,[2] Jodl had accepted the mixture of truth and rationalization with which Hitler had justified this decision, and he now presented Hitler's arguments to his subordinates. He said that the Führer considered 'a collision with Bolshevism was bound to come and that it was better therefore to have this campaign now, when we were at the height of our military power, than to have to call the German people to arms once more in the years to come.'[3] Admitting that the operation would take place even if the war against Britain had not been concluded, Jodl explained that it was 'the best method of forcing England to make peace if this had not proved possible by other means'.[4] As we shall see later, Jodl himself was by no means convinced by this argument.[5] But out of loyalty to Hitler he concealed his doubts from Warlimont and the others. When they protested against the prospect of a two-front war he engaged them in 'an hour of bitter argument' in which he 'countered every question'.[6] Finally, he sent them away to draw up a directive for the administrative preparations for the concentration of forces in Poland known as *Aufbau Ost*.[7]

### Three Decisions

Hitler's attempts to justify his decisions and to dramatize his historical role were repeated in the analysis of the war that he dictated to Martin Bormann in 1945. In this account he attributed his decision on when to attack Russia to three different dates. The first was in July 1940, 'as soon as I realised that Britain was determined to remain stubborn'. The second occasion was 'on the very anniversary of

[1] Warlimont, p. 111; see also Greiner, pp. 288 ff.

[2] See p. 43 above and Hillgruber, *Strategie*, pp. 157 ff.; *IMT* xxviii. 1776–PS, 301 ff.

[3] Warlimont, p. 112.                                    [4] Ibid., p. 111.

[5] See *KTB OKW* i. 981. Nevertheless, Jodl's support for Hitler's decision was so convincing that Warlimont was openly taken aback when the author drew his attention to the doubts expressed in Jodl's memorandum dated 3 Dec. 1940 revealed after the war.

[6] Op. cit., p. 112.

[7] *Testament of Adolf Hitler*, p. 96.

the signing of the Moscow Pact'.[1] on 28 September. The third was in mid November 1940 'immediately after Molotov's visit to Berlin'.[2] Subsequent writers including both generals and historians, who believe that Hitler's main motive in attacking Russia was the conquest of *Lebensraum* have selected the first date for the decision.[3] Those who see the eastern campaign as a preventive war or an indirect means of defeating Britain have chosen the last date, or have stated that the final decision came even later.[4] But none of these interpretations explains the significance of the Moscow Pact anniversary. Nor do they make it clear why Hitler should have found it necessary to make or reaffirm his decision to attack Russia on these separate occasions.

An examination of the situation facing Hitler on each occasion reveals that each one did in fact have a special significance. The initial decision, made in the last days of July 1940, remained constant and was reaffirmed on the two subsequent occasions. The factor which caused him to reappraise his grand strategy was not Russia but Great Britain. For once he had decided to strike at Russia in May 1941 it became desirable to make every attempt to defeat the British. Thus on 31 July 1940 Hitler's verbal orders for the preparations for the spring campaign in the East were accompanied by orders for immediate air attacks on Britain. When it was clear that these had failed, Hitler turned to an attempt to form a coalition directed against the British Empire, especially its bases in the Mediterranean. This was accompanied, on 28 September, by a definite confirmation of the decision to attack Russia as scheduled. Finally after the Molotov conversations, Hitler abandoned hope of defeating Britain before attacking Russia and had to be content to isolate her from Europe by eliminating her last footholds in Greece and Gibraltar. The reaffirmation of the decision to attack Russia in 1941 now caused Hitler to show signs of nervous anxiety, for this time it definitely meant that Germany would be fighting a two-front

[1] Ibid., p. 99. The Moscow Pact comprised the Non-Aggression Treaty of 23 Aug. and the Boundary and Friendship Treaty of 28 Sept. 1939. For reasons explained below, it is likely that Hitler was referring to the latter.

[2] Ibid., p. 65.

[3] For example: Warlimont, p. 114; Alan Clark, *Barbarossa, The Russian–German Conflict, 1941–1945* (London, 1965), pp. 19–20; Dallin, pp. 12–14; Weinberg, 'Der deutsche Entschluß, . . .', p. 313.

[4] Hinsley, p. 119; Halder, *Hitler as Warlord*, p. 39; Hans-Günther Seraphim and Andreas Hillgruber, 'Hitlers Entschluß zum Angriff auf Rußland', *VfZ* 2 (1954), p. 241.

war with a far more active enemy in the West than he had expected in July. By November 1940 the British had demonstrated that they were capable of striking back. They had bombed the Reich throughout the autumn and vigorously attacked the Italian fleet.[1] Nevertheless, Hitler subdued his doubts by deluding himself with optimistic assessments of Soviet weakness and the rationalization that the time which he had selected was 'especially favourable'.[2] Such arguments, stressing the importance of the timing of the Russian operation and its relationship to the war with Great Britain, were easy to use because at the conference with the Army leaders on 31 July Hitler had taken care to present his initial decision to attack Russia in the spring of 1941 in just such terms.

### The Conference on 31 July 1940

When Field-Marshal von Brauchitsch, General Halder, Admiral Raeder, Field-Marshal Keitel, and General Jodl gathered at the *Berghof* for a Führer Conference on the last day of July they had no unified ideas on the further prosecution of the war. The Army leaders wished to press for an invasion of England regardless of the difficulties revealed by the Naval Staff. Failing this, they preferred a strategy of attrition, including operations in the Mediterranean, to the alternative of an attack in the East, which ten days earlier they had optimistically supported. Admiral Raeder wished to postpone Operation 'Sea Lion', but he was not yet ready to abandon it altogether. Nor apparently was he prepared to advance the case for an attack on Russia recommended by some of his staff. The leaders of the OKW had accepted the idea of such an attack provided it was not attempted in the autumn of 1940. The Luftwaffe was not represented on this occasion.

The lack of co-ordination between the German military leaders was of little consequence because, as usual, Hitler had called them together not to seek their advice but to inform them of the decisions which he had made. So when Admiral Raeder opened the proceedings by proposing that Operation 'Sea Lion' should be postponed until the spring of 1941 he was overruled.[3] Nevertheless, Hitler reassured him that a landing would be attempted only if the air

---

[1] On 11 Nov. 1940 aircraft of the Fleet Air Arm seriously damaged three Italian battleships in Taranto harbour.

[2] *KTB OKW* i. 205, 5 Dec. 1940; see also 258, 9 Jan. 1941.

[3] *Halder KTB* ii. 47, 31 July 1940; see also p. 48, n. 5.

assault brought about a favourable situation. Similarly, when von
Brauchitsch attempted to suggest an operation in North Africa,
in accordance with the alternative strategy that he had discussed on
the previous evening with Halder, this was brushed aside by Hitler
as a 'diversionary manœuvre'.[1] However, the Army leaders were
relieved to hear that he still thought as they did that a 'really decisive
effect' could be achieved 'only by an attack on England',[1] and were
glad to drop the discussion of operations in the Mediterranean when
Hitler gave orders for the commencement of the air offensive which
was to become the Battle of Britain.[2]

The reason for Hitler's eagerness to seek a swift decision in the
West in preference to the longer but less risky alternative of a siege
of Britain and a war of attrition against the British Empire was
not revealed until Admiral Raeder had left the conference room.
Presumably Hitler assumed that his naval Commander-in-Chief
would object to the decision to attack Russia, and he kept him in
ignorance of it until September.[3] Even though he had no reason
to expect any criticism from the leaders of the Army or the OKW,
he approached the subject somewhat obliquely, carefully presenting
a strategic basis for his decision. If an invasion of England did not
take place, he stated, all factors that gave Britain hope of a change
in the situation must be eliminated. These, he stressed, were Russia
and America. But if Russia were to be destroyed, the corresponding
increase in the power of Japan would prevent America from aiding
Britain. Thus the key to the strategic problem facing Germany was the
destruction of Russia, 'for then Britain's last hope will be shattered'.[4]
All this led him to the decision that 'Russia must be defeated in the
course of this struggle. Spring 1941.'[4]

The whole charade was transparently weak. Hitler referred to
'overheard conversations' between the Soviet President, Kalinin,
and the Yugoslav Ambassador in Moscow, which revealed only an
understandable concern on the part of the Soviet leader at the
position of strength attained by Germany. There was no substantial
evidence that the Russians had any intention of aiding Britain.[5]

[1] Ibid.                                    [2] Ibid., p. 48, 31 July 1940.
[3] See Raeder, pp. 333, 335; see also Hinsley, p. 94; Hillgruber, *Strategie*,
p. 218, n. 53; Warlimont, p. 115.
[4] Op. cit., p. 49, 31 July 1940.
[5] *Halder KTB* ii. 49, 31 July; see also p. 34, 22 July 1940; *DGFP*(D) x. 321, n. 1.;
Philip W. Fabry, *Der Hitler-Stalin-Pakt, 1939–1941* (Darmstadt, 1962), pp. 257 ff.
Fabry lays considerable stress upon such incidents to support the argument

On the contrary Hitler was reported as stating only ten days earlier that 'even though Moscow is unenthusiastic about Germany's great success, she will nevertheless make no effort to enter the war against Germany of her own accord.'[1] Thus a German attack was the most certain way to force Stalin into the very alliance that Hitler claimed that he wished to avert. Furthermore, the predatory aims, including the annexation of the Ukraine, White Russia, and the Baltic States, which Hitler went on to describe, were hardly indicative of a purely preventive war to avert an alliance between Britain and Russia.[2]

Though he presented the whole concept as an alternative to the invasion of England,[3] these aims must have dispelled the idea that if Britain made peace before the spring the Russian campaign would have been cancelled as no longer necessary. Yet General Halder claimed after the war that in spite of the categorical nature of the entry in his diary neither he nor von Brauchitsch gained the impression from the conference on 31 July that Hitler made an 'irrevocable decision' to attack Russia, but only gave 'the starting shot [for preparations] for foreseeable possibilities'.[4] The Army's role in preparing plans for an eastern offensive in the autumn and Hitler's own admission that he would have preferred to attack Russia in 1940 indicated an eagerness to expand eastward, not merely to complete a plan for possible use if Russia became more hostile.[5] General Jodl, in briefing his staff two days earlier, expressed no doubt of the finality of Hitler's decision.[6] Furthermore, in spite of the fact that the date set was a long way off, and that Hitler had absolute power to change his mind on grand strategic matters, the changes in economic and foreign policies coupled with the decision to attack Russia placed growing limitations on his freedom of choice. These changes, the increase of the Army to 180 divisions, and the

that Hitler's decision to attack Russia was a reaction to Soviet political and military threats.

[1] *FNC* 1940, i. 81, 21 July 1940, quoted by Wheatley, p. 141, n. 2. Cf. *Halder KTB* ii. 32, 22 July 1940: 'There are no signs of Soviet activity directed against us.'
[2] Ibid., p. 50, 31 July 1940.
[3] See ibid., p. 49, n. 11. The entry 'Angenommen: England tritt nicht ein . . .' is interpreted as 'if the landing operation should not be carried out . . .'
[4] General Franz Halder, letter to Andreas Hillgruber, 5 Oct. 1954, quoted by Fabry, 498, n. 272.
[5] *Halder KTB* ii. 50, 31 July 1940. Note the words 'Standstill in winter conceivable. Therefore better wait [till 1941], but definite decision to finish off Russia.'
[6] See p. 66 above. General Warlimont was convinced that Hitler made a firm decision in the last week of July. Conversation with the author, 27 June 1969.

strengthening of German resistance to Soviet pressure on Rumania and Finland,[1] also reduced Hitler's flexibility after the failure of the Luftwaffe over England, when he sought alternative methods of defeating the British.

## The Second Decision, 28 September 1940

On 31 July Hitler stated that if the results of the air attacks on Britain were not favourable preparations for Operation 'Sea Lion' would be halted.[2] Nevertheless, in mid September when confronted with the bitter fact that the Luftwaffe had not achieved the prerequisites for an invasion Hitler showed great reluctance to abandon the operation.[3] It was not until late in the month that he turned to the Mediterranean in search of alternative means of defeating Britain. Since the end of July the OKW and OKH had been encouraged to study the possibilities there in case the Luftwaffe should fail.[4] But they had done so without enthusiasm, and it was Admiral Raeder who became the chief advocate of a major effort in the Mediterranean. Appalled when he finally heard of the decision to attack Russia without first ending the war in the West, he attempted to convince Hitler that German control of the Mediterranean and Middle East would not only defeat Britain but also enable Germany to threaten Russia from the south.[5] Though Hitler had no intention of changing his plans for the attack on Russia, the idea of bringing Britain to heel by striking at her overseas possessions seemed particularly favourable at that moment because the Tripartite Pact was to be signed the next day, 27 September, and von Ribbentrop was full of enthusiasm for the idea of inviting the Soviet Union to join its signatories in the partition of the British Empire.[6] So, while the representatives of Germany, Italy, and Japan gathered in the Reich Chancellery in Berlin, Keitel issued a short directive to the economic staffs stating that with immediate effect and until 15 November the Army construction programme, code name 'Axis',

[1] On 31 July Hitler named Finland as a possible ally in an attack on Russia. He also stated that Hungarian-Rumanian disagreements would have to be 'regulated' after which a guarantee would be given to Rumania. Op. cit.

[2] *Halder KTB* ii. 48, 31 July 1940.

[3] Ibid., p. 99, 14 Sept. 1940; see also Wheatley, pp. 85, 94–5.

[4] See Warlimont, pp. 109–10; *Halder KTB* ii. 79, 27 Aug. 1940. It seems likely from Warlimont's evidence that Jodl was the initiator of these studies.

[5] See FCNA, 26 Sept. 1940.

[6] See *NSR*, pp. 196–213, 255–8. See also *Halder KTB* ii, 118–19, 30 Sept. 1940.

would be given priority above the special programme for Operation 'Sea Lion'.[1] The strategy of direct assault on the British mainland having failed, the Wehrmacht was now to be turned to a strategy of coalition warfare against the British Empire.

This did not mean, however, that Hitler's resolve to attack Russia in May was in any way diminished. On the next day, 28 September, the first anniversary of the Russo-German Boundary and Friendship Treaty, he issued a major economic directive confirming the verbal orders of 31 July and the Führer Command of 26 August for an increase in the Army. The main features of the new war economic programme were:

*a.* In the Army, the preparation of armaments for 180 field divisions and certain occupation divisions by spring 1941;

*b.* In the Navy, unrestricted continuation of the U-boat programme beyond 1 January 1942;

*c.* In the Luftwaffe, raising of the anti-aircraft artillery priority and the speediest increase in anti-aircraft artillery.[2]

This directive, together with that issued by Keitel on the previous day, meant that the Army's immediate task would be to conduct certain limited operations in the Mediterranean theatre with the support of part of the Navy and the Luftwaffe.[3] Meanwhile, the remaining naval and air forces would maintain pressure on the British homeland and the bulk of the Army would prepare for the invasion of Russia. The stress on anti-aircraft artillery reflected Hitler's concern at the growing success of the R.A.F. night bombing on German cities and, perhaps also, the fear that the war in the East might expose important industrial targets to Soviet air attacks.[4]

On 29 September Field-Marshal von Brauchitsch was informed by Keitel that as a result of major changes in strategy Hitler was to meet Mussolini to discuss the conduct of the war in the Mediterranean.[5] But events in October showed that Hitler had left too late his bid to undertake a major effort in the Mediterranean. The opportunity had existed in July, but Hitler had gambled that he could

---

[1] Thomas, p. 430.          [2] Ibid., p. 432.

[3] The war-economic priority programme for code name 'Axis' was to last only until 15 Nov. 1940. Thus a sustained offensive in the south was evidently not envisaged.          [4] See *Halder KTB* ii. 33, 22 July 1940.

[5] Ibid. p. 118–19, 30 Sept. 1940. See also *DGFP*(D) x. 245 ff.; Warlimont, pp. 121–2; Galeazzo Ciano, *The Ciano Diaries. 1939–1943*, ed. Hugh Gibson (New York, 1946), pp. 298–9, Paul Schmidt, *Hitler's Interpreter* (New York, 1951), pp. 192, 194.

obtain a quick success by direct attacks on Britain and dismissed operations in the Mediterranean as 'diversionary manœuvres'.[1] On 31 July his divided and uncertain military leaders had accepted this decision without protest because none of them was able confidently to offer a better solution. Although on that occasion the Army leaders preferred operations in the Mediterranean to an attack on Russia,[2] they still gave priority to Operation 'Sea Lion' and clung to the hope that the Luftwaffe and the Navy would somehow produce conditions favouring a Channel crossing. For their part, Keitel and Jodl both would have welcomed an opportunity to avoid a two-front war. Jodl especially had consistently suggested anti-British operations in the Mediterranean in memoranda issued in January, March, and June 1940, and abandoned these views only in deference to Hitler.[3] Göring also preferred a Mediterranean campaign to the attack on Russia, but he stood too much in awe of Hitler to dispute his decisions.[4] Admiral Raeder, as we have seen, did not believe that Operation 'Sea Lion' could be undertaken until the spring of 1941, and although he did not suggest a Mediterranean effort until September, he probably would have done so earlier if he had been aware of Hitler's decision to attack Russia.

The political situation was also favourable in July 1940. France was cowed by defeat, Italy and Spain eager for easy gains, and Russia devoid of tangible grounds for suspecting Germany of ill faith. But Hitler's decisions to attack Britain immediately and directly and to strike Russia in the spring changed the entire situation. The failure of the German air attacks on Britain made the leaders of Spain and France wary of committing themselves to fight an enemy still capable of striking back. By October there was an even greater problem: the leaders of Italy, Spain, and Vichy France were each developing conflicting hopes and plans for the future of the French North African colonies. On 3 October von Etzdorf told Halder that Hitler took the cynical view that the solution could be found only by means of a 'grandiose deceit'.[5] Nevertheless,

[1] *Halder KTB* ii. 47, 31 July 1940.
[2] Ibid.
[3] See pp. 43, 66 above. See also Guderian, pp. 136–7.
[4] See Hillgruber, *Strategie.* pp. 396–7. Evidence of Göring's support for a Mediterranean strategy is slight. After the war he described 'his plan' for a huge drive to the south, but this was evidently calculated to demonstrate his military wisdom. See Milton Shulman, *Defeat in the West* (London, 1947), pp. 55–6; Liddell Hart, *On the Other Side . . .*, p. 233.
[5] *Halder KTB* ii. 124, 3 Oct. 1940.

in view of the urgent need to cripple the British before turning the Wehrmacht eastward, Hitler decided to undertake personally the task of persuading Mussolini, Pétain, and Franco to join in a 'continental coalition' against Britain. Thus, in contrast to his usual practice of summoning the heads of foreign states to Germany, he set out on a journey across Western Europe to Italy, France, and the frontier of Spain.

At the meetings with Mussolini, Laval, Franco, and Pétain Hitler unfolded a consistent grand strategy. He revealed only enough of his plans to make the proposed coalition appear as a convincing means of achieving his main aim. This, he stated, was to bring the war to an end as quickly as possible. Even if the gains were smaller, he preferred 'to achieve a swift victory . . . than to wage long dragged-out wars'.[1] He confessed with a show of frankness that direct assault on England had proved difficult. Germany lacked naval supremacy, and air superiority had not been decisive because of 'bad weather'. Britain's hopes lay in America and Russia. However, the Russians would not present any problem because the German Army was being reorganized and strengthened. While expressing the hope that the Russians might be encouraged to redirect their ambitions towards India or the Indian Ocean, Hitler admitted that it was doubtful whether they would in fact do anything in that direction.[2]

In Hitler's view, Britain's other hope, the United States, had been discouraged, like Russia, from entering the war by the world-wide strength of the Axis as expressed by the Tripartite Pact. However, he used the danger of American support for a British landing on the Atlantic coast of French Morocco in an attempt to win Italian and Spanish recognition of the need to bring Vichy France into the united front against Britain.

Throughout the planning for coalition warfare in the Mediterranean Hitler hesitated to commit large German land forces where they would depend upon the Italian fleet to defend their supply lines.[3] Thus his military strategy was based upon the commitment of army and Luftwaffe formations in support of Italian, Vichy French, and Spanish forces. Groups of Stukas and long-range fighters were to be established on bases in Spain and the Canary Islands to support the Vichy French land and naval defences of North Africa. The same air forces and heavy artillery units would support an assault

---

[1] Hillgruber, *Staatsmänner*, p. 139.    [2] Ibid., p. 109.
[3] *Halder KTB* ii. 164, 4 Nov. 1940.

on Gibraltar by a special force of mountain troops and assault pioneers.[1] Meanwhile, bombers were to mine the Suez Canal and Alexandria harbour and counter British naval supremacy in the eastern Mediterranean. These measures would open the way for the dispatch of Panzer and Stuka formations to spearhead Marshal Graziani's conquest of Egypt which would be followed by an advance through Palestine and Syria to Turkey.[2]

At a meeting on the Brenner Pass on 4 October Mussolini expressed full agreement with Hitler's Mediterranean strategy. He was won over by the Führer's assurance that Germany would never make peace with France without a fulfilment of Italian claims. Furthermore, the German plans for a vigorous prosecution of the war came as a relief to the Italian leaders who dreaded that Hitler might succeed in making peace with Britain before they had reaped a full harvest of spoils.

On 22 October Hitler met Laval at Montoire-sur-Loire and told him bluntly that the fate of France in the peace-making would depend largely upon her attitude towards the German attempt to end the war swiftly by means of a general continental mobilization against Britain. Laval replied that he identified French interests with the downfall of Britain, and Hitler, satisfied, moved his train on to the Spanish frontier at Hendaye. But the meeting next day proved disappointing. Hitler attempted to persuade General Franco that Spain must join the anti-British front even though her claims on the French Empire could not be fully met. The Spanish leader protested that his country's economy could not bear further burdens and refused to enter the war unless the reward was Gibraltar, the whole of French Morocco, and part of Algeria. The Germans came away from the meeting muttering about the 'false Spanish pride' of the 'Jesuit swine'.[3] Stopping again at Montoire on 24 October, Hitler was somewhat mollified by Marshal Pétain's readiness to endorse Laval's co-operative attitude. But in the early hours of the next morning the contents of a letter were transmitted to Hitler's train which revealed that Mussolini had completely changed his mind about accepting French membership in the Axis coalition. On the contrary, he now believed that the moment had come 'to define

[1] See Charles Burdick, *Germany's Military Strategy and Spain in World War II* (Syracuse, 1968).
[2] The main lines of Hitler's military strategy for the Mediterranean theatre were drawn at the conference with Raeder on 26 Sept. See FCNA 1940, p. 106.
[3] *Halder KTB* ii. 158, 1 Nov. 1940.

the shape of metropolitan and colonial France'.[1] As for Spain, that country would be more use to the Axis as a non-belligerent ally than as a weak and vulnerable combatant. Having destroyed the basis of the continental coalition, Mussolini proceeded to describe how Italy was about to strike alone at one of the last British bases on the continent—Greece.

Mussolini's self-assertive folly was his response to the arrival in Rumania of a German Military Mission. This was a direct result of Hitler's decision on 31 July to invade Russia. But to Mussolini, who was completely ignorant of the true nature of Hitler's strategy, it came as an unexpected affront because he had been repeatedly restrained by Hitler from any action that might precipitate a crisis in the Balkans and provoke Russian counter-measures there. Hitler's coup in Rumania reduced Mussolini's trust and revived his fears of a sudden agreement with France and a peace with Britain which would leave Italy almost empty-handed. He therefore decided to tell his German ally that he was 'putting an end to delays'.

Hitler's reaction was swift. He arranged to meet Mussolini in Florence and turned his train southward. His main aim was not to dissuade the Italians from the attack on Greece, but to gain a reaffirmation of Mussolini's willingness to accept Vichy France as an ally.[2] In this he was successful. He refrained from criticizing Mussolini for his decision to invade Greece, but he hinted at his concern at its possible consequences by offering a division of airborne troops and a division of parachute troops to seize Crete before the British got there. Halder was informed a few days later that in fact the Führer was 'very annoyed' about the Italians' action in Greece and had threatened to withhold German support. However, Hitler was still too concerned with patching up his coalition to reveal these feelings at Florence. Instead he surprised Mussolini and Ciano with the news that Molotov was coming to Berlin. This prompted the Duce to predict that Russia's entry into the common front would be a significant advantage, and that the very presence of the Soviet Foreign Minister in Berlin would constitute a 'heavy blow' to the British.

In fact Mussolini was quite wrong. Molotov's visit to Berlin in November proved to be the final blow to Hitler's hopes of waging

[1] Martin van Crefeld, '25 October 1940: a Historical Puzzle', *Journal of Contemporary History*, 6 (1971), 93.
[2] *Halder KTB* ii. 154, 29 Oct. 1940; 158, 1 Nov. 1940.

a swift coalition war against the British Empire in the winter of 1940–1. The methodical, impassive Russian ignored the blandishments of Hitler and von Ribbentrop and made it clear that German activities in Finland and Rumania and other Balkan countries had left the Soviet Union too suspicious of German intentions to participate in a war against Britain without further safeguards for her security.

There is no evidence to indicate what Hitler would have done if the Russians had proved gullible enough to co-operate with the Axis against Britain on his terms. It is doubtful, but not impossible, that with the Soviet Union thus committed, he might have postponed the attack in the East until the defeat of Britain was achieved.[1] Alternatively, he might have embroiled the Russians in the Middle East and then struck at them. However, one thing is clear; whatever Molotov's attitude Hitler would not have abandoned the attack on Russia. Directive No. 18 issued on 12 November 1940, the day of his arrival in Berlin, stated that irrespective of the results of the talks with the Soviet Foreign Minister, 'all preparations for the East already verbally ordered are to be continued'.[2]

## The Third Decision, November 1940

After the meeting with Molotov, Hitler remarked that he 'hadn't expected anything of it anyway',[3] and this was probably true. By the time the conversations took place Mussolini's folly and Franco's astute caution had already reduced his hopes of successful coalition warfare in the south.[4] Hitler was convinced that unless Russia was prepared to co-operate by advancing towards the Persian Gulf the risks of committing the Wehrmacht to operations in the Mediterranean theatre would be worse than those of a two-front war. Thus on 14 November Raeder, who had mistakenly believed that Hitler had adopted the plans for the Mediterranean as an alternative to the attack in the East, was disappointed to find that he was 'still

---

[1] Hitler thought that the United States would stay out of the war until 1942 Thus he had another year in which to defeat Britain while she was still isolated had he so wished. See ibid., p. 165, 4 Nov. 1940; *KTB OKW* i. 996.

[2] Hubatsch, p. 81.

[3] G. Engel, 'Tagebuch des Adjutanten des Heeres bei Hitler (Juni 1940—Mai 1941)', manuscript diary cited by Hillgruber, *Strategie*, p. 358.

[4] Hitler's doubts were already apparent on 4 Nov. See *Halder KTB* ii. 163–4, 4 Nov. 1940.

inclined to pursue the conflict with Russia'[1] and he appealed in vain for a postponement until after the defeat of Britain.

Hitler's determination to strike at Russia as soon as possible was fortified by the unco-operative attitude of the Soviet Foreign Minister in Berlin. He told his entourage that 'the conversations had shown where the Russian plans were leading. Molotov had let the cat out of the bag. This would not remain even a marriage of convenience. To let the Russians in . . . would mean the end of Central Europe.'[2] Thus the only change in Hitler's strategy resulting from the conversations with Molotov was that he now knew that the war against Britain could not be ended before the attack on Russia. His plans for the Mediterranean were therefore reduced to the ejection of the British from their last footholds on the Continent, Greece, and Gibraltar, and limited assistance to the Italians in North Africa.[3] Hitler's resolve to strike eastward in 1941 was thus further strengthened as the possible alternatives fell away. But he issued no orders after the failure of the Molotov conversations to confirm this because he saw no need for them. The processes of political, economic, administrative, and operational preparation had all been developing since July, and would be continued without further instructions. Nevertheless, this was not clear to the military leaders, to whom the operation in the East had been presented as an alternative to the invasion of England. Since they had not yet abandoned hope of carrying out Operation 'Sea Lion' they did not share Hitler's conviction that the spring of 1941 was the 'one most favourable moment' for the conquest of *Lebensraum*.

### The Attitude of the OKH to Hitler's Grand Strategy, August–December 1940

During the late summer and autumn of 1940 the General Staff of the Army was called upon to conduct planning for the invasion of England (Operation 'Sea Lion'), the capture of Gibraltar, the Azores,

[1] FCNA 14 Nov. 1940. Raeder conferred with Hitler only once, on 14 Oct., between 26 Sept. and this conference. Thus the Mediterranean strategy which he had advocated had been attempted and abandoned almost without his participation. See *KTB OKW* i. 166E, 177, 15 Nov. 1940.

[2] Engel, *Tagebuch*, 15 Nov. 1940, quoted by Hillgruber, *Strategie*, p. 358.

[3] *Halder KTB* ii. 207, 3 Dec. 1940. The offensive into Egypt was not to take place until the autumn of 1941.

Canary and Cape Verde Islands (Operation 'Felix'), the invasion of Greece (Operation 'Marita'), the defence of the Finnish nickel mines, the defence of the Rumanian oilfields, the support of the Italians in North Africa, and the invasion of Russia (Operation 'Otto'). But throughout this period the Army leaders were not called upon to offer advice on the grand strategy that these operations were to serve. Indeed, between August and November von Brauchitsch conferred with Hitler only once each month. Halder also met Hitler only four times, once in August, once in September, and twice in November. In October, a month of considerable grand strategic preparations for the war in the Mediterranean, he did not see Hitler at all.[1] The poor advice that these two generals had given in July can hardly have encouraged Hitler to consult them on the subsequent grand strategic problems. However, they preferred to place a different interpretation upon their neglect. On 3 September when von Brauchitsch complained bitterly that Hitler was even trying to keep him out of the public eye, Halder noted that it was 'apparently jealousy on the part of the Führer'.[2] Furthermore, resentment at their exclusion from the higher strategic counsels made von Brauchitsch and Halder hypercritical of Hitler's decisions even when these were little different from views they themselves had expressed.

Throughout July the OKH planned a Channel crossing with an optimism made possible only by a stubborn disregard for the difficulties facing the Navy and the Luftwaffe. But within a week of the conference on 31 July the Army leaders became disillusioned with Operation 'Sea Lion'. On 6 August Halder complained:

> We are in the peculiar situation where the Navy takes a narrow view, the Luftwaffe is unwilling to start on a task which is its alone at the onset, and the OKW, which for once is really confronted with a Wehrmacht operation, plays possum [*sich tot stellt*]. The only driving force comes from us [the OKH]. But we cannot succeed alone.[3]

Next day he told Admiral Schniewind that a landing attempt would be 'complete suicide'.[4] It does not seem to have occurred to Halder

[1] See *KTB OKW* i. 159E.
[2] *Halder KTB* ii. 85, 3 Sept. 1940. This entry again reflects von Brauchitsch's attitude of mind in 1940 and gives further support to the view expressed above that he was seeking means to reassert himself.
[3] Ibid., p. 57, 6 Aug. 1940.
[4] Naval Staff record, 7 Aug. 1940, quoted by Wheatley, p. 68.

that the unrealistic plans developed by the OKH might have contributed to Hitler's choice of a strategy of annihilation towards
Britain for which the Wehrmacht was ill equipped. Once committed, however, Hitler was determined to make a sustained attempt
to defeat the British by air attacks on their homeland culminating
in a cross-Channel landing. By 28 September Halder was petulantly
complaining that 'dragging out the continued existence [of Operation
'Sea Lion'] is intolerable.'[1] But what alternative had the OKH to
offer? On 30 July von Brauchitsch and Halder had agreed that a
strategy of attrition, including operations in the Mediterranean
theatre, was preferable to a campaign in the East as an alternative
to Operation 'Sea Lion'. But in August, when Hitler issued orders
for studies of Mediterranean operations that might be undertaken
before the attack on Russia if Operation 'Sea Lion' was abandoned,
Halder indignantly expostulated against the boundless schemes that
were drawn from the 'political kaleidoscope' without any establishment of priorities.[2]

On the 14 August the new field-marshals gathered at the Reich
Chancellery to receive their diamond-studded batons. At this time
Hitler evidently regarded as premature any open revelation of his
determination to attack Russia to all his senior commanders. But
over lunch he sounded a clear warning of the possibility of a conflict in the East.

Russia [he said], has once shown an inclination to overstep the agreements
made with us. However, she remains loyal at present. But should she reveal
the intention of conquering Finland or attacking Rumania we shall be
forced to strike. Russia should not be allowed to be sole master of the
eastern Baltic. Furthermore we need Rumania's oil. However, perhaps it
will suffice to send a German general with a 'ringing reputation' [to the
East] in order to keep Russia quiet.[3]

These remarks were still fresh in the mind of Field-Marshal von
Bock on 31 August when he received orders to move his Army
Group B Headquarters to Poland where it would take command over
the 18th Army, the 4th Army, and several army corps that were also
to be transferred there. 'What my task will be I don't know', he
noted in his diary. However, von Bock was not the man to underestimate his own reputation and he assumed that his initial role
would probably be 'to act as a scare-crow against any possible

[1] Op. cit., p. 117, 28 Sept. 1940.        [2] Ibid., p. 79, 27 Aug. 1940.
[3] Bock, *Tagebuch*, 18 Aug. 1940.

Russian desires [for expansion]'.[1] On the following day he met von Brauchitsch, but was disappointed to find that the Commander-in-Chief was unable to give him any precise directives for his new appointment. 'It seems', noted von Bock, 'that he too lacks any clear picture of the over-all situation or future intentions. Perhaps the political leadership has not yet come to a firm decision.'[2] All seemed to depend upon events in the West. The uncertainty of the outcome of the air battle over England made it difficult for von Bock to predict whether a landing would be attempted, and he was rather doubtful about the chances of defeating Britain by air and sea warfare alone.

As we have seen, these doubts were shared by Hitler, and in October it became clear that the struggle for the Mediterranean was to be the main task for the winter.[3] But Halder was still exasperated by the lack of purpose and direction from above.[4] By November, he was growing concerned that the operations planned in the Balkans would cause a delay in mounting the attack on Russia, especially if Turkey was provoked into a hostile reaction.[5] Furthermore, he doubted whether they would achieve a decisive success over Britain which was 'what really mattered',[6] and it appears that by late November he would have preferred a revival of Operation 'Sea Lion' in the spring to the attack on Russia.[6] He was also concerned that if 'Sea Lion' were abandoned, the alternative to it should be given clear priority.

In their post-war accounts of the period between July and December 1940 former members of the OKH have been at pains to belittle the planning and preparations for the invasion of Russia. When questioned on the plans drawn up by Lieutenant-Colonel Feyerabend and General Marcks, General Halder asked rather testily why there was so much interest in the staff studies conducted in 1940. These, he said, 'were mere "General Staff technicalities", preparations for possible future needs conducted by the most expert minds available. They were by no means decisive. The decisions were Hitler's. The OKH did not wish to encourage his ideas and fantasies about

[1] Ibid., 31 Aug. 1940.
[2] Ibid., 1 Sept. 1940.
[3] *Halder KTB* ii. 130, 8 Oct. 1940.
[4] See Halder's conversation with von Etzdorf (ibid., p. 129, 8 Oct. 1940) and von Brauchitsch (ibid., p. 133, 11 Oct. 1940).
[5] Ibid., p. 188, 18 Nov.; p. 191, 24 Nov. 1940.
[6] Ibid., p. 194, 25 Nov. 1940.

*Lebensraum.*[1] In the post-war biographical studies of Generals Wagner and Köstring the letters and papers on the subject of the early preparations for the invasion of Russia were missing. General Heusinger presented the attack on Russia as the 'last way out' from the strategic impasse resulting from Hitler's indecision in the second half of 1940, and ignored the planning resulting from the decision of July 1940.[2] However, on 22 October 1940, shortly after assuming the post of Chief of the Operations Department of the General Staff, Colonel Heusinger issued an order confirming the organization of his department into five groups. *Chefgruppe* 1a co-ordinated the work of the whole department, conducted strategic and operational studies, maintained liaison with the OKW and the Naval and Luftwaffe staffs. Group I was the 'East Group' under the direction of Major Gehlen. It was divided into two sections. Section I N (for North) under Captain Brandt, which was responsible for 'Questions of Strategy (*Kriegsführung*) in the north-eastern Theatre', including Russia, Finland, Scandinavia, and the area in which Army Group B was stationed, the General Government of Poland, Section I S (for South) under Captain Philippi was responsible for 'Questions of Strategy in the south-eastern Theatre', including south Russia, the Balkans, Slovakia, and the Protectorate. Group II, the West Group, was also divided into two sections, one dealing with strategic questions in Western Europe, and the other with the Mediterranean. Groups III and IV met the administrative and communications needs of the other groups.[3] The fact that Russia dominated the attention of two of the four sections devoted to detailed strategic planning indicates that it stood high in the planning priorities of the German Army in the autumn of 1940. The movement of forces to von Bock's new command was similarly significant. On 31 October the OKH also moved, leaving Fontainebleau for Zossen near Berlin.

Throughout the autumn of 1940 planning for Operation 'Otto', the invasion of Russia, continued, but there are few surviving documents available to reveal its details.[4] Halder's notes give very little

[1] Conversation with author, 23 June 1969. See also p. 70, n. 4 above.
[2] Adolf Heusinger, 'Die letzte Chance vertan', *Der Spiegel*, 16 (1966), 134.
[3] *Dokumentenbuch Heusinger*, Institut für Zeitgeschichte, 2871/62, F. 78. See also Chart V, p. 249.
[4] Documents cited by Besymenski, *Sonderakte Barbarossa*, pp. 307 ff., show that some of the missing OKH files for the period June–December 1940 are in Moscow.

indication of the attitude of the OKH towards it. His statements that the Balkan operation might delay the Russian campaign did not necessarily prove that he was eager to begin it. They may have been no more than further expressions of scepticism provoked by Hitler's failure to set clear priorities. On 4 November he noted in his diary 'the Commander-in-Chief wishes to present the operational plan for the eastern campaign on 18 or 20 November (will that be [time] enough?)'.[1] The question in parenthesis seemed to indicate that Halder doubted whether the plan would be ready in time for the date proposed.[2] But after the war he gave a more complex explanation, and stated that he attempted to restrain von Brauchitsch from taking the initiative in presenting the plan to Hitler. When the Field-Marshal insisted, Halder suggested that he should then do so before the visit of Molotov 'in order to draw Hitler's attention again to the difficulties of the campaign'.[3] This statement does not seem consistent with the optimism with which the General Staff conducted the operational planning during this period. But although the leaders of the Army were convinced that the defeat of Russia lay well within the operational capability of the Army, they doubted both the need and the wisdom of the attack in the East for grand strategic reasons.

This somewhat ambivalent attitude arose from their preference for a revival of Operation 'Sea Lion'.[4] In July when they had embarked on the planning for the East the situation seemed to offer them the opportunity to strike a blow at Russia which would 'force her to recognize Germany's dominant role in Europe'.[5] At the same time they would destroy the centre of Bolshevism, which as conservative nationalists they feared and detested. On the other hand the parallel problem of ending the war against Britain aroused in them increasing uneasiness about embarking prematurely upon a campaign in the East. In July Hitler had presented the idea of an attack on Russia as if it depended upon the condition that the invasion of England did not take place[6] so the generals still had reason to hope that he might still attempt to end the war in the West first. Since the postponement of Operation 'Sea Lion' in September Hitler had not given them a clear indication of his intentions. In the first draft of Directive

---

[1] *Halder, KTB* ii. 166, 4 Nov. 1940.
[2] The war game by which the operational plan for the East was tested was not completed until 7 Dec., two days after the plan was presented to Hitler. Ibid., p. 217, 7 Dec. 1940.
[3] Ibid., p. 166, n. 15, 4 Nov. 1940.  [4] Ibid., p. 194, 25 Nov. 1940.
[5] Ibid., p. 6, 3 July 1940.  [6] See p. 70, n. 3 above.

No. 18 General Warlimont placed operation 'Sea Lion' at the beginning and made it the primary operation for the spring of 1941. But he was informed by General Jodl that 'this order of things might well accord with the ideas of the OKH but not with those of Hitler'[1] and the section on England was transferred to the end of the directive. Nevertheless, it did state that Operation 'Sea Lion' might be revived in the spring if there were 'changes in the over-all situation . . .'.[2] The only possibility of such changes seemed to lie in the conversations with Molotov which might lead to an extension of the settlement between Russia and Germany. Thus, in spite of the instruction that 'all preparations for the East already verbally ordered'[3] were to continue, it appeared to the Army leaders that the choice between East and West was still open.

In fact, as already indicated, it was not. Hitler had made his decision in July and subsequent events had merely served to confirm it. His references to the campaign in the East as an alternative method of striking at Britain had begun as mere strategic rationalizations, but as Britain's resistance presented increasing problems it seems likely that Hitler became a victim of his own arguments. Nevertheless, his desire to conquer *Lebensraum* was still the dominant factor. If there had been any question of a choice still open until the talks with Molotov there would surely have been some indication of a decision made as a result of those talks at the first conference between Hitler and his Army leaders after the departure of the Soviet Foreign Minister.

### The Conference on 5 December 1940

The accounts of the conference on 5 December 1940 in the War Diary of the OKW and in General Halder's diary[4] reveal that Hitler took it for granted that the attack on Russia would take place in the spring of 1941 as decided in July. When von Brauchitsch asked him to give his views on the over-all situation, he did not refer to Russia as if making a new decision, or even specifically reaffirming an old one as a result of the conversations with Molotov. Instead, he delivered a rambling survey of his Mediterranean plans, in the course of which he casually remarked that even if the attack on Greece

---

[1] Warlimont, p. 116.
[2] Hubatsch, p. 81.                                    [3] Ibid.
[4] *KTB OKW* i. 203 ff.; *Halder KTB* ii. 209 ff., 5 Dec. 1940.

proved unnecessary the forces assembled for it could quite con-
veniently be used in the eastern campaign.[1]

This comment gave von Brauchitsch a cue for discussing the
danger of embarking on a two-front war. He was not concerned
about the ability of the Army but that of the Luftwaffe to meet the
simultaneous demands of the East and West. Hitler replied that
British aircraft production would not be able to keep pace with that
of Germany and that it would be possible to continue harassing the
British with night-bombing raids 'during a short eastern campaign'.[2]
The Field-Marshal's question evidently irritated Hitler, perhaps
because it aroused some uneasiness in his own mind and because it
suggested that the generals doubted his determination to adhere to
the decision of July. He reminded them that the inferiority of the
Soviet Army made the present time 'especially favourable' for a
German attack, and gave a comforting description of a swift and
victorious campaign culminating in the establishment of a row of
buffer states from the Ukraine to Finland.[3] In order to leave no
doubt about his grand strategy for 1941, he finished by summing up
the main operations: 'Felix' (Gibraltar) was to be carried out as
soon as possible, preparations for 'Marita' (Greece) and the eastern
campaign were to go ahead as ordered, and 'Sea Lion' was 'no longer
possible'.[4]

The generals did not argue. Jodl had stated in a memorandum two
days earlier that if economic difficulties made it necessary to choose
between the continuation of the siege of Britain and the invasion
of Russia then the latter 'would and could be postponed because
it is not a dire necessity for the victory over Britain'.[5] However, he
was not the man to question the decisions of the Führer, especially
in the presence of von Brauchitsch and Halder. Similarly, Halder
gave no expression to his recently recorded views that Operation
'Marita' threatened to delay the opening attack on Russia, or that
Operation 'Sea Lion' was 'the most certain way of hitting at Britain'.[6]
Halder, like the other German military leaders, was well aware that
Hitler's policy was founded upon the concept of eastern conquest.
Thus, he may well have suspected even then that the Führer could

[1] *KTB OKW* i. 204; *Halder KTB* ii. 211–13, 5 Dec. 1940.
[2] *KTB OKW* i. 205.
[3] Ibid., p. 207.
[4] Op. cit.; *Halder KTB* ii. 210, 5 Dec. 1940.
[5] Thomas, 437; *KTB OKW* i. 981.
[6] *Halder KTB* ii. 188, 18 Nov.; p. 191, 24 Nov. 1940.

not be persuaded to delay the attack on Russia until after Britain's defeat.

In July when Hitler announced his decision to attack Russia in May 1941, he had also accepted the possibility that Britain might still be fighting on and made provisions for sufficient forces to hold the West. Thus, the prior defeat of Britain was clearly not a prerequisite for the attack on Russia. Secondly, in spite of the inference he gave to his military leaders, events between July and November 1940 had shown that he did not regard operations against the British Isles or against Britain's Mediterranean bases as *alternatives* to the attack on Russia. His 'definite decision to finish off Russia' in May 1941 was made by 29 July 1940 before either of those operations had begun. His long-range economic planning was geared to this decision. The priorities given to the operations in the West and the South were short-term, limited measures to meet a stop-gap strategy designed to fill a period of time made available because an attempt to carry out an invasion of Russia in 1940 might not be completed before winter. But significantly Hitler admitted that he would have preferred to attack Russia in 1940 if more time had been available.

What made the Russian operation so urgent that it was to be carried out as soon as possible irrespective of the situation in the West? The main factor was probably Hitler's desire to take advantage of the military weakness of the Soviet Union before the Russian leaders could modernize their forces and retrain them in the light of their experiences in Finland and their observations of the *Blitzkrieg*. Hitler was also anxious to establish his great empire dominating Europe before the United States entered the war. On 5 December 1940, General Halder was not yet convinced that these factors justified the risks of a war on two fronts. Nevertheless, he dutifully presented the General Staff's operational plan for the campaign in the East.

# CHAPTER IV

# German Military Strategic Planning
# July–December 1940

## *Operational Plan or Formula?*

MILITARY plans usually follow an accepted sequence of development and presentation. Their first stage is an appreciation, or assessment, of the situation and the definition of aims. The relevant factors are set out. These include the forces available to both sides, time, distance, terrain, and logistics. From them are derived the courses open. The planner then makes a choice of action and develops a written plan. This presents a summary of the situation, the strength and state of the forces on both sides, a statement of the aim, and an outline of the method to be used for its attainment. In the following examination of the operational plan for the invasion of Russia it will be noted that each element of this sequence in the German military strategic planning contained serious omissions or defects which contributed to the failure of the *Blitzkrieg* in the East.

Normally military strategic planning is based upon information and tasks defined by the grand strategic planners. The first duty of the military strategists must be to ensure that the tasks set are possible with the available means. If they are not it is their responsibility to advise their superiors and recommend alternatives. Once the grand strategic aims have been adjusted to the means by this process, the military strategic planners define their aims, which in turn set the tasks to be passed on to the operational level in the form of an operational plan. The entire procedure of which this forms a part should involve the careful assessment and reassessment of the relevant factors at each level from policy through grand and military strategy to operations and tactics, for it is upon such assessments that the feasibility of the aims and methods of plans must rest.

The plan for the German invasion of Russia did not, however, result from the careful assessment of the relevant factors. It was based upon a serious underestimation of the strength of the Soviet Union and of the problems presented by its terrain and climate, and upon a crass over-confidence in the invincibility of the Wehrmacht. The aims were defined, not upon the basis of what was feasible, but upon vague and shifting expressions of what was desirable. The economic and logistic factors were almost completely ignored until after the operational plan was completed. The operational method consisted of the repetition of *Blitzkrieg* techniques which had succeeded elsewhere under very different circumstances. This choice was made inevitable by the nature of the equipment, organization, and experience of the Wehrmacht, but any attempt to adapt the *Blitzkrieg* to the more difficult conditions and greater spaces in Russia was ruled out by Hitler's insistence on the achievement of victory in one campaign of five months' duration.[1]

The flaws in German military strategic planning in the East cannot, however, be blamed entirely on Hitler on the grounds that he imposed arbitrary decisions upon a row of helpless subordinates. Even before he had announced his decision to attack Russia in 1941 the Army leaders had defined their own military strategic aims and ordered their operational planners to conduct studies for a campaign in the East. Their basic approach to the problem differed little from Hitler's. Thus they later accepted his aims, timing, and methods because they shared his optimistic assumptions about the weakness of Russia and the invincibility of the Wehrmacht.

Since the assessments of the enemy and of their own troops and the aims and methods of the campaign were accepted without question by the operational planners, they considered that they had little to do but apply the *Blitzkrieg* doctrine to the terrain of the Soviet Union. Their approach to military planning differed little from that of military staffs in the age of von Moltke or Napoleon, when operational decisions were less dependent upon administrative considerations. They selected the best ground on which to concentrate their forces for the battle of destruction and the best routes over which to pursue and envelop the shattered remnants of the enemy army. Administrative details they left to the Quartermaster-General. Yet the feasibility of their operational plans depended upon logistics. The maintenance of the advance of the motorized and armoured forces in Russia presented problems of supplying gasoline and diesel, lubricants, spare parts, replacements, ammunition, and

[1] *Halder KTB* ii. 49–50, 31 July 1940.

food on a scale that the German General Staff had never experienced. But these problems were not studied in detail until the objectives, lines of advance, and timing of the campaign had been decided upon.

In retrospect it seems incredible that the operational plan for a vast mobile campaign should have been completed without a careful examination of the economic and logistic difficulties. However, it must be remembered that the great majority of the senior German generals and staff officers had little or no technical training or experience in mechanized warfare. The only large-scale manœuvres involving Panzer divisions had been carried out in 1937.[1] Since then the Army had been too preoccupied with the operational tasks in Austria, Czechoslovakia, Poland, and the West to extend training in the direction of mechanized formations beyond the small group of senior officers directly involved in their development. Most of the German generals had conducted their soldiering on horseback, and had led units and formations in which the guns and transport had been horsedrawn.[2] In the German Army of 1940 they still did; only the Panzer and motorized divisions and certain anti-tank, medium, and heavy artillery regiments, engineer, signals, and supply units were motorized. Thus the problem of supplying and maintaining great mechanized forces was something new. In Poland a great deal of experiment and reorganization had taken place on the basis of experience gained. But the senior generals and staff officers still regarded these newfangled formations and their tactical and administrative improvisations with scepticism. This contributed to their pessimism in 1939 and 1940 when confronted with the task of attacking in the West. The subsequent campaign in France revived their confidence and the mechanized formation commanders gained further experience. However, the very ease of supply there may have encouraged neglect in the field of administration,[3] and a lack of understanding for the logistical problems of modern mobile warfare still prevailed among the conservative, equestrian-minded senior officers.

[1] See Hauptmann Martin, 'Wehrmachtmanoever, 1937', *Jahrbuch des deutschen Heeres*, 1938, ed. Walter Jost (Leipzig, 1937), pp. 169–73.

[2] Senior officers devoted much energy and time to riding. See Wagner, p. 192. General Freiherr von Geyr described von Rundstedt as 'incredibly idle . . . clever, but horse-minded'. Conversation with author, 27 June 1969.

[3] See Guderian, p. 113, n. 1: 'During the campaign in France there was no lack of fuel—good staff work can avoid this calamity . . . it was only a question of transport and easy to solve.'

The men responsible for the initial planning of the eastern campaign were all from the artillery or the infantry.[1] Only with the appointment of General Paulus as *Oberquartiermeister I* did the General Staff acquire a senior planner with experience in the operational and administrative problems of Panzer and motorized forces.[2] But by that time the basic concepts of the operational plan had already been established by Hitler and the OKH, and Paulus was not the man to question or reject what they had done and begin again. He had a reputation for patient devotion to duty, for meticulous attention to detail, but he lacked the sort of flair and insight that had led von Manstein to criticize the unimaginative planning of von Brauchitsch and Halder before the campaign in the West. He accepted the approach to the problem taken by General Marcks, amending it in detail, but not questioning the feasibility of defeating Russia in a single campaign. In contrast, von Manstein later criticized his superiors for having produced 'nothing more or less than a strategic or even a tactical formula' which, he continued, 'could never replace an operations plan . . . which, in view of the relative strengths of the opposing armies and the tremendous distances involved, accepted the premise that it might take *two* campaigns to destroy the Soviet armed forces'.[3]

This was not the first time that German leaders had committed such an error. The Schlieffen Plan in 1914 and Ludendorff's offensive in 1918 were based upon military strategic and tactical doctrines which became rigid formulae. Like the plans of von Schlieffen and Ludendorff, the *Blitzkrieg* formula of Hitler and his generals also became sacrosanct. After the completion of the plan for the invasion of Russia, disconcerting changes in the grand strategic situation and inadequacies in the German war economy and military supply systems came to light. These cast considerable doubt upon the feasibility of Operation 'Barbarossa' as Hitler now entitled the plan.[4]

[1] Field-Marshal von Brauchitsch and Generals Halder and Marcks had served in the artillery; General von Greiffenberg and Colonel Kinzel were from the infantry.

[2] General Paulus succeeded Guderian as Chief of Staff of the Panzer Troops Command in 1935. He served as Chief of Staff of the 10th Army in Poland and the 6th Army in the West, both of which contained Panzer and motorized formations. See Görlitz, *Paulus*, pp. 16–19, 21–4.

[3] Manstein, *Lost Victories*, pp. 177–8. General von Manstein played no part in the planning for the Russian campaign. He was preparing XXXVIII Army Corps for Operation 'Sea Lion' at this time. See ibid., pp. 150 ff.

[4] The code name 'Barbarossa' was adopted by Hitler in December 1940 in

Nevertheless, it remained unamended. Later, marked increases in the assessed strength and potential of the Soviet Union were also reported. But again there was no basic reassessment of the German plan. The only changes were those necessitated by the increased German commitments in the West, the Mediterranean, and the Balkans, which led to a reduction both in the time and the strength available for the defeat of the Soviet forces.

## The Underestimation of Soviet Strength

The basic error in German planning for Operation 'Barbarossa' was the underestimation of the strength of the Soviet Union. This was mainly due to two factors: the paucity of accurate information on the Russian armed forces and war potential, and the poor use that was made of what little information was received. The first factor was explained quite simply by General Köstring, the German Military Attaché in Moscow, when he told the head of the *Abwehr*, Admiral Canaris, that 'it would be easier for an Arab in flowing burnous to walk unnoticed through Berlin, than for a foreign agent to pass through Russia!'[1] Thus, apart from a few agents in the new Baltic republics and eastern Poland and the staff of the German Embassy in Moscow, the Germans had no reliable internal sources of information on Russia.[2] The files of the intelligence services of Poland and France revealed that they, too, had been baffled by Soviet security.[3] The external means of surveillance, radio listening, and air photography by the 'Rowehl' squadron, were limited to a range of 300 kilometres.[4]

place of 'Otto' and 'Fritz' used by the OKH and OKW. It was the nickname of the Emperor Frederick I, who, according to legend would return at Germany's hour of greatest need. He drowned in a Balkan stream while on his way to a crusade.

[1] Hermann Teske (ed.), *General Ernst Köstring, Der militärische Mittler zwischen dem deutschen Reich und der Sowjetunion, 1921–1941. Profile bedeutender Soldaten*, Herausgegeben vom Bundesarchiv/Militärarchiv (Frankfurt a.M., 1966), p. 93.

[2] See Louis de Jong, *The German Fifth Column in the Second World War*, trans. C. M. Geyl (Chicago, 1956), p. 235. See also Teske, pp. 89 ff.; *IMT* xxxvi. C–170, 690; Paul Leverkühn, *German Military Intelligence*, trans. R. A. Stevens and Constantine FitzGibbon (London, 1954), pp. 155 ff.

[3] See Bor, p. 191; Leverkühn, p. 156.

[4] See Helmuth Greiner, *Die Oberste Wehrmachtführung* (Wiesbaden, 1951), pp. 312–13; *Halder KTB* ii. 120, 1 Oct. 1940; p. 419, 17 May; p. 426, 22 May; p. 448, 7 June 1941; Plocher, p. 11.

The reasons for the poor use made of information about Russia
were more complex. In Hitler's Germany the traditional West European tendency to regard Russia as a primitive, semi-Asiatic country
was reinforced by the Nazi racial and ideological attitudes towards
the Slavs and Bolshevism, which prevailed in spite of the Russo-
German Pact. The Army leaders were also influenced by their desire
not to repeat the pessimistic overestimation of the enemy that had
brought Hitler's scorn and anger upon the General Staff in 1938 and
1939. In fact, there was at first little apparent reason for pessimism.
In 1937 and 1938 Stalin had inflicted upon his officer corps a crippling
blow in the form of a purge unequalled in modern history.[1] The
view that the Red Army would need years to recover seemed confirmed by the inept leadership displayed in the Winter War against
Finland.[2]

Under these circumstances it was understandable that the German generals, fresh from their victories in Poland, Norway, and the
West, viewed the task of attacking Russia with equanimity.[3] Nevertheless, the estimate given to Hitler on 21 July 1940 that Russia
had only 50 to 73 good divisions and could therefore be defeated in
the autumn by a German force of 80 to 100 divisions, reflected a
remarkable departure from the caution shown hitherto by the OKH.
Even when the inaccuracy of this estimate of Soviet strength was
acknowledged the general staff planners continued to underestimate
Soviet combat capabilities, equipment, and war potential. General
Marcks, for instance, based the plan that he produced in late July
and August 1940 upon the assumption that the forces of the two
sides would be numerically equal because the subtraction of the
Russian divisions tied down on frontiers facing the Japanese, Turks,
and Finns would leave only 96 infantry divisions, 23 cavalry divisions,
and 28 mechanized brigades to face a German attack by 24 Panzer,
12 motorized, 110 infantry, and 1 cavalry divisions.[4] He stated that
the Russians would not be able to increase their strength appreciably
by next spring and, though the creation of a strong mobile reserve

[1] See Erickson, pp. 504 ff.; Leonard Schapiro, 'The Great Purge', *The Soviet
Army*, ed. B. H. Liddell Hart (London, 1956), pp. 65 ff. The number of victims
was estimated at 35,000 or about half of the total officer corps.

[2] See *Halder KTB* ii. 86, 3 Sept. 1940; p. 395, 5 May 1941; see also p. 382,
26 Apr. 1941; *KTB OKW* i. 297, 3 Feb., p. 393, 8 May 1941. Cf. Teske, pp. 102,
107, for Köstring's rather different post-war view of the effect of the purge.

[3] See Görlitz, *Paulus*, p. 129.

[4] See Appendix I, 'The Marcks Plan'. The total of 24 Panzer divisions was
ordered by Hitler in June but later reduced to 20.

of armoured, motorized, and cavalry forces was possible, there was no sign of such a force. He therefore predicted optimistically that:

Because the Russians no longer possess the superiority of numbers they had in the [First] World War it is likely that once the long, extended line of their forces has been broken through they will be unable to concentrate or coordinate counter measures. Fighting in isolated battles they will soon succumb to the superiority of the German troops and leadership.[1]

Similar over-confidence caused Marcks and the subsequent planners to underestimate the strength of the Soviet industrial potential. They focused their gaze upon the narrow strip of western Russia about which they were better informed and in which they assumed the decisive battles would be fought. Reports of what lay beyond were mostly discounted.[2] It was assumed that the *Blitzkrieg* would again achieve a swift defeat of their opponents' field forces and the early capture of the main Soviet industrial centres. The remaining Soviet war potential in the Urals could be neutralized by bombing raids.[3] The Germans showed little concern about the possibility that Russia might mobilize replacement armies from her enormous reserves of manpower, and equip them from the current production of her war industries in the interior. In this respect their thinking seems to have been influenced by their own *Blitzkrieg* economy which stockpiled the required armaments and munitions by a short burst of high production before each campaign.[4] They knew that much of the Soviet war industry would lie outside the reach of their ground forces during the early phases of the campaign, and that the Luftwaffe would lack the strength to attack it.[5] Yet the German Army leaders seem to have assumed that from the moment of their onslaught the Soviet political and military authorities, industry, and communications systems would be seized with a sort of paralysis.

Hitler was eager to encourage such views to counter any revival of the caution he had witnessed in his Army leaders prior to earlier campaigns. On 5 December he assured von Brauchitsch and Halder

[1] See Appendix I, 'The Marcks Plan'.

[2] General Köstring stated after the war that he warned Marcks that Soviet resistance would continue in the interior. But it seems doubtful whether his warnings were really as clear as he later claimed. See *Halder KTB* ii. 86, n. 2; Hillgruber, *Hitlers Strategie*, p. 228, n. 93; George E. Blau, *The German Campaign in Russia—Planning and Operations (1940–1942)*. Department of the Army Pamphlet No. 20–261a (Washington, 1955), p. 12.

[3] See *KTB OKW* i. 208, 5 Dec. 1940.

[4] See Milward, pp. 7–9, 16.

[5] See *Halder KTB* ii. 468.

that the Russian Army once struck 'would suffer an even greater collapse than that of France'.[1] But he was quite capable of sounding a different note if it suited his purpose. A month later he stressed the temporary nature of the Soviet weaknesses as a further justification for his choice of the spring of 1941 for the attack. 'The Russian armed forces', he told his military chiefs, 'were indeed a clay colossus without a head, but their future development could not be safely predicted. . . . the Russians should not be underestimated even now. The German attack must therefore be delivered with the strongest forces.'[2]

### The Strength of the Wehrmacht

The size of the forces available for the invasion of Russia was influenced by both economic and strategic factors. The German reliance on a limited war economy restricted the quantity of equipment and ammunition available for the campaign to what could be produced by a concentrated spate of production in the winter of 1940–1.[3] Shortages of oil, gasoline, and vehicles imposed limits on the number of mechanized formations that could be put in the field. Thus hopes of raising twenty-four Panzer and twelve motorized divisions were not fulfilled. The demands of the war against Britain further reduced the forces available in the East. As a result the German planners were able to reckon with only two-thirds of their field divisions.[4] These included nineteen Panzer divisions, with a total of 3,350 tanks, ten motorized divisions, and six SS divisions, supported by 2,770 of the total of 4,300 combat aircraft available to the Luftwaffe.[5] The German Navy was able to allocate only five submarines, several minelayers, and a few dozen other small vessels to the Baltic and Black Seas. None of the surviving heavy

---

[1] *KTB OKW* i. 205, 5 Dec. 1940.

[2] Ibid., p. 258, 9 Jan. 1941.

[3] See Milward, pp. 40–3. See also Appendix V.

[4] See *Halder KTB* ii. 50, 31 July 1940. Hitler suggested that of the 180 divisions planned, 7 should go to Norway, 50 to France, 3 to Holland and Belgium, and 120 to the East. The actual distribution on 22 June 1941 was: 7 to Norway, 39 to France and the Low Countries, 1 to Denmark, 1 to Germany, 8 to the Balkans, 2 to Africa, 149 to the East. See Müller-Hillebrand, *Das Heer* ii. 186–91.

[5] Most of the remaining aircraft were distributed as follows: 370 to Mediterranean, 660 to the West, 120 to Norway. See Plocher, pp. 23 ff. According to Bekker (pp. 313, 552) only 1,945 aircraft were available on the Eastern Front on 22 June 1941. Of these, a bare two-thirds, 1,280 machines, were serviceable.

warships could be permanently stationed in the Baltic.[1] Nevertheless, even after reassessments of the Soviet forces had revealed far greater numbers of tanks, aircraft, and warships than the Wehrmacht could muster, the German leaders believed that they could compensate for their numerical inferiority by means of the superior equipment, tactics, and leadership that had served them so well in Poland and the West.[2] In taking this view they forgot the improvised nature and narrow economic basis of the *Blitzkrieg* doctrine which had made Hitler's strategy seem so risky in 1938 and 1939. They also ignored the vast differences between their previous campaigns and the one that confronted them now in Russia.

### The Problems of a Blitzkrieg in the East

The German victories in 1939 and 1940 had been won over nations that were vulnerable to the *Blitzkrieg* because the amount of psychological pressure, industrial damage, military failure, and territorial loss they could endure was limited. Thus the degree and duration of violence necessary for their defeat could also be limited. Much could be achieved by propaganda and bluff while the real military effort could be concentrated into short periods of time and directed against specific vital objectives. Under these circumstances the *Blitzkrieg* had great advantages. It provided a tactical means to overcome the military stalemate of the First World War and achieve a 'battle of destruction' which was not also suicidal. Psychologically it had all the sound and fury of total war but only the material cost and duration of limited war. But in Russia the *Blitzkrieg* was confronted with a state whose totalitarian regime, economic and human resources, and territorial extent gave it the ability to wage total war.[3] Thus to defeat Russia the Germans had to achieve a decisive military

---

[1] See Alfred Philippi and Ferdinand Heim, *Der Feldzug gegen Sowjetrussland, 1941–1945* (Stuttgart, 1962), p. 37. Cf. Höhn, pp. 274 ff. See also Appendix VII.

[2] See Hoth, p. 146.

[3] The expression 'total war' is used in the sense described by Erich Ludendorff in *Der totale Krieg* (Munich, 1935). It is summarized by Hans Speier, 'Ludendorff: The German Concept of Total War', *Makers of Modern Strategy*, ed. E. M. Earle (Princeton, 1943), p. 315, as follows: Total war (1) extends over the whole territory of the belligerents; (2) involves the active participation of the whole population and national economy; (3) uses propaganda to strengthen the morale at home and weaken that of the enemy; (4) must be prepared before the outbreak of hostilities; (5) must be directed by one supreme authority. The Soviet Union was able to meet all these requirements.

success so swiftly that it would prevent the Soviet regime from completing the mobilization of its full human and material resources.

The swiftness of the operational and tactical successes in Poland and the West resulted mainly from the Germans' skilful use of surprise, economy and concentration of force, and mobility. However, in Russia the psychological and physical effects of these factors were reduced by the great depth of the theatre of operations and the primitive state of its roads, the size of the Soviet armed forces, and the fact that the Russian soldier's mind was less open to German propaganda vaunting the strength and invincibility of the Wehrmacht.

By the summer of 1941 the Germans' tactical innovations in the use of armoured, motorized, and airborne forces had been demonstrated. Apart from the employment of submersible tanks for crossing rivers and the use of detachments of the special 'Brandenburg Regiment' in Russian uniforms to seize bridges there was nothing new in the *Blitzkrieg* operations planned for the East. Surprise could be achieved by striking without warning, but the difficulty of assembling an army of such size undetected on the frontiers of so notoriously suspicious a neighbour left the planners with little hope of taking the Russians completely off guard.[1] Nevertheless, they hoped that the concentration, direction, and speed of their armoured spearheads would enable them to surprise and overwhelm the defenders in the opening surge of the attack.

The concentrations of force that had delivered the main German thrusts in Poland and the West were made possible by reducing to a minimum the number of formations in the static defences of the *Ostwall* facing central Poland, and in the *Westwall* facing the heavily garrisoned Maginot Line. But in Russia the Germans were not able to achieve a comparable economy of force by the use of defensive positions. On the contrary the vulnerability of the Rumanian oilfields and East Prussia to Soviet counter-thrusts from the territories Russia had acquired under the terms of the secret protocol to the Non-Aggression Pact of August 1939 made it necessary to advance on both flanks. As a result the German forces were extended across a wide front which, because of the diverging directions of the Baltic and Black Sea coasts, would become wider as they advanced

---

[1] See Erickson, pp. 574, 585-6. Shortly before the campaign a Luftwaffe photographic reconnaissance aircraft crashed in bad weather near Vinnitsa. The crew was captured and released a few weeks later by the advancing German troops. See also Plocher, p. 17.

eastwards. Furthermore, the need for the deep penetrating thrusts that characterized the *Blitzkrieg* operations added the problem of dispersion in depth to that of extension in width.

Nevertheless, in the mood of optimism prevailing after the triumph in the West, the German planners expected even greater successes from vast enveloping movements in the East. The studies produced by Colonel von Greiffenberg and Lieutenant-Colonel Feyerabend in the last week of July suggested a single major thrust cutting off a large part of the Soviet forces in the Ukraine in a manner similar to that achieved in the Low Countries in May 1940.[1] General Halder preferred a major thrust towards Moscow with its flank on the Baltic coast turning south to make the Soviet armies in the Ukraine fight with an inverted front, just as the French armies in the Maginot Line had been forced to do in June.[2] These concepts failed to take into account the difference in the distances involved between swinging a flanking operation across northern France and a similar movement covering over 1,000 miles between the Baltic States and the Black Sea.

This error prevailed throughout the German planning for the East. On 9 January 1941 Hitler stated that 'the distances in Russia are indeed great, but no greater than those distances that the German Armed Forces have already mastered'.[3] However, this statement ignored the facts. The initial thrust to the English Channel in May 1940, a distance of about 250 miles, had lasted ten days and had been followed by a few days of sporadic fighting and a long pause for recuperation and redeployment lasting until 5 June, when the second phase of the campaign began. The pursuit following the collapse of the Weygand Line was sustained over distances of 200 to 300 miles for a further period of about ten days. But even these comparatively short distances had imposed unexpected strains on the German command and communication system. The Quarter-master-General wrote during the campaign: 'We thought our Army High Command to be mobile compared with the last war [1914–18]. But even so our communications are proving inadequate. Ten days' construction time are required, and there is as yet no such thing as a secure radio network.'[4]

In Russia the distances were not only much greater, but the

[1] See *Halder KTB* ii. 39, 27 July 1940.
[2] Ibid., p. 37, 26 July; p. 39, 27 July 1940.
[3] *KTB OKW* i. 258, 9 Jan. 1941.                        [4] Wagner, p. 185.

chances of long pauses for recuperation were reduced by the need not only to penetrate the defences on the border but also to cut off the retreat of the Soviet forces outflanked and prevent the creation of new lines of defence.[1] Furthermore, the maintenance of a rapid advance over longer distances would increase the gap between the Panzer spearheads and the infantry divisions following them on foot. Thus there was a considerable danger that the mobile formations would often be isolated from their infantry support and from each other by large tracts of marsh and swampy forest. The resultant dispersion of force in rough terrain compounded the physical problem of containing the enemy in vast envelopment operations and of inducing in him a psychological collapse similar to that of his western counterpart, who was more imaginative and susceptible to a sense of isolation, and who had been subjected to *Blitzkrieg* propaganda without the counter-influence of any strong political indoctrination.

This problem could only have been solved by the provision of adequate mobile forces. But, considering the size of the enemy forces, the distances to be covered, the obstacles to be overcome, and the poor state of the roads, the relative striking power of the German Panzer and motorized forces available for the Russian campaign was much lower than in the West. The increase from six motorized, four *Waffen* SS divisions, and ten Panzer divisions with 2,570 tanks employed in France to ten motorized, six *Waffen* SS divisions, and nineteen Panzer divisions with 3,350 tanks was quite inadequate to meet the greater demands of the mobile operations required in the East.[2]

The primitive Russian road network added to these problems. Competition for road space between the infantry divisions and the motorized supply columns following the Panzer spearheads was bound to lead to congestion because inadequate maps and unpredictable combat and weather conditions limited the value of meticulous staff planning.[3]

The comparative reduction in the striking power and flexibility

---

[1] See Hoth, p. 146.

[2] The *Waffen* SS divisions were organized as motorized infantry divisions until 1942 when they were converted into Panzer Grenadier divisions.

[3] Bad maps were to prove a severe handicap to the Germans in Russia. Some use was made of air photographs but the situation was only eased when quantities of Russian maps were captured and reproduced. See Karl Allmendinger, *Terrain Factors in the Russian Campaign*, U.S. Army Pamphlet No. 20–290 (Washington, 1951), p. 13; *Halder KTB* ii. 279, 13 Feb. 1941. Cf. Paul Carell, *Unternehmen Barbarossa, Der Marsch nach Russland* (Frankfurt a. M., 1963), p. 363.

of the *Blitzkrieg* forces on the ground was matched by similar limitations in the air. In Poland and the West the Luftwaffe had concentrated first upon the winning of air supremacy by destroying the enemy air force and its bases. Then the weight of the air attacks shifted to the direct support of the ground forces and the disruption of road and rail communications behind the enemy front. In the final stage, the air offensive was extended to industrial targets and the cities for the purpose of breaking the morale of the government. By means of a carefully planned concentration of effort on vital targets in each phase the Luftwaffe had achieved considerable success. But it had been less effective in large-scale interdiction and had failed to prevent the withdrawal of the British Expeditionary Force from Dunkirk. Later its failure over Britain further demonstrated its limitations in range, flexibility, and striking power. In the eastern campaign the Luftwaffe appeared to be reverting to the role for which it was designed. But whereas in the West it had employed 3,530 aircraft, most of which operated over an area about 200 miles square, in Russia only 2,770 aircraft were available in a theatre 1,000 miles wide and of such depth that many important industrial targets were beyond the range of the standard bombers. The OKH, therefore, warned the field commanders in its Deployment Directive that since it was unlikely that complete air superiority could be won they must expect greater interference from the enemy air force than in previous campaigns.[1] Nevertheless, neither this factor nor the others mentioned above were sufficient to foster any doubt that in the course of a single summer the aims of the campaign could be achieved.

### The Aims of the Russian Campaign

The initial operational planning for the eastern campaign began on 3 July when General Halder ordered Colonel von Greiffenberg of the Operations Branch of the General Staff to study 'how to deliver a military blow at Russia which will force her to recognize Germany's dominant role in Europe'.[2] More specific goals and military objectives were presented at the Führer Conference on 21 July. Hitler added the Rumanian oilfields to the areas to be protected against Soviet bombing and asked what operational

---

[1] *Halder KTB* ii. 468; Hoth, p. 146. See also Appendix II of this study.
[2] *Halder KTB* ii. 6, 3 July 1940.

objectives should be set. In the subsequent discussion thrusts through the Baltic States to Finland and through the Ukraine were mentioned.

The political, military, strategic, and operational aims presented to Hitler on 21 July were confirmed by him at the Führer Conference ten days later. To them he added the grand strategic aim of depriving Britain of her last hope on the Continent.[1] But this attempt to give the operations in the East some relevance to the war already being fought in the West was a rationalization for the ears of the generals. The true purpose of the campaign was the fulfilment of Hitler's *Lebensraumpolitik*. However, Hitler clearly recognized that from the military viewpoint the 'winning of a certain area would not be enough'.[1] The military strategic aim must be 'the destruction of Russia's vital power'.[2] Furthermore, Hitler stated that the operation would make sense only if this aim was achieved in a single campaign completed in five months. Not content with these arbitrary decisions, which simultaneously set the aims on every level of political and strategic planning without any consideration of feasibility, he proceeded next to suggest the lines of operation to be followed.

## Operational Lines and Objectives

There should be two main thrusts, Hitler proposed, one towards Kiev and down the Dnieper and a second through the Baltic States and towards Moscow. These thrusts should then turn inwards to meet in the interior of Russia. Finally, a subsidiary operation should be directed towards the Baku oilfields.[3] The only significant difference between these ideas and those developed by the Chief of the General Staff at this time was their comparative moderation.

Five days earlier, after examining the outline of Soviet dispositions presented by Colonel Kinzel of the Foreign Armies East Branch, General Halder concluded that the most favourable operation would be a thrust along the Baltic coast swinging south via Moscow to attack the Russian forces in the Ukraine and Black Sea in the rear.[4] This manœuvre would have covered a distance of over 1,000 miles, but when Colonel von Greiffenberg and Lieutenant-Colonel Feyerabend presented their recommendations for a more cautious operation

---

[1] *Halder KTB* ii. 49, 31 July 1940.
[2] Ibid. The meaning of this phrase was made clearer at later conferences. See *KTB OKW* i. 258, 9 Jan. 1941.
[3] Ibid., p. 50, 31 July 1940.
[4] Ibid., p. 37, 26 July 1940.

with the main blow in the Ukraine, Halder repeated his preference for the enormous swinging operation traversing the whole of European Russia.[1] On 29 July Halder decided to seek a further opinion and summoned General Marcks, Chief of Staff of the 18th Army, who had not yet departed for his new headquarters in the East, and charged him with the conduct of an independent study of the eastern campaign.[2] The draft plan produced by Marcks on 1 August rejected the concept of a single thrust and came very close to the ideas presented by Hitler at the conference on the previous day.[3]

The military strategic aims of the 'Marcks Plan'[4] were, first, to strike the Russian armed forces, and second, to protect Germany against Soviet air attacks by occupying Russia up to the line Rostov–Gorki–Archangel.[5] Marcks assumed that the Russians would be forced to stand and fight west of the rivers Pruth, Dniester, Dnieper, and Dvina in order to defend their main centres of supply, the Ukraine, Donets Basin, Leningrad, and, above all, Moscow. Since the capture of the capital, 'the economic, political and spiritual centre of the USSR' would '. . . destroy the co-ordination of the Soviet States',[6] Marcks made it his main operational objective, and proposed a direct approach to the city because a good road system extended from Warsaw and East Prussia to Moscow via Sluzk, Minsk, and Vitebsk, over the 'Orsha Corridor' between the Dvina and Dnieper, and through the narrowest part of the great swampy forest region extending from the White Sea, passing south of Leningrad to the Pripet Marsh. An approach from the Baltic States would have to pass through the worst part of this region north and south of Lake Ilmen. Nevertheless, the size of the front and its division by the Pripet Marsh and the presence of strong Soviet forces in the Ukraine prompted Marcks to plan two separate offensives, one directly towards Moscow with a special force directed via Pskov towards Leningrad, and the second towards Kiev which should join the right flank of the northern force east of the Pripet Marsh.

Since it was virtually a frontal attack the enemy was to be enveloped

[1] *KTB OKW* i. 39, 27 July 1940.          [2] Ibid., p. 41, 29 July 1940.
[3] Ibid., p. 51, 1 Aug. 1940.
[4] Extracts from the Marcks Plan are attached in Appendix I. They are translated from Hans-Adolf Jacobsen, *1939–1945. Der Zweite Weltkrieg in Chronik und Dokumenten* (Darmstadt, 1962), pp. 142–7. See also Alfred Philippi, *Das Pripjet Problem* (Frankfurt a. M., 1956), pp. 69–72.
[5] These aims were derived from the earlier General Staff studies as presented at the Führer Conference on 21 July. See *Halder KTB* ii. 32–3, 22 July 1940.
[6] Jacobsen, op. cit., p. 143.

MAP I. THE MARCKS PLAN

by the deep penetration and pincer movements of armoured thrusts. But by increasing the depth of the battlefield this solution also compounded the problem of the relationship between space and the forces available. Marcks sought to overcome this by allocating a third of the 110 available infantry divisions, as well as four Panzer and four motorized divisions to a large reserve. This was to be committed to protect the flanks of the armoured thrusts, to enclose the Soviet forces that they outflanked and to maintain the advance to the line Rostov–Gorki–Archangel.

After reading the 'Marcks Plan' Halder accepted the concept of thrusts north and south of the Pripet Marsh. He was probably influenced too by Hitler's choice of a similar solution. But he still stressed the danger of relying upon 'politically unsafe' Rumania as the concentration area for the thrust on Kiev.[1] He also warned against extending the group directed towards Moscow too far northward. Instead he proposed a subsidiary operation in the Baltic States independent from the main thrust through White Russia.

Halder's views were confirmed by General Friedrich Paulus who, on taking up the appointment of Deputy Chief of the General Staff, *Oberquartiermeister I*, on 3 September, was given the task of co-ordinating all the operational planning for the operation in the East. To give each of the thrusts towards Moscow, Kiev, and Leningrad sufficient strength to operate independently Paulus reduced the number of divisions that Marcks had allocated to the reserve and divided most of the available forces into three army groups, 'North', 'Centre', and 'South', each of which was to conduct a separate envelopment battle in the first stage of the invasion.[2]

The main striking-forces of each army group lay in the Panzer groups. Field-Marshal von Bock's Army Group 'Centre' was allocated Panzer Group 2, commanded by General Guderian, and Panzer Group 3, under General Hoth. These were to drive eastward on the flanks of the Bialystok salient and meet in the area of Smolensk to enclose the Soviet forces around Minsk. The infantry divisions of the 4th and 9th Armies were to follow the armoured columns and surround the enemy. Field-Marshal von Leeb's Army Group 'North' was to direct its Panzer Group 4, commanded by General Hoepner, via Dvinsk towards Leningrad, while the 18th

---

[1] *Halder KTB* ii. 51, 1 Aug. 1940. On 17 Mar. 1941 Hitler cancelled the plan to launch a major thrust from Rumania. See ibid., pp. 319–20, 17 Mar. 1941.

[2] Ibid., p. 103, 17 Sept.; p. 155, n. 5, 29 Oct. 1940.

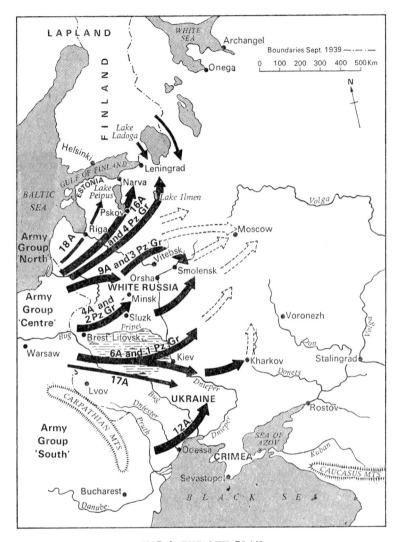

MAP 2. THE OKH PLAN

and 16th Armies defeated the Russians cut off between the armoured drive and the Baltic coast. Field-Marshal von Rundstedt's Army Group 'South' was to achieve a double envelopment of the Soviet forces in the Ukraine by attacking towards Kiev and down the Dnieper with the 6th Army and Panzer Group 1, under General von Kleist, to meet the advance of the 12th Army from Rumania. The 17th Army had the task of pinning down the Soviet forces between the two enveloping arms.[1]

In November and December General Paulus conducted a General Staff war game to test the plan. He later admitted that in the exercise 'the exchange of views was confined purely to questions of military strategy . . .'.[2] Although 'consideration was to be given to the effect of the supply situation on the time table',[3] the logistic difficulties of the campaign were apparently not yet fully recognized. Co-operation with the Navy was not discussed at all. As before, the Russian forces were assumed to be 'inferior in armour, artillery and, particularly, in the air'.[4] The first objective to be attained after the first twenty days was the general line between Upper Dnieper–Dvina River–Lake Peipus. This line was selected 'partly for reasons of the terrain and partly because it was recognized that the troops would require a breathing space and the opportunity to organise a defensive line, before embarking on the imminent and decisive battles before them'.[5] The pause for recuperation was to last for almost three weeks so that on about the fortieth day 'the decisive advance on Moscow' could be resumed.[6]

During the course of the exercise it became clear that the diverging advance of the three army groups would lead to the creation of dangerous gaps between them in the areas Lake Ilmen–Veleiki–Luki and south of Gomel. Nevertheless, in view of the 'paramount importance' of keeping Army Group 'Centre' at maximum possible strength for the attack on Moscow,[7] it was decided that the other two army groups should clear these gaps of the enemy with their own forces. Thus Army Groups 'North' and 'South' were to concentrate their weight on the flanks of Army Group 'Centre' for the

---

[1] See Görlitz, *Paulus*, pp. 109–10; *Halder KTB* ii. 464 ff. The OKH Deployment Directive, dated 31 Jan. 1941 is attached as Appendix II.

[2] Görlitz, *Paulus*, p. 100. In the original, Paulus used the phrase 'rein strategische Führungsfragen' (*Ich stehe hier auf Befehl*, ed. Walter Görlitz (Frankfurt a. M., 1960), p. 110).

[3] Ibid., p. 101.          [4] Ibid., p. 105.          [5] Ibid., p. 103.
[6] Ibid., p. 116.                                        [7] Ibid., p. 117.

'ultimate and decisive advance on Moscow' which was to take place 'at the latest on $x+40$ days'.[1] General Halder confirmed that the capture of the Don Basin and of Leningrad 'would depend on the progress of the general offensive against Moscow'.[2] The General Staff felt that this attack 'should be delivered on as wide a front as possible, in order to prevent massive Russian counter-attacks on individual and perhaps isolated formations'.[3] Paulus stated that 'this was not to be interpreted as meaning that the whole front would advance simultaneously'.[3] But earlier in the exercise the General Staff had regarded as an 'extreme solution' the idea expressed by the OKW and the Panzer generals that 'the Panzer arm was an independent entity, to be used in independent operations at long range'.[4] Thus there was a real danger that the second phase of the campaign would deteriorate into a broad, frontal advance and merely push the Russians back into the interior.

The cause of this tendency was revealed in the general conclusion to the exercise, which was 'that the German forces were barely sufficient for the purpose'.[5] Since the army groups were already over-extended in width, the planners hesitated to expose the flanks of the thrusts on Moscow by over-extending the depth of the Panzer groups' attacks.

Under these circumstances, Paulus admitted in retrospect that the final objective, Volga–Archangel, was 'far beyond anything the German forces available could hope to achieve'.[5] But although he blamed this on the 'megalomaniac extravagance of National Socialist political thinking',[5] he made no attempt to modify these aims or to question the feasibility of their achievement in the course of a single campaign. Instead he relied upon the achievement of a decisive victory by means of 'the final and ultimate onslaught on Moscow'.[6]

## The Army Group Studies

While Paulus was conducting his war game, the Chiefs of Staff of Army Groups A, B, and C were instructed to carry out independent operational studies for an invasion of Russia.[7] Generals Brennecke and von Salmuth, Chiefs of Staff of Army Groups C and B respect-

[1] Görlitz, *Paulus*, pp. 118, 120.    [2] Ibid., p. 120.
[3] Ibid., p. 118.    [4] Ibid., p. 100.
[5] Ibid., p. 106.
[6] Ibid., p. 117.    [7] OKH Befehl Nr. 88/40 dated 28 Nov. 1940.

ively, each completed a draft operational plan which was similar to that developed by Paulus. Both placed the main weight with the central army group north of the Pripet Marsh in the direction Smolensk–Moscow. The flanks of this thrust were to be secured by two smaller army groups; one directed towards Leningrad, the other towards the Don Basin.[1]

The third study, that of General von Sodenstern of Army Group A, differed from all other proposals. This was perhaps due to the fact that von Sodenstern was the only senior member of the General Staff who was openly appalled when informed of the decision to attack Russia. He responded with the words 'Do you realize that now the war is lost?'[2] Confronted with the task of producing a plan for an operation that he considered to be hopeless, von Sodenstern contented himself with the aim not of destroying the Soviet forces but of crippling the Russian leadership by capturing Moscow, Leningrad, and Kharkov.[3] Recognizing the danger of allowing these objectives to draw the German Army into eccentric operations, he placed the main weight of the attack on the north and south wings which were to swing inwards to meet east of the Pripet Marsh near Gomel. Thus concentrated, the main forces were then to drive on to Moscow with their flanks covered by subsidiary thrusts towards Pskov, Toropez, Kursk, and Kharkov. Von Sodenstern's plan involved only one major envelopment operation between Kiev and Gomel, but he hoped that the Germans could achieve a strong position from which to negotiate a favourable peace by seizing the industrial areas of Leningrad, Kharkov, and, above all, Moscow.

## The Importance of Moscow

The General Staff studies and war games were still incomplete when Field-Marshal von Brauchitsch and General Halder took the draft Army plan to the Führer Conference on 5 December 1940.[4] The generals had no cause to doubt that Hitler would accept their proposals because they had turned out to be remarkably similar to the operational suggestions that he had made on 31 July.[5] But although

---

[1] See W. E. Paulus, 'Die Entwicklung der Planung des Russland Feldzuges', Typescript, University of Bonn 1957, pp. 179–80.

[2] Uhlig, p. 176, n. 3.

[3] See Philippi, pp. 13–15, 73–5.

[4] See Halder KTB ii. 210–11, 213–14, 5 Dec. 1940; KTB OKW i. 208–9.

[5] See Halder KTB ii. 50, 31 July 1940.

he first expressed agreement with the Army plan, his subsequent remarks revealed that he did not share the view that the Soviet capital was the key objective. He stated that 'Moscow is not very important' and stressed that the primary aim was to envelop the Soviet forces before they could withdraw.[1] For this reason he suggested that part of Army Group 'Centre' should be turned north to assist in cutting off the enemy in the Baltic States. Similarly, the main envelopment in the Ukraine should be achieved by a strong thrust southwards. Thus, in contrast to the Army's plan, the operation that he described involved a dispersion of the main effort, initially concentrated in the centre, towards the Baltic and Black Seas.

It is possible that Hitler got this idea from General Jodl who had ordered Lieutenant-Colonel von Lossberg to carry out an independent examination of the problems of an eastern campaign. In his study, dated 15 September 1941, von Lossberg defined a fourfold aim:

... to destroy the mass of the Soviet Army in Western Russia; to prevent the withdrawal of battle-worthy elements into the depth of Russia, and then, having cut Western Russia off from the seas, to advance to a line which will place the most important part of Russia in our hands . . .[2]

For the achievement of the first two aims he advocated a concentration of force in the centre of the front using most of the Panzer and motorized formations for deep thrusts towards Minsk–Smolensk–Moscow. However, in order to envelop the Russians on the Baltic coast he suggested that forces should be turned from the central army group to the North, 'possibly east of the Dvina'. However, he added that the enormous spaces to be covered in this phase would necessitate a pause for supply purposes before attempting the fourth phase of operations. Lossberg believed that 'all German operations must be supported in their later stages by reliable Russian railways, because in the vast spaces a transport system based only on roads will be insufficient'.[3] However, this involved capturing sufficient Russian locomotives and rolling-stock for use on part of the railway

---

[1] See *Halder KTB* ii. 211, 5 Dec. 1940.

[2] See Appendix II. See also Besymenski, pp. 307–13; Blau, p. 13; Philippi–Heim, p. 43; Hillgruber, *Strategie*, p. 230; Uhlig, p. 173; Greiner, p. 322. Greiner states that von Lossberg's study was never shown to Hitler. However its contents probably reached him through Jodl. See Warlimont, pp. 138–9, 151. In the summer of 1940 the *Wehrmachtführungsamt* was renamed the *Wehrmachtführungsstab*.

[3] Besymenski, pp. 309–10.

MAP 3. THE LOSSBERG STUDY

system and resetting the lines on the rest to the German gauge. Thus the early capture of the Baltic harbours and the elimination of the Russian Fleet would make the coastal waters available for supply, and would help to ease the logistic situation. Later the Baltic area would constitute a well-stocked base from which to launch the final phase of the campaign beyond Moscow to the Volga, Gorki, and Archangel.

Hitler's adoption of the idea of securing the Baltic region by turning forces from the central sector involved a major departure from the plan of the OKH. It has been cited by many former generals and historians as an example of the way in which a meddling and fanatical amateur ruined a sound strategic plan. Such critics assert that Hitler was drawn away from strategic realities by his psychological aversion to treading 'the same path as Napoleon',[1] by his ideological desire to capture Leningrad because it was 'the cradle of Bolshevism',[2] and by the attraction of economic gains in the Don Basin and the Caucasus.[3] These opinions were not without some justification, especially in view of the importance with which Hitler regarded the psychological factors in war. Nevertheless, his objection to the direct thrust towards Moscow was based on strategic considerations. His intention was the same as that of the Army leaders, to envelop and destroy the Russian forces. But he believed that this was more likely to be achieved by large turning operations than by the frontal thrusts proposed by the Army.[4] Furthermore, Hitler appreciated the logistical difficulties of the campaign and felt that the delivery of quantities of supplies for the later phase would be made easier by the use of Baltic sea-routes. Subsequently in Directive No. 21 he ordered that after the Soviet Fleet had been destroyed the German Navy should 'protect the entire maritime traffic in the Baltic and the transportation by sea of supplies to the northern flank of the Army'.[5] At this time Hitler showed no hesitation in subordinating his political and economic aims to the prior achievement of the military strategic aim.

[1] Heusinger, *Befehl im Widerstreit*, p. 133; see also Warlimont, p. 189.

[2] Manstein, *Lost Victories*, p. 176. See also Görlitz, *Paulus*, p. 107; Halder, *Hitler as Warlord*, p. 41; Höhn, p. 446.

[3] See Günther Blumentritt, 'Moscow', *The Fatal Decisions*, eds. William Richardson and Seymour Freidin, trans. Constantine FitzGibbon (London, 1956), p. 40; Bor, p. 199; Kurt Assmann, 'The Battle for Moscow, Turning Point of the War', *Foreign Affairs*, 28 (January 1950), 310.

[4] See *KTB OKW* i. 996; see also p. 258, 9 Jan. 1941.

[5] Hubatsch, p. 100. See also Besymenski, pp. 314, 320; Höhn, p. 448.

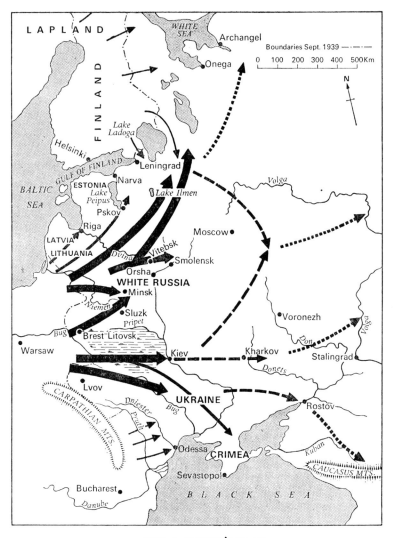

MAP 4. HITLER'S PLAN

Hitler's refusal at the conference on 5 December to make Moscow the main operational objective was accepted by the OKH without protest.[1] On 18 December he amended Directive No. 21, to state that after the initial battles in White Russia, strong mobile formations would swing north to co-operate in the destruction of the Soviet forces in the Baltic States and in the capture of Leningrad and Kronstadt. Only after the completion of these tasks were further operations towards Moscow to be undertaken in order to destroy the remaining Soviet forces and seize the industries in the area.[2] Hitler confirmed his views on 9 January when he told von Brauchitsch that the attack

should on no account turn into a frontal pushing back of the Russians. Therefore the most brutal break-throughs are necessary. The most important task is the swift envelopment of the Baltic area, thus the right flank of the German forces thrusting north of the Pripet Marsh must be made especially strong. The aims of the operation must be the destruction of the Russian Army, the seizure of the most important industrial areas and the destruction of the remaining industrial areas . . ., in addition the Baku area must be occupied.[3]

With the exception of Baku, these aims and the new operational objective, Leningrad, were duly incorporated into the Deployment Directive issued by the OKH on 31 January 1941.[4]

According to General Paulus, the OKH continued to regard the capture of Moscow as the principal objective.[5] However, Hitler's proposal for the prior capture of Leningrad was accepted, and with it the diversion of the Panzer forces of Army Group 'Centre', in order to

deprive the Baltic fleet of its main base, the Russian war effort of the armament production of the city and, above all, the Russian Army of a strategic assembly area for a counter-offensive against the flank and rear of the German forces advancing on Moscow. For this last reason alone it was essential that Leningrad should be the first objective.[6]

Nevertheless, the manner in which the Army leaders later directed

[1] *Halder KTB* ii. 211, 5 Dec. 1940.
[2] See Hubatsch, pp. 96 ff.; Warlimont, pp. 138–9; *KTB OKW* i. 996.
[3] Ibid., p. 258, 9 Jan. 1941.
[4] See Appendix III.
[5] See Görlitz, *Paulus*, p. 127. See also Liddell Hart, *On the Other Side* . . ., pp. 263–5; Hoth, p. 40; Uhlig, p. 175.
[6] Görlitz, *Paulus*, p. 127.

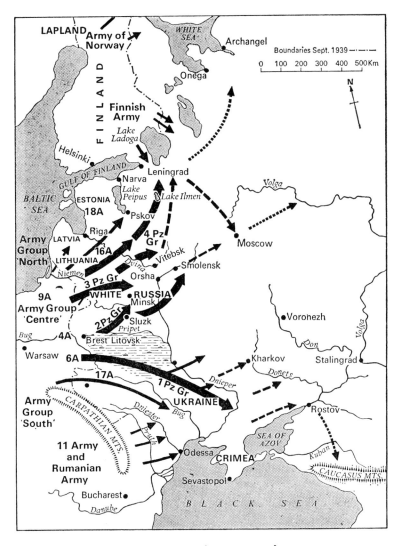

MAP 5. PLAN 'BARBAROSSA'

operations towards Moscow casts some doubt on this view. It is by no means clear whether in accepting Hitler's demand for a turning movement towards Leningrad von Brauchitsch really abandoned the OKH plan for a direct thrust on Moscow, only to revive it in July when such an operation seemed opportune, or merely concealed his intention to adhere to the Army plan in spite of Hitler's views. Certainly he was guilty of either inconsistency or deception when he attempted to change the 'Barbarossa' plan agreed upon in December, and caused a serious delay in the course of the campaign. As on so many occasions in the planning of the Russian operation, arrogant over-confidence was probably the true cause of von Brauchitsch's failure to settle this question before the opening of the attack. It appears that the choice between Leningrad and Moscow as the operational objective for the second phase of the campaign was regarded as unimportant during the planning. The Army Commander-in-Chief was confident that the decision would be reached west of the Dvina and Dnieper Rivers. 'The great frontier battles . . . of up to four weeks duration', he assured General Warlimont, would be followed by a mopping-up operation against 'slight opposition.'[1] The sequence in which cities were occupied in the course of this process seemed perhaps a matter to be settled according to the situation at the time, and of no more importance than the choice between Paris and Cherbourg as the initial objective of the final phase of the German *Blitzkrieg* in the West.

The field commanders, however, were disturbed by the vagueness and uncertainty of the OKH on this crucial question. General Hoth was particularly concerned because the direction to be taken by his Panzer Group in the opening battles would be partly determined by the choice between Leningrad or Moscow. If the former was to have priority, as indicated in Directive No. 21, his main weight should be on the left flank advancing from Vilna to take bridge-heads across the Dvina west of Vitebsk for a further thrust to the north-east. But the OKH Deployment Directive gave priority to the movement

---

[1] *IMT* xxvi. 873–PS, 400. See also *IMT* xxxviii. 221–L, 94; cf. Assmann, 'Moscow', p. 311. General Heusinger confirmed in a post-war statement that in the second phase of the campaign 'armoured thrusts' (*Panzerstiche*) would suffice to '. . . push over the crumbling remnants and occupy important centres'. Hillgruber, *Strategie*, p. 373. Cf. H. Teske, *Die silbernen Spiegel* (Heidelberg, 1952), p. 109. Halder, visiting H.Q. 17th Army predicted 'hard and bloody' battles lasting several weeks on the border, but after that a general collapse of Russian resistance.

towards Minsk, which would draw much of his strength away from Vitebsk.

From the start the army group studies and war games convinced von Bock and Hoth that the success of the campaign depended upon preventing the Russians from evading battle by means of a rapid retreat behind the Dvina and Dnieper Rivers. On 31 January 1941 at the first discussion of 'Barbarossa' between the army group commanders and OKH von Bock immediately expressed to Halder his concern on this point, and repeated it next day to Hitler himself.[1] On returning to his headquarters von Bock encouraged the view that the main, initial task of his Panzer groups must be to get to the Dvina and Dnieper crossings and the corridor between the upper reaches of the two rivers west of Smolensk before the retreating Russians. To Hoth this also meant that his group would be well placed to cross the Dvina in order to advance towards Leningrad in accordance with Hitler's wishes. In March 1941 the matter was still unresolved, so Hoth referred it to von Bock, who answered that the completion of an envelopment of the Russians west of Minsk would demand a south-easterly swing of the bulk of Hoth's armour to meet Guderian's arm of the pincer movement. However, he foresaw arguments and sent his Operations Staff Officer, von Tresckow, to discuss the question at the OKH. But the most von Brauchitsch would say was that the direction to be taken by Hoth's Panzer Group beyond Vilna would depend upon the situation, especially upon the results of Guderian's attack, and that Army Group 'Centre' headquarters would be responsible for making the decision on the spot.[2] A week later, on 27 March, von Bock himself went to the OKH at Zossen, but was disgusted by the preoccupation with 'petty details' he found there. He stressed the importance of obtaining a clear operational decision because the land east of Minsk between the upper reaches of the Dvina, Dnieper, and Beresina was marshy and likely to prove an unsuitable area in which to concentrate the bulk of his armour prior to its further advance. But he was no more successful than von Tresckow in obtaining a decision. Three days later the gathering of all the senior generals to hear Hitler's views on the campaign gave von Bock a further opportunity to raise the question. When Hitler underlined the 'decisive importance' of

---

[1] Bock, *Tagebuch*, 31 Jan. 1941.
[2] Ibid., 18 Mar. 1941; see also Heusinger, *Dokumentenbuch*, p. 56, 21 Mar. 1941.

turning the Panzer groups of Army Group 'Centre' towards Leningrad, the Field-Marshal drew attention to the difficulty of doing this
from Minsk. Von Brauchitsch, evidently annoyed that this matter
had been raised in front of the Führer, hastily interposed that 'only
the broad area around Minsk was meant'. Sensing his embarrassment
von Bock dropped the subject. But on leaving he complained to
Halder that his written orders stated that the two Panzer groups of
Army Group 'Centre' should continue the advance 'in close contact'.
To this Halder laughingly retorted: 'Spiritual contact was meant!'
Von Bock, a lover of precision in plans and orders, noted angrily in
his diary later that 'This makes nothing clearer!'[1]

The matter remained on this uncertain basis until mid May when
von Tresckow finally wrested from Field-Marshal von Brauchitsch
clear confirmation that the OKH expected Hoth's Panzer group to
direct its main strength through Molodetzno to Minsk where it would
meet Guderian's thrust and close the ring around the Russians in
the Bialystok area. After that Hoth's Panzer Group would shift its
weight northwards and advance around the marshes of the Beresina
River. On hearing this von Bock declared satisfaction that the
problem was finally cleared up, but in fact he was not really happy
with the OKH solution and as soon as the campaign began both
he and Hoth attempted to revive their own plan. However, he did
not agree with Hitler's concept of a north-easterly thrust from
Vitebsk towards the Baltic. Like Halder, von Bock preferred Moscow
to Leningrad as the main objective of the second phase. This would
retain the main effort on his sector of the front. In 1940 he had
experienced the disappointment of losing the bulk of the Panzer
forces when the weight of the initial offensive was shifted to von
Rundstedt's Army Group. Since a conspiracy of silence might reduce
the chance of this happening again in 1941 with the movement of
his Panzer Groups into von Leeb's sector he was probably tempted
to let the matter rest. He could rationalize this attitude not only
because it was encouraged by the evasiveness of von Brauchitsch
and Halder, but also because he considered that the capture of
Moscow would have more decisive results than that of Leningrad.

This conviction was probably the result of the impression made
upon him by the collapse of French morale when Paris fell. During
his convalescence in December 1940 he had read an article in a

[1] Bock, *Tagebuch*, 27 and 30 Mar. 1941.

Swiss newspaper entitled 'How France lost the War'. From it he copied into his diary the words, 'After the loss of Paris, France became a headless body. The war was lost.'[1] It is not unlikely that von Bock hoped that a similar psychological effect could be achieved if his troops could march into Moscow as they had marched into Paris in 1940.

There was no further discussion of the choice between Leningrad and Moscow until after the campaign had begun.[2] Only in July 1941 did von Brauchitsch perceive the need for a decisive operational objective for the second phase in Russia, because by then the difficulties and delays in completing the first envelopment battles, the dogged resistance of the Soviet troops, the quality of the new Soviet tanks, and the size of the Soviet reserves began to open the eyes of the Army Commander-in-Chief to his terrible underestimation of the enemy.

## The Final Operational Objectives

The confidence of the OKH that a decisive victory would be won in the initial phase of the campaign—the envelopment battles west of the Dvina and Dnieper—caused them to accept the view that the capture of Moscow would present little difficulty. It also made them careless in planning the final phase. Marcks defined the final operational objective as the line 'Rostov–Gorki–Archangel'.[3] In the 'Barbarossa' Directive of 18 December 1940, it was 'Volga–Archangel'.[4] Presumably the idea of stopping at Rostov was dropped to allow for the 'subsidiary operation' to seize the Baku oilfields which Hitler had mentioned on 31 July.[5] However, Marcks did not expect that the attainment of this line would result in an end of hostilities. He warned that the offensive might have to be extended to the Urals and that a Soviet government in Asia might continue the war indefinitely.[6] Hitler shared this view. He envisaged the political disintegration of Western Russia into separate states with which peace could be made.[7] But further east a force of forty to fifty German divisions would be required as a 'shield against Asiatic Russia', while an air fleet of the Luftwaffe launched raids on the remaining

---

[1] Ibid., 14 Nov. 1940.                    [2] Guderian, p. 150.
[3] Jacobsen, *1939–1945*, p. 145. Cf. Appendix II, The Lossberg Study.
[4] Hubatsch, p. 97.                    [5] *Halder KTB* ii. 50, 31 July 1940.
[6] See Blau, p. 12.                    [7] *Halder KTB* ii. 341, 3 Mar. 1941.

Soviet war industrial centres in the Urals.[1] Later, when Field-Marshal von Bock expressed doubt about the ability of the Wehrmacht to force the Russians to make peace, Hitler replied that, if necessary, German motorized forces would have to advance to the Urals.[2] These vague aims involving operations of indefinite duration and territorial extent were compatible neither with Hitler's earlier insistence that the Soviet State must be 'heavily defeated in a single sweep', nor with the opening sentence of Directive No. 21 which called upon the Wehrmacht to be prepared '*to defeat Soviet Russia in one rapid campaign*'.[3] About a third of the Wehrmacht would be tied down in Russia under winter combat conditions even if Operation 'Barbarossa' attained its full objectives. Some attempt was made to prepare winter clothing, equipment, and shelter but it was inadequate even for the needs of an army of occupation.[4] Throughout the operational planning the assumption persisted that the campaign would be decisively ended before the onset of winter. In making this assumption, the Germans conducted their planning, in the words of Marshal Eremenko, as if 'they thought they would "overfulfil" their plan'.[5]

Thus, the German military strategy in the East was characterized by a lack of caution, of imagination, of flexibility and of attention to logistical problems. Any one of these omissions would seem remarkable in the General Staff, which since 1870 has been regarded as a paragon of military methods and skills. But the presence of all of them demands a reassessment of the reputation for efficiency that the heirs of Moltke have attempted to uphold.

## The Responsibility of the Chief of the General Staff

One of the most remarkable features of German history in the twentieth century is the extent to which the German General Staff has continued to maintain its reputation for efficiency in spite of its terrible errors in both world wars. This has often been achieved by

[1] See *KTB OKW* i. 209, 5 Dec.; p. 258, 9 Jan. 1941. See also Hubatsch, pp. 97, 152. Directive No. 32 dated 11 June 1941 increased the land force required to 60 divisions.

[2] Bock, *Tagebuch*, 1 Feb. 1941. See also *KTB OKW* i. 90E.

[3] *Halder KTB* ii. 49, 31 July 1940; Hubatsch, p. 96. Italicized in original.

[4] Guderian, pp. 151, 267; Blumentritt, 'Moscow', pp. 62–3.

[5] A. Eremenko, *The Arduous Beginning*, trans. Vic Schneierson (Moscow, 1966), p. 319.

shifting the blame for military failures on to the political leadership of Germany. The defeat of the invasion of Russia has been no exception, and Adolf Hitler was the natural scapegoat on which to push the errors of its planning and execution. After the Second World War the most unabashed writer in this endeavour was the former Chief of the General Staff, General Franz Halder. His pamphlet *Hitler as Warlord* and the book of conversations edited by Peter Bor were obvious attempts to clear the General Staff of all responsibility for the defects in the planning for the East.[1] In their pages Halder blamed the major mistakes or omissions of the German operational plan on Hitler, a man 'to whom the artistry of a modern General Staff map was a complete mystery'.[2]

According to Halder, on 3 February 1941 Hitler 'brushed aside' arguments stressing the strength of the Soviet Union.[3] Yet the contemporary evidence of Halder's own notes and those of the OKW War Diary suggest that on this occasion he presented not 'arguments' but a report indicating that the German forces had qualitative superiority over those of Russia.[4] It has been shown above that this optimism in fact typified the attitude of the Army leaders from the start of the planning. Similarly, it was evident that the military planners completely shared Hitler's confidence that Russia could be defeated in a single campaign. Yet Halder described this belief as 'in contrast to that of the General Staff'.[5]

In an attempt to explain away the erroneous German assessment of what was feasible in Russia, Halder resorted to the excuse that there was a marked difference between the limited aims of the Army and the over-ambitious predatory aims of Hitler, who 'had never made known his intentions in these clear terms to the men who were charged with the command of the operation'.[6] According to Halder, the military leaders believed that the German forces were 'just about sufficient to defeat the Russian levies facing them' and thus to win 'a strategic foreground . . . by the occupation of sizeable parts of the Ukraine, of White Russia and of the Baltic States—thereby providing a bargaining counter for peace'.[6] Yet it is again Halder's own contemporary notes that show that there were no basic disagreements

---

[1] See Introduction, p. 2, n. 2.
[2] Halder, *Hitler as Warlord*, p. 23.
[3] Ibid., p. 19.
[4] See *Halder KTB* ii. 266–7; *KTB OKW* i. 297, 3 Feb. 1941.
[5] Bor, p. 199.
[6] Halder, *Hitler as Warlord*, p. 40.

over the territorial and political aims of the campaign. Those proposed by von Brauchitsch on 21 July 1940 were very similar to those
described by Hitler ten days later. The only major difference lay in
Hitler's addition of the Caucasus to the territories to be conquered.[1]
The Army planners evidently preferred to postpone consideration
of the 'subsidiary operation' required to reach the Baku oilfields, but
they were not allowed to forget it altogether because Hitler took
care to remind them of it in January 1941.[2]

Halder's mendacious statements about the military leaders'
ignorance of Hitler's real aims in the East were matched by a gross
misrepresentation of Hitler's concept of the operation plan. He
envisaged, Halder stated, an 'enormous, completely fantastic pincer
[movement] with the jaws on Leningrad and Stalingrad'.[3] However,
Hitler's statements at the planning conferences for the campaign of
1941 made no mention of Stalingrad. As suggested above, his main
concern was to achieve the envelopment of the Soviet forces, and he
was not without justification in fearing that the Army's concept of
the campaign would deteriorate into a frontal advance.

Halder also managed to blame Hitler for the failure of the Army
to prepare sufficient winter clothing for the troops. This was not a
question upon which Hitler needed to be consulted since it was a
matter of internal Army administration to provide suitable clothing
for the large number of formations that would have to garrison
Russia and hold the eastern boundaries even if 'Barbarossa' was
successful. Nevertheless, he stated: 'When the Commander-in-Chief
asked for immediate preparations for the provision of special winter
clothes, he received a curt refusal with the remark that by the beginning of winter, the fighting would long since have been over.'[4] What
Halder failed to point out was that if this request was indeed ever
made, the readiness of von Brauchitsch to accept such a reply can
be explained only by his agreement with it.[5]

The German neglect in the administrative preparations was not
confined to their winter equipment. But Halder carefully evaded the
fact that the crucial factors of supply and transportation, indeed the
whole logistic and economic foundations of the campaign, were
ignored by the Army leaders until after the operational plan had
been completed.

---

[1] *Halder KTB* ii. 50, 31 July 1940.
[2] See *KTB OKW* i. 258, 9 Jan. 1941.          [3] Bor, p. 199.
[4] Ibid., p. 198.                              [5] Ibid., p. 173, n. 82.

The man chiefly responsible for the errors in the operational plan was of course the Chief of the General Staff, General Halder himself. His performance as a strategist had been unimpressive in previous campaigns. When planning the invasion of Czechoslovakia in September 1938, he had provoked Hitler's anger by allocating the Panzer and motorized divisions to supporting roles which made little use of their mobile striking power.[1] The success of the invasion of Poland reflected no great credit on Halder because as he himself admitted 'the Germans would have had to be very poor soldiers not to win the war in Poland with one hand tied behind their backs'.[2] Halder's operational plan for an offensive in the West was an un-imaginative repetition of the initial phase of the Schlieffen Plan of 1914, which could have led only to a 'partial victory'.[3] The German success in 1940 was due to Hitler's recognition of the superiority of the rival plan produced by the Chief of Staff of von Rundstedt's Army Group, von Manstein. Thus, by the summer of 1940, in spite of his 'remarkable grasp of every aspect of staff duties',[4] Halder had not demonstrated any great flair or insight as a strategic planner.

Halder's limitations in this respect were made worse by the very nature of the German High Command organization, which pre-vented him from concentrating effectively upon matters of strategy. It is interesting to compare his diaries with those of the British Chief of the Imperial General Staff, General Sir Alan Brooke, who was 'freed . . . from a host of unnecessary distractions and enabled . . . to concentrate on his main task of formulating and guiding strategy'.[5] In contrast to those of Brooke, Halder's daily notes are mainly con-cerned with the minutiae of tactical, technical, administrative, and personnel matters. Of course, Halder's position was not strictly equivalent to Brooke's because, as von Manstein later complained, Hitler had failed to create a 'Reich Chief-of-Staff responsible for grand strategy'.[6] Nevertheless, this omission made it all the more necessary that the German Army Chief of Staff should endeavour to

[1] See *IMT* xxv. 338–PS, 429–32, 441–5, 463–4, 466–9.

[2] Conversation with General Halder, 23 June 1969. See also Manstein, *Lost Victories*, p. 62: 'the Germans were *bound* to win this campaign by virtue of their superiority and the infinitely more favourable starting conditions'.

[3] Ibid., p. 99. See also Bock, *Tagebuch*, 25 Oct. 1939.

[4] Manstein, *Lost Victories*, p. 79.

[5] Arthur Bryant, *The Turn of the Tide, 1939–1943, A Study based on the Diaries and Autobiographical Notes of Field Marshal The Viscount Alanbrooke, K.G., O.M.* (London, 1957), p. 263.

[6] Manstein, *Lost Victories*, p. 153.

take the widest possible responsibility for military strategy. Thus it is curious that Halder should have chosen to involve himself in a mass of staff detail and to delegate so important a task as the planning of the *Blitzkrieg* in the East to a number of his subordinates. Perhaps he was prompted by an awareness of his limitations as a strategist.[1] But it seems more likely that his action was merely a further example of the German tendency to reduce strategy to an exercise of staff procedure. As Chief of the General Staff, Halder was free to organize his daily work and that of his subordinates as he wished. His choice reflected a bureaucratic diligence which had lost sight of priorities.

The fact was that the General Staff had acquired such an aura of competence and infallibility that the need to incorporate individuals of genius within its structure was ignored. It felt that from principles laid down by Clausewitz and the practices developed by the elder Moltke it had developed a 'doctrine that would make the conduct of war no longer the personal secret of the great captain, but the permanent property of the whole leadership: a solid body of knowledge capable of being handed on from generation to generation and adapted to the ever changing conditions of strategy'.[2] But the very reputation won by the German General Staff in the nineteenth century gradually reduced its ability to adapt its doctrine or to accept innovators into its ranks. As a result in the twentieth century it lost the philosophical breadth of the early masters, Scharnhorst and Clausewitz, who saw war related to policy as 'an organic whole'.[3] By 1940 it had deteriorated into 'an almost anonymous syndicate' which displayed merely 'a virtuosity of operational technique' and was incapable of adjusting to entirely new technological and grand strategic problems.[3] Halder was unable to recognize these limitations and believed that by using the team approach to planning he was conforming to the best traditions of the General Staff.

The decision to delegate and divide the planning of the eastern campaign undoubtedly contributed to the omissions, errors, and lack of unity which, as indicated above, characterized the final plan. The studies of von Greiffenberg, Kinzel, Marcks, Paulus, and Wagner and the proposals of Hitler were not combined into a con-

---

[1] This is implied in von Manstein's remark that this delegation of the planning was due to his 'high sense of responsibility', Manstein, *Lost Victories*, p. 79.

[2] Herbert Rosinski, *The German Army* (New York, 1966), p. 113.

[3] Ibid., pp. 314–15.

sistent whole, and for this General Halder must bear the main responsibility. For, as von Manstein later commented, 'the fact remains that the basic concept of a campaign plan should be born in the mind of the man who has to direct the campaign'.[1]

[1] Manstein, *Lost Victories*, p. 79.

CHAPTER V

# Strategic, Economic, and Political Problems December 1940–May 1941

## *Grand-Strategic Doubts*

THE German operational plan for the invasion of Russia which General Halder presented to Hitler on 5 December was amended and issued to the three services on 18 December in Directive No. 21.[1] On 31 January, the field commanders received it in the form of 'Deployment Directive Barbarossa' issued by the OKH.[2] During and after this process, the German military leaders became increasingly doubtful about embarking upon a major operation in the East before ending the war in the West. Nevertheless, there were no strong or unified attempts by the service chiefs to present a concerted argument against the attack in the East. Instead, they showed an ambivalent attitude of confidence in the operational feasibility of the Russian campaign, and doubt about its grand-strategic wisdom or political necessity. These doubts increased as the economic difficulties of the campaign became apparent. But they found little expression because they lay outside the narrow confines of operational and military strategic competence that the service chiefs had accepted. Inter-service jealousy and rivalry between the OKH and OKW prevented a frank and searching discussion between the military leaders of the problems of the grand strategy of the war, especially of the relation between the war in the West and the proposed attack in the East. Hitler dominated the grand-strategic level of planning and decision-making, and the generals were seldom permitted to discuss political or economic factors at Führer Conferences. If they were mentioned, they were used by Hitler as evidence of a deteriorating situation. Since the political and economic position of Germany could only become worse in relation to those of Britain,

[1] See Hubatsch, pp. 96 ff.    [2] See Appendix III.

the United States, and Russia, he argued, the blow for the completion of a German hegemony over Europe must be launched as soon as possible. Furthermore, it must also be as brutal as possible in order to ensure a swift and decisive result. Confronted by the sweeping confidence of their Führer, most of the military leaders had little difficulty in subduing their doubts. Nevertheless, between December 1940 and February 1941 they passed through a phase of disturbing uncertainties.

With all the advantages of hindsight it now seems incredible that these uncertainties did not result in a thorough and frank reassessment of the situation. But in addition to the difficulties of serving a dictator, the German military leaders were also subject to the weaknesses and frustrations that mar most human affairs. Field-Marshal Lord Wavell once remarked,

it has always seemed to me that most people seeing the muddles of war forget the muddles of peace and the general inefficiency of the human race in ordering its affairs. War is a wasteful, boring, muddled affair; and people of fine intelligence either resign themselves to it or fret badly, especially if they are near the heart of things and can see matters which ought to be done, or done better, and cannot contrive to get them set right.[1]

On another occasion Wavell wrote that the principles of strategy and tactics, and the logistics of war were 'really absurdly simple'. What made war 'so complicated and so difficult' were its 'actualities . . .—the effects of tiredness, hunger, fear, lack of sleep, weather, inaccurate information, the time factor and so forth'.[1] Of these only one, inaccurate information, could be applied to the men who planned the German invasion of Russia, but it had most important effects. Information about the enemy was limited and ill assessed. Information about their own troops was distorted by the fact that the basis of the planning for the invasion of Russia was laid down in the period of relief and elation, of optimism and unreality that followed the victory over France.

During the further development of the planning, inaccurate information or incomplete knowledge played a major role in discouraging criticism. The need for secrecy and deception and the standing order that knowledge of military plans should be strictly limited to those who had to possess it, discouraged any wide discussion of the

[1] Quoted in John Connell, *Wavell, Scholar and Soldier* (London, 1964), p. 22.

problems involved.[1] Such restrictions, obviously necessary for military reasons, always impose intellectual limitations on the original concept of planning, and discourage processes of amendment which might further endanger security. Furthermore, most of the men who were fully informed of the operational planning from the start had been severely strained by the controversies, heated argument, breach of security, and changes of plan that had occurred during the preparations for the campaign in the West. A desire to avoid a repetition of such experiences must have exercised a restraining influence on those tempted to reveal anxiety about Operation 'Barbarossa'.

Under these circumstances, once the operational plan was established it became difficult for the German military leaders to adjust their thinking or react decisively to the changes that took place in the general situation in the months that followed.

In July 1940 when the OKH began the operational planning for the Russian campaign, the grand-strategic situation appeared to be very favourable for such an undertaking. In the West the only surviving enemy had been flung off the Continent and was threatened with air assault and, perhaps, invasion. To the south, Italy had joined the war and Spain had offered to follow suit. France, resentful towards her former ally who had deserted her army and sunk her fleet, seemed prepared to comply with the conqueror's demands. But by December the picture had greatly changed. The British had successfully defended their island and struck back at the Axis. In so doing they had discouraged Spain from entering the war.[2] Italy had suffered serious reverses at sea, in Greece, and North Africa. These had encouraged an independent attitude in the French leaders, especially General Weygand, and this, in turn, had necessitated preparations for a German occupation of Vichy France, Operation 'Attila'.[3]

When called upon to discuss this situation with Hitler on 9 December, General Halder took the opportunity to stress the need to concentrate all means for the invasion of the British Isles, and, secondly, to counter the possibility of a strengthening of the British position in North Africa or the formation of a Balkan front. Hitler expressed agreement with his views but apparently nothing was said

---

[1] See Appendix II, 'The Lossberg Study'. See also *KTB OKW* i. 151E.

[2] See *Halder KTB* ii. 218, 8 Dec. 1940.

[3] See ibid. See also Bock, *Tagebuch*, 12 Dec. 1940.

about a postponement of the Russian operation.[1] Four days later
Halder gave the Chiefs of Staff of the army groups and armies an
outline of the situation. Ostensibly this was based upon the views
presented by Hitler at the conference on 5 December, but Halder's
own opinions, especially his preference for an attack on Britain,
intruded upon his discourse. He stated that Operation 'Sea Lion'
might be carried out if an internal weakening of Britain presented
the opportunity for a 'death blow'.[2] This was hardly an accurate
account of Hitler's view at this time. Similarly, Halder's remarks
about the Russian campaign reflected the ambivalent attitude of the
OKH. Though he echoed Hitler's assertion that 'the decision over
the hegemony in Europe would be achieved in a struggle with Russia',
he also stated that preparations should be made to permit an attack
'if the political situation demands it . . .'.[3] 'We do not seek a conflict with Russia,' he continued, 'but from the spring of 1941 we
must be ready for this task also.'[4] He then gave the Operations
Branch a list of possible future operations: 'Sea Lion', Gibraltar,
Vichy France, Bulgaria, Russia, and he warned that 'Political uncertainty is possible for a long while yet, therefore [we must be]
flexible.'[4]

Directive No. 21, which Hitler issued on 18 December, left little
room for flexibility. Nevertheless, at the OKH there was still an
unwillingness to believe that Hitler was determined to go ahead with
the eastern campaign irrespective of the situation in the West or
of the attitude of the Russians. Field-Marshal von Brauchitsch even
asked Major Engel, Army Adjutant to the Führer, 'to establish
whether Hitler really intended to resort to force or was only bluff-
ing'.[5] The attitude of the Army leaders at this time was the result of
a number of factors. They were not opposed to the campaign in
Russia on principle. They were hostile towards Bolshevism, suspicious
of Stalin's intentions, and eager to end Slavic rivalry for the domination of eastern Europe. Furthermore, they were convinced that the
Army could beat the Russians and that they had adequate land
forces for the tasks in both the East and the West. Indeed, having
pushed Britain off the Continent, they claimed that for the Army
the war in the East could be regarded as a single-front war. But in
spite of this they were nagged by the uneasy feeling that the British

[1] See *Halder KTB* ii. 219, 9 Dec. 1940.          [2] Ibid., p. 226, 13 Dec. 1940.
[3] Ibid., p. 227.                                         [4] Ibid., p. 228.
[5] G. Engel, *Tagebuch*, 18 Dec. 1940, quoted by Hillgruber, *Strategie*, p. 369.

should be completely defeated before the campaign in the East began. This feeling was strengthened by the naval and military defeats inflicted on Italy in November and December 1940. But just as the British could not strike at them, so they were forced to admit that they could not inflict a death-blow on the British. For this they needed naval and air superiority and there was no immediate prospect of achieving either.[1] Thus, while clinging stubbornly to 'Sea Lion', the OKH had no real hope of carrying it out.

The Army's dependence upon the support of the Luftwaffe was also a cause of uneasiness in the East. The only note of pessimism or even caution in the operational planning for Russia arose from the likelihood that the Luftwaffe would be unable to fulfil its primary tasks of winning air superiority and providing support to the ground troops. But the brusque manner in which Hitler had dismissed the doubts of von Brauchitsch on this point on 5 December, made it clear that he would not tolerate any interference from the Army in Reichsmarschall Göring's sphere of competence.[2]

Göring's attitude towards the decision to attack Russia was also one of mixed feelings. According to General Schmid, Chief of the Luftwaffe Intelligence Branch, he dreaded 'the boundless extension of the war, the unending size of Russia, and, on the other side, America's entry into the war'.[3] But in view of his confidence in German technical superiority, his long adherence to the Nazi policy of eastern conquest, and his loyalty to Hitler, it is unlikely that warnings which he claimed to have made against the Russian operation were strongly worded.[4] His Chief of Staff, General Hans Jeschonnek, who had served in Russia in the period of co-operation between the Reichswehr and Red Army in the 1920s, had a low opinion of the Soviet Union and was definitely in favour of striking in the East, even though the Luftwaffe Chief of Operations, von Waldau, and Chief of Intelligence, Schmid, disagreed with him.[5]

Like Göring, Field-Marshal Keitel also stated at Nuremberg after the war that he expressed his opposition to a two-front war. But when Hitler refused to accept the arguments of the memorandum that he drew up in August 1940 and also the resignation that he offered, Keitel resumed his normal obsequious role.[6]

[1] See *Halder KTB* ii. 226, 13 Dec. 1940.
[2] *KTB OKW* i. 205, 5 Dec. 1940.
[3] Quoted by Hillgruber, *Strategie*, p. 396, n. 17.
[4] See *IMT* ix. 59 ff., 386; x. 493, 590 ff.
[5] Op. cit. See also Plocher, p. 6.        [6] Görlitz, *Keitel*, pp. 243-4.

The most serious military criticism of the attack on Russia came from Admiral Raeder. On 27 December, he told Hitler that it was 'absolutely essential to recognize that the greater task of the hour is to concentrate all our resources against England'.[1] But Hitler insisted that this could not be done until the last continental enemy had been eliminated, after which production priorities could be shifted to the Luftwaffe and Navy.[2] From this reply, Raeder concluded that further warnings 'were completely useless'.[3]

Once the Naval and Air Force Chiefs had abandoned their attempts to dissuade Hitler from his decision to attack Russia their staffs began planning the details of their roles in the East. It is significant that they had not even been asked to contribute their advice during the development of the operational plan. Like the logistical planners, they were merely confronted with a *fait accompli* and expected to conform to it.

## The Luftwaffe's Planning for 'Barbarossa'

For the sake of secrecy only a small number of Luftwaffe staff officers were involved in the initial planning for the air war in the East. During January and February 1941 the allocation of reconnaissance and fighter aircraft and anti-aircraft artillery and the organization of the supply services were discussed with the Army General Staff. On 27 February the Chief of Staff of the Luftwaffe, General Jeschonnek, conferred with General Halder on the problems of air support. An enormous administrative organization was necessary to prepare bases in the East to which two-thirds of the Luftwaffe could suddenly fly in May from their aerodromes in the West. As the advance progressed short-ranged fighters and Stukas would have to be provided with new airfields close to the front. The consequent movement of ground staff and equipment would place a heavy strain on the transport and road system. Special administrative staffs were formed, commanded by officers selected for their foresight, ability to give clear orders, and 'talent for improvisation'.[4]

[1] FCNA 1940, pp. 138–9.

[2] See *IMT* xxxiv. 170–C, 674 ff.

[3] *IMT* xxxiv. 066–C, 276 ff. A warning similar to Raeder's was expressed by State Secretary von Weizsäcker, who was a former naval officer. See *NSR*, pp. 333–4. See also the Naval Staff Memorandum of 6 June 1941 on the relationship between 'Barbarossa' and the Mediterranean theatre. *KTB SKL, Teil C VII*, 1941, 173, quoted by W. E. Paulus, p. 289.

[4] Plocher, p. 285.

The main operational problem was the low ratio of aircraft to space. From the start it was clear that the available formations would have to concentrate upon attacks most vital to the achievement of the operational goals. Discussion of the details of air support to be given to Army Group 'Centre' was conducted by Field-Marshal Kesselring, commanding Air Fleet 2, at a war game in Brussels. On 25 March he visited von Bock and his Panzer Group commanders, Guderian and Hoth. Similar co-ordination was achieved between General Keller, commanding Air Fleet 1, and Field-Marshal von Leeb. But in the south von Rundstedt was served during the planning by only a small Luftwaffe staff detached from Air Fleet 4, which was engaged in the Balkans until the very eve of 'Barbarossa'.

A total of 2,770 aircraft out of the Luftwaffe's first-line strength of 4,300 were allocated to the East. Of these Air Fleet 2 had about 1,500, Air Fleet 4 was given 750, Air Fleet 1 about 400, and the rest were flown from Air Fleet 5's bases in Norway against targets in the far north. Spread over 1,000 miles of front these formations seemed weak indeed. But in spite of this dispersion and the estimates of the strength of the Soviet Air Force, which varied between 8,000 and 10,000 aircraft, the planners voiced no doubt that the Luftwaffe would be able to fulfil its normal *Blitzkrieg* roles: the winning of air supremacy by destroying the enemy's air force; the support of the land operations by engaging ground targets; the shattering of morale of the civil population and government by bombing selected cities. In addition the Luftwaffe also accepted the task of crippling the major units of the Soviet fleets, because the German Navy could not operate in strength in the Baltic or Black Seas.

### Naval Planning

On 30 January 1941 the Naval Staff completed a study of the Navy's role in 'Barbarossa'.[1] It concluded that the tasks of securing German and Rumanian coasts, preventing the Russian Baltic fleet from escaping into the North Sea and safeguarding the iron-ore sea traffic from Sweden could be achieved only with considerable co-operation from the Luftwaffe. Air attacks would have to be conducted on Soviet ships in the Baltic and Black Seas and the Arctic Ocean and on the locks in the White Sea Canal to prevent the Baltic fleet from escaping

[1] Nuremberg Document, NOKW–2270, SKL B Nr. 1, I Op/94/41 g.k. Chefs. 30 Jan. 1941.

north. Luftwaffe help was also needed in the tasks of minelaying and coast defence and in the provision of further anti-aircraft artillery around naval bases. The co-operation of the navies of Finland and Rumania was anticipated, and although they still out-numbered those of the Axis it was thought that the Soviet fleets would attempt only defensive operations with their surface vessels. Their use of heavy warships was likely to be limited through fear of mines laid by aircraft. However, the Russians were expected to make full offensive use of their 152 submarines.[1]

Admiral Raeder presented the naval plans for the East to Hitler on 4 February 1941, but on the following day these plans were upset because the Luftwaffe announced its inability to meet all the Navy's requests for support. This confirmed the Naval Staff's belief that the destruction of the Soviet fleet could only be achieved by the capture of the main naval bases.[2] However, Hitler had made it clear in Directive No. 21 that he did not expect more of the Navy. Its main task would be the continuation of the war against Great Britain.[3] Two days after his acceptance of the Navy's eastern plans he issued Directive No. 23 'Directions for Operations against the English War Economy'.[4] Thus Raeder turned his main attention to the West and tried to ignore the dismay he felt at the grand strategic error of starting a new war in the East.

Since both Raeder and Göring, the service chiefs most directly concerned with the problem of a two-front war, were unwilling or unable to make any impression on Hitler, von Brauchitsch and Halder were discouraged from voicing grand-strategic arguments against Operation 'Barbarossa'. They were even less inclined to question its political origins.

### The Political Danger of Russia

Between July and December 1940, Hitler was able to assemble an impressive array of evidence of Soviet hostility with which to justify his resolve to attack Russia. Further Soviet expansion in Finland and Rumania had apparently been averted only by demon-strative German troop movements in August and September. After

---

[1] See Appendix VII, 'Axis and Soviet Naval Strengths, 1941'. Friedrich Ruge, *Der Seekrieg, The German Navy's Story, 1939–1945*, trans. M. G. Saunders (Annapolis, 1957), pp. 197–201, 203–4.
[2] N.D. 033C. SKL *Tagebuch*, 19 Feb. 1941.
[3] Hubatsch, p. 100.                                         [4] Ibid., p. 118.

the meeting with Molotov, Hitler, in a conversation with Field-Marshal von Bock, began to revive the idea of liaison between Russia and Britain and to this he added hints of 'contacts between Russia and America'.[1] The note replying to the proposals placed before Molotov in Berlin was treated by Hitler as proof of the expansionist tendencies of that 'incomparable and imperturbable blackmailer, Stalin, who was trying to gain time in order to consolidate his advanced bases in Finland and the Balkans'.[2] Hitler admitted that the Russian leader was wise enough not to 'start anything openly with Germany'.[3] He would, however, do all he could to make Germany's situation more difficult.

Very similar views had already been expressed by General Halder on 13 December when he told the senior staff officers, 'Every weakening of the position of the Axis leads to a Russian advance. Russia cannot take the initiative of her own accord, but she will use every opportunity to weaken our position.'[4] After the war, General Halder continued to describe the German attack on Russia as a response to a 'long but steadily rising political danger'.[5] He preferred, however, not to go into details, because, as he put it, politics was 'not my area'.[6] Halder's evasiveness is understandable, for any delusions he had about the reasons for Hitler's decision to attack Russia must have been dispelled on 17 February when von Etzdorf, the liaison officer from the Foreign Office, reported Hitler as saying that 'if Britain were defeated, then he would no longer be able to rouse the German people against Russia. Thus, Russia would have to be attacked first.'[7] From then on Halder well knew that Hitler's aggressive aims in the East were inflexible, and that the Soviet Union had good reason to seek the means of improving her own strategic position and weakening that of Germany.[8] Thus the deterioration of Russo-German relations was a result rather than the cause of the German preparations for the invasion of Russia. Nevertheless, until 17 February 1941 Halder and several other German military leaders remained

[1] Bock, *Tagebuch*, 3 Dec. 1940.
[2] *Hitler's Testament*, p. 97. See also FCNA 1941, pp. 8–13.
[3] *KTB OKW* i. 257, 9 Jan. 1941.
[4] *Halder KTB* ii. 227, 13 Dec. 1940.
[5] Bor, p. 194.
[6] Ibid. See also Günther Blumentritt, *Von Rundstedt, the Soldier and the Man*, trans. Cuthbert Reavely (London, 1952), p. 41, for a further example of the incredible political *naïveté* from a senior officer of the German General Staff.
[7] *Halder KTB* ii. 283, 17 Feb. 1941.
[8] The belief that the conflict with Russia was the result of a steady deterioration

unwilling to accept the inflexibility of Hitler's grand strategy, especially when they became aware of the enormous economic and logistic difficulties of the campaign in the East.

### Economic Preparations for the East, July–December, 1940

As already described, economic and logistical factors were almost ignored in the initial planning conducted by the Army General Staff for the invasion of Russia. In the OKW, however, economic and logistical preparations for the East began as soon as Hitler announced his decision to Keitel and Jodl in the last week of July 1940. On 29 July Jodl ordered Section 'L' of the *Wehrmachtführungs- stab* to start work on the communications system, accommodation, and depot facilities required in the eastern concentration and deployment areas.[1] In August the Reich Defence Council and War Economy and Armament Office of the OKW began to draw up economic plans for the field army of 180 divisions ordered by Hitler on the 31 July, and, at the same time, to make increases in the strength of the Luftwaffe and Navy made necessary by Hitler's wish to step up the air and sea war against Britain in the time available before the Wehrmacht turned eastward.

The economic planners were well aware of the size of their task. On 14 August Göring told General Thomas, Head of the War Economy and Armament Office, that 'only now was real rearmament production starting'.[2] A few days later, Field-Marshal Keitel expressed doubt that the new demands could be met because the *Blitzkrieg* economy was already extended to full capacity. Nevertheless, manpower and raw materials would have to be made available by ruthless cuts in the civil and consumer goods sectors and by the

of Russo-German political relations persisted. Admiral Assmann, for instance, collected in 1943 from the files of the Naval Staff an account of this process. His illusions were shattered in 1944 when Admiral Raeder bluntly informed him that Hitler was 'firmly resolved on a surprise attack against Russia, regardless of what was the Russian attitude to Germany', *IMT* xxxiv. 066–C, 278. Cf. *IMT* xxxiv. 170–C, 674 ff.

[1] See Warlimont, p. 112. This work was conducted in close co-operation with the General Staff's Transport Branch. On 11 Oct. 1940 General Gercke reported to Halder on the progress in railway and road improvements in the East. *Halder KTB* ii. 133, 11 Oct. 1940.

[2] Thomas, p. 512. Göring also told Thomas that German deliveries of goods to Russia should continue till the spring of 1941 after which 'we will not be interested in a full satisfaction of Russian wishes'.

employment of women, prisoners of war, and foreign workers.[1] In short, Keitel felt that the time had come to place the economy upon a total-war footing.[2] These ideas were, however, rejected by Hitler.[3] He regarded the maintenance of the civilian economy as essential to morale, and for racial and social reasons he opposed employment of women.[4] Since the *Blitzkrieg* economy had succeeded in providing the necessary armaments and munitions for the earlier campaigns, he saw no reason to doubt that it would also meet the requirements of a victory in the East. Thus Keitel had to be content with an increase in foreign workers and an attempt to offset deficiencies in raw material by concentrating upon essential elements in each of the services: armour and motorized artillery, fighter aircraft and anti-aircraft guns, and U-boats.[5] Nevertheless, Keitel's fear proved fully justified. On 3 September General Fromm, Commander of the Reserve Army, wrote to General Thomas detailing the needs of the expanded Army for a major campaign.[6] Sufficient munitions would be required to bring 200 divisions up to full-scale holdings, plus reserves totalling twelve times the monthly 'major combat expenditure' based on the amount used during the campaign in the West between 10 May and 20 June 1940. A full-scale issue of weapons and equipment would also be needed, plus only one month's 'major combat expenditure'. Evidently the losses in Russia were not expected to exceed those in the West. Even so it was doubtful, wrote Fromm, whether these requirements could be met in the mere six months left. The attempt could only be made if more labour was made available. But in view of Hitler's decision, the OKW was able to meet the Army's needs for the eastern campaign only by cuts and compromises. Aircraft production declined throughout the second half of 1940,[7] and the doubling of the number of Panzer divisions was achieved only by halving the tank strength of each

[1] *KTB OKW* i. 76–77E.
[2] For Keitel's views on Ludendorff's concept of total war see Görlitz, *Keitel*, pp. 154 ff.
[3] Keitel, while urging the adoption of a total-war economy, also, according to his own account, attempted to dissuade Hitler from his eastern plans. Ibid., pp. 243–4.
[4] See Rauschning, pp. 207–8; Milward, pp. 12, 28–30, 34–5, 46; Klein, pp. 140–1.
[5] See Thomas, p. 432.
[6] *OKH* Stab II (Rüst) Nr. 1702/40 g. Kdos, 3 Sept. 1940. See also W. E. Paulus, p. 137.
[7] See Milward, p. 42. See also Appendix VIII, 'The *Blitzkrieg* War Economy'.

division and using captured French cars and trucks.[1] In December the OKW issued a Führer Command which contained measures to ensure that key workers on extended leave of absence from the Army should not be recalled too early. As soon as 'Barbarossa' began the production of army munitions was to be ruthlessly cut and priority shifted to anti-aircraft ammunition and equipment.[2] Thus the economic planners were forced to gamble that the predictions of a quick victory in Russia would be fulfilled. In fact the production of army weapons fell by an average of 38 per cent between July and December 1941.[3]

General Jodl shared Keitel's doubts about the economic basis of the war in the East. On 3 December 1940 he wrote a note stating that if the armament situation required it, the Russian campaign 'can and must be postponed because it is by no means necessary for the victory over Britain'.[4] Furthermore, he was very critical of the reduction of the strength of the Panzer divisions and commented:

If this great campaign has to be fought soon, then it can be done just as well with 12 Panzer divisions as 24 Panzer brigades, because there won't be any more by the spring [of 1941]. We would thus save a mass of [units from] the supporting arms and rear services.[4]

There is, however, no evidence that Jodl expressed these critical views to Hitler, who, either through ignorance or self-delusion, remained confident that German armament production was equal to all demands. Nor did Jodl discuss these matters with the Army General Staff, which at this time was beginning its first major examination of the logistical problems of the eastern campaign.[5]

## The Logistical Planning in the General Staff

Throughout the summer and autumn of 1940 the Quartermaster-General's Branch of the General Staff was kept so ignorant of the planning for the East that even after the war some of its senior

---

[1] See Guderian, pp. 138, 143; Walter Krüger, *The Conduct of Operations in the East, 1941–1943*, U.S. Army Historical Division, MSC–050 (H.Q. U.S. Army Europe, 1949), p. 2; Müller-Hillebrand, *Das Heer*, ii. 105 ff.; Hoth, pp. 44–5; Bock, *Tagebuch*, 20 Mar. 1941.

[2] *Führer Befehl* 'Personelle Massnahmen für Ruestungsindustrie und Bergbau', OKE/Wfst/Abt. Lll Nr. 2295/40 g Kdos, 20 Dec. 1940.

[3] Milward, p. 45. Anti-aircraft guns are excluded. See also Appendix VIII.

[4] Thomas, p. 437; *KTB OKW* i. 981.

[5] See Blau, p. 20; Wagner, pp. 196–7, 315.

officers were convinced that until December 1940 the Operations Branch had only some 'very broad plans and ideas for "Barbarossa" which had not as yet been subjected to any sort of proper staff planning'.[1] As a result 'the operational basis for a campaign in Russia was not so far developed that the Quartermaster General could draw positive conclusions for the conduct of supply expected from him'.[2] General Wagner was able to begin the logistical plan only a bare six months before the campaign was due to begin. During the second half of 1940 his department might have worked closely with the Operations Branch in shaping the plan of campaign. The exceptionally great difficulties posed by the size and poor communications of the Russian theatre would have justified a special consideration of the supply and administrative factors. But this did not occur. As in previous campaigns 'strategic considerations formed the basis for the preparation and subsequent administration of the Army supply system'.[3] Thus the Quartermaster-General had to conform to the decisions already made by the Operations Branch and overcome the problems created by some of these decisions as best he could.

The problems confronting the Quartermaster-General were made greater by the comparatively small and primitive nature of the supply system at his disposal. Just as the General Staff gave priority to operational planning, so the organization of the German Army laid stress upon combat formations and kept the administrative tail to a minimum. This enabled Germany, with less than double the population of Great Britain to put nearly ten times as many fighting divisions in the field in the Second World War.[4] Nevertheless, it left the German Army with an administrative system suited only to limited wars or campaigns of short range and duration.

In peacetime the formations of the German Army were raised, trained, equipped, and supplied in the military districts into which the nation was divided. On the outbreak of war in 1939 the commander of the military district became a corps commander and took the formations from his district into the field. The deputy corps commander, normally a general whose health or age rendered him unfit for further active service, then assumed command of the mili-

[1] Wagner, p. 197.
[2] Ibid., p. 315.
[3] General Alfred Toppe *et al.*, *Problems of Supply in Far Reaching Operations*, U.S. Army Historical Division MS T8, p. 12.
[4] See Liddell Hart, *Defence of the West* (London, 1950), pp. 212–14.

tary district with the task of maintaining the flow of reinforcements and replacements to the field formations. On mobilization the corps would procure additional horses and vehicles from government agencies, such as the postal organization, and from private owners within the military districts. The supply organizations of the divisions were particularly dependent upon such additions to their transport to carry into the field the equipment, ammunition, fuel, and supplies required for operations.

In the field the headquarters of corps and army groups were left free to concentrate on the direction of operations, and the task of organizing the further supply of the fighting troops was conducted by administrative staffs on the headquarters of armies and divisions. Delivery was carried out by the railway system and by army and divisional motor transport units many of which were equipped with the trucks temporarily impressed from civilian road-haulage companies. This supply system had proved adequate in Poland, but in the West a number of improvisations were necessary in order to sustain the offensive as the spearheads thrust deep into France.[1] Even before the campaign was over Hitler summoned Wagner and demanded a complete reorganization of the Army's supply services.[2] It was evidently clear to him that if they were strained by the range of operations in the West they would certainly not be adequate to support a conquest of Russia.

There were two major tasks confronting Wagner: the stockpiling of adequate supplies before the opening of hostilities; and the delivery of supplies during the campaign. Since the *Blitzkreig* was expected to overwhelm the Russians as quickly as it had defeated the Poles and the French the logistic planners at first made the totally false assumption that 'available stocks of ammunition and fuel and the expected output of these two items . . . were adequate to supply the planned operation in the light of the time schedule set for it...'.[3] But the difficulties involved in delivering these items to the advancing combat columns were recognized from the very start of logistic planning.[4] Logistical staff exercises were held in December 1940 'to determine the deficiencies and gaps in the supply structure'.[5] These led to the establishment of a new supply organization designed to operate in depth. A 'Quartermaster-General's Field Agency'

[1] Toppe, p. 29.
[2] Wagner, p. 184.
[3] Toppe, p. 22; see also Milward, p. 45.
[4] Wagner, pp. 196–7.
[5] Toppe, p. 23.

comprising a 'supply command echelon' and a 'supply district' was set up in each of the three army groups in the East. The supply command echelons were not made part of the Army Group Headquarters but retained their independence as detachments of the Quartermaster-General's Branch of the General Staff. They enabled General Wagner to exercise close control and co-ordination of the limited resources allocated to the supply districts. Each district operated a supply base containing stockpiles, heavy motor transport units, and technical service troops. It was planned that at the start of the offensive the supply districts should contain three basic loads of artillery ammunition (i.e. sufficient to replenish the carrying capacity of combat units three times), one and a half basic loads of infantry ammunition, and eight consumption units of fuel and lubricating oils. Each consumption unit was sufficient for a particular vehicle to travel 100 kilometres.

A major difficulty in the initial logistical planning lay in the estimates of the rates of consumption of all supplies except rations. General Fromm's letter of 3 September to General Thomas had made a broad, arbitrary estimate of the Army's ammunition and equipment needs.[1] But after the war members of the Quartermaster-General's staff admitted that the ammunition requirement was unknown and the fuel need was based upon an uncertain estimate of the pace of the advance.[2] Finally the quantities were decided on the basis of what could be carried by the vehicles available rather than upon any estimate of probable combat expenditures. Troops were to cross the border with one basic ammunition load, five consumption units of motor fuel, and four daily rations. It was expected that for some time the infantry would be able to replenish their supplies by sending back their own horse-drawn supply columns to the supply base near the border. This would leave the heavy motor transport units free for the more difficult task of supplying the Panzer groups thrusting quickly and deeply into enemy territory. Some of these transport units, nicknamed 'hand baggage', were incorporated fully loaded into Panzer formations. Between two-thirds and three-quarters of the truck space was filled with motor fuels and rations. The rest was used for ammunition, mainly for tank and artillery guns. The 'hand baggage' columns had orders to issue their supplies as required in the course of the initial battles and to dump the remainder once a suitable point was reached 100 kilo-

See p. 134 above.        [2] Toppe, p. 49.

metres from the start line. The Panzer units would then collect from such supply points while the trucks raced back to the supply base to reload. Meanwhile the rest of the heavy motor transport units would follow the advance in order to reach the 100-kilometres supply point on the second day. A second supply point, 200 kilometres from the start line, would be established on the fifth day. This system of supply could be continued after the fifth day but with diminishing efficiency because of the increase in range, deterioration of road surfaces, and the fall-out due to mechanical breakdowns and enemy action. General Wagner considered that it could be successfully maintained only to a line through Minsk which Guderian later estimated would be reached after five or six days.[1] However, at the war games conducted by Paulus in December 1940 the operational planners decided that the first pause in operations of sufficient length to permit a reorganization of the supply system and the establishment of new supply bases would take place only when the line of the Upper Dnieper and Dvina Rivers was reached after twenty days of combat. Undismayed by this discrepancy, General Halder later confirmed that the supply system would have to operate with motor transport alone over almost twice the distance regarded as feasible by Wagner. Since the Quartermaster-General and his field agencies 'had to co-ordinate their resources with the intentions of the High Command',[2] they were not able to change the time-table of the operations plan for administrative reasons. Yet even had this been permitted Wagner could not have requested an earlier halt in operations in order to build up forward supply bases because his motor transport units could not possibly carry the quantities of materials required. The pause could only be effectively used when sufficient Russian railway lines had been converted to the German gauge, and this was unlikely to take less than the twenty days proposed for the first phase by the operational planners. Thus there was a period of two weeks between the time when the motor transport units would be unable to keep up with the demand for supplies and the time when the railways could take over their burden. The problem of this hiatus was never solved before the campaign. Indeed it had scarcely been recognized when it was overshadowed by the discovery that all the assumptions made by the Quartermaster-General's Branch about the sufficiency of material for the campaign were totally false.

[1] Ibid., p. 65; Guderian, p. 150.     [2] Toppe, p. 43.

*Economics, Logistics, and Strategy*

On 23 December General Fromm, the Commander-in-Chief of the Reserve Army, drew the attention of General Halder to the shortages of steel, non-ferrous metals, and rubber, and warned him that food requirements could be met only by 'cheating our way through 1941'.[1] On returning from leave a month later, General Halder summoned the senior administrators of the Army and the Luftwaffe to a conference on 28 January.[2] He began by emphasizing the strain that the speed and distance of the campaign in Russia would place upon the supply system. Demolition and the difference in gauge between the German and Russian railways would rule out their early use. Therefore, motor transport would have to provide an uninterrupted flow of supplies to support an advance of 600 miles.[3] General Thomas then presented the shattering information that there was a deficiency of almost 50 per cent in tyre requirements, and sufficient fuel oil only for the concentration of the forces and two months of combat.[4]

The purpose of this conference was to find an 'adequate solution' to the supply problems in the East, or, failing this, to present a clear basis upon which 'a decision could be requested from the Führer'.[5] So Halder immediately went to von Brauchitsch to discuss the effect of the morning's revelations on the grand-strategic situation. Afterwards, he noted in his diary:

The purpose [of Barbarossa] is not clear. We do not strike at the British and our economic potential will not be improved. The risk in the West should not be underestimated. It is even possible that Italy might collapse after losing her colonies and we find ourselves with a southern front through Spain, Italy, and Greece. If we are then committed against Russia our position will become increasingly difficult.[6]

They resumed this unusually broad discussion of the economic and strategic risks of the eastern operation next day.[7] Their desire to

---

[1] *Halder KTB* ii. 240, 24 Dec. 1940; cf. *IMT* xxxi. 2718–ps, 84.

[2] It was attended by General Fromm, Commander-in-Chief, Reserve Army, Generals Thomas and Hannecken of the War Economy and Armament Office, General Emil Leeb, Chief of the Army Armaments Office, General Seidel, Quartermaster-General of the Luftwaffe. See *Halder KTB* ii. 256 ff., 28 Jan. 1941.

[3] Ibid., p. 258. The OKH disagreed with the OKW on this point. The Lossberg Study, 15 Sept. 1940, stated that the railways must support the later stages of all operations because 'in the vast spaces a transport system based only on roads will be insufficient', See Appendix II; see also Besymenski, p. 309.

[4] Op. cit. See also *KTB OKW* i. 997.

[5] *Halder KTB* ii. 259, 28 Jan. 1941.

[6] Ibid., p. 261, 28 Jan. 1941.          [7] Ibid., p. 262, 29 Jan. 1941.

avoid a rigid commitment was reflected in the opening words of the Deployment Directive for Operation 'Barbarossa' which they issued on 31 January: 'In case Russia should change her present attitude towards Germany all preparations are to be taken as precautionary measures to make it possible to defeat the Soviet Union in a quick campaign even before the end of the war against Britain.'[1] At a gloomy luncheon meeting that day von Brauchitsch and Halder discussed 'Barbarossa' for the first time with all three army group commanders designated for the East: Field-Marshals von Leeb, von Bock, and von Rundstedt.[2] They confirmed that they too had misgivings about the over-all strategic situation. Von Bock made the following notes after the meeting:

Brauchitsch gives a picture of the situation which does not please me. He states that the attack on England did not take place in the autumn because the OKW and the Navy devoted themselves too late and too slowly to the task, and because the successes of the air attacks fell considerably short of the expectations of OKL. He confirmed that the Italian attack on Greece took us by surprise. Brauchitsch's proposals to take Gibraltar and to intervene in Libya were unfortunately not taken up. His suggestion for a negotiated peace with Greece, which would have been readily accepted by that country, was also rejected. No agreement over Gibraltar could be reached with Spain. With France there are tensions which have been increased by the dismissal of Laval . . . The attitude of the French colonies, in so far as they are under government control, is unpredictable. Weygand is no friend of Germany, but it can be assumed that he will follow Petain's directives.[3]

Von Bock also expressed doubts about the plan for the invasion of Russia, and he bluntly asked Halder if he had any firm grounds for assuming that the Russians would fight west of the Dvina–Dnieper Line. To this Halder gave the discouraging reply 'that it might well turn out differently'.[4] According to post-war accounts

[1] Ibid., p. 464. See also Appendix II below. The German sentence structure is deliberately retained to convey the laboured attempt to give the statement a conditional basis.

[2] Ibid., p. 264, n. 1, 31 Jan. 1941.

[3] Von Bock, *Tagebuch*, 31 Jan. 1941.

[4] Ibid. Halder had also expressed scepticism about the chance of reaching the line Leningrad–Smolensk–Kiev–lower-Dnieper in a commentary on the Deployment Directive 'Barbarossa' which he wrote on 20 Jan. 1941. (File: *OKH. Chef d Gen St d.H. Durchführung Barbarossa Nr. 138*. Quoted by Besymenski, p. 335.) He felt that any attempt to plan operations beyond that line would be so hypothetical that the effort would be wasted.

both von Leeb and von Rundstedt had similar doubts about the operation in the East. It appears, however, that von Brauchitsch was loath to resume the task of carrying their misgivings to the Führer, and it was von Bock who, two days later, raised the subject of 'Barbarossa' during an audience with Hitler.

The lean, austere Field-Marshal explained as tactfully as possible that he had no doubt that the Russians would be defeated if they chose to give battle. But he questioned whether it would be possible to force the Russians to make peace. Hitler replied that he was confident that the loss of Leningrad, Moscow, and the Ukraine would cause them to abandon the struggle. If not, then German motorized forces would have to drive on beyond Moscow to Ekaterinburg.

In any event, [he continued] I am happy that our war production is equal to any demand. We have such an abundance of material that we had to reconvert some of our war plants [to civilian production]. The armed forces now have more manpower than at the beginning of the war, and our economy is in an excellent condition.[1]

He dismissed any thought of dissuading him from the operation with the blunt assurance, 'I shall fight.'[2]

This categorical rejection of criticism on economic grounds ended the matter as far as the Army leaders were concerned. On the next day, 3 February, at a conference with Hitler, General Halder referred to the difficulties of supply in the East, but omitted those details that made the whole operation seem a questionable risk. Instead, he described methods by which he hoped the transportation problems might be overcome: the concentration of motorized supply columns in support of the armoured thrusts, co-operation between the Army and the Luftwaffe to ensure the fullest use of all available truck space. He also accepted Hitler's suggestion that the Baltic coast as far as Leningrad should be occupied as soon as possible in order to provide the supply base for further operations, thus seeming to confirm his agreement with the decision to give the capture of Leningrad priority over that of Moscow.[3]

The establishment of a firm base on the Baltic coast was also favoured by Field-Marshal von Rundstedt. But he thought that

---

[1] Von Boch, *Tagebuch*, 1 Feb. 1941. Bock's doubts were far from quelled; see ibid., 6 June 1941. See also Blau, p. 30.

[2] Ibid. See also Heusinger, p. 122.

[3] *KTB OKW* i. 298–9.

the subsequent development of thrusts southward from Leningrad towards Moscow might have to be postponed until the following year.[1] However, the concept of an operation extending over two summer seasons was compatible neither with Hitler's demand that Russia should be defeated in a single campaign nor with the recent discovery that there was sufficient fuel oil only for two months of fighting. As a result, while paying lip service to Hitler's idea of building up 'the most favourable supply base' on the Baltic, the Army leaders neglected to conduct any detailed planning for such a base, from which the Dvina and Narva river systems might have been used as major supply arteries for a southward advance. Instead they continued to hope that the success of the initial attack would be so great that the problems of supplying the subsequent operations would disappear. This attitude evaded the crucial question of whether victory could be won in a single campaign and was the root cause of the attempt by von Brauchitsch to depart from the 'Barbarossa' plan in the midst of the operation in order to revert to the idea of a swift, direct thrust on Moscow. It was also the cause of the Army's failure to make adequate and timely preparations for operations under winter conditions.

Although on 3 February von Brauchitsch and Halder had shown greater confidence in Operation 'Barbarossa' than von Bock, Hitler did not ignore the warnings of the Army Group commander. On 5 February he called for a study of the various major Soviet industrial areas to test their ability to sustain centres of resistance even as far east as the Urals.[2] To this the OKW replied that Field-Marshal Keitel had requested such a study and that the War Economy and Armament Office had already submitted material on the subject to General Jodl. Three days later Keitel summoned General Thomas to discuss the matter further. In his notes on the interview Thomas stated that he informed the Chief of the OKW that if operations in the East took place, the fuel situation would be as follows: 'Aircraft fuel will last until autumn 1941 . . . Vehicle fuel only sufficient for the deployment and two months of combat . . . The same situation applied to diesel oil . . .'[3] He also warned Keitel that rubber production of about 7,500 tons per month could be maintained only until

[1] See Blumentritt, *Rundstedt*, pp. 103–4; 'Moscow', p. 41. See also Liddell Hart, *On the Other Side* . . ., p. 277. Guderian after the war came to express similar views. See Guderian, pp. 149–50.
[2] *KTB OKW* i. 306, 5 Feb. 1941.
[3] Thomas, p. 17.

the end of March. If there were no further imports in April, Germany would be left with a reserve of 2,600 tons.[1] These and other economic statistics related to the operation in Russia were included in a written report which Thomas gave Keitel to pass on to Hitler. However, Keitel brusquely told him that 'the Führer would not allow himself to be influenced in his planning by such economic difficulties'.[2] Thus, it is unlikely that this report ever reached Hitler.

On 13 February, General Thomas completed a bigger study entitled 'The Effects of an Operation in the East on the War Economy'.[3] This document presented statistics from which Thomas and his staff attempted to predict the outcome of the occupation of European Russia excluding the Urals. During the first few months, Germany's economic position would be relieved in the field of nutrition and raw materials if a rapid conquest should succeed in preventing the destruction of stocks, capturing the oilfields of the Caucasus intact, and solving the transport problem. In the case of a longer war, effective relief would depend on the following: the solution of the transport problem; the prevention of the evacuation of the population which would have to be won over to collaboration; the prevention of the destruction of Russian motor transport; the replacement of Russian tractors by a resumption of production; the seizure of fuel supplies and power stations; the securing of the delivery of raw materials not existing in European Russia. The resumption of supplies of rubber, tungsten, copper, platinum, tin, asbestos, and manila hemp would depend on the re-establishment of communication with the Far East.

General Thomas also stated that the area south of the mouths of the Volga and Don must be included in the operation because the oil of the Caucasus would be essential for the exploitation of the rest of occupied Russia. His final conclusion was that the campaign would lead to the capture of 75 per cent of the Soviet war industry and almost 100 per cent of the precision tool and optical instrument industries.

Later, Thomas stated that from his report emerged 'the clear recognition that a collapse of the Soviet Union on purely war

---

[1] Thomas., pp. 17–18.

[2] Ibid., p. 18. See also *KTB OKW* i. 316–17, 11 Feb. 1941.

[3] Thomas, pp. 515 ff. Confusion over the date of this document (13 Feb. 1941) has arisen through Thomas's references to it at conferences before and after the date of its completion. See Hillgruber, *Strategic*, pp. 265–9; Fabry, pp. 389–90; *IMT* xxx. 2353–PS, is not dated.

economic grounds could be expected only with the loss or destruction of the industrial areas in the Urals'.[1] Furthermore, the report
has been described as a deliberate attempt to discourage Hitler from
attempting an attack on Russia.[2] However, Thomas himself admitted
in retrospect that it was too optimistic, and the prediction that the
campaign would overrun all but 25 per cent of the Soviet war
industry was hardly discouraging. In spite of the obvious difficulties
of capturing Soviet economic resources and industrial plants intact,
the urgent needs that the report reflected served to justify an invasion
of Russia as a solution for Germany's economic problems.

This was indeed the attitude taken by Göring on 26 February when
Thomas submitted the report to him as head of the Four Year Plan
Organization.[3] He showed no sign of wishing to avoid the Russian
operation but began to cast about wildly for means to overcome the
problems involved. He expressed vague hopes of persuading the
Japanese to co-operate in 're-opening the Trans-Siberian railway as
quickly as possible'.[4] He also claimed that he had constantly warned
Hitler that the failure of the supply organization could endanger
the entire operation. To ease the strain, he suggested that the number
of divisions committed in the East should be restricted. He evidently
envisaged that as in France the brunt of the fighting would be borne
by the mobile forces and the infantry divisions would play a 'walking-
on' part, for he suggested that 'only a portion of them would come
under fire'.[5] In the same unrealistic vein, he ordered General von
Schell, the Plenipotentiary for Motor Transport, to find a way to
produce synthetic tyres for heavy trucks. 'It would be unthinkable',
he added, 'to allow our last rubber supplies to be wasted on the bad
Russian roads.'[5]

When General Thomas repeated the warning that there was
sufficient fuel for only two months of operations, Göring replied
that he would suggest to Antonescu that Rumanian oil production
should be increased. Ignoring the limited range and striking power
of his Luftwaffe he spoke of seizing the Baku oilfields by means of
an airborne attack.[6]

[1] Thomas, p. 270.  [2] Fabry, p. 390.
[3] Göring ordered Thomas to begin work on the report in November 1940.
[4] Thomas, p. 18.
[5] Ibid., p. 19.
[6] For an indication of the weakness of the Luftwaffe in 1941, see *KTB OKW*
i. 1016. Göring later called for plans for the bombing of war industries in the
Urals. See ibid., p. 346, 6 Mar. 1941.

### The Caucasian Oilfields as a Strategic Objective

The idea of seizing the Caucasian oilfields had from the start been part of Hitler's concept of the campaign in Russia.[1] Although he mentioned it at the conference on 31 July 1940 and again on 9 January 1941 the leaders of the OKH made no attempt to include it in their planning. On the 4 May 1941 Keitel sought to rectify this omission and sent to the OKH a request that the possibility of an early occupation of the Caucasian oilfields should be examined in co-operation with the Commanders-in-Chief of the Luftwaffe and Navy.[2] Appended to this letter was a report on the oil situation based on statistics provided by General von Hannecken, an Assistant State Secretary in the Armament and War Economy Office. This was evidently intended to demonstrate the urgent need to win new sources of oil. The European Axis Powers, stated the report, required 1·15 million tons of oil monthly. By the end of August 1941 only 850,000 tons would be available per month. Assuming that Iraq need not be taken into consideration, the Caucasus offered the sole source from which the deficiency of 300,000 tons per month could be met. Even if damaged in the course of military operations the oilfields there, which yielded two and a quarter million tons per month, could also be expected to provide the 900,000 tons required to keep Russia's agriculture and industry operating for the conquerors. This optimistic assumption was based upon the belief that, though it was impossible to use military means to prevent serious damage to the oil wells, the encouragement of Caucasian hopes of political independence might cause the local population to protect their main source of economic wealth.

Even assuming that the Caucasian oilfields were captured reasonably intact, the problem of transporting the oil to Germany and Italy still had to be surmounted. A maximum of only 100,000 tons per month could be carried overland. The Danube river tankers were working to capacity transporting Rumanian oil. The only remaining route was across the Black Sea, through the Dardanelles and the Aegean Sea. *'Thus'*, ran the report, *'the opening of the sea routes and the security of the tankers in the Black Sea is the prerequisite for the use of Russian supply sources in sufficient quantity to support*

[1] See *Halder KTB* ii. 50, 31 July 1940; *KTB OKW* i. 258, 9 Jan. 1941.
[2] OKW/Wfst/LTV *Chefsachen 'Barbarossa'* (Feb.–Mar. 1941) Bundesarchiv-Militärarchiv III W 59/2, p. 5.

*the further continuation of the war.*[1] The main conclusion of the report was that Maikop, Grozny, and the sea-routes through the Dardanelles must be captured as soon as possible. But the means to attain these far-flung objectives were completely lacking. The bulk of the Wehrmacht was concentrated north of the Pripet Marsh and directed towards Leningrad and Moscow. A seaborne force could not be employed as long as the Russian Black Sea Fleet was still afloat. The only remaining possibility was to use airborne forces. But even for them the distance involved presented enormous problems. Landings at Krasnodar and Maikop could be conducted with fighter protection only from airfields in the Rostov area and it could not be expected that these could be won until the final phase of Operation 'Barbarossa'. A landing at Grozny would require the establishment of Luftwaffe bases at Maikop, or better still at Georgievsk, 170 miles further east. As for Baku, it might be captured by airborne forces flown from Tiflis or Grozny, but the operation would involve air communications over the Caucasus Mountains, fighter protection would be impossible and a period of bad weather might leave the force isolated from sources of supply and reinforcement. To make matters worse, the report stated, while the Germans were establishing this precarious hold on the Caucasus the British might respond to a Russian call for help by sending naval forces from the eastern Mediterranean into the Black Sea and by moving land forces and supplies by road and rail through Iraq and Iran. In the event that a pro-German Caucasian state declared its independence from the Soviet Union the British might set the oil wells ablaze by air attacks from their bases in Iraq.

The most effective way to counter these dangers was to give Army Group 'South' sufficient force, range, and speed to capture the Caucasian oilfields before they could be adequately defended or destroyed. But this would have meant abandoning the 'Barbarossa' plan and shifting the main blow to the sector south of the Pripet Marshes.

The idea of placing the weight of the campaign on the southern sector had been favoured by Colonel von Greiffenberg and Lieutenant-Colonel Feyerabend in the early stages of the operational planning in July 1940.[2] But this had been overruled by Halder mainly because Rumania was not a favourable base for operations of such

[1] Ibid., p. 8. Italics in the original.
[2] See *Halder KTB* ii. 39, 27 July 1940.

magnitude. Although by the spring of 1941 the political situation in Rumania had radically changed in Germany's favour, the Wehrmacht was too deeply committed to the 'Barbarossa' plan to consider such a drastic change of strategy. It is significant to note, however, that Hitler's first major attempt to modify the conduct of campaign was the proposal made on 23 July 1941, a month after the opening of the invasion, to combine Panzer Groups 1 and 2 under the command of Field-Marshal von Kluge for a thrust via Kharkhov and over the Don to the Caucasus. Furthermore, when the campaign of 1941 failed it was towards the Caucasus that the major German effort was directed in the following year only to meet defeat because the objective lay beyond the strength and range of the Wehrmacht.

There was, however, an alternative strategy which still lay open to the Germans in 1941. Namely, to follow the Balkan campaign with operations in the Middle East. These would not only seriously weaken the position of Britain, but would give the Axis the oil of the Arab lands and Persia and place the Wehrmacht in a position to strike Russia at her most vulnerable quarter, seizing the oil of the Caucasus at the first blow. This was the proposal made by Admiral Raeder on 26 September and again on 27 December 1940. Both the other service chiefs, von Brauchitsch and Göring, shared the admiral's opinion.[1] However, neither was prepared to give him effective support against Hitler.

Göring by this time was living a life of semi-retirement from his duties. He was capable of work only with the stimulation of drugs. As Commander-in-Chief of the Luftwaffe he probably saw the strategic possibilities in the eastern Mediterranean, but as director of the Four Year Plan Organization he was attracted by the idea of a direct attack on Russia which seemed to offer an immediate solution to all Germany's economic problems. He had never been capable of standing up to Hitler in an argument, and now his influence with the Führer was considerably weakened by the failure of the Luftwaffe in the war against Britain. Already convinced of the need to conquer Russia and eager to regain the favour of Hitler, Göring was easily persuaded that the invasion of Russia would be like the Polish Campaign on a grander scale and that the conquest of the Middle East should be left till after 'Barbarossa'.

Field-Marshal von Brauchitsch also accepted this view, though,

[1] Liddell Hart, *On the Other Side* . . ., p. 233.

according to General Siewert, his First General Staff Officer at that time, he was deeply perturbed at Hitler's refusal to concentrate German efforts towards the Middle East in the spring of 1941.[1] The failure of von Brauchitsch to demand that 'Barbarossa' should be postponed must be partially attributed to the fact that he was not supported by Halder. The Chief of the General Staff was doubtful about the 'extremely difficult problem' of undertaking operations into the Middle East as long as the British fleet based on Alexandria was still intact.[2] He regarded the Naval Staff as possessed of strategic ideas out of all proportion to the strength and capability of the German fleet. Halder felt that the Navy had let the Army down by its inconsistent planning for the invasion of England in the summer of 1940, and was likely to do the same in the eastern Mediterranean. He was even more uneasy about relying upon the Italian fleet to protect the sea communications of long-range operations in the eastern Mediterranean. In Halder's view Turkey was also an uncertain factor. Looking back, he commented that 'under pressure from Britain and afraid of Russia, the Turks knew that an attempt to co-operate with us might unite the British and Russians and perhaps even provoke a Russian attack on Germany'.[3] In November 1940 he expressed the view that significant operations by the Army in the Middle East would take so long that the time would be better used for direct attacks on the British Isles by air and naval forces.[4] His attitude had not changed by the spring of 1941, so it is unlikely that he encouraged von Brauchitsch to urge a postponement of 'Barbarossa' for the sake of operations in the Middle East.

Thus, arriving in May, the OKW report on the need to conquer the Caucasus was too late to be more than a source of uneasiness to the three service chiefs. But even had it been written earlier it is doubtful whether its implications would have provoked the OKH to a reappraisal of German strategy. Adhering to the orthodox Clausewitzian view that the first aim of military strategy must be the destruction of the enemy forces, the General Staff considered that economic objectives in Russia could be attained only after the forces

[1] Conversation with General Siewert, 8 July 1969. Von Brauchitsch's concern on this subject is also apparent in von Bock's account of the conference with him on 31 Jan. 1941.
[2] Notes for a General Staff Conference, 2 Nov. 1940, *Bundesarchiv-Militärarchiv*, H 25/1.
[3] General Halder, Conversation with author, 23 June 1969.
[4] Op. cit.

barring the way to them had been decisively defeated. Confronted with the choice between the now familiar *Blitzkrieg* form of land campaign against the Soviet Army and the uncertainties of thrusting across Asia Minor and the Middle East against the elusive British, most German staff officers preferred the former course. Furthermore, since they still thought first and foremost in terms of operations and tactics rather than of war economics and logistics, they did not consider the Caucasian oilfields to be of such crucial importance that German strategy should give priority to their immediate capture. In 1942 when the attempts to defeat the Soviet Army had failed, they accepted the need to concentrate a major part of their striking force on the southern front in Russia for a thrust towards the Caucasus. But even then they did so only upon Hitler's insistence and without any real assessment of the war-economic factors involved. General Blumentritt, who succeeded Paulus as *Oberquartiermeister I* in January 1942, later admitted to Sir Basil Liddell Hart that he 'was not acquainted with the economic side of the war'.[1] He was unable to verify the accuracy of Hitler's assertion that he could not continue the war unless the Caucasian oilfields were captured in 1942 because 'the General Staff was not represented at conferences on these issues . . .'.[1]

Although in 1941 the Army leaders still refused to allow economic needs to determine the form and direction of operations, they accepted, like Keitel and Göring, the weakness of the German war economy as very real proof of the urgent need to conduct Operation 'Barbarossa' without further delay.

## The Economic Staff East

The economic necessity for the conquest of Russia was confirmed by the work of the Economic Staff East, formed by General Thomas in April 1941 under the command of General Schubert. Its three main inspectorates covered the areas of the three army groups extending as far east as Vologda, Gorki, and Stalingrad. A special inspectorate was responsible for the Caucasian oilfields. A memorandum issued by this staff on 2 May left no doubt about the nature of their task. It opened with the statement:

The war can only be continued if all the armed forces are fed by Russia in the third year of the war [1941–2]. There is no doubt that many millions

---

[1] Liddell Hart, *On the other Side* . . ., p. 296.

of people will starve to death in Russia if we take out of the country the things necessary to us.[1]

Thus, ultimately, the War Economic and Armament Office merely confirmed the views expressed on 28 July 1940 in the Naval Staff's memorandum 'Observations on Russia'. This had stated:

The future safety of our homeland requires the build-up of a spatial impregnability, i.e. an expansion which will prevent an unhindered, surprise entry into vital parts of German territory, a buffer zone so to speak . . . Further it requires if possible an autarkic economy especially in goods vital in war time (e.g. oil, foodstuffs). The build-up of Germany requires raw materials and, to the same degree, markets for its products. For both Russia is . . . well suited. . . .[2]

Such views on the achievement of economic self-sufficiency by means of conquest in the East were completely in accordance with Hitler's ideas. Two days before the opening of 'Barbarossa' he stated:

The course of the war shows that we have gone too far in our efforts to set up an autarky. It is impossible . . . to try to produce by synthetic means all those things we lack . . . We must follow another course and conquer that which we need . . . So the aim must be to secure by conquest all areas which are of special importance to our war industry.[3]

On an earlier occasion, he told his military leaders that after the destruction of Russia Germany would be 'unassailable'. 'The vast Russian space', he continued, 'heaped up immeasurable riches. Germany must dominate it economically and politically. . . .'[4]

### Political Warfare in Russia

In the interview with General Thomas on 26 February Göring dismissed the warning that the Russians would destroy all industrial machinery and railways in the wake of their withdrawals. He shared the view of the Führer that 'with the entry of German troops into Russia, the entire Bolshevist State would collapse'.[5] To speed this, Göring stated, it would be necessary 'swiftly to wipe out the Bolshevist leadership'.[5] Such remarks showed that the programme of

---

[1] *IMT* xxxi. 2718–PS, 84. Cf. Fromm's statement on 23 Dec. 1940, *Halder KTB* ii. 240; and Bock, *Tagebuch*, 6 June 1941.
[2] Hillgruber, *Strategie*, p. 221.
[3] *IMT* xxxvii. 1456–PS, 220, Bock, *Tagebuch*, 14 June 1941.
[4] *KTB OKW* i. 258, 9 Jan. 1941.
[5] Thomas, p. 18.

ideological warfare directed against the Communist intelligentsia and bureaucracy was intended to form part of the campaign. It would add a further element of terror to the *Blitzkrieg* which would speed its effect and help to achieve the rapid victory essential to prevent the Soviet Union from either mobilizing its full resources or from destroying them before the Germans could seize them. The ideological war in the East, which the German Army leaders have attempted to depict as a distasteful element imposed upon them against their will, had, in fact, an important relationship to German military strategy and economic policy in Russia.

Detailed planning for this process began early in March when Hitler rejected the draft of a directive for a military administration in the East prepared by the *Wehrmachtführungsstab*. He returned it with a long commentary which opened as follows:

The coming campaign is more than a mere clash of arms; it is also a conflict between two ideologies. In view of the extent of the space involved, the striking down of the enemy armed forces will not suffice to bring about an end to the war. The whole area must be divided into [separate] states each with its own government with which peace can be made.[1]

This, Hitler explained, would require great 'political skills and well-prepared principles'. The socialist idea, he admitted, was too deeply entrenched in Russia to be just 'washed away'. It would constitute the basis for the foundation of new states and governments. 'The Jewish-Bolshevist intelligentsia' and the former 'middle-class and aristocratic intelligentsia' including that of the Baltic States and *émigrés* would, therefore, have to be 'removed', and a revival of Russian nationalism prevented. The task of establishing dependent 'socialist states' in the East was so difficult that Hitler 'could not entrust it to the Army'.[1] Three days later, he stressed that the German political leadership must be established in the East as soon as possible 'in order to conduct the ideological struggle simultaneously with the military struggle'.[2] An annexe to Directive No. 21, outlining the relationship between the political, economic, and military administrations in Russia, was accordingly issued by Keitel on 13 March.[3] Field-Marshal von Brauchitsch immediately attempted to counter it with the suggestion that the occupied territories in the East should be controlled by a military administration similar to those in Belgium and France. This was sharply refused by Hitler on the grounds that

[1] *KTB OKW* i. 341, 3 Mar. 1941.    [2] Ibid., p. 346, 6 Mar. 1941.
[3] Hubatsch, pp. 101–5.

'a military administration is useless . . . the Army understands nothing of politics'.[1]

Nevertheless, Hitler intended to ensure that the Army played an active role in the political terror campaign which was to increase the impact of the *Blitzkrieg* in the East. At the Führer Conference on 17 March he told von Brauchitsch, Halder, Heusinger, Keitel, and Jodl: 'The leadership structure of the Russian empire must be destroyed . . . the most brutal use of force would be necessary. Ideological bonds did not yet hold the Russian nation firmly enough together. It would fall apart with the removal of the [communist] functionaries.'[2]

The same theme was stressed on 30 March when Hitler told a large assembly of senior generals that the aim of the coming struggle between two ideologies must be the total destruction of Bolshevism and the establishment of a German 'protectorate' embracing the Baltic States, White Russia, and the Ukraine. The Army officers would have to sacrifice their scruples and play a leading role on the elimination of Bolshevist commissars and the Communist intelligentsia.[3]

At the Nuremberg Trial von Brauchitsch described the generals crowding round him in outraged remonstration when Hitler left the hall at the close of this speech.[4] In fact the scene was very different. According to Halder, the generals had lunch with Hitler and spent the afternoon presenting to him the plans of the various army groups and armies. To this Halder added the comment 'Nothing new', which Warlimont later regarded as an indication that 'none of those present availed themselves of the opportunity even to mention the demands made by Hitler in the morning.'[5] Warlimont is probably correct in this assumption, but his explanation of the generals' failure to protest is far-fetched. The majority of them, he stated, had probably 'not followed Hitler's long diatribe in detail, . . . others had not grasped the full meaning of his proposals and others . . . thought it better first to look into these questions more deeply or to follow normal military practice and await the reaction of their superiors'.[5] There can be little doubt that Halder grasped the full meaning of Hitler's words. After his account he noted 'C. in C. Order' as a

[1] Engel, *Tagebuch*, 16 Mar. 1941, quoted by Hillgruber, *Strategie*, p. 524, n. 34.
[2] *Halder KTB* ii. 320, 17 Mar. 1941.
[3] Ibid., p. 337, 30 Mar. 1941.　　　　　　　　　　　[4] *IMT* xx. 581–2,
[5] Warlimont, p. 162. See also Reitlinger, pp. 68 ff,

reminder for future action,[1] and early in May a draft order entitled 'General Instructions for dealing with Political Leaders and for the Co-ordinated Execution of the Task allotted on 31 [*sic*] March 1941' was sent to the OKW.[2] This document stated that any Russian identified as 'a political personality or leader (commissar)' would be executed. On the day of its dispatch Halder told General Müller and the Judge-Advocate-General that 'during the eastern campaign the troops must be aware of the ideological struggle'.[3] On learning that von Brauchitsch and Halder had accepted Hitler's 'brutal and uncontrolled measures . . . against the Bolshevists', Ulrich von Hassell wrote in his diary that 'the Army must assume the onus of the murders and burnings which up to now have been confined to the S.S.'.[4]

Meanwhile, the OKW had issued orders that partisans and Russian civilians attacking the Wehrmacht would be shot without trial or court martial. Anticipating criticism, Keitel ended the instruction with the reminder that no German had forgotten that 'the German collapse in 1918, the German people's subsequent period of woe, and the fight against National Socialism, with its countless bloody sacrifices by the Movement, were mainly attributable to the influence of Bolshevism'.[5]

In an attempt to mitigate the effect of both this instruction and the 'Commissar Order' von Brauchitsch issued a further order on 24 May 1941 calling for the traditional discipline and restraint in the East.[6] Field-Marshal von Bock used the latter as an excuse for ignoring the 'Commissar Order', but neither von Leeb nor von Rundstedt followed his example in their army groups. Von Bock also rejected the orders for the unrestricted shooting of partisans and civilian suspects as incompatible with the very discipline that the OKH was attempting to maintain.[7] His first protest, personally conveyed to von Brauchitsch by his Chief of Staff, von Greiffenberg,

[1] Halder KTB ii. 337, 30 March 1941.
[2] See Warlimont, p. 163. See also *ND* 1471-PS; *Vollmacht des Gewissens*, pp. 358 ff.
[3] *Halder KTB* ii. 399, 6 May 1941. General Eugen Müller, Formerly Quarter-master-General, was appointed General Officer on Special Duties and acted as the Army's senior liaison officer for legal affairs.
[4] Hassell, p. 181.
[5] Führer HQu. 30/41 g Kdos Ch. WR. 28 April 1941. *Bundesarchiv-Militär-archiv*, OKW/Wfst/LTV, p. 71.
[6] See Reitlinger, p. 72; *IMT* xxi. 25; xx. 582.
[7] Bock, *Tagebuch*, 4 June 1941.

was ignored. So three days later von Bock telephoned the Commander-in-Chief to insist that such orders should be worded in a form acceptable to the Army. After considerable argument von Bock cynically concluded that von Brauchitsch's reason for tolerating summary executions during the campaign was that the alternative of insisting on a court martial in every case would result in a wearisome burden of paperwork.[1] In fact, there were other reasons for the readiness of the Army leaders to issue such orders. One was their wish to prevent political interference in the battle zone. When General Warlimont expressed his surprise at the decision of the OKH to send out the 'Commissar Order' in writing, General Wagner, the Quartermaster-General, categorically refused to withdraw it on the grounds that 'there was a danger that Hitler would send the SD right up into the forward areas so that it could be used to carry out his wishes'.[2]

However, the main reason for the acceptance of Hitler's ideological policies by the majority of the generals was that they welcomed them as a means of increasing the effects of terror and paralysis of the *Blitzkrieg* in the East. After the war, Field-Marshal von Kleist stated that:

Hopes of victory were largely built on the prospect that the invasion would produce a political upheaval in Russia. Most of us generals realised beforehand that if the Russians chose to fall back there was very little chance of achieving a final victory without the help of such an upheaval.[3]

Not all Germans agreed that Hitler's policy was the best way to achieve an internal collapse. Particularly in the Army there was support for the formation of anti-Bolshevist movements in Russia, especially in the Ukraine and in the Baltic States. But such ideas were discouraged because they were incompatible with the Nazi racial policy and with the vague and often contradictory schemes for dependent 'socialist' states in the East described by Hitler and by his Minister for Eastern Territories, Alfred Rosenberg.[4]

The 'Directive for Handling Propaganda for Operation Barbarossa' issued in June 1941[5] outlawed appeals to nationalistic sentiments or

[1] Ibid., 7 June 1941.
[2] Warlimont, p. 165; see also p. 151. Cf. Hubatsch, p. 102.
[3] Liddell Hart, *On the Other Side* . . ., p. 259.
[4] See Reitlinger, pp. 128 ff., 160 ff.; Dallin, pp. 44 ff., 107 ff.
[5] See Edgar M. Howell, *The Soviet Partisan Movement, 1941–1944.* Department of the Army Pamphlet 20–244 (Washington, 1956), pp. 22–3. See also *IMT* 221-L; *KTB OKW* i. 89–90E.

ambitions of ethnic minorities, and references to new pro-German national governments. Instead, vague assurances were to be made that the Wehrmacht was entering Russia to free the Russian people from Jewish-Bolshevist rule. Nevertheless, civilians should not attempt to take part in the fighting but remain 'calm and orderly'. The importance of 'work as usual' was stressed and warnings were to be issued that looting, waste, or the destruction of industrial machinery would lead to famine. For the same reason the break-up of collective farms and distribution of land would be delayed to a later date. The Russian press and radio were to be used to exert a calming influence and to discourage acts of sabotage. This negative approach combined with the ruthless extermination of the Communist intelligentsia and Jewish people was hardly likely to sustain enthusiasm for the new German rule. Still less would it stir Russian people into a 'political upheaval' against Stalin only to exchange one form of terror for another.

The success of terror policy depended, like the German military strategy and economic policy, upon swift and decisive results. If the Soviet state collapsed under the impact of the initial blow, the long-term adverse effects on Russia and German morale would be of no consequence. But if the war in the East deteriorated into a protracted struggle then brutal ideological warfare and immediate economic exploitation would prove double-edged weapons.

For this reason the crucial question was whether twenty years of Communist ideology, organization, and discipline had given the Soviet state the strength and resilience to withstand the shock of the *Blitzkrieg*. Later, Hitler admitted his doubts on this point when he told his aides,

at the moment of our attack, we were entering upon a totally unknown world. . . .

On the 22 June a door opened before us, and we didn't know what was behind it . . . the heavy uncertainty took me by the throat. Here we were faced by beings who are [*sic*] complete strangers to us.[1]

There is evidence that this was not mere self-dramatization. On the day before the attack Himmler gave Heydrich the impression that 'the Führer is not so optimistic as his military advisers'.[2]

In spite of Hitler's warning that 'the struggle in the East will be

---

[1] *Hitler's Secret Conversations*, pp. 59, 94. See also Joachim von Ribbentrop, *The Ribbentrop Memoirs*, trans. Oliver Watson (London, 1954), p. 153.

[2] Schellenberg, p. 223.

very different from the struggle in the West',[1] only a few of his generals showed any sign of recognizing the true extent of the risks involved in all aspects—military, economic, and ideological— of the campaign. Their plans remained based upon a repetition of the *Blitzkrieg* of 1939 or 1940 on a grander scale. They spoke of the difficulties in terms of their experiences as junior officers on the eastern front in the First World War.[2] Recognition of the enormity of their error came late, for some incredibly late. Field-Marshal Keitel, with the air of one confidentially revealing a surprising discovery, told an American psychiatrist at Nuremberg in 1946 that Hitler 'talked as if the Russian campaign were a sure thing. . . . But now that I look back, I am sure it was just a desperate gamble.'[3]

At the root of the military, economic, and political problems which made the campaign in Russia such a gamble lay the flaws in Hitler's original grand strategy for the conquest of *Lebensraum*. The basic assumption that a conflict between Germany and Britain could be avoided had caused Hitler to neglect the German Navy and to develop a Wehrmacht for short-range *Blitzkrieg* operations on land. Thus, in 1940 and early 1941, the resistance of Britain confronted the Germans with a military problem for which they were ill equipped. They were unable to wage a war of attrition in the West while maintaining a large land army for a possible conflict in the East. By the time the full extent of this problem had become apparent Hitler had already decided to attack Russia. Thus the German military leaders accepted his solution as the only way out of their dilemma, in spite of the fact that it involved the deliberate acceptance of a two-front war.

But the German hope of winning a quick victory and making immediate economic gains in Russia was reduced by the second basic flaw in Hitler's *Lebensraumpolitik*, the belief that for racial reasons the Soviet state would be internally rotten. This made it seem unnecessary to back the invasion of Russia with any positive political appeal to the Russian people. Thus in Russia their contempt for the enemy caused the Germans to abandon their skilful use of propaganda and subversion and to rely instead upon the hope that the Soviet state would succumb to the mere application of force.

[1] *Halder KTB* ii. 337, 30 Mar. 1941.
[2] See Liddell Hart, *On the Other Side* . . ., pp. 256–7; Blumentritt, 'Moscow', pp. 31, 38.
[3] G. M. Gilbert, *The Psychology of Dictatorship* (New York, 1950), p. 222.

The anxiety that some of his closest advisers observed in Hitler was probably due to his awareness that under the circumstances prevailing in 1941 'Barbarossa' was not far removed from the 'intoxicating Alexandrian campaign' against which he had warned in *Mein Kampf*.[1]

[1] *MK*, p. 557.

CHAPTER VI

# Changes in the Operational Plan

## Military Strategy

THE growing anxiety that lay behind Hitler's attitude towards Operation 'Barbarossa' was not sufficiently great to cause a basic reassessment of German grand strategy in the spring of 1941. Nevertheless, it prompted him to subject the operational plans of the Wehrmacht to constant scrutiny and amendment. In December 1940 the reply that Major Engel gave to von Brauchitsch's query about the seriousness of Hitler's intention of attacking Russia revealed the doubts behind the outward show of confidence. He reported: 'The Führer doesn't yet know himself how things should go. He is constantly preoccupied with mistrust towards his military leaders, uncertain over the Russian's strength and disappointed at the toughness of the British.'[1] Hitler's main fear was that his generals would conduct the operations in the East as a frontal attack towards Moscow and allow the Russians to elude the German spearheads and withdraw into the interior.[2] He suspected that the OKH underestimated the ability of the Soviet Army to strike at the flanks of the German advance, especially from the Pripet Marsh. Furthermore, he was not fully convinced by the encouraging reports given by General Köstring on the weakness of the Soviet war industry.[3] He also expected that the British would react with great vigour when he moved his forces eastward and attempt to land on the coast of Norway or to support the Russians through the Arctic port of Murmansk. Later in March, he feared that the *coup d'état* of General Simovich in Yugoslavia would result in a strengthening of the British position in the Balkans. Hitler's fears had contradictory effects. His effort to increase the power of the thrusts in Russia was

---

[1] Engel, *Tagebuch*, 18 Dec. 1940, quoted by Hillgruber, *Strategie*, p. 369, n. 93.

[2] See *Halder KTB* ii. 210–11, 5 Dec. 1940; *KTB OKW* i. 209, 5 Dec. 1940.

[3] Engel's statement (op. cit.) that Hitler was reassured on this point by General Köstring's reports is not correct. On 5 Feb. Hitler requested a special study of the Soviet war industries' ability to sustain Russian resistance. See *KTB OKW* ii. 306, 5 Feb. 1941.

offset by the dispersion of force on the coast of Norway and in Finnish Lapland and by the postponement of 'Barbarossa' necessitated by the decision to attack Yugoslavia. To make matters worse, German intelligence estimates of Soviet strength began to rise sharply in the spring of 1941. So when the Germans attacked on 22 June 1941 they had less time for the operation and a lower relative strength than they had expected when planning commenced. Thus, Hitler had greater cause to demand quick, decisive successes by the audacious use of mobile and air forces in the opening phase of the campaign.

Hitler's restless anxiety about the ability of his generals to conduct Operation 'Barbarossa' with sufficient daring and determination was apparent at all the major military conferences in the early months of 1941. On 9 January he lectured the Army leaders on the need to envelop and destroy the Russian forces in bold encircling operations.[1] This theme was repeated on 3 February when General Halder presented the operational plan for 'Barbarossa'.

It is important [Hitler warned] to destroy the greater part of the enemy [forces] not just to make them run. This will only be achieved by occupying the areas on the flanks with the strongest forces, while standing fast in the centre, and then outmanoeuvering the enemy in the centre [by attacks] from the flanks.[2]

On the following day Hitler revealed his intention of following the Army's preparations in detail. He requested copies of the maps used by General Halder during his presentation and also situation maps showing the deployment of German and Russian forces in the East at the middle of each month until deployment was completed.[3] On 5 February he called for a study of the Pripet Marsh to examine the possibility that it might become a centre of Soviet resistance on the flanks of the German advance.[4] As described above, he also requested a study on the ability of the Soviet war industries to sustain resistance in the interior of Russia.[4] The General Staff study on the Pripet Marsh was submitted to Hitler on 1 March.[5] It concluded that only cavalry divisions and other formations of up to a regiment in

[1] *KTB OKW* i. 258, 9 Jan. 1941.
[2] Ibid., p. 298, 3 Feb. 1941.
[3] Ibid., p. 303, 4 Feb. 1941.
[4] Ibid., p. 306, 5 Feb. 1941. General von Sodenstern shared Hitler's anxiety on this point. See *Halder KTB* ii. 272, 5 Feb. 1941; Philippi, *Pripjetproblem*, pp. 22–3.
[5] Ibid., p. 339, 1 Mar. 1941.

strength could operate there against the flanks of the German advance and recommended air patrols in order to locate such forces.

A few days later Hitler's anxiety was again aroused when the British carried out a successful raid on the Lofoten Islands.[1] This seemed to justify the demands he had made in February for a reinforcement of the Norwegian coast.[2] It also provoked fears of British action in north Finland and Russia after the start of 'Barbarossa' and contributed to his decision to reinforce the German formations there with a motorized group including heavy tanks.[3]

The alacrity with which Field-Marshal von Brauchitsch allocated forces to meet Hitler's demands for increased security on the coasts of Europe was regarded with scorn by General Halder, who noted that 'it is not a matter of ensuring 100 per cent security everywhere, but of making do with the most essential security for the sake of ensuring the full success of Operation "Barbarossa"'.[4]

The inadequacy of the forces available for 'Barbarossa' had become very clear to Halder at a discussion conducted by the Operations Branch on the previous day. The most prevalent problem was over-extension of force, especially in the 12th and 17th Armies in the Ukraine and in the 16th Army in the northern swamps and forests. The 6th and 4th Armies both lacked sufficient flank protection towards the Pripet Marsh, and the 9th and 18th Armies were both required to allocate part of their infantry strength to support the Panzer groups. Halder sought to solve these problems by making greater use of the armies of Rumania, Slovakia, and Hungary in support of the 12th and 17th Armies, and by allocating reserve divisions to the 16th Army to give it 'added punch'.[5] In his notes for the Führer Conference scheduled for 17 March, he listed the satellite forces that could be used to reinforce Army Group 'South'. The OKH Reserve, he noted, was twenty-one divisions, including one motorized and two Panzer divisions. But of these, nine were allocated to the attack on Greece, Operation 'Marita', which left 'only twelve divisions definitely available, (very few!) of which five are still in the West'.[6] Thus he stressed that a further subtraction of force would be impossible without jeopardizing 'Barbarossa', and

[1] *KTB OKW* i. 346-7, 7-8 Mar. 1941.
[2] Ibid., pp. 317-18, 12 Feb.; p. 326, 15 Feb. 1941.
[3] Ibid., p. 349, 8 Mar. 1941.
[4] *Halder KTB* ii. 313, 15 Mar. 1941.
[5] Ibid., p. 312, 14 Mar. 1941.
[6] Ibid., p. 316, 16 Mar. 1941.

**M**

that if the operation was to begin as planned on 15 or 16 May then no further forces should be sent to the Balkans.[1]

Hitler was also determined to solve the problems of achieving effective concentration of force, especially in Army Group 'South' and of safeguarding the flanks of the advance both sides of the Pripet Marsh. But he was not content to improvise solutions by pushing in reserves or by using satellite armies. Instead he amended the operational plan. This decision was announced at the conference on 17 March attended by Keitel, Jodl, von Brauchitsch, Halder, Wagner, and Heusinger.[2]

### The Conference on 17 March

Hitler opened his comments on Operation 'Barbarossa' with the observation that success must be won from the start and that there must be no reverses. Therefore, no operations should include 'forces that we cannot count on with certainty'.[3] He then proceeded to overthrow Halder's concept of obtaining substantial help from the satellite states by stating that only German and, to a limited degree, Finnish forces could be relied upon. The Rumanians, he stated, lacked offensive capability. The Hungarians could not be relied upon because they had no reason to attack Russia. The Slovaks, he said contemptuously, were Slavs. They might be used later as occupation troops.

Since little use could be made of Germany's allies greater concentration of force on vital sectors could only be achieved by greater economy in the deployment of German forces elsewhere. Thus once again Hitler stressed that Army Group 'North' and 'Centre' should advance to the Dnieper and then, using the river as protection, concentrate their strength towards the north. The capture of Moscow he described as 'completely irrelevant'.[3] The reason for this repetition of a point he had already stressed at three earlier conferences evidently lay in his continued distrust of the generals' ability to resist the temptation to rush headlong into Russia.[4] To this was added his anxiety about the danger of a Soviet attack from the Pripet Marsh

---

[1] *Halder KTB* ii. 314, 316, 16 Mar. 1941. Halder's notes on Soviet strengths were surprisingly inaccurate. His estimate of 155 Russian divisions was 22 divisions *lower* than his estimate on 2 Feb. 1941. See ibid., p. 266, 2 Feb. 1941.

[2] See ibid., pp. 318–21, 17 Mar. 1941.

[3] Ibid., p. 319, 17 Mar. 1941.

[4] See *KTB OKW* i. 209, 5 Dec. 1940; p. 258, 9 Jan.; p. 298, 3 Feb. 1941.

on the south side of Army Group 'Centre'. Contradicting the study made by the General Staff,[1] he asserted that the Pripet Marsh was really no obstacle to movement and that entire armies could be deployed there.[2] Thus he was anxious to avoid the dispersion that might result if Army Group 'Centre' allowed its forces to be drawn in a southerly direction to counter this danger.[3]

In Army Group 'South' Hitler made a drastic change of the operational plan. On the grounds that it was 'basically false to attack everywhere',[4] Hitler decided to abandon the concept of a double envelopment in the Ukraine. The German forces in Rumania were to be reduced to those required to safeguard the oilfields and the remainder, including all armoured formations, were to be added to the main striking force north of the Carpathians for a single thrust towards Kiev and down the Dnieper. Hitler further justified this elimination of the 12th Army's offensive role with the assertion that its attacks were bound to have been blocked on the broad lower reaches of the Pruth and Dniester Rivers. Furthermore, he added, 'we would drive the Russians away, where we should invite them to stay put [for envelopment].'[5]

Hitler's decisions on this occasion intruded into the Army's area of operational planning, contradicted the OKH report on the Pripet Marsh and some of the findings of the war games conducted on the operations of Army Group 'South' by Generals Paulus and von Sodenstern.[6] Nevertheless, neither these factors nor Hitler's subsequent remarks about the extermination of the Russian intelligentsia provoked any complaint from von Brauchitsch or Halder. Indeed, in spite of Halder's subsequent criticisms of the cancellation of the 12th Army's operation, there was 'cheerful agreement between the [Army] Commander-in-Chief and Chief of the General Staff and Hitler over the deployment plan and concentrations of force'.[7]

However, the Commander of Army Group 'South', Field-Marshal

[1] See *KTB OKW* i. 339, 1 Mar. 1941.
[2] *Halder KTB* ii. 319, 17 Mar. 1941.
[3] In fact both of these fears were proved fully justified in July and August when Guderian's Panzer Group was divided between the effort to extend the advance eastward and to ward off threats to its south flank. See Guderian, pp. 183 ff.
[4] Op. cit.
[5] Ibid.; see also *KTB OKW* i. 361, 18 Mar. 1941.
[6] See Görlitz, *Paulus*, pp. 111–12; *Halder KTB* ii. 272, 5 Feb. 1941.
[7] Engel, *Tagebuch*, 17 Mar. 1941, quoted by Hillgruber, *Strategie*, p. 504. Cf. *Halder KTB* iii. 7, 23 June 1941.

von Rundstedt, showed himself less disposed to accept the arbitrary abandonment of the plan for a double envelopment battle in the Ukraine. On 30 March he was summoned, together with the other army group and army commanders, to hear Hitler personally explain the decisions he had announced on 17 March. He could not deny the truth of Hitler's argument that 'the endless expanse of the [Russian] space necessitates . . . the massive concentration of the Luftwaffe and Panzer forces'.[1] Nor could he reject Hitler's warning that 'the fate of major German formations may not be made dependent upon the staying power of Rumanian formations'.[1] Nevertheless, Army Group 'South' was confronted by a large Soviet concentration in the centre of its very wide front and von Rundstedt feared that unless this was pinned down by Hungarian attacks on the Carpathian sector it might prove a serious threat to the south flank of his main thrust on Kiev. Thus he alone argued against the change of plan. Though von Rundstedt failed to convince Hitler, he evidently impressed Halder with his 'very skilful' presentation.[2] Later, the Chief of the General Staff encouraged the active participation of Hungarian and Rumanian troops in the campaign. Nevertheless, Hitler's decision to concentrate the main striking force of Army Group 'South' in the northern sector was maintained and was later justified by the difficulties experienced by the 6th Army and Panzer Group 1 in breaking through the Russian defences and warding off Soviet counter-attacks from the Pripet Marsh.

Hitler's effort to achieve greater concentrations of force on the eastern front were somewhat contradicted by the decision, which he confirmed on 17 March, to reinforce the German garrison in northern Norway with two or three divisions from the West, and at the expense of forces needed in Finnish Lapland.[3] Here further dispersion resulted from the decision to deliver two attacks eastward. In the far north two mountain divisions were to secure Petsamo and, if possible, take Murmansk. Further south, a German infantry division and an SS brigade and supporting formations were to drive for Kandalaksha and the Murmansk railway.[4] Later, Halder expressed regret that valuable forces had been committed to this 'expedition'.[5]

Halder's efforts to prevent the further dispersion of force to another

[1] *Halder KTB* ii. 336, 30 Mar. 1941.
[2] Ibid., p. 338, 30 Mar. 1941.
[3] Ibid., p. 320, 17 Mar. 1941.
[4] See Ziemke, p. 130; *KTB OKW* i. 362, 18 Mar. 1941.
[5] Op. cit., p. 411, 14 May 1941.

such 'expedition' were more successful in the case of the *Afrikakorps*. On 17 March Hitler approved his rejection of the appeal by General Erwin Rommel for two motorized divisions in addition to the 5th Light Division and part of the 15th Panzer Division which he was deploying in Libya.[1] Nevertheless, the demands of the southern theatre of war, especially the Balkans, had serious effects upon Operation 'Barbarossa'.

### The Effects of the Balkan Campaign

Planning for an operation in the Balkans began on 4 November, seven days after Italy had attacked Greece and four days after the British had responded by occupying Crete and Limnos.[2] The German invasion of Greece then became part of the plan that Hitler had developed since late September, to deprive Britain of all her Mediter- ranean bases. Even when the operations for the capture of Gibraltar and Suez were postponed until after 'Barbarossa',[3] Hitler remained determined to eliminate the British air bases in Greece because they were a threat to the Rumanian oilfields and to the Italian mainland. For this reason, he issued Directive No. 29, Operation 'Marita', on 13 December 1940.[4]

Even in November, General Halder had expressed concern that this operation might cause a postponement of the attack on Russia, especially if Turkey entered the war against Germany.[5] However, changes in the date and deployment for Operation 'Barbarossa' did not result until 27 March, when Hitler decided to invade Yugoslavia. To provide the necessary forces, nine divisions and two corps head- quarters were diverted from their assembly areas in the East.[6] The effects of this on 'Barbarossa' were discussed in the General Staff on the same day,[7] and on 7 April 1941 an OKH Order was issued stating that the opening of the attack on Russia would have to be

[1] *KTB OKW* i. 315, 16 Mar.; pp. 320–1, 17 Mar. 1941. Halder's distaste for the African 'expedition' was increased by his personal antipathy for Rommel. See ibid., pp. 377–8, 23 Apr. 1941.

[2] See ibid., p. 164, 4 Nov. 1941. See also Burckhard Müller-Hillebrand, *The German Campaigns in the Balkans, Spring 1941*, U.S. Army Pamphlet No. 20–260 (Washington, 1953), p. 4.

[3] See *Halder KTB* ii. 223, 12 Dec. 1940; p. 315, 16 Mar. 1941.

[4] Hubatsch, pp. 91–3.

[5] Op. cit., p. 188, 18 Nov.; p. 191, 24 Nov. 1940.

[6] See Müller-Hillebrand, *Balkans*, p. 150.

[7] *Halder KTB* ii. 331, 27 Mar. 1941.

delayed by about four weeks.[1] Directive No. 21 set 15 May 1941 as the date by which all preparations were to be ready and although the 'end of May' was mentioned on 5 December, General Halder wished to start sooner.[2] However, there was agreement later among the generals that the weather and ground conditions would not have been favourable earlier than the first week of June.[3] Thus, the Balkan campaign cannot be regarded as causing a delay of more than three weeks in the opening of Operation 'Barbarossa'.

Although the postponement of the start of 'Barbarossa' was prompted by the decision to attack Yugoslavia, the campaign there had less effect on the availability or condition of the forces required for Russia than the operations in Greece. Six of the nine divisions diverted to Yugoslavia were replaced by OKH reserves, so the infantry used there virtually became the reserve for 'Barbarossa'. All combat divisions had been withdrawn from Yugoslavia to their assembly areas for 'Barbarossa' by the end of May.[4]

The situation was very different in the Greek campaign, which involved longer approach marches and lengthier operations, and thus cost more in wear and tear and time. The long return journey to Poland by road and rail via Yugoslavia, Austria, and Bohemia–Moravia or Germany caused further delays so that the 2nd and 5th Panzer Divisions and the *Leibstandarte SS Adolf Hitler* failed to arrive in time for the opening of the Russian campaign on 22 June. Their absence was especially felt by Army Group 'South' which thus lacked about a third of its tank strength in the initial attack.[5]

Although the tank losses in the Balkans were few, the damage incurred through bad road conditions placed a heavy demand on spare parts and gave the tank repair depots in Germany and Poland considerable work right up until the start of Operation 'Barbarossa'. In spite of their efforts the effects of the Balkan campaign must have contributed to the high fall-out rate due to engine and track wear in the summer of 1941.[6]

[1] See *DGFP*(D) xii. Doc. 217, 374. U.S.N.A., Microfilm Guide No. 30, Serial T78–335, Frame 6291347, OKH Order, 7 Apr. 1941.
[2] See op. cit., p. 201, 5 Dec. 1940; p. 315, 16 Mar. 1941.
[3] Interview with Lieutenant-General Müller-Hillebrand, 18 July 1965. See Guderian, p. 145; Philippi–Heim, p. 49; Blumentritt, 'Moscow', p. 36; *Rundstedt*, p. 101, 457; *Halder KTB* ii. 457, 19 June 1941; Hillgruber, *Strategie*, pp. 506–7; Plocher, p. 37; Müller-Hillebrand, *Balkans*, p. 150.
[4] Ibid., p. 149.
[5] See Appendix V.
[6] See *Halder KTB* ii. 481; iii. 109, 29 July 1941; Blumentritt, 'Moscow', p. 36;

The attack on Crete, which was improvised late in April,[1] delayed the return to Poland of the VIII Air Corps. It also had other far-reaching effects. The loss of 170 transport aircraft and over 4,000 of the 22,000 parachute and airborne troops of the XI Air Corps discouraged Hitler from making further use of large-scale airborne operations.[2] Thus the XI Air Corps was never employed on the Russian front, though there were many occasions during the deep advances towards river crossings when this force might have been invaluable.

In spite of its cost in men, equipment, and time, the victory in the Balkans prompted Admiral Raeder to urge Hitler on 6 June to exploit the favourable situation before Britain could restore her position in the Middle East with the help of the United States. This must be done, he said, 'in spite of the burden placed on the German armed forces by Operation "Barbarossa" '.[3] But Hitler was not inclined to commit forces to further operations in the Mediterranean. The attack on Russia was only two weeks away, and he felt that once it was successfully concluded Germany would have the added advantage of land bases in the Caucasus and sea bases in the Black Sea from which to extend her power into the Middle East.

As events turned out, the long-term effects of the conquest of the Balkans were similar to those of the Norwegian campaign, in that the Wehrmacht was obliged to commit considerable strength to garrison the peninsular and yet lacked the sea power to exploit its strategic advantages. The ruthless *Blitzkrieg* unleashed on Yugoslavia, instead of having the paralysing effect intended by Hitler, provoked hatred in the population which contributed to the bitter partisan warfare in the following years. In their haste to return to the assembly areas for Operation 'Barbarossa', the Germans failed thoroughly to disarm the Yugoslav forces or to destroy stocks of arms before they were hidden in the mountains.[4] The security forces that replaced

Burckhard Müller-Hillebrand, *German Tank Maintenance in World War II*, U.S. Army Pamphlet No. 20–202 (Washington, 1954), p. 1; Blau, p. 72; Guderian, p. 190; Wolfgang Werthen, *Geschichte der 16, Panzer Division, 1939–1945* (Bad Neuheim, 1958), p. 40; Liddell Hart, *On the Other Side . . .*, p. 251.

[1] See *KTB OKW* i. 411–12, 28 May 1941; *Halder KTB* ii. 408, 12 May 1941; Hubatsch, pp. 134–5.

[2] *Rise and Fall of the German Air Force*, p. 125; Liddell Hart, *On the Other Side . . .*, p. 242.

[3] W. E. Paulus, p. 289. See also Bock, *Tagebuch*, 30 Mar. 1940.

[4] See Robert M. Kennedy, *German Antiguerrilla Operations in the Balkans, 1941–1944*, U.S. Army Pamphlet No. 20–243 (Washington, 1954), pp. 16–17.

the combat divisions never regained full control of the situation and the struggle against the partisans remained a constant drain on German military resources throughout the war.

## Comparative Strengths, April–June 1941

As a result of events in Norway, the Balkans, and the Mediterranean in the spring of 1941 General Halder was unable to make any substantial reduction in the sixty German divisions that had been allocated to the western, Scandinavian, and Mediterranean theatres on 31 July 1940. Although on 17 March Hitler had dismissed the danger of a British landing in the West, since December 1940 the Germans had felt it necessary to hold considerable forces in readiness for the occupation of Vichy France (Operation 'Attila') as a response to any hostile actions in the French North African colonies. As a further justification for holding forces in the West Jodl told Warlimont on 1 May 1941 that Hitler expected that once 'Barbarossa' was launched the British would attempt to repeat the strategy used against Napoleon by landing forces in Portugal. They might also occupy territory north of Gibraltar and establish air bases in Morocco perhaps with American support.[1] For these reasons thirty-nine divisions were retained in France and the Low Countries. Together with eight in Norway and Denmark, eight in the Balkans, two in Africa and two in Germany, this left 149 for 'Barbarossa'.[2] But although this number exceeded the requirement of 130 to 140 estimated in December, marked increases in Soviet strength gave cause for concern. The hopes expressed in the early plans that the two sides would be approximately equal in numerical strength were abandoned as the estimated number of Soviet formations in European Russia rose from 141 in July 1940 to $226\frac{1}{2}$ in June 1941.[3] Nevertheless, the German military leaders clung to the conviction that the disparity would be offset by achieving some measure of surprise, and by making full use of their battle experience, and superior equipment and tactics.

Few of the German leaders believed that it would be possible to achieve complete initial surprise because the concentration of so many army formations and supporting air forces could scarcely be

[1] OKW/Wfst/LTV, Conference notes *Chef L*, 30 Apr. 1941, *Bundesarchiv-Militärarchiv* III W 59/1. See also Bock, *Tagebuch*, 30 Mar. 1941.

[2] See Müller-Hillebrand, *Das Heer*, ii. 186–91.

[3] See Appendix IV.

1a. Victory in the West, June 1940. The Army Commander-in-Chief, von Brauchitsch (*centre*), overshadowed by the Army and Air Force Field Commanders. Von Bock is beside Hitler, and Kesselring is shaking hands

1b. Führer Conference, Berlin, 21 July 1940. Grand-Admiral Raeder and Field-Marshal von Brauchitsch advise Hitler on Operation 'Sea Lion', while the taciturn Jodl looks on. After Raeder's departure the idea of an attack on Russia in the autumn of 1940 was discussed

2a. Colonel-General von Küchler, Commander of the 18th Army, was ordered to take command in the East early in July 1940. His Chief of Staff, General Marcks (*left centre*) was charged with drafting a plan for operations against Russia

2b. Colonel Siewert, Chief General Staff Officer to the Army Commander-in-Chief (*left*) with Colonel Heusinger (*right*), who was appointed Chief of the Operations Branch in October 1940

3. The South-Eastern Ally. Marshal Antonescu, the Rumanian Head of State, receives his instructions from Hitler, backed by Field-Marshal Keitel and Colonel-General Halder

4*a*. Army Group 'Centre' Headquarters, 4 August 1941. Hitler and Keitel listen while von Bock brings Guderian (*right*) to report on the situation

4*b*. Army Group 'South' Headquarters, 6 August 1941. Field-Marshal von Rundstedt accompanied by his supporting Air Fleet Commander, General Löhr, describes the operations on his sector to the Dictators and General Cavallero, the Chief of Staff of the Italian Army

concealed even if most of them were kept away from the frontier area until the latest possible moment.[1] The best the General Staff could do with the railways available was a concentration spread over the months between February and June as follows:

### Strength in the East

| | |
|---|---|
| by 21 December 1940 | 34 divisions |
| February–April 1941: | |
| 1st and 2nd Phases of Deployment East | 103 divisions |
| by 20 May 1941: | |
| 3rd Phase of Deployment East | 120 divisions |
| by 2 June 1941: | |
| most formations from Balkans and Luftwaffe ground staffs | 129 divisions |

Since this massive movement could not be hidden the OKW issued an instruction on 15 February 1941 entitled 'Directions for the Deception of the Enemy'. This laid down that the movement of troops to the East should be presented as an elaborate deception to cover preparations for an invasion of England in 1941. Army Group 'Centre' was ordered to employ troops in building defences near the eastern frontier as long as this activity did not interfere with training for 'Barbarossa'. Poles were to be used as labourers on the fortifications to start rumours seeming to confirm the Germans' lack of aggressive intentions. Later the German operations in the Balkans gave a further means of explaining the shift of forces to the East. Meanwhile, the OKH ordered that the movement of formation headquarters should be staggered. Those headed by well-known generals who might be recognized were to remain as late as possible in the West. There, on 24 April, the OKH issued 'Instruction for the Preparation of Operation "Shark" (*Haifisch*)' which revived the cross-Channel invasion plans made for 'Sea Lion' in 1940. Another deception operation, code-named 'Harpoon', ordered troops in Brittany and Scandinavia to prepare for seaborne operations against the British Isles.[2]

These measures certainly caused confusion in the German ranks and convinced many senior officers that Hitler's decision to invade Russia was made in the spring of 1941 only under the threat of a

[1] See Appendix II, 'The Lossberg Study', p. 261.
[2] Wheatley, pp. 97–8.

Soviet attack on Germany. Even General Hoepner, who was later hanged for his part in the attempt to kill Hitler on 20 July 1944, remarked after the final Führer Conference a week before the start of the campaign, 'Now I am really convinced that we must strike in the East.'[1]

Nevertheless, the Germans could not feel certain that their deception would succeed. They were disquieted by the fact that Soviet spy activity increased in the winter of 1940. This was attributed to the work of the new Soviet Ambassador in Berlin, Dekanosov, who was believed to hold a high rank in the N.K.V.D. He and his assistant, Kobolov, established a spy ring in the German capital, and the Soviet consuls in Danzig and Prague attempted to set up a secret radio system in Poland and Czechoslovakia.[2] One of the agents in Czechoslovakia sent in reports of German troop concentrations in the East and stated that the Skoda Works had been instructed by the Germans not to fulfil Soviet orders.[3] This report was ignored in Moscow. So too were those of Richard Sorge, the Soviet agent who won the confidence of the German Ambassador in Tokyo, of Alexander Rado, the Intelligence Director operating out of Geneva, and of the *Rote Kapelle* spy network. Stalin was convinced that such warnings were 'English provocations' engineered to confirm the pernicious reports given to Soviet diplomats by Sumner Welles on 20 March 1941 and by the British Ambassador in Moscow, Sir Stafford Cripps, in April.[4] When the German Naval Attaché in Moscow was secretly informed of the British Ambassador's warning that the Germans would attack on 22 June he reported this 'manifestly absurd' prediction to Berlin where it must have caused grave concern. The Germans were forced to expect that these warnings and the increased frequency of flights by air reconnaissance aircraft of the Luftwaffe would provoke Stalin into vigorous defensive preparations. Thus, they had to place their major hopes in the moral and technical advantages gained from their victories elsewhere.

In fact the bold tactics of armoured warfare by which the Germans

[1] W. E. Paulus, p. 254.

[2] Ibid., p. 217.

[3] D. J. Dallin, 'Die Sowjetespionage', *Beilage zur Wochenzeitung Das Parlament*, 48 (1955), 742 ff.

[4] See Gille Perrault, *The Red Orchestra*, trans. Peter Wiles (New York, 1969), pp. 44–5. For accounts of Stalin's refusal to believe indications of a forthcoming German attack see Harrison E. Salisbury, *The 900 Days: the Siege of Leningrad* (New York, 1969), pp. 4, 37–8, 67–81.

had won such successes were gradually overshadowed by caution in the spring of 1941. The small size of the mobile forces in relation to the extent of their tasks in Russia led to a revival of conservative attitudes towards their tactical deployment. Von Brauchitsch and Halder and infantry generals like von Kluge, Strauss, and Busch urged that the Panzer divisions should be held back during the initial phase of the attack in order to save their strength for the exploitation phase. They also supported the subordination of the Panzer groups to infantry army commanders so that the armoured thrusts could be prevented from outrunning the infantry divisions following them on foot. To the Panzer group commanders, Guderian, Hoth, Hoepner, and von Kleist, these proposals sounded like the death-knell of the *Blitzkrieg*.[1] The speed of the infantry advance for which they would have to wait was reduced by the shortage of supply trucks which meant, General Halder warned, that 'regular and complete supply of all troops would not always be possible' and that the infantry divisions would have to make 'extensive use of the land'.[2] The problem was finally settled by placing one or two infantry corps under the operational command of each Panzer group for the initial attack. The Panzer groups were in turn subordinated to an infantry army commander in the same period. Once the break-through had been achieved, the Panzer groups would be divested of the slow-moving infantry and freed for the deep thrusts in the rear of the enemy. It was in these mobile operations that the Germans expected that the superiority of their equipment would prove decisive in countering the numerical superiority of the Russian divisions.

Such optimism could have been justified only if the German intelligence estimates had been based upon reliable statistics. They were not. Yet such was the reputation of the General Staff that even rumour and optimistic guesswork took on the sanctity of truth once it had passed through the hands of the Foreign Armies East Branch. Belatedly and ruefully, General Halder recorded the admission of this error in his diary on 11 August 1941, the fifty-first day of the campaign.[3] It was the same story with tanks and aircraft. The

[1] See *Halder KTB* ii. 312, 14 Mar.; p. 323, 19 Mar.; p. 325, 21 Mar.; p. 330, 27 Mar.; p. 420, 19 May; pp. 438–9, 4 June; p. 445, 6 June 1941; Guderian, p. 149; Hoth, pp. 49–50. Görlitz, *Paulus*, p. 100. Bock, *Tagebuch*, 27 Feb., 14 May, 7 June 1941; Heusinger, *Dokumentenbuch*, p. 56, 21 Mar. 1941.
[2] U.S.N.A., Microfilm Guide No. 30, Serial T78–335, Frame 6291349, 'Anordnung für die Versorgung', signed Halder, no date.
[3] *Halder KTB* iii. 170, 11 Aug. 1941.

Germans had expected large numbers of obsolete models, 10,000 and 8,000 respectively.[1] But soon after the opening of hostilities it became clear that these figures fell far short of the true totals, and in the following months the Germans literally wore themselves out in the process of destroying enormous quantities of inferior Russian equipment.[2]

The fact that the quality of the new Russian tanks, the T34 and KV, also came as a surprise to the German Army was hardly justified.[3] In view of the obsolescence of the standard Russian models, the T26, T28, BT, and T35, and the lead already taken by the Red Army in tank technology, rumours of new Soviet tanks should have been given more credence.[4] On 2 February Halder admitted that in the field of armour 'surprises were not impossible'.[5] Yet, the OKH continued to base its judgements on the equipment used by the Red Army in the occupation of eastern Poland and the war in Finland. The German Ordnance Office ignored Hitler's instructions about the improvement of tank guns and the German anti-tank units retained the 3·7 cm. gun which proved inadequate against the T34 and KV.[6] The use of 8·8 cm. and 10 cm. anti-aircraft guns in the anti-tank role was limited by orders which stated that, in view of the commitment of a large part of the Luftwaffe in the West and the size of the Soviet Air Force, anti-aircraft guns would be used against ground targets only in emergency.[7]

Throughout the spring Hitler continued to stress that once struck the Soviet forces and state would collapse, and that the blow must not be delayed because the condition of the Soviet forces could only

[1] See U.S.N.A., Microfilm Guide No. 30, Serial T78–335, Frames 6291302–3. Intelligence Summary, 15 Jan. 1941; *Halder KTB* ii. 267, 2 Feb. 1941; Blau, p. 42; Plocher, p. 30; Raymond L. Garthoff, *How Russia Makes War* (London, 1954), p. 429.

[2] See *Halder KTB* iii. 32, 1 July; 36, 3 July 1941. By the end of 1941 the Germans claimed to have destroyed or captured 11,627 tanks. See Richard Weber and Karl Korbe (eds.), *Kartenskizzen zum Weltkrieg und zum Grossdeutschen Freiheitskampf für den Unterricht in Kriegsgeschichte*, OKH (Berlin, 1944), p. 30. See also U.S.N.A., Microfilm Guide No. 30, Serial T78–464, Frame 6443755; Plocher, pp. 39–42; *Halder KTB*, iii. 32–3, 2 July 1941.

[3] See Guderian, p. 162.

[4] See R. M. Ogorkiewicz, 'Soviet Tanks', *The Soviet Army*, p. 300; Philippi–Heim, p. 39; Guderian, p. 143; *Halder KTB* ii. 336, 30 Mar. 1941; V. Mostovenko, 'History of the T34 Tank', *Soviet Military Review*, 3 (1967), 38–9.

[5] *Halder KTB* ii. 267, 2 Feb. 1941.

[6] See Guderian, pp. 143–4.

[7] U.S.N.A. Microfilm Guide No. 30, Serial T78–335, Frame 6291346; see also *Halder KTB* ii. 465.

improve.[1] Thus, he treated evidence of any growth in Russian strength not as a reason for caution but as a justification for acting as swiftly and ruthlessly as possible. Normally, Hitler emphasized the obsolete equipment and poor leadership of the Soviet forces.[2] But on 30 March 1941, when he wanted to demonstrate the need for brutal methods in Russia, he deliberately drew the attention of the generals to the strength of the 'respectable' Soviet tank arm, its numbers and its good guns, and a 'new giant type with a long 10 cm. gun . . .'.[3] But he considered a short dose of the truth sufficient for the Army, and when the German Embassy in Moscow obtained permission for a group of German army officers to visit Soviet war plants Hitler promptly cancelled the arrangement.[4]

Nevertheless, the German Army's estimate of Soviet industrial potential also rose considerably. In December 1940 Colonel Heusinger reported to Halder that only 24 per cent of Soviet war industry was located in the Urals and the Far East.[5] This was confirmed by the report completed by General Thomas on 13 February.[6] But an OKH intelligence survey issued a month later indicated that a third of the most important small arms and artillery works and 40 per cent of the tank factories were located in the Urals alone.[7] This led, however, only to the guarded conclusion that 'it is not possible to predict whether the supply [of the Red Army] can be maintained by longer and more intense use of the entire war industry'.[8] This report caused grave misgivings among the intelligence officers to whom it was distributed, especially in view of the acknowledged inability of the Luftwaffe to bomb the industries of the Urals effectively.[9]

Improvements in the Soviet Air Force also caused concern. On this subject Hitler displayed the same ambivalence he had shown towards the Soviet tank arm. On 17 March he encouraged the

[1] See Engel, *Tagebuch*, 10 Aug. 1940, quoted by Hillgruber, *Strategie*, pp. 226–7; *KTB OKW* i. 205, 5 Dec. 1940; p. 208, 9 Jan. 1941.

[2] *Halder KTB* ii. 214, 5 Dec. 1940.

[3] Ibid., p. 336, 30 Mar. 1941. Cf. Engel, op. cit., p. 504; Hilger and Meyer, p. 297.

[4] See Uhlig, p. 172.

[5] *Halder KTB* ii. 236, 17 Dec. 1940.

[6] See Thomas, pp. 525–7, 532.

[7] U.S.N.A., Microfilm Guide No. 30, Serial T78–335, Frames 6291302–3, Intelligence Summary, 15 Jan. 1941.

[8] Ibid., Frame 6291302.

[9] Interview with Baron von Hahn, 17 July 1967.

optimism of von Brauchitsch and Halder with references to the Russians' 'obsolete equipment and especially few [modern] aircraft'.[1] But if it suited his purpose he justified his decision to attack Russia by pointing out the vulnerability of Berlin, Silesia, and the Rumanian oilfields to Russian bombers. When Colonel Aschenbrenner, the Air Attaché in Moscow, returned from a tour of Russian aircraft factories in April 1941 and delivered a report which exposed 'the myth of Soviet deficiencies in the area of workmanship' Hitler greeted it with the comment, 'Well, there you see how far these people are already. We must begin immediately.'[2]

By this time even the pedantic Halder began to speculate on the implications of the strength and deployment of the Soviet Army. On 7 April he noted that:

If one frees oneself from the accepted belief that the Russian wants peace and will not attack of his own accord, then one must admit that the Russian organization would very easily permit a quick change-over to the offensive, which could be very uncomfortable for us.[3]

However, such fears were eased a month later when Colonel Krebs, the acting Military Attaché in Moscow, reported that 'Russia will do everything possible to avoid a war.'[4] On 20 May the Foreign Armies East Branch of the General Staff stated that a Russian preventive offensive was unlikely in view of the weakness of the Soviet Army which was undergoing an extensive reorganization on the basis of lessons learned in the Finnish War.[5]

Subsequent studies have shown this view to have been correct. The Soviet forces, which had been trained and organized in accordance with the doctrine that 'attack is the best defence', were thrown into a state of confusion by Stalin's determination to avoid any military measures which could be judged 'provocative'. Thus the Soviet leaders had neither the wish nor the ability to launch a major offensive in 1941, and it is doubtful whether they had even worked out any comprehensive defensive strategy before the German attack.[6]

[1] Engel, *Tagebuch*, 17 Mar. 1941, quoted by Hillgruber, *Strategie*, p. 504.
[2] Plocher, pp. 17–18.
[3] *Halder KTB* ii. 353, 7 Apr. 1941; see also p. 382, 26 Apr. 1941.
[4] Ibid., pp. 396–7, 5 May 1941.
[5] Erickson, p. 583.
[6] Ibid.; see also Alexander Werth, *Russia at War, 1941–1945* (London, 1964), pp. 133 ff. Papers found on the body of a senior commissar at Kiev in September 1941 contained notes of speeches given before the war by Stalin in which he stressed that he wanted no war with Germany and would fight only if Soviet

Nevertheless, the German military leaders were aware that the armed forces of the Soviet Union were more formidable than their assessments had indicated in 1940 when they conducted their operational planning. By the spring of 1941 they had allocated as much of the Wehrmacht as Hitler would allow to reduce the numerical disparity between their forces and those of Russia. The only remaining possibility was to force the Russian leaders to disperse their forces further by threatening the Soviet Union from every side with a well-co-ordinated coalition grand strategy, making full use of all the possibilities offered by the Axis alliance.

vital interests in the Baltic and Black Sea areas were endangered. (Conversation with General Freiherr von Geyr, 27 June 1969.) See also Salisbury, pp. 28, 56 ff.

CHAPTER VII

# The Weakness of the Coalition Strategy in the East

## The Axis and Operation 'Barbarossa'

BY the early spring of 1941 Hitler appeared to be in an excellent position to establish a great coalition against the Soviet Union. On 27 September 1940 Japan had signed the Tripartite Pact with Germany and Italy, thus strengthening the world-wide influence of the Axis. The subsequent adherence of Slovakia, Hungary, Rumania, and Bulgaria to the Tripartite Pact had given Germany a dominant position on the south-western borders of the Soviet Union and the opportunity to exert pressure upon Turkey. In the north, military liaison between the Germans and the Finns had developed cautiously but firmly during the winter.

Yet Hitler failed to take full advantage of these possibilities. Though founded upon the Anti-Comintern Pact of 1936, the Axis alliance had stemmed mainly from Hitler's desire to neutralize France and, later, to counter Britain's hostility to Germany.[1] Now that Germany was turning to the great task of conquest in Russia Hitler still looked to the Axis alliance to cover his rear by threatening the British in the Mediterranean and Far East and by discouraging the United States from entering the war. Thus, no provision was made in German planning for the active participation of either Italy or Japan in the war against the Soviet Union. The governments in Tokyo and Rome were officially notified of the German attack only in the early hours of 22 June 1941.

Although Mussolini was the last of Hitler's allies to be informed of 'Barbarossa' he succeeded in being the first to declare war on Russia and insisted that the legions of the modern Rome should be represented on the battlefields of the Ukraine. Hitler permitted his fellow dictator to indulge in his foolish wish and send a corps of

[1] See Burkhard Müller-Hillebrand, *Germany and Her Allies in World War II*, U.S. Army Historical Division MS. P-108, 2 vols. (1954), i. 11 ff.

40,000 men to the eastern front, but he shared the view of the German and Italian generals that it would have been of more value committed against the British.[1] The presence of the Italian Expeditionary Force in Russia in 1941 was of negligible value and its subsequent losses in a campaign that promised no direct gains to Italy only added to the war-weariness of the Italian people.

It was typical that the whims of the dictators should have decided this question, for no joint planning staff or committee was established to direct Axis coalition strategy. Keitel's attempts in 1938 to prepare the groundwork by means of high-level staff discussions were discouraged by Hitler[2] and later foundered on Italian lack of readiness for war.[3] There was no further meeting between the Chiefs of the German and Italian High Commands until 14 November 1940, five months after Italy's entry into the war, and two weeks after the opening of Mussolini's disastrous 'parallel war' against Greece.[4] But still no attempt was made to replace the loose system of meetings and exchanges of correspondence between Hitler and Mussolini with a more closely co-ordinated system. Finally, in December the critical situation of the Italian forces in Greece and Libya led to the commitment of German air and land formations to assist them. As a result, German-Italian discussions on military strategy in the Mediterranean were held in January 1941 and closer co-ordinating activity between the military attachés of the two countries followed. Nevertheless, Hitler's acceptance of the Italian contribution to the Russian campaign and its subsequent employment in roles of secondary importance reflected the uneasy mixture of consideration for Mussolini's prestige and mistrust of Italian military capabilities that typified the Germans' attitude toward their ally.

While the presence of an Italian corps in Russia was of little value, the Italian war effort in the Mediterranean proved a serious liability. Italy's entry into the war merely gave the British direct means of striking at the Axis, and forced Germany to tie down mobile and air formations in North Africa and Sicily and to conduct the Balkan operation at the cost of valuable time and effort. From the German viewpoint, a neutral Italy, hostile to Britain, might have been of more value. She would have forced Britain to keep considerable

[1] See *Halder KTB* iii. 53, 8 July 1941.
[2] See *DGFP*(D) vi, Appendix I.
[3] See Müller-Hillebrand, *Germany and Her Allies*, ii. 1–2; Taylor, *Origins*, p. 14.
[4] See Müller-Hillebrand, *Germany and Her Allies*, ii. 9; *KTB OKW* i. 195E.

forces idle in the Mediterranean and Africa merely to discourage her from entering the war, yet she would not have required the support of German forces which could have been used in Russia.

There were even greater obstacles to the formulation of a coalition grand strategy between Germany and Japan. The main Japanese advocates of the Tripartite Pact, Yosuke Matsuoka, the Foreign Minister, and General Oshima, the Japanese Ambassador in Berlin, never commanded the lasting support of the government in Tokyo. Their temporary ascendency resulted from the success of the former in persuading Prince Konoye and his colleagues late in 1940 that Britain was beaten and that the United States could be intimidated into remaining neutral.[1] But until late in 1941 there was little agreement in the Japanese Cabinet or even between the Army and the Navy on how best to take advantage of the events in Europe and the Axis alliance. A military commission, headed by General Yamashita, visited Germany in the first half of 1941, but it confined its activities to studies of the tactical and operational aspects of the *Blitzkrieg*. In spite of his enthusiasm for the Axis, General Oshima was unable to obtain any clear strategic direction from Tokyo because there was none to give. Thus it was left to Hitler to take the first step in defining aims for a coalition strategy.

These appeared on 5 March 1941 in Directive No. 24, 'Regarding Co-operation with Japan'.[2] This stated that the common war aim was to defeat Britain quickly and so keep the United States out of the war. Hitler specified the capture of Singapore as the best way in which Japan could contribute to this aim. But he concealed the fact that his underlying purpose was to achieve a dispersal of British strength while Germany was invading Russia. He did not consider that he needed the aid of the Japanese in defeating the Soviet Union, and, for security reasons, he felt justified in ordering that they were 'not to be given any intimation of the "Barbarossa" operation'.[3]

Though he strongly supported the idea of a Japanese attack on Singapore, Admiral Raeder urged Hitler in March also to advise the Japanese Foreign Minister of the German intentions in Russia during his forthcoming visit.[4] Hitler refused Raeder's request. Nevertheless, a number of broad hints of a possible deterioration

---

[1] Sir Robert Craigie, *Behind the Japanese Mask* (London, 1945), p. 109. Paul W. Schroeder, *The Axis Alliance and Japanese-American Relations, 1941* (Cornell, New York, 1958), pp. 117–18, 125. See also Robertson, *Origins*, pp. 253–4.          [2] Hubatsch, pp. 121–3.
[3] Ibid., p. 123.          [4] FCNA 1941, p. 37; *NCA* vi. 966–7.

in Russian-German relations were dropped in the course of the conversations between Matsuoka and the German leaders. On 27 March von Ribbentrop stated that if some day Russia were to become a threat to Germany she would be totally crushed.[1] He hastened to point out to his guest that 'he did not believe that Stalin would pursue an unwise policy',[1] and later Hitler himself repeated this assurance.[2] Two days later, however, von Ribbentrop revived the topic and suggested that 'if the Russians should pursue a foolish policy and force Germany to strike', the Japanese Army should not attack Russia. 'Japan would best help the common cause', he explained, 'if she did not allow herself to be diverted by anything from the attack on Singapore'.[3] This and other statements during the conversations gave the Japanese the clear impression that the main aim of the Axis grand strategy in 1941 was to defeat Britain.[4]

The result of this impression was that on 13 April the Japanese Foreign Minister stopped in Moscow on his way home and concluded a Neutrality Pact with the Soviet Union, which made conditions more favourable for a Japanese attack on the British Empire. Furthermore, the Japanese probably believed that the pact would improve the contact between Japan and her European allies by assuring her of a safe land route across Eurasia and by giving her a relationship with Russia similar to that negotiated by Germany in August 1939.

For his part, Stalin was delighted with this development which seemed to reduce the danger of an Axis encirclement of the Soviet Union. He made a rare and unscheduled appearance at the Moscow railway station to bid the Japanese a jovial farewell. Then turning to the attendent diplomats, he sought out the German ambassador, Count von der Schulenberg, enveloped him in a hug and told him, 'We must remain friends and you must do everything to that end!'[5] Colonel Krebs, acting German Military Attaché, was also singled out for the same treatment and was assured by Stalin, 'We will remain friends with you in any event (*auf jeden Fall*).'[5]

Hitler was not perturbed by the Russo-Japanese Pact. On the contrary he welcomed it as a confirmation that the Japanese would meet the German request for an attack on Singapore. This attitude confirms that the anxieties he felt at this time about the coming campaign in the East were confined to the operational level. He

[1] *NSR*, p. 285.                              [2] Ibid., p. 291.
[3] Ibid., p. 309.      [4] See *Halder KTB* ii. 334, 29 Mar. 1941.
[5] Op. cit., p. 324.

anticipated some difficulties, but none great enough to cause him
to doubt the outcome of the invasion or to attempt to develop a
coalition strategy in which Japan would share the task of defeating
the Soviet Union. Hitler's attitude was all the more remarkable
in view of the economic need to open up the Trans-Siberian railway
as soon as possible which was stressed by General Thomas in his
discussion with Göring on 26 February.[1]

Hitler's confidence was evidently not shared by the German Military Attaché in Tokyo, General Alfred Kretschmer. Soon after the
German attack on Russia opened, he began on his own initiative to
urge the Japanese General Staff to impose a blockade on Vladivostok
and to tie down Soviet forces by means of military deceptions in
Manchuria.[2] The OKH promptly repudiated these requests. But on
28 June, von Ribbentrop, also acting on his own initiative,[3] sent
a long cable to the German Ambassador in Tokyo, General Eugen
Ott, ordering him to appeal to the Japanese to attack the Soviet
Union in the rear. Such a move, he asserted, would 'convince the
United States of the utter futility of entering the war on the side of
a Great Britain entirely isolated and confronted by the most powerful
alliance in the world'.[4] The argument was probably designed to
appeal also to Hitler who still felt that the main contribution of
Japan should be to pin down British forces and to discourage the
entry of the United States into the war.[5] On 10 July von Ribbentrop
again cabled an urgent request for efforts to persuade the Japanese
to attack Vladivostok. 'The natural objective', he told Ott, 'still
remains that we and the Japanese join hands on the Trans-Siberian
railway before winter starts.'[6]

The German appeals for a Japanese attack on Russia won support
only from Matsuoka and a small faction of Japanese Army leaders.
In July they suffered a set-back when Matsuoka was manœuvred
out of office. Furthermore, General Yamashita returned and reported
the aversion for Operation 'Barbarossa' expressed by 'a high-ranking
officer of the German General Staff' who had compared the problems

[1] See Thomas, pp. 18–19.
[2] See Müller-Hillebrand, *Germany and Her Allies*, ii. 280.
[3] See Hillgruber, *Strategie*, p. 485, n. 8.
[4] Nuremberg Document NG-3437, Document Book VIIIB, Weizsäecker
Case, quoted by Shirer, p. 1148.
[5] For Hitler's attitude towards the Japanese at this time see Hillgruber,
*Staatsmänner*, pp. 600 ff.
[6] *IMT* xxxi. 2896–PS, 261.

of a war with Russia with those of the Japanese struggle in China.[1] Yamashita's report strengthened the doubts of the Japanese about the wisdom of again challenging the Red Army, which had inflicted a sharp defeat on their forces during the Khalkim-Gol incident on the Mongolian border in August 1939.[2] Their experience in China also made them wary of extending their forces in further operations in pursuit of vague and distant aims on the vast mainland of Asia. The embargo placed by the United States on oil shipments to Japan forced the Army and Navy leaders to unite in seeking strategic objectives that would solve their most acute economic problems. They now began to agree on plans for expansion to the south-west, to the oilfields of the Dutch East Indies and Burma. Furthermore, the Japanese leaders no longer shared Hitler's belief that attacks could be carried out on British possessions in the Far East without bringing the United States into the war. Their strategic decisions were influenced by the awareness that, if Singapore threatened the flank, the United States' bases on the Philippines dominated the centre of their routes to the essential oil of the East Indies. The conviction that a war with the United States and Britain was unavoidable made the Japanese most anxious to see an end to the Russo-German war and a revival of the war against Britain. On 15 July Hitler had assured General Oshima that he hoped to free a major part of the land and air forces from operations in Russia in three or four weeks and in six weeks he would be 'just about ready'.[3] But by October the Japanese were becoming impatient. General Tojo, the War Minister, told the German Ambassador, General Ott, that the war in Russia had been a mistake and that Germany should end it as soon as possible, if necessary by negotiation. She should then transfer her main effort to the Middle East to seize the Suez Canal and the seaways to the East, while Japan would strike 'in an East Indian direction'.[4]

[1] See Müller-Hillebrand, *Germany and Her Allies*, ii. 281. The officer referred to was probably General Matzky who became *Oberquartiermeister IV* (Intelligence) on the German General Staff in January 1941, having been German Military Attaché in Tokyo prior to that date. Most of the planning for 'Barbarossa' was completed before his arrival, and his criticisms do not seem to have had any effect upon his colleagues.

[2] See Erickson, pp. 536-7. Nevertheless, Yamashita was sent to Manchuria and given command of the forces facing Vladivostok. For a time preparations were made for war. Early in August the Kwantung Army was authorized to bombard Soviet territory in the event of a Soviet air attack. See Robertson, *Origins*, p. 254.

[3] Hillgruber, *Staatsmänner*, p. 603.

[4] Op. cit., pp. 283-4.

Later in the month, after the resignation of Prince Konoye and his Cabinet, Tojo became Prime Minister and the concept of a war of expansion south and south-west of the Japanese islands became the policy of the State. With their oil reserves diminishing the Japanese could not wait for the German forces to complete the conquest of Russia and turn to the Middle East. Nor had they any intention of tying down further forces on the mainland of Asia by attacking Russia. Thus the renewal of the Anti-Comintern Pact which took place in Berlin on 25 November 1941 was perhaps the most empty of the many hollow diplomatic gestures ceremoniously conducted by the Axis powers. In spite of its name the pact was not a prelude to a Japanese entry into the war with the Soviet Union. Indeed, on the very day of its signature the Japanese naval task force set sail for the attack on Pearl Harbour.

## The Satellite States

Although the attack on Russia could not satisfy the aims of Hitler's main Axis partners, there were two states, Finland and Rumania, whose territorial aspirations gave them a direct motive for participation. Others were also prepared to contribute forces to the war in the East in order to win the esteem of the German leaders. But Hitler did not form a true coalition in which the partners all met to work out a unified strategy. Instead he controlled them on a unilaterial basis through a German military liaison staff in each of their capitals. He manipulated them just as he used his own staffs, taking advantage of their rivalries to keep them divided and dependent upon his support. While encouraging his allies to follow policies that suited his purpose, he entrusted them with the minimum information about his own plans. Their military contributions, even those of Finland, he regarded as of limited value.[1] The participation of a large number of European states lent a semblance of reality to the propaganda myth of a 'crusade against Bolshevism', but the main value of Rumania, Hungary, Slovakia, and Finland lay rather in their road and rail communications, giving access to the Russian southern and northern flanks. Turkey had this value also, but since

[1] Hitler stated 'the Finns will fight bravely, but they are numerically weak and have not yet recovered [from the Winter War, 1939–40]'. *Halder KTB* ii. 336, 30 Mar. 1941. In fact, the Finns were later unimpressed by the performance of the German troops on the far northern sectors. See Seaton, pp. 155 ff.

she lay on the outer edge of the area of German political and military influence Hitler was uncertain about her participation in the attack. Finland and Rumania were both also of great economic importance to Germany. Since the nickel mines of Petsamo and the oil of Ploesti were vulnerable to Russian counter-moves in the event of a German attack, the commitment of German forces to their defence was regarded as a necessity from the very start of the German planning.[1]

The leaders of Finland and Rumania were receptive to German proposals for military co-operation. They felt themselves to be defenceless against further Russian pressure and were eager not only to recover their recent territorial losses but also to extend their boundaries eastward. Such aspirations were well suited to serve Hitler's purposes. The first steps in preparing for German-Finnish and German-Rumanian military co-operation were taken in 1940,[2] but the detailed co-ordination of plans between the German military staffs and those of the prospective eastern allies was delayed as long as possible for security reasons. On 1 May 1941 Keitel issued an order stating that staff talks with Hungary would commence 'in the last ten days of May' and Rumania 'as late as possible'.[3] Finland, on the other hand, was to send staff officers to Berlin 'within the next few days'.[3] Greater trust was placed in the Finns, but the main reason for their preferential treatment was the need to start preparations earlier in the far north because of the lack of good road and rail communications.

## Finland

The probable participation of Finland was mentioned in the early planning of the campaign in Russia in July 1940.[4] One of the political aims defined by Hitler was the extension of Finland to the White Sea. His readiness to encourage the establishment of an independent 'Greater Finland' was due entirely to the fact that it suited his own racial and territorial concepts. Hitler considered the lands of the north too cold for settlement by Germans and he preferred to have

[1] *Halder KTB* ii. 33, 22 July 1940.
[2] See Ziemke, pp. 115 ff. for an outline of German-Finnish military negotiations and Hillgruber, *Hitler, König Carol und Marschall Antonescu*, pp. 118 ff. for an account of the establishment of the German Military Mission in Rumania.
[3] See Hubatsch, p. 106.
[4] See *Halder KTB* ii. 33, 22 July; p. 50, 31 July 1940.

Finns there rather than Russians.[1] In fact, Hitler's policy toward the Finns was based primarily upon deceit. In August 1939 he used Finland as a pawn in his pact with Stalin, and had offered help in blockading her in the Winter War of 1939–40.[2] Even while seeking the co-operation of Finland he considered giving her Aaland Islands to Sweden as a bribe for assistance.[3] Early in 1941 he sent a diplomat to describe in Helsinki how he was struggling with Russia's leaders to preserve Finnish independence without having to resort to war. Meanwhile, the military operations to be conducted from Finland were being discussed and planned by the OKW and OKH.

Directive No. 21 Operation 'Barbarossa' of 18 December 1940 outlined three main lines of attack from Finland.[4] Like the operations on the main front in Russia, they were based on what was operationally desirable rather than what was feasible in view of the logistical problems involved. Furthermore, they bore little relation to the aims of the Finns. In the far north, an operation proposed by Hitler in August had as its aims the occupation and defence of the Petsamo nickel mines and later the investment of Murmansk (Operation 'Reindeer').[5] Further south, an attempt would be made to cut the Murmansk railway if Sweden permitted German troops to cross her territory (Operation 'Silver Fox'). It was assumed that the third operation would be conducted by the Finns to tie down Soviet forces on their southern border.[6] Staff discussions were conducted on a 'hypothetical' basis with the Finnish Generals Talvela, in December, and Heinrichs, in January 1941.[7] Between January and April detailed planning for the two northern operations was conducted by General von Falkenhorst's Army of Norway.[8]

Joint planning became more specific late in May when a Finnish staff delegation headed by General Heinrichs arrived in Berlin. General Jodl greeted the Finns with a speech in which he stated that if attempts through diplomatic channels failed to bring about a reduction of the Soviet troop concentrations on the German border a preventive attack would be necessary. After the subsequent 'crusade against Bolshevism', he said, Russia would 'cease to be a great power'.[9]

[1] See *Hitler's Secret Conversations*, p. 380; *KTB OKW* i. 90E.
[2] See Uhlig, p. 163.          [3] See *KTB OKW* i. 299, 3 Feb. 1941.
[4] See Hubatsch, p. 99.          [5] See op. cit., p. 27, 13 Aug. 1940.
[6] See op. cit.          [7] See Ziemke, p. 119.          [8] See ibid., pp. 124–8.
[9] Ibid., p. 132. See also Anthony F. Upton, *Finland in Crisis, 1940–1941* (London, 1964), p. 256.

The Finns regarded these blandishments with caution. They had no wish to see their country taken over like Denmark and Norway and used for the furtherance of German aims. In a later talk, Heinrichs bluntly warned the representatives of the Wehrmacht that any attempt to install a 'Quisling-type' government would result in an end of Finnish-German collaboration.[1] Furthermore, they were determined to avoid any premature action that might expose them to Soviet counter-measures before Germany was ready to help them. On the other hand, a conflict between Germany and Russia would present them with a unique opportunity to regain the territories occupied by Russia after the Winter War, and perhaps even to realize their claim to Eastern Karelia as far as the White Sea.[2]

For this reason the Finns were eager to undertake offensive operations that would serve their political aims. They were, therefore, disappointed when Jodl allotted them the passive role of merely pinning down the Russian force in the Lake Ladoga area.[3] This was done in accordance with the instructions given by Hitler on 17 March when he stated that the forces of Finland should undertake offensive operations only against the Russian coastal batteries at Hangö.[4]

On the following day, however, the wishes of the Finnish delegation received a more responsive hearing when they visited the Army General Staff. Unlike Jodl, General Halder was evidently not prepared to accept Hitler's view that the allied forces should not be committed to offensive operations. He urged the creation of a strong striking force which could be employed on either shore of Lake Ladoga.[5] The Finnish military leaders were eager to concentrate the bulk of the Finnish Army for the attack on the Lake Ladoga front, but at their next conference with the Germans in June it became clear that this was not possible.[6]

The subsequent dispersion of military effort in Finland was the result of a complex division of command which placed demands upon the Finnish forces from three directions—their own general headquarters, the OKW, and OKH. The unnecessary and confusing division of the German command in Finland originated from the

[1] Ziemke, p. 134.
[2] Ibid., p. 193. See also Charles Lundin, *Finland in the Second World War* (Indiana, 1957), pp. 113 ff., 147 ff.; J. Wuorinen (ed.), *Finland and World War II, 1939–44* (New York, 1948), p. 125.
[3] Ziemke, p. 132.
[4] *Halder KTB* ii. 319, 17 Mar. 1941.
[5] See op. cit., pp. 132–3; ibid., p. 429, 26 May 1941.
[6] Ziemke, p. 134.

jealous hostility between von Brauchitsch and Keitel. The former had long harboured a 'smouldering resentment' at the exclusion of the OKH from the Norwegian campaign that had been planned and directed by the OKW.[1] This was apparently aggravated by the changes in the plans for the Army of Norway ordered by Hitler on 17 March, and on the following day von Brauchitsch petulantly declared that 'he was leaving it to the OKW to issue all orders'[2] for the operations in Finnish Lapland. Later the OKW offered the command of all operations in Finland to Marshal Mannerheim, but he refused to take responsibility for the attacks conducted by predominantly German forces to attain Hitler's strategic objectives in the far north. So he retained command only in the south where Finnish formations were in the majority.[3] As a result the operations in Finnish Lapland were controlled by the OKW through the Army of Norway, the headquarters of which was split into two parts, one in Norway and the other over 1,000 miles away in Finland. However, because the OKW lacked the necessary administrative organizations, the supply of all the German forces in Finland was conducted by the OKH. The OKH also advised Marshal Mannerheim, the commander in the south of Finland, on operational matters there through General Erfurth, Head of the German Liaison Staff.

Since neither the OKW nor the OKH could commit sufficient formations in Finland to achieve their respective military strategic aims, they both requested the allotment of Finnish formations to support their attacks. These requests and the demands of their own political and strategic aims forced the Finns to divide their army in June between five separate operations. The main force of thirteen divisions, reinforced by one German division, was to advance from Lake Ladoga to the Svir River. A corps of two divisions was to take part in Operation 'Silver Fox' and a battalion group was committed to Petsamo. In addition, the Finns agreed to occupy the Aaland Islands and seal off the Russian base at Hangö. Later, they launched an attack on the Karelian Isthmus.[4] Once committed to these operations the Finnish and German forces were prevented from swift or easy concentration by the sparse lines of road and rail communications in Finland. Even if the command structure had made a

[1] See Warlimont, p. 142.
[2] Ibid. See also *Halder KTB* ii. 322, 18 Mar. 1941; *KTB OKW* i. 363, 18 Mar. 1941.
[3] See Ziemke, pp. 133–4.
[4] See ibid., p. 192.

unified strategic direction possible in this theatre it would have been difficult to implement any major shift of forces in the short campaigning season in the north.

### Rumania

At the other extremity of the great eastern front Rumania presented fewer problems than Finland. German relations with the Rumanian leaders were simpler and even more unscrupulous than those with the Finns. By means of the secret protocol to the Russo-German Pact of 1939 and the Vienna Award of August 1940, Hitler encouraged the annexation of huge portions of Rumanian territory. Then, in September 1940, he took up the role of protector of the shattered remnant. General Antonescu, who had been installed as dictator with German help, eagerly welcomed Hitler's aid and offered military support in the event of a war between Germany and Russia.[1] In return he hoped to recover Bessarabia, northern Bukhovina, and perhaps even some of Transylvania, and also to annex the so-called Transnistrian Regions as far east as the Dnieper.[2] Hitler did not discourage these hopes, but he secretly admitted that he had no intention of giving Rumania more than 'Odessa and a strip of land leading west-north-west from the city'.[3] Hitler had a low opinion of the Rumanian people and their armed forces, and though he admired Antonescu as a political leader he gave him only ten days' notice of the coming attack on Russia.[4] Antonescu promptly agreed to take command of the Rumanian 3rd and 4th Armies and the German 11th Army.[5] However, the real control of operations was retained by the 11th Army commander, General Ritter von Schobert. Even before the attack had begun Hitler requested that 'in the interests of maintaining a unified and consistent system of command' Antonescu should accept directions for the employment of the 11th Army given by Field-Marshal von Rundstedt, commanding Army

[1] See Hillgruber, *Hitler, König Carol und Marschall Antonescu*, pp. 118, 127; Jon Gheorge, *Rumäniens Weg zum Satalliten-Staat* (Heidelberg, 1952), pp. 50 ff.
[2] See *IMT* vii. 317–20.
[3] *KTS OKW* i. 90E.
[4] See *Halder KTB* ii. 319, 17 Mar.; 337, 30 Mar. 1941; *NCA* vi. 945; Schmidt, p. 244, for Hitler's views on the Rumanians and their leader. Gheorge reveals (pp. 143 ff.) that Antonescu evidently guessed Hitler's intention of attacking Russia much earlier.
[5] See *Halder KTB* ii. 455, 14 June 1941. The 11th Army headquarters replaced that of the 12th Army under Field-Marshal List which had moved to the Balkans.

Group 'South'.[1] This virtually excluded Antonescu from any real
operational function and after a few ineffectual weeks in the field
he returned to Bucharest, leaving the Rumanian forces under German
command.

## Hungary

In spite of its one-sided nature, the growth of co-operation between
Germany and Rumania was observed with jealous suspicion by
Hungary. In April 1941 Admiral Horthy, the Regent, was prompted
by rumours of an impending 'preventative war' against the Soviet
Union to write to Hitler assuring him that such a blow would win
him 'not only the inexhaustible treasures of Russia's soil' but also
'the blessing of history . . . for centuries to come'.[2] However, he took
occasion to warn the German leader not to place trust in the Rumanians, who 'in the course of their short history . . . have betrayed and
defrauded all their friends and allies'. Nevertheless, Horthy's
obsequious arguments could hardly outweigh the importance of
Rumania's oil and geographical position. In contrast, Hungary's
strategic importance to Germany was limited to her road and rail
communications to Rumania. Her mountainous eastern border was
not a suitable jumping-off place for a major attack on the Soviet
Union. Thus Hitler's revised plans for Operation 'Barbarossa' envisaged only a limited, primarily defensive, role for the Hungarian
Army.[3]

However, as in the case of Finland, General Halder did not agree
with Hitler. He sympathized with the view expressed by Field-
Marshal von Rundstedt that the Hungarians should be encouraged
to attack on the Carpathian sector in order more effectively to pin
down the Russian forces there.[4] Since a request for such an attack
was a contradiction of Hitler's orders it had to be made in secrecy
through General Himer, the OKH representative on the Hungarian

[1] Müller-Hillebrand, *Germany and Her Allies*, ii. 157.
[2] Miklós Szinai and Lósló Szües (eds.), *Horthy's Confidential Papers* (Budapest,
1965), pp. 180-1. Horthy spoke in a similar vein a month later to General Baron
von Weichs, commander of the German army that invaded Yugoslavia. The
Chief of the Hungarian General Staff, von Werth, told the visitor that 'in a war
against the Soviets the whole Hungarian Army would fight shoulder to shoulder
with the Germans.' Nachlass von Weichs, *Erinnerungen*, vol. 5, *Bundesarchiv-
Militärarchiv* HO8-19/9.
[3] See *Halder KTB* ii. 319, 17 Mar. 1941; Hubatsch, p. 106.
[4] See *Halder KTB* ii. 338, 30 Mar. 1941.

General Staff, and couched in such terms that the Hungarians could not expect some sort of compensation for their action.[1] The problem of bringing the Hungarians into the war without offering them a specific reward was overcome when the town of Kassa was bombed on 26 June. An officer of the Hungarian Air Force identified the aircraft as German, but he was ordered by the Prime Minister, Bardossy, to remain silent. A post-war account suggests that the bombers were of German make but were flown by members of the Slovakian Air Force who were deserting to the Russians and deliberately jettisoned their bombs on Hungary.[2] Nevertheless, the attack was blamed on Russia, and Hungary declared war next day. In mid July the Hungarian Mobile Corps was placed at the disposal of Army Group 'South' with the request that it should not be deployed beside a Rumanian formation.[3]

## Turkey

Even though the enmity for Russia and Bolshevism displayed by Horthy's Hungary was shared by the Turks, they hesitated to commit themselves to an active role until the success of Germany was assured. Hitler had stated on 31 July 1940 that 'it remained to be seen to what degree Finland and Turkey would be interested [in the invasion of Russia]'.[4] On 17 March 1941 he suggested that after its resources had been exhausted, the Caucasus might be given to Turkey,[5] and he told the Turkish Ambassador in Berlin that in the November conversations with Molotov he 'had prevented the liquidation of the Balkans and Turkey by Russia'.[6] But the Turks refused to abandon their neutrality and the German-Turkish Pact of Friendship which was signed in Ankara on 18 June 1941 did little more than prevent Britain from sending aid to Russia over Turkish territory. Though the German attack on Russia was welcomed by the Turks, their leaders held back from any direct involvement.

[1] *KTB des deutschen Generals beim Oberkommando der Kgl. Ungar. Wehrmacht*, 23 June 1941, quoted in *Horthy's Confidential Papers*, p. 183, See also *Halder KTB* iii. 6, 22 June 1941.

[2] See C. A. Macartney, 'Hungary's Declaration of War on the USSR in 1941', *Studies in Diplomatic History and Historiography in Honour of G. P. Gooch* (London, 1961), p. 164.

[3] See *Halder KTB* iii. 20, 27 June 1941; *KTB OKW* i. 421.

[4] *Halder KTB* ii. 50, 31 July 1940.

[5] Ibid., p. 320, 17 Mar. 1941.

[6] Hillgruber, *Strategie*, p. 496; *DGFP*(D) xii, Doc. 177.

### The 'Crusade against Bolshevism'

Few countries in Europe were able, like Turkey, to avoid commitment. Sweden permitted the transportation of a German division
across her territory to Finland. Many felt obliged to win favour
with Germany by offering forces for Operation 'Barbarossa'. Hitler
gave orders that such contributions should be 'enthusiastically
accepted'.[1] Their participation served, not to strengthen a true
coalition, but to support the propaganda of the Führer Proclamation
issued on the eve of the attack, which closed with an exhortation
to the troops to save European civilization and culture.[2] Later, Hitler
stated that the 'crusade' in the East was developing for the first time
'a feeling of European solidarity'.[3] This, he said, would be most
important for the future because a later generation would have to
face the problem of a conflict between 'the European economic area'
and the United States of America.[3] So contingents from the armies
of Italy, Slovakia, and Croatia, and volunteer formations from France
and Spain were sent to fight in Russia and volunteers from Norway,
Denmark, Finland, Holland, and Belgium were formed into Waffen
SS formations.[4] But none of these was militarily significant. Indeed
some were a liability because their training and equipment were not
equal to the rigours of the campaign and their different weapons and
vehicles served only to complicate the supply and maintenance
systems.[5]

Many German soldiers would have welcomed the support of anti-
Communist Russians.[6] But Hitler refused to accept such aid until
it was too late. Although the German Army made considerable use
of volunteer help from Russian prisoners of war, the recruiting of
entire Russian formations began only when the hope of a German
victory had disappeared.[7] The fact that even then an entire army

---

[1] *KTB OKW* i. 409.

[2] U.S.N.A., Microfilm Guide No. 30, Serial T78–335, Frame 6291693 ff. See
also Domarus, ii. 1725 ff.; Bramstead, pp. 244 ff.; Dallin, pp. 67–8. Cf. Telegram
to the Führer from the Ecclesiastical Council of the German Evangelical Church,
30 June 1941, quoted in J. S. Conway, *The Nazi Persecution of the Churches,
1933–45* (Toronto, 1969), p. 398.

[3] Op. cit., p. 92E.

[4] See Müller-Hillebrand, *Das Heer*, ii. 113.

[5] To reduce this difficulty, the Spanish and French formations were issued
with German equipment for the Russian campaign.

[6] See Dallin, pp. 515 ff., 533 ff.; Teske, pp. 11–12, 323–4.

[7] See Dallin, pp. 535 ff.; Reitlinger, pp. 309 ff. See also Wilfried Strik-Strikfeld,
*Against Stalin and Hitler*, trans. David Footman (London, 1970).

was raised under the command of General Vlassov showed what might have been achieved if such a force had been formed, backed by a positive political movement, in 1941 when the disillusionment with the Soviet regime provoked by the military defeats was at its height.

Thus, the German policies towards their allies and potential allies were filled with missed opportunities. In spite of the appearance of a great coalition, the Axis and its satellites did not possess a true coalition strategy and therefore failed to bring their full resources to bear upon their opponents. The lack of any central body for co-ordinating the efforts of all the members made the Axis somewhat less than the sum of its parts. The dispersion of effort in Finland, the disparagement of the satellite forces in Army Group 'South', the failure to involve Turkey and Japan in the war against Russia, all reflect the same arrogant over-confidence that marred German military strategy. Even in periods of success too much effort was diverted into the pursuit of individual aims, and co-operation rested too often upon deceit. These weaknesses not only contributed to the failure of German strategy in the East, but also involved Germany in the war that the Japanese decided to launch upon the United States. Thus Hitler led Germany into the very revival of the great coalition struggle of the First World War which he had always sought to avoid.

# CHAPTER VIII

# The Failure of the 'Barbarossa' Plan

## The Great Gamble

OPERATION 'Barbarossa' began on 22 June 1941 when 3,000,000 German soldiers advanced across the Soviet frontier.[1] The planning on which their fate depended was based upon a grand strategy which accepted the risks of a two-front war and yet failed to establish a well-co-ordinated coalition. It was a grand strategy accepted by Hitler because it seemed to lead to the achievement of his main goal, the establishment of a great eastern empire. Most of his military leaders accepted it because they too were lured by the vision of a great autarkic German state, the triumphant victor over Bolshevism and master of Europe. Those who had doubts suppressed them because they could offer no acceptable alternative to the problem of winning the war in the West, and because they were confident that the victory in Russia would be so swiftly won that the risks of a two-front war would be short-lived.

But the hope of a successful *Blitzkrieg* in the East rested upon the delusion of invincibility fostered by earlier victories and upon an underestimation of Soviet strength and of the terrain factors in Russia. The limited quantity of fuel oil and the lack of winter equipment turned the campaign into a gamble. German military strategy lacked flexibility. If the *Blitzkrieg* formula failed there was no alternative except an improvised defence. But this would convert the temporary risks of a two-front or multi-front war into a grand

---

[1] The General Staff 'Barbarossa' file contained the following Statistics for the Eastern Armies:

| | |
|---|---|
| Officers and men | 3,050,000 |
| Horses | 625,000 |
| Motor vehicles (including armoured cars) | 600,000 |
| Tanks | 3,350 |
| Artillery pieces | 7,184 |

U.S.N.A., Microfilm Guide No. 30, Serial T78–335, Frame 6291687. See also Charts III and IV and Appendix VI below.

strategic problem for which the Wehrmacht, with its inadequate air and naval forces, had no solution.

All operational plans are bound to contain uncertainties, but the 'Barbarossa' plan also contained serious omissions. It envisaged four phases: envelopment battles west of the Dvina and Dnieper; the capture of the Baltic States and Leningrad; the envelopment of the remaining Soviet forces around Moscow; and, finally, thrusts to the Volga and the Caucasus. In the development of this sequence, the crucial question was when and where to turn the mobile forces concentrated in the centre of the front toward the Baltic and Leningrad. The success of the second and subsequent phases depended upon the answer. Yet no studies or plans had been made by the OKH to provide it.[1]

As already suggested, the main reason for this omission seems to have been confidence that the 'Barbarossa' plan would prove unnecessary. Both Directive No. 21 and the OKH Deployment Directive stated that in the event of a surprisingly sudden collapse of enemy resistance in northern Russia, the Panzer forces of Army Group 'Centre' might abandon the turning movement towards Leningrad and drive directly towards Moscow.[2] The Army leaders were convinced that such a collapse would result from the first battles, and so they assumed that it would be unnecessary to turn strong elements of the mobile forces of Army Group 'Centre' northward to assist in the conquest of the Baltic States.[3]

Furthermore, the postponement of the opening of the campaign from May until the 22 June made it doubtful whether it was feasible to complete all four phases of the 'Barbarossa' plan before the winter. The movements of the mobile forces north through the swampy forests all the way to Leningrad and then south-east to the area beyond Moscow and thence to the Volga and Caucasus would

---

[1] Allmendinger, *Terrain Factors*, p. 8, attributes the Army's failure to plan the advance beyond the line Dnieper–Smolensk–Leningrad to 'Hitler's belief in the collapse of the Communist regime in the interior of the Soviet Union'. This view ignores the fact that it was Hitler who urged the planning of the later stages of the campaign.

[2] See Hubatsch, 99; *Halder KTB* ii. 465; Appendix II. See also *KTB OKW* i. 298, 3 Feb. 1941; Hitler stated that the quick capture of Leningrad and the Baltic States would be essential 'if the Russians succeeded in conducting a large-scale withdrawal to a new defensive line further east'. This seemed to imply that if they did not conduct such a withdrawal the operations in the Baltic States would be less important.

[3] See *IMT* xxvi. 873-PS, 400; Cf. *Halder KTB* iii. 39, 3 July 1941.

have taken more time than was available. However, no detailed time-tables or studies of the difficulties of these operations appear to have been made.[1] Thus on 22 June 1941 the German Army began to carry out an operational plan which had not been completely prepared and which its leaders had every intention of abandoning if they possibly could in order to revert to their own plan for a direct thrust on Moscow after the battles west of the Dvina and Dnieper Rivers.

What followed was a curious half-concealed struggle between the Army and Hitler, in the course of which the 'Barbarossa' plan was amended, reasserted by Hitler and finally abandoned in favour of a serious of hasty improvisations designed to achieve a decisive victory before winter. Since these shifts and changes of plan were responses to the situation at the front, German strategy in Russia during the crucial period between June and December 1941 can be understood only by examining some aspects of the operations and the influence upon the minds of the field commanders, staff officers, and Hitler.

In the very first days of the campaign Hitler continued to express anxiety that the conduct of operations would depart from the concept of controlled envelopments and deteriorate into an over-extended frontal advance. On the 24 June he told von Brauchitsch that the encirclement of Bialystok was not tight enough. Next day he repeated this concern in a written order, but Halder merely noted 'The same old song! This won't change our conduct of operations.'[2] However, Hitler's anxiety that the encircled Russians might break through the over-extended Panzer forces was not without foundation. The commander of Army Group 'Centre', who in May had accepted the idea of closing the encirclement at Minsk, now suddenly became convinced that he had been right in the first place and that Hoth's Panzer group should plunge on to block the Russian retreat on the Dvina between Vitebsk and Polozk.[3] At the headquarters of Panzer Group 3 von Bock's view was fully supported. Hoth was most

---

[1] See Walter Chales de Beaulieu, *Der Vorstoss der Panzergruppe 4 auf Leningrad—1941* (Neckargemünd, 1961). pp. 132–3. On 20 January 1941 Halder commented that the objective Leningrad–Smolensk–Kiev–Dnieper envisaged for the second phase of the campaign was 'so distant that it exceeded all normal standards based upon previous experience'. Besymenski, p. 335. See also pp. 321, 328, for comments on the disadvantages of the advance from Smolensk to Leningrad written by an unknown staff officer shortly before the start of the campaign.

[2] *Halder KTB* iii. 10, 24 June; p. 15, 25 June 1941.

[3] Bock, *Tagebuch*, 23 June 1941.

reluctant to turn to meet Guderian if this meant missing the opportunity of reaching the Dvina in full strength. Lieutenant-Colonel Kahlden, a liaison officer placed by the OKH on Hoth's staff, volunteered to fly back to von Brauchitsch in order to persuade him to allow Hoth to drive on north-eastwards.

Halder was understandably irritated at being caught between these attempts to revise the plan for the initial battle. While ignoring Hitler's wish to reduce the size of the envelopment, he also rejected the appeals from von Bock and Hoth on the grounds that committing Hoth further north would place an 'almost impassable strip of water and swamp' between the two Panzer groups and enable the Russians to attack each singly. This decision had a 'shattering' effect at the headquarters of Panzer Group 3 where orders had been prepared for the continuation of the drive to the Dvina. While conceding that it was a safer decision to close the ring at Minsk, Hoth was convinced that it involved a crucial loss of time.[1]

With advantage of hindsight it now seems that Hoth was right and that Halder, on 23 June, was still tending to overestimate the Russians' ability to conduct a withdrawal from the Bialystok salient. It is also possible that Halder was not eager to see Hoth lead the operations of Army Group 'Centre' in a direction which would well serve the purposes of Hitler's plan for an advance on Leningrad. It is significant that a few days later when Guderian decided to turn a considerable portion of his forces away from Minsk in a rush to seize a bridgehead over the Dnieper Halder did not intervene. Instead he commented that 'had he not done so it would have been a great mistake'. He also expressed the hope that the field commanders would 'do the right thing on their own initiative without specific orders, which we may not give . . .'.[2]

Meanwhile, the Luftwaffe, unaware of the Army's unauthorized departure from the 'Barbarossa' plan, began to make preparations for a concentration of its formations against Leningrad. When the Chief of Air Operations came to co-ordinate these measures with Halder, the latter petulantly described them as 'totally muddled conceptions'.[3] By the first week of July Halder was confident that:

Once we have crossed the Dnieper and the Dvina, it will be less a question

[1] See Hoth, pp. 61–3.
[2] *Halder KTB* iii. 25, 29 June 1941. However, next day some Russian forces broke out of the Bialystok pocket through Guderian's over-extended forces (ibid., p. 30, 30 June 1941).
[3] Ibid., p. 32, 1 July 1941.

of defeating the enemy's formations than of taking over his centre of production and so preventing him from setting up new armed forces out of the enormous potential of his industry and his unlimited reserves of manpower.[1]

He continued with the optimistic assertion that as soon as this stage was reached the Wehrmacht could return to the tasks of the war against Britain. These included operations against the Middle East from Libya, Turkey, and perhaps over the Caucasus into Persia.[2]

In the Führer Headquarters the success of the German operations had inspired similar optimism. On 16 July Hitler called together the *Ostminister*, Alfred Rosenberg, *Reichsmarschall* Göring, Field-Marshal Keitel, *Reichsminister* Lammers, and Martin Bormann. To this select group the Führer laid down the basic lines for Nazi policy in Russia. This he summed up as a matter of 'dividing up the huge cake into handy pieces, so that we can first dominate, second govern, and third exploit'.[3] But even with the Wehrmacht thrusting deep into Russia Hitler considered it essential to conceal his objectives from the world behind a veil of deceit. Echoing the phrases used by Dr. Goebbels in his secret speech on 5 April 1940, Hitler stressed that 'The main thing is that we ourselves know what we want . . . Under no circumstances should we make our path more difficult by superfluous statements.'[4] The occupation authorities should appear as 'bearers of freedom'. Their actions would be justified on grounds of order and security 'in the interests of the inhabitants'. But this should not prevent the implementation of all 'necessary measures' such as shooting or resettling elements of the population. The Crimea and parts of Galicia, for instance, were to be depopulated to make way for German settlers.

The deception was not confined to his victims. Even his allies were to be swindled. The new boundaries with Rumania would be drawn, not in the light of present good relations but in consideration of the uncertainty of future relations. Only the Germans would be allowed to bear arms, Hitler warned. 'The creation of a military power west of the Urals must never again become possible even if we have to wage war for a hundred years to prevent it.' This one aim must be pursued with a single-mindedness like that of the

[1] *Halder KTB* iii. 38–9, 3 July 1941.
[2] Ibid., p. 39, 3 July 1941. See also *KTB OKW* i. 1038; *Halder KTB* iii. 53, 8 July 1941.
[3] N.D. L–221; *KTB OKW* i. 89–90E; Jacobsen, *Grundzüge*, pp. 183–4.
[4] Cf. Jacobsen, *Grundzüge*, pp. 180–1. See also ch. i, p. 22, note 7 above.

British in India. 'The soldier must always guard the regime!', for
the newly won territories in the East are 'vital to us', he stressed.
Compared to them, the traditional overseas colonies would play a
subsidiary role. Nevertheless, for the moment it was necessary to
speak 'not of a new Reichs territory but of a task made necessary
by the war . . .'.

This was the argument he had used a year earlier to justify to his
military leaders his decision to attack Russia. Now it was to be
used to weaken not only the resistance of the Russian people to their
systematic destruction but also that of Germans who might criticize
Nazi policy on grounds of what Himmler called *sentimentale Gefühls-
duselei*, 'slushy sentimentality'. Before the invasion of Russia the
German military planners had been confused by the duplicity in
Hitler's strategic arguments. So, too, after the invasion, the occupation authorities were bewildered by the deceptions and contradic-
tions of Hitler's eastern policy. Since the war these same factors
have convinced some historians that Hitler was a feckless opportunist. But his statement on 16 July 1941 confirms the ruthless consistency with which Hitler pursued his aim of eastern conquest.

Furthermore, the need for caution which he stressed throughout
the speech was not merely the result of a lifelong habit of political
deceit. Hitler was well aware at this time of the military issues at
stake. On 4 July he had described the task of determining the
direction of future operations in the East as 'perhaps the most
difficult decision of this campaign'.[1] He recognized three choices.
First, he could adhere to the 'Barbarossa' plan as described in
Directive No. 21. Second, he could amend 'Barbarossa' so that part
of the Panzer forces of Army Group 'Centre' would turn south to
link up with von Rundstedt's army group for a deep thrust across
the Donets Basin towards the Caucasus. Third, he could keep the
concentration of Panzer forces in the centre and head for Moscow.[2]
At a conference on 8 July he announced his decision. The mobile
forces of Army Group 'Centre' would not need to turn towards
Leningrad, he said, instead they would conduct a further 'pincer
attack' to envelop the remaining Soviet forces astride the road to
Moscow. However, neither the capital nor Leningrad were to be
captured, Hitler stated, but surrounded and levelled with the ground
by the Luftwaffe so that their population need not be supported
throughout the winter. Meanwhile, the mobile forces should be used

[1] *KTB OKW* i. 1020.        [2] Bock, *Tagebuch*, 5 July 1941.

in 'expeditions' towards the Volga to destroy the remaining Soviet industrial centres.[1]

The amended plan which Hitler revealed at this conference was not unlike that developed by Marcks and Paulus between July and December 1940. Yet four days later, instead of welcoming this reversion to the Army plan, Halder told Brauchitsch,

> I am not all that wedded to the idea of hurrying the Panzer groups eastwards. I can well visualize the necessity for turning Hoth with considerable portions [of Panzer Group 3] to the north . . . Guderian [Panzer Group 2] must turn to the south . . . perhaps to drive down even as far as the Kiev area . . .[2]

This statement was remarkable in view of the bitter conflict between the OKH and Hitler which resulted from the latter's decision in August to carry out the very operations described here. But, as will be indicated later, by then Halder had reverted to the belief that only by the swift capture of Moscow could Germany achieve a decisive victory before the winter.

In the next few days the Army arrived at a compromise plan which was incorporated into Directive No. 33 on 19 July.[3] But four days later Hitler produced a supplement to that directive which was in fact a desperate bid to revive the 'Barbarossa' plan, including the capture of Leningrad, the envelopment of the Russians around Moscow, the drive to the Volga, and an operation to the Caucasus.[4]

In order to compensate for the failure of the OKH to include the operation for the capture of the Caucasian oilfields in their plans Hitler now gave it special stress and proposed the union of Panzer Groups 2 and 3 under the command of Field-Marshal von Kluge. This powerful armoured force, together with infantry and mountain divisions was to be called the 4th Panzer Army. It was to capture Kharkhov, thrust across the Don and into the Caucasus before the onset of winter. This involved a considerable shift of forces to the south-east. Nevertheless, Hitler had regarded a drive to Baku as an

---

[1] Plans for 'expeditions' beyond the Volga were also prepared later in July. See *KTB OKW* i. 1037: 'Allocation of Forces for Operations against the Industrial Areas of the Urals', dated 27 July 1941.

[2] *Halder KTB* iii. 69, 12 July 1941.

[3] Hubatsch, pp. 163–5.

[4] Ibid., pp. 166–8. Blau was in error when he stated (p. 52) that the supplement was the result of the Führer Conference on 23 July. Halder referred to the supplement at the conference. See op. cit., pp. 107–8, 23 July 1941. See also Warlimont, p. 183.

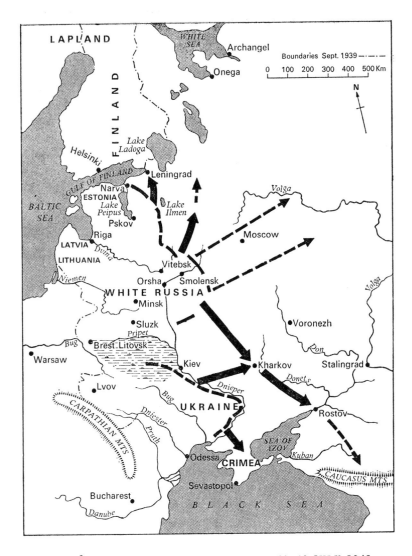

MAP 6. THE SUPPLEMENT TO DIRECTIVE 33, 23 JULY 1941

important part of the invasion of Russia ever since the conference of 31 July 1940.[1] Thus the Supplement to Directive No. 33 did not constitute a departure from the 'Barbarossa' plan but a forceful expression of the way Hitler had interpreted it from the start.

Confronted by the reality of the plan they had helped to make before the campaign, the Army leaders refused to recognize, or at least to accept, it. Now at last they openly proposed the adoption of their original plan, and the concentration of all available forces for a great offensive towards Moscow.[2] Earlier in July they had preferred this course because they believed that the Russians were defeated and there was therefore no need to carry out the circuitous manœuvres of the 'Barbarossa' plan.[3] Now they had even stronger reasons for wishing to adopt the swifter and simpler course of a direct thrust on Moscow. They were beginning to recognize the serious miscalculations of comparative strengths, terrain difficulties, logistics, and timing upon which their plans had been based.

### The Reappraisal of the Soviet Forces

The serious defeats and enormous losses initially suffered by the Soviet Armed Forces in 1941 seemed to confirm the German intelligence estimates of Russian weaknesses. Much of the Soviet equipment was inferior or obsolete. The leadership of the Russian forces at all levels was frequently inept. The training of the troops was inadequate for the requirements of flexible, mobile warfare.

The achievement of tactical surprise on the frontier and the failure of the Russians there to elude the German envelopment operations came as a great relief to the Germans.[4] The extent of the material successes was first indicated by the war in the air. At 13.30 hours on the first day of the attack, Halder recorded that the Luftwaffe had claimed the destruction of 800 Soviet aircraft. Its own losses totalled only ten aircraft.[5] On the second day the German claims reached 2,500 aircraft shot down or destroyed on airfields. When Göring refused to believe this score it was rechecked and found to be 200 to 300 short of the actual total.[6]

[1] See *Halder KTB* ii. 50, 31 July 1940.
[2] See *KTB OKW* i. 1031–4.
[3] See *Halder KTB* iii. 38–9, 3 July; p. 41, 4 July 1941.
[4] See ibid., pp. 3, 5, 22 June; p. 12, 25 June 1941.
[5] Ibid., p. 4.
[6] See Albert Kesselring, *Memoirs* (London, 1952), p. 98; Plocher, pp. 41–2.

On the ground the Panzer groups north of the Pripet Marsh had also achieved spectacular successes. On 26 June the right wing of Hoepner's Panzer Group 4 had reached the Dvina River and seized the bridges at Dvinsk.[1] Next day the two Panzer groups of Army Group 'Centre' met at Minsk thus closing the ring around the Russian forces in the Bialystok salient.[2] From there Guderian thrust eastward with part of his Panzer Group 2 in an endeavour to establish a bridgehead across the Dnieper.[3] Yet even amid the reports of the first victories came indications that the Russians were meeting the *Blitzkrieg* attacks with a determination seldom encountered in the earlier German campaigns. 'Reports from the front', Halder noted on 29 June, 'indicate that everywhere the Russians are fighting to the last man.'[3] General Ott, the Inspector-General of Infantry, reported with an air of professional vindication: 'Now, for once, our troops are compelled by the stubborn Russian resistance to fight according to their combat manuals. In Poland and the West they could take liberties, but here they cannot get away with it.'[3] By mid July, a note of deeper concern was creeping into Halder's notes. 'The Russian troops', he wrote on 15 July, 'are fighting as ever with wild ferocity and enormous human sacrifice.'[4]

The size of the Russian losses in ill-directed frontal counter-attacks[5] and the large numbers of prisoners taken in the envelopment battles encouraged German belief that Russian resistance must soon slacken.[6] On 5 July reports of unusually high rail movements from Briansk and Orel puzzled Halder and caused him to remark that 'the forces still available to the enemy can hardly permit the establishment of an operational reserve'.[7] The Foreign Armies East Branch of the General Staff estimated at this time that of the total of 164 Soviet divisions 89 had been entirely or partly destroyed, and only 9 of the 29 Soviet tank divisions were still fit for combat.[8] The danger that the Russians might raise new divisions was dismissed by Halder as unlikely on the grounds that officers, technical specialists, and artillery equipment would be lacking. But a month later he was forced

---

[1] See Manstein, *Lost Victories*, p. 183.
[2] See Hoth, p. 64; Guderian, p. 158.
[3] See *Halder KTB* iii. 25, 29 June 1941.
[4] Ibid., p. 79, 15 July 1941.
[5] Ibid., p. 47, 6 July 1941.
[6] See ibid., p. 56, 9 July 1941; Weber and Korbe, p. 30.
[7] Op. cit., p. 43, 5 July 1941.
[8] Ibid., p. 52, 8 July 1941.

to admit that the structure, economy, transportation system, and military capability of 'the Russian colossus' had been underestimated.

At the beginning of the war we reckoned with about 200 divisions. We have already counted 360. Admittedly, these divisions are not armed and equipped to our standards, and their tactical leadership is often inadequate. But they are there, and when a dozen of them are destroyed, then the Russians replace them with a dozen more.[1]

The size of the Soviet tank forces and the quality of its new tanks also came as an unpleasant surprise. The Germans had re-estimated Russian strength at 15,000 tanks,[2] but the total was probably nearer to 24,000, of which 1,475 were new T34 and KV tanks which had begun to come into service in April.[3] The armament and thickness of armour of these new types came as a shock to the Germans.[4] By the end of 1941 the Soviet armament industry was concentrated upon their production with a target figure of 22,000 to 25,000 for the year 1942.[5]

The Germans made a very similar underestimation both of the size of the Soviet Air Force and of the quality of its new equipment. Even on 1 July Halder admitted that the Luftwaffe had seriously underestimated the strength of the Soviet Air Force which 'evidently had far more than 8,000 aircraft'.[6] After a month of fighting the Luftwaffe claimed the staggering total of 7,564 destroyed. But of these a very large proportion were knocked out on the ground, which meant that the Russian losses in crews were not so severe.[7] The demands for air support for the ground troops forced the Luftwaffe to reduce the attacks on the Soviet Air Force before it had won complete air superiority. As a result the Russians gradually rebuilt their air formations from the current production of their aircraft industry in the Moscow, Voronezh, and Ural areas, which the Luftwaffe was unable to bomb effectively through lack of suitable aircraft.[8]

---

[1] *Halder KTB* iii. 170, 11 Aug. 1941.

[2] Ibid., p. 36, 2 July 1941.

[3] See R. E. Sherwood, *Roosevelt and Hopkins. An Intimate History* (New York, 1948), pp. 317 ff.; Ogorkiewicz, *The Soviet Army*, p. 300; Erickson, p. 567.

[4] See *Halder KTB* iii. 14, 25 June; p. 223, 12 Sept. 1941; Erickson, p. 616.

[5] Werth, p. 223.

[6] Op. cit., pp. 32–3, 1 July 1941.

[7] See Plocher, p. 42. The availability of air crews is described by Eremenko, p. 208.

[8] See Plocher, pp. 43–4.

## The Decline of German Strength

The size and fighting spirit of the Soviet forces and the quality of their new equipment, especially tanks and aircraft, confronted the Wehrmacht with unexpected difficulties. By the third week of July the combat strength of the Panzer and motorized divisions had fallen to about 60 per cent of normal in Army Group 'Centre'.[1] In some of the Panzer divisions of Army Group 'South' it was down to 40 per cent.[2] Early in July Halder calculated that by the end of the month only 431 tanks would be available from the OKH reserve and current production to replace those destroyed or broken down out of the original total of 3,350.[3] But to make matters worse, Hitler gave orders that new tanks should be kept in Germany for equipping fresh Panzer divisions for use in the offensives planned for 1942 in the Middle East.[4] Under pressure from the Army leaders, he agreed on 8 July to release seventy Mark III and fifteen Mark IV tanks, and all the captured Czech tanks available.[5] Later in the month Hitler insisted that Panzer divisions suffering heavy losses in Russia should be disbanded and their personnel and equipment used to reinforce the remainder.[6] However, on 4 August Guderian persuaded him to provide 350 new engines for Mark III tanks,[7] and with this meagre allocation the Panzer group commanders had to patch up their tank units for the far-reaching operations by which Russia was to be conquered. Not only the lack of tank replacements but also the shortage of vehicles, tyres, and fuel made it impossible to maintain the strength even of the inadequate mobile forces allocated to the Russian front.[8]

In view of their inferior strength, the German Panzer forces achieved remarkable victories. Their success was due to the superior tactics and leadership that resulted from their training and experience, especially in the use of radio communications for the co-ordination of supporting fire and in the tactical use of the ground. Thus they were frequently able to outmanœuvre and defeat even the Soviet

---

[1] *Halder KTB* iii. 90, 18 July 1941.
[2] Ibid., p. 97, 20 July 1941.
[3] Ibid., p. 34, 2 July 1941.
[4] Ibid., p. 39, 3 July; p. 53, 8 July 1941.
[5] Ibid., p. 54, 8 July 1941.
[6] Ibid., p. 109, 24 July; p. 115, 25 July 1941.
[7] See ibid., p. 152, 4 Aug. 1941. Guderian mentions only 300 new engines (p. 190).
[8] *Halder KTB* ii. 343, 3 Apr. 1941.

units equipped with KV and T34 tanks. Nevertheless, the new Russian tanks presented serious problems to the German infantry divisions because only the medium artillery and the heaviest anti-tank guns were capable of penetrating their armour.[1] Under these circumstances, the order forbidding the employment of anti-aircraft artillery against ground targets was frequently waived, and in the first three weeks of the campaign the II Flak Corps, for instance, destroyed 250 Russian tanks in addition to ninety-two aircraft.[2]

The use of anti-aircraft artillery in this manner was possible only in the first weeks of the campaign when the Soviet Air Force was still suffering from the effects of the initial blows inflicted by the Luftwaffe. In the opening days, German bombers flew from four to six missions daily, dive-bombers seven to eight, and fighters between five and nine sorties.[3] During the period 22 to 25 June the V Air Corps, one of five such formations allocated to the eastern front, flew 1,600 sorties against seventy-seven Russian airfields and destroyed 774 Russian aircraft on the ground and shot down a further 136.[4] After shifting the weight of its attacks to the support of the ground forces, it destroyed in one day, 1 July, forty tanks and 180 other vehicles.[5] But it was impossible to keep up this level of effort. By the end of July German losses totalled 774 aircraft destroyed and 510 damaged. Air crews were showing signs of exhaustion and maintenance problems further reduced the number of serviceable aircraft to only 1,045 in the whole theatre. As a result, when Hitler demanded 'terror attacks' on the city of Moscow, the Luftwaffe was unable to deliver raids of more than 100 sorties, and they usually consisted of harassing attacks of only thirty to forty sorties.[6]

The exhaustion, which by late July was reducing the *Blitzkrieg* impact of the air and mobile forces, was also having its effect on the infantry divisions. Though their strength still averaged about 80 per cent of normal establishment,[7] they were seriously fatigued by a month of intermittent, often severe, fighting and continuous marching on hot dusty roads. The general weariness influenced the morale of the senior commanders,[8] who were becoming increasingly aware

[1] *Halder KTB* iii. 42, 4 July 1941.                    [2] Plocher, p. 75.
[3] Ibid., p. 39.                                        [4] Ibid., p. 52.
[5] Ibid. See also *Europäische Beitrag, die deutsche Luftwaffe*, pp. 51, 58, 64.
[6] *Rise and Fall of the German Air Force*, p. 167.
[7] *Halder KTB* iii. 104, 23 July 1941.
[8] Ibid., p. 98, 20 July 1941.

that the dogged resistance of the Soviet troops even when surrounded was causing a constant drain in casualties, which by 31 July had reached 213,301 officers and men.[1] Furthermore, it had imposed repeated delays which were bound to affect the time-table of the campaign.

In the original operational plan developed at the end of 1940, General Paulus had allowed twenty days for the first phase of the campaign culminating in the attainment of the line Dnieper–Smolensk–Dvina. There would then be a pause of almost three weeks for recuperation, redeployment, and the establishment of new supply bases. The second phase of the campaign was to start on the fortieth day at the latest.[2] In fact, the first phase of the campaign was still not completed on the fortieth day, 31 July, and the troops had received no significant pause for rest. It was evident, therefore, that most of August would be required for the elimination of the Soviet forces enveloped near Smolensk and for recuperation and replenishment. This left six weeks at the most in which to complete major operations before the autumn rains began.

### The Logistical Situation, July 1941

It was only by prodigious efforts on the part of the supply organization that the momentum of the German advance had been sustained until mid July. The Quartermaster-General's field agencies were to have their supply districts organized by the middle of May, but by then only three-quarters of their work had been accomplished. Although the postponement of the attack on Russia until 22 June gave them time in which to complete most of their preparations, there were serious difficulties until the very eve of the attack. The needs of industry in Germany prevented the release of trucks for the heavy motor transport units until a week before the campaign. Their arrival in the supply districts coincided with the movement of the Panzer and motorized formations into their concentration areas. The resultant traffic was so congested that it had to be controlled from the air.

After the opening of operations it soon became clear that the estimates of the fuel needs of the mobile formations were far too low. On the appalling roads and difficult terrain all vehicles consumed almost twice the quantity of fuel expected. Furthermore, the larger

---

[1] *Halder KTB* iii. 151, 4 Aug. 1941.     [2] See Görlitz, *Paulus*, pp. 115, 120.

supply trucks, most of which lacked four-wheel drive, proved too heavy for the unsurfaced roads. When the roads were churned up the larger horse-drawn vehicles also had difficulty in moving at their accustomed rates, and the Germans soon found it better to replace them with small Russian *Panje* waggons pulled by light, agile Russian horses.

The prolongation of the initial frontier battles into deeper operations towards Vitebsk and Smolensk placed enormous strains on the road supply system. However, just as it seemed impossible to meet the mobile formations' fuel needs large stocks of gasoline and oil were captured at Baranovichi and Minsk. Another unexpected occurrence was the capture in June of sufficient Russian locomotives and rolling-stock to bring the railway line Warsaw–Molodetzno–Polozk into immediate use. Meanwhile, working round the clock, railway engineers converted the line Vilna–Molodetzno–Minsk–Borissov to the German gauge and had it in use early in July.

The addition of these rail lines enabled the Quartermaster-General's field agency to sustain the eastward advance of Army Group 'Centre' but the depth and direction of these operations necessitated a radical change in the logistical plan for the next phase of the campaign. The intention of setting up a forward supply base at Molodetzno was abandoned early in July and a new site was selected near Borissov. Nevertheless, due to lack of transport it was still impossible to move more than the Command Echelon and part of the Supply District forward. The rest of the Supply District remained near Warsaw. This split in the supply organization caused some confusion and on 20 July General Wagner sent a senior staff officer, Colonel Baensch, to Borissov to supervise a further reorganization. Ten days later the first pause in offensive operations took place on the central sector and 'Supply District Dnieper' was established.

The decision to establish Army Group 'Centre''s Supply District at Borissov rather that at Molodetzno which lay on the more northerly axis was in part the result of the abandonment of the plan to swing the mobile formations north-east towards Leningrad. The subsequent uncertainty about the alternative direction to be followed made long-term planning and stockpiling very difficult for the Quartermaster-General's staffs. Initial logistic planning had been based upon the optimistic assumption that after the attainment of the line Leningrad–Dnieper subsequent operations would be merely a matter of occupying the territory of the defeated enemy.[1] In the absence of any clear new priorities the logistic planners endeavoured to replenish all three army groups and to build up reserves in all supply districts. The assumption prevailing in the OKH that Moscow would be the next objective probably influenced the priorities set by the Quartermaster-General's Branch. But, as in the initial planning for 'Barbarossa', General Wagner appears to have been consulted neither on the choice of that objective nor on the feasibility of supplying operations to attain it. The selection was determined by the belief prevailing in the General Staff and the field commands that in a battle for Moscow the German Army would win the decisive victory which seemed to have eluded its grasp in the battles on the frontiers.

### The Abandonment of the 'Barbarossa' Plan

In the second half of July the German Army leaders recognized that, in spite of the enormous efforts of the Wehrmacht, the Soviet forces had only been weakened and not eliminated. No longer were they able to justify their clandestine revival of their own plan on the grounds that the collapse of the enemy made the second phase of the 'Barbarossa' plan unnecessary. Now they were forced openly to advocate a direct assault on Moscow for the new and disquieting reason that there was no longer time to carry out the 'Barbarossa' plan as restated in the Supplement to Directive No. 33 before the arrival of winter. If reduced to static warfare, they warned, the Wehrmacht would be confronted in the spring by new and re-equipped Soviet formations which would pin down even more German forces in the East. As a result, 'it would not be possible to achieve the military aim of the war against Russia, the swift overthrow of one opponent in a two-front war in order to tackle the other [Britain] with all forces'.[2] The choice of Moscow as the next major objective was justified by the expectation that the Russians would commit the major portion of their remaining forces to battle in its defence. Furthermore, the capture of the centre of the Soviet 'leadership apparatus' and communications system, in addition to the significant industries of the city, would split Russia in two parts and 'render

[1] Toppe, p. 43. See also Adolf Heusinger, *Der Ostfeldzug, 1941–1942. Ein operativer Überblick*, U.S. Army Historical Division MS. T6, p. 11.
[2] *KTB OKW* i. 1033.

unified resistance difficult'.[1] Behind these cautious words lay the hope that the fall of the capital would bring about a collapse of the Soviet Union.

At the OKW Jodl was converted by the Army's arguments and on 27 July he asked Hitler to reconsider his plans.[2] But Hitler was not impressed. He considered that the capture of the industries at Kharkhov and the Donets Basin and the cutting off of Soviet oil supplies would have far more significant effects on the Russian ability to resist than the capture of Moscow.[3] Furthermore, he adhered to the view, which he had expressed repeatedly since December 1940, that a great frontal offensive would not succeed in enveloping the Russians, but would merely push them back into the interior. The experiences of the Bialystok–Minsk and Smolensk operations served only to confirm this view. Therefore, apart from the bold thrust of the 4th Panzer Army to capture economic objectives, the Army should concentrate upon 'tactical battles of destruction over smaller areas in which the enemy would be pinned down and completely destroyed'.[4] When von Brauchitsch also expressed this view Halder sarcastically reported that the avoidance of all tactical risks and the methodical elimination of all gaps between the army groups could indeed be achieved and the end result would be positional warfare.[5] On 26 July, he bluntly informed Hitler that to resort to 'tactical envelopments' would be to play into the hands of the enemy. Such operations, he warned, would be too prolonged to permit the attainment of the objectives on the Volga.[6]

Shortly after this conference, General Paulus returned from a visit to Army Group 'North' and reported that the area between Lake Peipus and Lake Ilmen was, in the opinion of General Hoepner and his corps commanders, Reinhardt and von Manstein, quite unsuitable for mobile warfare.[7] This was hardly new information. General Marcks, in the study he compiled in July and August 1940,

---

[1] *KTB OKW* i. 1033.                                          [2] Ibid., pp. 1036–7.
[3] Ibid., pp. 1037, 1040.                                        [4] Ibid., p. 1035.
[5] *Halder KTB* iii. 121, 26 July 1941.          [6] Ibid., p. 123, 26 July 1941.
[7] Ibid., p. 124, 26 July 1941. See also Manstein, *Lost Victories*, p. 187. The supply trucks in this terrain averaged 7 m.p.h. Up to 50 per cent were off the road with broken springs. Delays of 24 hours due to traffic congestion were not unusual. The average day's journey for a truck was only 68 miles. In October conditions became worse. See U.S. Army Europe, Historical Division, Heidelberg, 'Transportation Problems of the 18th Army during the advance to Leningrad (22 June–3 September 1941)', typescript report submitted to the OKH by the Chief of Supply, 18th Army, February, 1942.

had rejected the idea of an advance on Moscow from the Baltic States because the swampy forests were 'most extensive between Leningrad and Moscow'.[1] Nevertheless, the 'Barbarossa' plan required that the Panzer groups north of the Pripet Marsh should traverse this forest region twice, first to reach Leningrad and then to drive east of Moscow. Awareness that the OKH should have openly questioned the feasibility of these movements when they were first proposed only added to Halder's irritation at Hitler's determination to go through with them now. Three days later he was still grumbling to the unfortunate von Brauchitsch—who, as usual, was the whipping boy for both Hitler and the General Staff—that the forthcoming operations would lead only to 'a dispersal of force and a standstill in the decisive direction towards Moscow'.[2]

Though Halder did not yet know it, Hitler had in fact decided 'in view of . . . the arrival of new, strong enemy forces on the front and flank of Army Group "Centre" . . .'.[3] to cancel the Supplement to Directive No. 33. On 30 July, news of this change, coupled with reports that Panzer Group 1 had at last broken through into the rear of the Russian forces west of the Lower Dnieper, provoked from Halder an uncharacteristic burst of enthusiasm:

This solution means that all thinking soldiers are now freed from the frightful spectre of the last few days during which it looked as if the entire eastern operation would be bogged down as a result of the Führer's stubbornness. At last a little light on the horizon once more.[4]

However, the contents of Directive No. 34,[5] which arrived next day, rather dampened Halder's spirits again. It called for operations to envelop Leningrad and link up with the Finns, and to destroy the Soviet forces at Kiev and in the Ukraine west of the Dnieper. Army Group 'Centre' including both its Panzer Groups, was to go over to the defensive for recuperation. But there was no indication how it would be employed when it was ready for further operations.[6]

Hitler's decision to divert forces from Army Group 'Centre' for the envelopment of Kiev was regarded by many of his generals as one of the major errors of his military strategy. Since the war, historians have echoed this criticism. But in view of the logistical situation

[1] Appendix I.
[2] Op. cit., p. 129, 28 July 1941.
[3] *KTB OKW* i. 1040.
[4] *Halder KTB* iii. 134, 30 July 1941.
[5] See Hubatsch, pp. 168–71.
[6] Op. cit., pp. 138–9, 1 Aug.; pp. 142–4, 2 Aug. 1941.

the envelopment of Kiev was probably the only major operation feasible in the late summer of 1941. This was not the main factor influencing Hitler's choice at the time. He allowed logistics to determine his strategy no more than he allowed economics to shape his policies. In his view the problems they both presented could be solved by the exertion of will and determination. But if Hitler paid scant attention to the logistical factors in choosing his next objective, his generals were no different. Though well aware of the difficulties already encountered in supplying the fighting troops, they failed to consult the Quartermaster-General's staff before urging Hitler to permit Army Group 'Centre' to push on towards Moscow. Yet at the very time when the argument over objectives was at its height and Hitler was visiting the front for personal conferences with von Bock and von Rundstedt, the Quartermaster-General's staff reached the conclusion that a simultaneous attack by three armies on the central sector was simply not feasible.[1] Army Group 'Centre' required twenty-five goods trains to meet its daily needs, but on some days in late July and early August as few as eight arrived, and the best day produced only fifteen. This rate of supply not only ruled out a triple-pronged thrust on Moscow in August, but it made it difficult to support simultaneous operations by both Panzer Groups 2 and 3. Hitler's idea of pushing the latter over the Valdai Hills towards Leningrad was especially questionable in the eyes of the Quartermaster-General's staff because this move cut across the main lines of road and rail communications.[1]

The supply of Guderian's Panzer Group 2 for a southward thrust towards Kiev was more feasible, especially when major supply points had been established at Roslavl and Gomel. Nevertheless, the Kiev operation still presented great difficulties because the road and rail situation in von Rundstedt's Army Group 'South' was no better than in that of von Bock. The high rate of vehicle fuel consumption was temporarily met by drawing from captured stocks at Lvov. But the shortage of trucks was even more serious than in Army Group 'Centre'. Worse road conditions and heavier losses through enemy ground and air action had reduced motor transport units to almost half strength by late July. In early August the daily average of ten trains was still not sufficient to bring deliveries up to the demand.

In the north the situation was quite different. Von Leeb's was the

[1] Toppe, p. 125.

smallest of the three army groups and thus required less supplies. Furthermore, the Baltic States had quite good road and rail facilities especially near the coast. By August a daily average of eighteen trains proved adequate. After the capture of Riga some supplies were delivered by sea and by river as far as Grodno.[1] Later the ships on Lake Peipus were also brought into use as the invaders advanced along its shores. The use of boats on the navigable rivers was conducted only on a 'minor scale' because it proved 'time-consuming and not worth the effort'.[2] Had the situation demanded it, greater use could have been made of sea and river supply lines. The Russian Baltic Fleet made no serious sorties. A plan was made in September to form a German Baltic Fleet comprising the battleship *Tirpitz*, the pocket battleship *Admiral Scheer*, two light cruisers, three destroyers, a flotilla of torpedo boats, and several minelayers. But the idea was abandoned because the Russians had only two battleships in the Baltic and both were put out of action by bombing attacks.[3]

As a result of these factors Army Group 'North' accumulated sufficient supplies 'to make up shortages in its area, sustain operations, and even aid the adjacent . . . [9th Army of Army Group "Centre"]'.[4] This seems to show that Hitler had been right all along in urging the early capture of the Baltic coast region as a major base. But the situation in the north was not as favourable for further operations as it might appear. The Baltic coast region proved easy to enter from the south-west, but the further north or east the invaders pushed the more unfavourable became the terrain. A large army group deployed in the narrow coastal sector served by good communications would probably have had the greatest difficulty in breaking out across the marshy forests that lay between Leningrad and Moscow.[5] The report submitted by Paulus after visiting Army Group 'North' had made it clear that the roads in such areas were worse even than those in White Russia and the Ukraine. Truck breakdowns and 'bog-downs' averaged 39 per cent in July. Some units had as much as 56 per cent of their vehicles out of action. Trailers had long been abandoned on all but the coast roads in von Leeb's army group.

---

[1] *Halder KTB* iii. 138, 1 Aug. 1941.          [2] Toppe, p. 145.
[3] Ruge, pp. 203–4.                              [4] Toppe, p. 138.
[5] When von Leeb suggested operations from his sector against the north flank of Timoshenko's forces west of Moscow his proposal was rejected by the OKH on the grounds that the terrain was unsuitable. *Halder KTB* iii. 211, 1 Sept. 1941.

In short, by August, the supply organizations of Army Groups 'Centre' and 'South' were able to support the shared burden of the Kiev operation but not more. At the same time Army Group 'North' was able to supply that part of the mobile forces of Army Group 'Centre' diverted to assist it, but its operational opportunities were severely limited. Nevertheless, the relief thus offered to Army Group 'Centre' until the autumn enabled von Bock to build up stocks for an offensive towards Moscow in October on a scale that was impossible in August.

It might be argued that the Moscow attack could have taken place in September if the essential Panzer groups had not been engaged elsewhere. But it is questionable whether the generals would have been content to remain on the defensive till then, ignoring the opportunities to clear the flanks at Kiev and the Valdai Hills. Even von Bock was forced to admit that 'the elimination of the enemy on both of the trailing wings of the army group is a prerequisite for all future operations'.[1] It should be noted that this admission was made on 5 August, the day after Hitler's visit to the headquarters of Army Group 'Centre' when von Bock and his Panzer group commanders had done their best to persuade the Führer to give priority to the thrust on Moscow.

While Hitler was away discussing future operations with his army group and army commanders Halder found time to turn to the problems of supply, including that of providing winter clothing and accommodation. The difficulties lay less in obtaining clothing and prefabricated buildings than in getting them to the troops on the inadequate transport system. It was clear that as long as all railway rolling-stock and road transport was committed to carry ammunition, fuel, and food for the current operations the delivery of winter clothing and equipment would be impossible. This problem could only be solved if Russia was defeated before winter set in.

The utter inadequacy of the German logistical plans and capability became obvious to every soldier of the *Ostfront* in the terrible winter of 1941–2. But the soldiers of the Soviet Army unfortunate enough to be captured were immediately aware of the inability of their captors to cater to their simplest needs. The German operational plan was based upon a series of envelopment battles and the capture of vast numbers of the enemy was anticipated. Yet there was no corresponding administrative plan for providing food, shelter, or the

[1] Bock, *Tagebuch*, 5 Aug. 1941.

minimum medical care for the millions of prisoners. As a result, of the five and a half million prisoners taken in the East, over three million died in conditions 'almost too nauseating to quote'.[1] In November 1941 Halder was told that 20,000 prisoners of war in a camp at Molodetzno were 'doomed to die', and in neighbouring camps 'considerable numbers' were dying daily of starvation. All this made a 'horrible impression' upon the Chief of the General Staff. But he could only note that 'relief appears impossible at the moment'.[2] Later he explained that the OKH had made the necessary preparations for the evacuation of prisoners, but Hitler's refusal to allow them to enter Germany had ruined the Army's plan and obliged its leaders to disclaim responsibility for the consequences.[3] The OKW agreed to share the problem but was no better equipped to solve it than the OKH.[4] Early in 1942 Rosenberg, the Minister for Occupied Eastern Territories, complained that out of 3,600,000 Russian prisoners only a few hundred thousand were fit for work. Göring was also concerned at the loss of labour, but this did not prevent him from making a joke about the cannibalism in the P.O.W. camps. It had gone a bit far, he told Ciano, 'they had even eaten a German sentry!'[5]

The scenes of human degradation in the camps were used by the Nazis to demonstrate that the Russian was indeed an *Untermensch*. In Russia even those military leaders who did not share the most extreme ideological views of the Nazis abandoned the usual standards of behaviour towards prisoners and the civil population. This was partly due to their fear of Communism and their contempt for the Slavs. But it was also due to the sense of desperation of men confronted by an enormous failure of their own making. Under these circumstances von Brauchitsch, whom Halder described as a man of 'deeply Christian thought', was able to issue an order authorizing the use of Russian prisoners of war to clear minefields in order to 'save German blood'.[6] The same desperation enabled staff officers, educated in a tradition which made much use of the word 'chivalry', to discuss whether their troops would have the nerve to shoot women

---

[1] See Eugene Davidson, *The Trial of the Germans* (New York, 1966), p. 568; Werth, pp. 211–12, 703–9; Clark, p. 128, Besymenski, p. 218.
[2] *Halder KTB* iii. 289, 14 Nov. 1941.
[3] Ibid., note 2.  [4] Werth, p. 708.
[5] Ibid., p. 703.
[6] U.S.N.A., Microfilm Guide 12, Serial 7, Roll 7, *OKH Heeresarchiv*, Telegram dated 29 Oct. 1941.

THE FAILURE OF THE

and children trying to get out of Leningrad where, it was hoped, 2,000,000 people would starve to death.[1] Confronted with these monstrous crimes even the individuals most deeply involved felt themselves to be helpless victims of circumstances beyond their control. The only solution seemed to be the attainment of victory, after which the 'abnormalities' would disappear.

Even in August there were doubts whether that victory could be won. On the 4th Halder discussed the early resumption of vigorous operations with the Commander-in-Chief. To achieve a decisive victory, he said, the Wehrmacht must either deprive the enemy of the industries of the Ukraine and the Caucasus, or defeat the last of the enemy armed forces. If the second choice was made, Halder warned von Brauchitsch, then the Army would have to be given full operational freedom, instead of being 'talked into' courses of action with which it disagreed. Operations in 1941 would end not on the Volga, but at Moscow. Further conquest of territory would depend on the situation. However, he stated, it was 'unlikely that we shall be in the Caucasus before winter sets in'.[2] With these words Halder dismissed the hope of achieving the aims of Directive No. 21 and so admitted that operation 'Barbarossa' had failed.

### The Responsibility for the Failure of 'Barbarossa'

On 22 August, in the course of the argument over the future conduct of operations in the East, Hitler wrote a study in which he blamed the Army leaders for the failure of the 'Barbarossa' plan.[3] His main criticism was that the OKH had lost control of the campaign by giving excessive freedom of action to the army group and army commanders who had been able to 'threaten or question the over-all concept [of the operation]'.[4] The Army, he stated, had wrongly assumed that, because the main weight of the German forces had been deployed in the centre of the front, the decisive objective also lay there. In fact, the real reason for this form of deployment was that from the centre the enemy front could best be rolled up to the north and south. There was no room for doubt that on reaching a certain line—he himself had placed it on the Dnieper[5]—Army Group 'Centre' should have halted in order to free its two Panzer groups

---

[1] *Bundesarchiv-Militärarchiv*, III W 59/2 *Chefsachen Barbarossa, Vortragsnotiz Leningrad, Abteilung L*, 21 Sept. 1941, 144.
[2] *Halder KTB* iii. 153, 4 Aug. 1941.
[3] *KTB OKW* i. 1063–8.       [4] Ibid., p. 1064,
[5] Ibid. Cf. *Halder KTB* ii. 319, 17 Mar. 1941.

to assist Army Groups 'North' and 'South'. Instead, Army Group 'Centre' had sought to extend its attack eastwards towards Moscow. As a result the Panzer forces had lost contact with the infantry following them, and valuable weeks had been lost in re-establishing co-ordination while many Russian formations had broken out of the envelopments to form a new front.

What made Hitler's study particularly invidious to the OKH was its unfavourable comparison between the manner in which *Reichsmarschall* Göring had concentrated the Luftwaffe for decisive operations 'in keeping with the requirements of the over-all campaign plan',[1] and the manner in which the Army had employed its mobile formations. By allowing the field commanders to follow their own selfish or independent wishes, Hitler asserted, the Army leaders had made it necessary to abandon 'proven fundamentals' of the plan because they were no longer compatible with the general situation.[2]

Hitler's criticisms were not without foundation. From the start of the campaign, Halder, von Bock, and Guderian had not directed operations in accordance with the intentions of the 'Barbarossa' plan, but had fixed their eyes upon Moscow as the main objective. Von Brauchitsch had failed to assert himself in the role of Commander-in-Chief, either by clearly proposing a reversion to the OKH plan or by ordering a strict adherence to the 'Barbarossa' plan.

In the opinion of General Hoth, the commander of the 3 Panzer Group, his forces could only have carried out a successful turning movement to the north in accordance with the 'Barbarossa' plan if it had been ordered between 1 and 10 July.[3] At that time the mobile forces could have moved through favourable terrain in the rear of the enemy pinned down by Army Group 'North' and thus achieved the envelopment victory in the north that Hitler had evidently envisaged. In its Deployment Directive, the OKH acknowledged its responsibility for deciding when they should turn.[4] But once Guderian crossed the Dnieper and drew half of Army Group 'Centre' after him, the chance of an early northward movement was lost. Later,

---

[1] Ibid., p. 1065. See also op. cit. iii. 193, 22 Aug. 1941. Halder suggested to von Brauchitsch that they should resign in protest. In fact, Hitler was right. General Schmid later described the inability of the OKL to obtain from the OKH the formulation of a clear plan 'for the subsequent operation to be conducted after the [initial] smashing of the Russian armed forces' (Plocher, p. 5). See also *Halder KTB* iii. 32, 1 July 1941.

[2] *KTB OKW* i. 1065.     [3] See Hoth, p. 105.

[4] See Appendix III, § 4(c).

after the battle of Smolensk, neither the terrain nor the state of the enemy presented a favourable opportunity for a decisive envelopment battle on the north flank of Army Group 'Centre'.

Nevertheless, Hitler must also share with his Army commanders some of the blame for the failure to order the turning operation at the decisive moment early in July. It may be said that it was not his responsibility to make an operational decision of this sort. But he was in fact meddling at this level, and had done so since the beginning of planning. Significantly, at this time Hitler himself had departed from the 'Barbarossa' plan. On 8 July he told von Brauchitsch and Halder that the 'ideal solution' would be to leave Army Group 'North' to fulfil its objective 'with its own forces'.[1] This optimism, he revealed later, resulted from the successful crossing of the Dvina achieved by von Leeb's forces which temporarily convinced him that Army Group 'North' needed no help.[2]

Hitler's criticism of the Army's failure to keep the mobile forces concentrated for operations in accordance with the spirit of the 'over-all campaign plan'[3] was hardly justified in view of his own indecision and inconsistency over the selection of objectives. The directives and supplements, orders and counter-orders about the direction to be taken by the mobile forces resulted in the splitting and dispersion of Panzer Groups 3 and 4 in the swamps and forests between Lake Peipus and Lake Ilmen, the diversion of part of Panzer Group 2 to the south in July, and strong disagreements with the OKH and Army Group 'South' over the objective of Panzer Group 1 in the first phase of the battle of Uman.[4]

Hitler's complaint that the OKH had allowed its plans to be directed by the tactical concepts and needs of the individual army groups and armies was partly due to his failure to understand the freedom to act upon their own responsibility traditionally granted to field commanders in the German Army. It was also due to Hitler's preference for placing men with weaker personalities in the top appointments of the Army. Von Brauchitsch had been made Commander-in-Chief over the heads of all of the three men who now served him as army group commanders. It seems likely that the command of the OKH would have been exercised rather more firmly by von Leeb, von Rundstedt, or von Bock. Similarly, the man

[1] See *Halder KTB* iii. 53, 8 July 1941; *KTB OKW* i. 1021.
[2] Ibid., p. 1041.                                    [3] Ibid., p. 1065.
[4] Op. cit., p. 58, 9 July; p. 61, 10 July 1941.

whom Ludwig Beck nominated as his successor as Chief of the General Staff, Erich von Manstein, would undoubtedly have kept a far tighter control over the planning and direction of the campaign than Halder.

The failure of Halder personally to conduct the planning for the eastern campaign has been remarked upon in an earlier chapter.[1] Later, he accepted Hitler's concepts and incorporated them into the written operational plan. But he evidently harboured mental reservations and even criticisms[2] which remained unexpressed, yet which were sufficient to mar his direction of the campaign. His ideas seemed to shift in such a way that they were always diametrically opposed to Hitler's. When Hitler wanted to swing von Bock's Panzer groups north, Halder's eyes were on the road to Moscow. When Hitler became optimistic and was inclined to retain the armour in the centre, Halder began to worry about the flanks, even as far as Kiev. By the time Hitler was drawn towards Kiev, Halder had reverted to his preference for Moscow. Whether these shifts were a subconscious expression of antipathy for Hitler or merely the result of an earlier recognition of the needs of the situation it is impossible to say. What is certain was that neither he nor von Brauchitsch shared a real understanding with Hitler of the over-all concept of the 'Barbarossa' plan. As a result, the unsettled points on which they differed became the cause of mutual recrimination over errors for which all three shared responsibility.

[1] See Chapter IV.
[2] See *Halder KTB* iii. 7, 23 June 1941. Halder's belated criticism of change of plan in Rumania was quite unjustified since he had accepted the change in March.

# CHAPTER IX

# The Improvised Plans

## *The Choices Open*

AFTER the abandonment of the 'Barbarossa' plan the German leaders were left with three alternatives: to seek a political solution by means of peace negotiations; to adopt a new military strategy based on an acceptance of a period of static warfare in the winter and a second campaign in 1942; to improvise a decisive victory in 1941. The first solution could have been combined with the second so that if the negotiations failed, operations could be resumed in 1942. But the German leaders were not sufficiently convinced that the situation warranted a negotiated peace. The victorious encirclement battles completed in early August at Smolensk and Uman seemed to pave the way for further successes even though the objectives of Operation 'Barbarossa' were now out of reach. The military leaders would probably have settled for the establishment of a series of buffer states between the Black Sea and the Baltic and the transfer of most of the Wehrmacht for the completion of the war in the West. But Hitler's war in Russia was not merely an indirect solution of the grand strategic problem of defeating Britain. His political, economic, and territorial aims were too extensive to be satisfied with a mere revival of the Treaty of Brest Litovsk. In 1938, confronted by unexpected difficulties, he had told his service chiefs that he would adapt circumstances to aims.[1] Now by the same token there was no question of modifying the aims of winning *Lebensraum* and of destroying Bolshevism.

Hitler had decided to fight a two-front war on the assumption that he could win a quick victory. With Britain, and perhaps later the United States, threatening the south and west of Europe, the Wehrmacht could not accept a protracted war in the East.[2] Furthermore, it lacked the equipment and training for such a war. Thus

[1] *IMT* xxxvii. 079–L, 548.
[2] See *KTB OKW* i. 1033. Cf. Bock, *Tagebuch*, 30 Mar. 1941.

the idea of deliberately adopting a military strategy based on *two* campaigning seasons was barely considered until it was too late.[1]

Hitler had from the start accepted the idea that about one-third of the Wehrmacht in the East would have to fight on against Soviet resistance in the winter and if necessary for years after the completion of the campaign of 1941.[2] On 11 June 1941 he had issued Directive No. 32, 'Preparations for the Period after Barbarossa', which estimated that a force of sixty divisions and one air fleet would be needed in Russia in the winter of 1941–2.[3] In July he told his political leaders that the creation of a Soviet military force west of the Urals must be prevented 'even if we have to wage war for a hundred years in order to achieve this'.[4] Nevertheless, neither Hitler nor his military leaders had envisaged that the further operations in the East would be on the scale of a full campaign. They would be 'expeditions' by motorized columns and perhaps later some sorties into the Ural Mountains not unlike those of the Indian Army into the Afghan mountain passes.[5] However, a change of attitude was apparent in the OKW memorandum issued with Hitler's approval on 13 September 1941, which considered the situation confronting Germany 'if . . . the campaign in the East in 1941 failed to achieve the complete destruction of the Soviet powers of resistance'. Although it was careful to state that this was a situation 'with which the Supreme Command had presumably always reckoned', there was an implication that something more might be required in 1942 than mere mopping-up expeditions.[6] However, no plans were developed for calling a timely

---

[1] See Liddell Hart, *On the Other Side* . . ., pp. 284–5. See also U.S. Army Europe, Historical Division, Heidelberg, 'Construction of a Strategic Defence Line in the East proposed by General of Infantry Olbricht, Chief of the General Army Office, January–February 1942', typescript.

[2] See above, p. 117–18.                                    [3] Hubatsch, p. 152.

[4] *KTB OKW*, p. 90E. Cf. *Hitler's Secret Conversations*, p. 62, 17–18 Sept. 1941.

[5] *KTB OKW*, p. 1037; *Hitler's Secret Conversations*, p. 60, 17–18 Sept. 1941.

[6] *Halder KTB* iii. 226, 13 Sept. 1941. The possibility of an extension of the campaign into 1942 was voiced in a document entitled 'The Planning of the Offensive Operation' found by the Russians in a file with the Marcks Plan and the Lossberg Study after the war. It appears to have been written before the campaign began by the Military Historical Division of the OKW or the Historical Section (OQuV) of the General Staff. It suggests the possibility that the Russians might withdraw into the interior and evade destruction in the initial battles. There would be little hope of destroying the Russian Army before the onset of winter. This would create a critical situation, the document predicted, because 'the campaign against Russia must be decided before the entry of the United States into the war which was expected in 1942'. See Besymenski, pp. 314–15.

halt to operations in 1941 in order to take up suitable defensive positions until the next summer.

There remained the third choice, a resumption of *Blitzkrieg* operations to seek a decisive victory before winter. This would be an improvisation because the forces were still deployed for the un-attainable 'Barbarossa' plan. It would also be a gamble since success was not certain and failure could mean the loss of the war. Above all it required a fresh analysis of the situation and a clear expression of operational aims which were attainable with the force and time available.[1] However, General Halder had no confidence in the ability of von Brauchitsch to demand such aims from Hitler. He was, Halder had noted earlier, dominated by his anxiety not to reveal any opinions which contradicted those of the Führer.[2] As a result, on 7 August, the Chief of the General Staff took the unusual step of discussing the selection of new operational objectives with his rival on the OKW, General Jodl.[3]

Halder's first question was 'Do we want to defeat the enemy forces or go after economic objectives (Ukraine, Caucasus)?' Jodl replied that the 'Führer thinks we can do both at the same time'.[4] However, Halder was not convinced that this was entirely possible since he considered that a major defeat of the Soviet forces could only be achieved by concentrating German forces for an operation with a 'far-reaching, decisive objective',[4] namely Moscow. Thus Leningrad would have to be reached with the forces already avail-able in Army Group 'North'. Similarly, Army Group 'South' would have to take advantage of its recent victory at Uman to seize the Ukraine and eliminate the Korosten bastion, north-west of Kiev, with its own forces. Although this meant postponing the Caucasus operation, it was, Halder said, not a question of Moscow *or* the Ukraine, but of Moscow *and* the Ukraine; otherwise, the source of enemy strength would not be conquered before the autumn. Finally, Halder urged Jodl to impress upon Hitler the need to concentrate all forces for the operation against Moscow and to 'play down' the importance of the Russian forces near Kiev.[5]

Although Jodl supported the OKH proposal with a situation report recommending a concerted attack on Moscow for the end of August,[6]

[1] See *Halder KTB* iii. 153, 4 Aug.; p. 155, 5 Aug. 1941.
[2] Ibid., p. 136, 31 July 1941.
[3] See ibid., p. 159, 7 Aug. 1941; Warlimont, p. 186.          [4] Ibid.
[5] Ibid., p. 160, 7 Aug. 1941.
[6] *KTB OKW* i. 1044.

Hitler refused to give priority to such an operation. He attempted at
first to adhere to some of the operational objectives set for Operation
'Barbarossa', Leningrad, then the Donets Basin, and finally Moscow.[1]
His desire to conduct enveloping operations on the flanks of the army
groups led him into the concept of a great envelopment battle around
Kiev.

The arguments between Hitler and the Army leaders over the
order of priority between Kiev and Moscow were a more open
repetition of their disagreements over Leningrad and Moscow. Their
exchanges of views have been described elsewhere and need not be
detailed here. Hitler's view was clearly expressed in the same
strategic study dated 22 August in which he criticized the Army
leaders' handling of the 'Barbarossa' plan.[2] Although prepared to
carry out a post-mortem of this plan, Hitler refused to believe that
it was quite dead. He sought to adhere to the general sequence of
operations it contained but limited the range of its aims since the
line Archangel–Volga–Caucasus was no longer attainable. The first
aim continued to be the destruction of the Soviet armed forces. The
second was the prevention of rearmament by depriving the Russians
of their major sources of raw material and industrial centres. In
addition, the protection of the supplies of Swedish iron ore and
Rumanian oil also had to be ensured by establishing German control
over the Baltic and over the Crimea and South Ukraine. Compared
with these aims the capture of Moscow was less important. 'However,' Hitler reminded his Army leaders, 'this is no new concept, but
one that I have made clear and plain from the beginning of the
campaign.'[3]

The essential aim of clearing the Baltic coast could be achieved,
Hitler insisted, only with the help of forces from Army Group
'Centre'. Even more important was the need to send forces southward to envelop the Russian salient at Kiev. Hitler was convinced
that the opportunity presented here would be far more decisive than
the capture of Moscow. For at Kiev the Wehrmacht could destroy
large Soviet formations and at the same time open the way for the
capture of the economic objectives in the Ukraine and Donets Basin
and the elimination of the Soviet air threat to the Rumanian oilfields.

---

[1] Ibid., p. 1043.
[2] Ibid., pp. 1063–8. See also Guderian, pp. 189 ff.; Clark, pp. 96 ff.; Carell,
pp. 80 ff.; Philippi–Heim, pp. 70–5; Blau, pp. 61–70; Seaton, pp. 141 ff.
[3] Ibid., p. 1064.

Furthermore, Hitler pointed out, the arguments that the Kiev operation would be time-consuming and perhaps cause the Moscow offensive to open too late, or that it would impose too great a strain upon the mechanized forces, were not acceptable. Indeed, the elimination of the Russian threat to the south flank of Army Group 'Centre' would make its subsequent task of attacking Moscow easier, not more difficult.[1] While on this subject, Hitler took the opportunity to stress yet again that when the Moscow offensive was launched, after the Kiev operation, it should have the task, 'not of storming forward into endless space', but of destroying the enemy forces in tight envelopments.[1]

The victory at Kiev which resulted from Hitler's decision to override the OKH has been described as 'the greatest cauldron battle in history'.[2] According to the OKW report, the operation yielded 665,000 prisoners, 884 tanks, and 3,718 guns captured or destroyed.[3] Meanwhile, the operations of Army Group 'North' near Lake Ilmen led to the capture of a further 53,000 prisoners and the capture or destruction of 320 tanks and 695 guns.[4] The elimination of the Russian army group at Kiev enabled von Rundstedt to occupy the Ukraine, most of the Crimea and the Donets Basin. In the course of these operations, Army Group 'South' took a further 400,000 prisoners, and captured or destroyed 753 tanks and 2,800 guns.[4] Early in October Army Group 'Centre' launched Operation 'Typhoon', the offensive towards Moscow. At the double-envelopment battle of Viasma and Briansk von Bock's forces took 663,000 prisoners, and captured or destroyed 1,242 tanks and 5,452 guns.[4] But in spite of these enormous losses the Russians continued to resist the German advance. As the autumn rains turned the roads to quagmires, the German armies bogged down. They made sporadic attempts to resume their attacks when the ground froze hard, but Russian counter-attacks flung them back from Rostov in the south, Tikhvin in the north, and Moscow in the centre.

In spite of the claims to the contrary,[5] it seems very doubtful

---

[1] *KTB OKW* i. 1067.

[2] See Werner Haupt, *Kiev, die größte Kesselschlacht der Geschichte* (Bad Neuheim, 1964).

[3] Ibid., p. 180.

[4] See Weber and Korbe, p. 30.

[5] See especially Carl Wagener, *Moskau, 1941. Der Angriff auf die russische Hauptstadt* (Bad Neuheim), pp. 199 ff. Wagener presents a hypothetical construction of what might have happened if the OKH had had its way.

whether the OKH plan for a direct advance on Moscow could have achieved a more decisive result. The Russians were expecting such an attack and had prepared their defence to meet it.[1] The frontal attack proposed by the OKH towards Moscow would have had little chance of eliminating the Soviet forces on its flanks. At most it could have pushed them back. The envelopment of the enemy between Viasma and Briansk with two Panzer groups would probably not have achieved a greater success than that conducted by three Panzer groups in October. Thus even if the Germans had reached Moscow they could hardly have inflicted losses upon the enemy as great as those that resulted from the battle of Kiev and the operations that followed it. After reaching the city, their forces, extended in a great salient would not have been favourably deployed to deal with the enemy threats to its base and flanks south of Lake Ilmen and north of Kiev. Subsequent German attempts at envelopment operations from this salient would have lacked the 'tightness' that Hitler rightly insisted was essential to their success. The economic conquests in the Moscow area would not have exceeded those actually gained in the south. The Russian railway network would have lost its most important junction, but contact between the eastern industrial areas and the front could still have been maintained on the lines north and south of the city. Thus the capture of Moscow could have been decisive only if it had resulted in a psychological or political collapse. But in view of the terrible losses of human life and resources stoically borne by the Russian people in 1941 and in the following year, it does not seem likely that such a collapse would have resulted from the loss of the capital to a second *Grande Armée*.

Some have argued that the early capture of Moscow would have given the German Army a better chance to prepare winter positions and to complete its victory in the following year.[2] This view ignores the fact that the OKH plan assumed a continuation of operations after the fall of the city, to capture Leningrad, the Ukraine, the Donets Basin, and if possible the route to the Caucasus. Furthermore, Hitler had ordered that Moscow and Leningrad should be razed to the ground. They would therefore have offered few advantages to the German winter defence. Even if these orders had been abandoned and the great salient with Moscow at its apex had been defended, it might only have offered the Russian winter offensive a more specific

[1] See Eremenko, pp. 202–4, 216.
[2] See op. cit., p. 206.

objective to envelop and destroy as occurred at Stalingrad in the following year.

It is pointless to indulge in speculations of this nature except to suggest that even if Moscow had been placed first instead of last in Hitler's list of priorities the Germans would still have fallen short of complete victory. The tasks that they had set themselves in Russia exceeded their resources. On 7 August the Quartermaster-General reminded Halder that after 1 October fuel oil and gasoline would be in such short supply that a major military operation would no longer be possible. For the offensive towards Moscow the Germans scraped together last available supplies. By 27 November General Wagner reported 'We have reached the end of our resources in personnel and material.'[1] The *Blitzkrieg* economy was simply not equal to the task imposed upon it. The arguments of the Army leaders and most of the field commanders had served only to waste valuable time in discussion. With the means and time available they were unable to destroy sufficient Russian formations or capture enough Russian territory, industrial plants or raw material to deprive the Soviet Union of its power to offer further resistance. The many flaws in their planning of the campaign in the East had tended both to conceal and to compound the difficulties that lay before them. The mis-assessment of the comparative strengths, the miscalculation of the time required to conduct the envelopment battles, the failure to base operations on the logistical needs of the mobile forces, the half-concealed lack of accord, and inconsistency over the objectives and lines of operation, all these lay at the root of the failure of the *Blitzkrieg* in Russia.

The failure of the *Blitzkrieg* had serious repercussions on the command structure of the German Army in the East. On 10 November Field-Marshal von Brauchitsch suffered a heart attack.[2] At the end of November Field-Marshal von Rundstedt, whose health had also begun to deteriorate,[3] bluntly refused to obey Hitler's order to hold the over-extended positions at Rostov and was replaced as commander of Army Group 'South' by von Reichenau. At the same time von Brauchitsch began to show signs of further physical collapse, and on 5 December he told Halder that he had decided to resign.[4]

---

[1] *KTB OKW*, p. 99E.
[2] *Halder KTB* iii. 285, 10 Nov. 1941.
[3] Ibid., p. 280, 4 Nov. 1941.
[4] Ibid., pp. 322, 327, 328, 1, 4, and 5 Dec. 1941.

But Hitler who had so often refused his advice now rejected his request to be released from his post. The Commander-in-Chief then flew to the front where Army Group 'Centre' was suffering heavy blows from Marshal Zhukhov's great counter-offensive before Moscow. Meanwhile, Hitler had decided to honour a verbal assurance given to the Japanese Foreign Minister in April, and on 11 December he declared war on the United States. But von Brauchitsch was so overwhelmed by the situation in Russia that the true extent of this additional folly, which brought the world's greatest industrial power into the war against Germany, was probably lost to him. He returned from the front on 15 December very depressed and unable to see any way out of the crisis. Two days later he again requested his release and this time it was accepted, though it was not announced until 19 December. Von Brauchitsch became the main scapegoat for the failure of Operation 'Barbarossa'. Three months later Goebbels noted in his diary that

By his constant interference and consistent disobedience he had completely spoiled the entire plan for the eastern campaign as it was designed with crystal clarity by the Führer . . . The Führer had no intention whatever of going to Moscow. He wanted to cut off the Caucasus and thereby strike the Soviet system at its most vulnerable point. But Brauchitsch and his general staff knew better.[1]

This statement distorted the facts. Hitler's plan did not rule out an attack on Moscow altogether, nor did it give priority to cutting off the Caucasus. Furthermore, Goebbels's assertion that 'the Führer's plan was bound to lead to victory' was without any justification, for whichever direction the campaign had taken it would have suffered from the same material shortages. Nevertheless, there was an element of truth in the criticism of von Brauchitsch. Halder was well aware of this. The Field-Marshal had become a growing embarrassment and his Chief of Staff was probably relieved to see him go. This partly explains Halder's decision to remain in his post even though Hitler announced himself as the successor to von Brauchitsch in 'the little job of directing operations'.

The strain of events also proved too much for the health of Generals Strauss and von Weichs, Commanders of the 9th and 2nd Armies. In the north Field-Marshal Ritter von Leeb resigned from his command, and in Army Group 'South' General von Stülpnagel gave up

[1] Joseph Goebbels, *Diaries*, ed. Louis P. Lochner (London, 1948) p. 136, 20 Mar. 1942.

his command of the 17th Army. In February Field-Marshal von Reichenau died of a heart attack.

Meanwhile, Field-Marshal von Bock had also been taken ill and forced into retirement. His replacement as Commander of Army Group 'Centre', Field-Marshal von Kluge, displayed his zeal in carrying out Hitler's commands to the letter by recommending the dismissal of two of his Panzer group commanders, Hoepner and Guderian. The latter ended his farewell message to the troops who had served him so well with the words 'My thoughts will be with you in your hard struggle.' It was a struggle that they were to endure for another four ghastly years. It culminated in the destruction of the *Großdeutschland* and the dreams of *Lebensraum*, which for a fleeting moment in history had almost come within their grasp.

# CHAPTER X

# Conclusions

THE purpose of this study has been to seek in the German planning for the campaign in the East the answers to four questions: Did Hitler follow a great preconceived plan? Why did he decide to invade Russia before ending the war against Britain? What role did the German military leaders play in the planning for the invasion of Russia? Why did the *Blitzkrieg* fail in Russia? The conclusions are, therefore, presented in the form of answers to these questions and to the further question of Hitler's responsibility for the failure of the campaign which arises from them.

## *Did Hitler Follow a Great Plan?*

What light does the German planning for the invasion of Russia cast upon the question of whether Hitler followed a great preconceived plan? At first the absence of any planning for such an operation until after the defeat of France would seem to suggest that Hitler was an opportunist and that the policies expressed in *Mein Kampf* and in his public speeches had little relation to his actions. This, however, is a false impression. Hitler did indeed follow a preconceived plan. Throughout his career, though he used the flexible methods of an opportunist, he adhered rigidly to the aim of winning a great eastern empire.

His consistency of purpose was partly veiled by his failure to create a staff responsible for grand-strategic planning. Thus there is a lack of documentary evidence of the grand-strategic connection between Nazi foreign policy and the military operations of the Second World War. German grand strategy must be traced less in the files of the military staffs than in the sweeping statements and vague hints of Hitler's secret speeches and casual conversations. But even though this evidence sometimes appears slight, especially in the eyes of soldiers or archivists, it is substantial enough to belie the assertion that Hitler had no grand strategy.

The Army leaders by refusing until July 1940 to accept Hitler's

ideas as a valid grand-strategic basis for their planning, neither
served Hitler loyally nor opposed him effectively. Since the war it
has been in their interest to minimize their responsibility for aggression and for the strategic errors that contributed to the German
defeat by stressing that there was no over-all 'war plan'. They have
supported General Halder's assertion that Hitler produced 'a chaos
of improvisation which has already become next to impossible for
the historian to unravel'.[1] This, however, was an expression of hope
rather than fact. For a close examination of the secret speeches,
decisions, and directives that Hitler gave to his military leaders
confirms that they were consistently related to the *Lebensraumpolitik*
described in his early writings and public speeches.

Events did not always turn out the way Hitler hoped. So, in order
to continue the relentless pursuit of his aims, he was forced to adapt
his methods to the new circumstances. In 1938 he wanted to invade
Czechoslovakia but Britain and France forced him to negotiate. He
made a drastic departure from his usual line of policy when the
refusal of Poland to become a satellite forced him to isolate her by
means of a pact with Russia in 1939. The declaration of war by the
Western Powers forced him to improvise an attack on France earlier
than he would have chosen. But these actions were quite consistent
with the internal and external policies and grand strategy he had
followed since 1933, which were intended to create in Germany and
Europe a favourable situation for a war of conquest against Russia.

Hitler's grand strategy was based upon his determination to win
his eastern empire without a repetition of the long coalition struggle
that had led to the German defeat in the First World War. He sought
to attain his aims by a series of political coups and limited wars.
This demanded a readiness to strike when internal weaknesses or
divisions between potential enemies presented the opportunity. Once
the process of conquering territory occupied by non-Germans had
begun in Czechoslovakia in 1939, Hitler was driven by a desperate
determination to achieve his aims before a great coalition of enemies
united to oppose him. This explains the urgency behind his decisions
to destroy Poland and to strike in the West. For the same reason he
felt compelled to invade Russia even though the war in the West
was not completely won and finally to gamble on a *Blitzkrieg* victory
even when the aims of Operation 'Barbarossa' eluded his grasp.

He could at any time have modified his aims. After 1938 he had

[1] Halder, *Hitler as Warlord*, p. 11.

CONCLUSIONS 229

surpassed Bismarck by unifying Greater Germany including the German-speaking territories of Austria. In the winter of 1939 he could have made genuine attempts to use the territories he had won in central and eastern Europe as bargaining counters with which to negotiate a favourable peace. In the summer of 1940 great opportunities for conquest lay open to him in the south. In August or September 1941, he could have sought to impose a second Treaty of Brest Litovsk upon the Soviet Union. But on each occasion he chose a riskier course because it led him nearer to his inflexible goal, the conquest of a great empire in the East.

### Why did Hitler Invade Russia Before Defeating Britain?

Hitler decided to attack Russia before ending the war against Britain because he was determined to complete the conquest of *Lebensraum* in the East as soon as possible. His aim in the West in 1940 had been to inflict upon France and Britain a defeat which would prevent them from interfering with German expansion into Russia. By June he thought he had succeeded and he began to make long-term economic preparations for the eastern campaign. But he soon began to realize that the British would require another demonstration of German power to make them give up. This, however, did not need to interfere with the plans for the East, especially since, in the last week of July, Hitler decided that the Russian campaign would require a full summer season and would, therefore, have to be delayed until 1941. This left only enough time to deliver a swift, direct attack on Britain.

Some historians have expressed surprise at Hitler's preference for a quick solution to the problem of Britain because there seemed 'to be no compelling reason for its adoption'.[1] Telford Taylor has questioned whether the air attack on Britain and Operation 'Sea Lion' were 'secondary operations—speculative ventures in the nature of time-killers, pending the maturation of eastern plans. . . .'[2] The evidence certainly supports an affirmative answer.

Throughout his political career Hitler had pursued the aim of eastward expansion. It is hardly likely that at the moment of his triumph in France he lost sight of his ultimate objective. The reason why there was insufficient time for a war of attrition against Britain was because the great task in the East, the attack on Russia, was on no account

[1] Wheatley, p. 141.　　　[2] Taylor, *Breaking Wave*, p. 75.

to be delayed by these interim activities in the West. The Soviet forces were undergoing modernization, and, furthermore, Hitler suspected that by 1942, the United States might be prepared to enter the war.

He decided, therefore, to launch an air offensive, gambling that it might cause a collapse of the British will to resist great enough to permit a Channel-crossing. The collapse would have to be considerable, because he envisaged Operation 'Sea Lion', not so much as a seaborne assault as the transportation of an army to occupy a defeated nation. In contrast to his attitude towards the other operations of the war, Hitler avoided active participation in the preparation and conduct of the aerial assault on Britain as if he did not wish to be directly connected with it. On 31 July 1940, before the battle of Britain had begun, he ordered an increase in the Army to 180 divisions in order to have 60 with which to garrison the West and 120 for the attack on Russia. This shows that he was not optimistic about the attack on Britain and began to prepare for a two-front war even before the Luftwaffe had made its bid for air supremacy over England.

It seems probable that Hitler expected the idea of a two-front war to provoke from his military leaders more of the tiresome and pessimistic criticism of the type that he had heard during the planning of operations against Czechoslovakia and France. He therefore presented his decision to attack Russia not as the fulfilment of his dream of conquering *Lebensraum*, which might be considered irresponsible with a war still unfinished in the West, but as a grand-strategic means of defeating Britain by depriving her of her last hope of finding a continental ally. If this had been the true reason, the prior defeat of Britain would have removed the necessity for an attack on Russia. But since the territorial aims he outlined in the East were clearly those of the *Lebensraumpolitik* which was the very cornerstone of Nazism it is difficult to believe that Hitler really would have abandoned the plans for an eastern campaign in the event of a British collapse. Later, he even admitted that he feared that such a collapse would make it difficult to arouse the German people against Russia, and 'therefore Russia must be attacked first.' This statement contained, however, an element of rationalization, for it was made in February 1941 when Hitler knew that there was no longer any hope of defeating Britain before the attack on Russia. While there was still time he continued to attempt the prior defeat of Britain.

By the end of September 1940 it was clear that the attacks of the Luftwaffe had failed. While confirming his intention of attacking Russia in the spring of 1941, Hitler turned to the possibility of defeating Britain by means of a number of quick, decisive blows in the Mediterranean theatre. Like the Battle of Britain, these operations did not constitute an alternative to the invasion of Russia, but were a further set of stop-gap improvisations, which Hitler regarded with some scepticism from the start. By the end of November 1940, the unco-operative attitudes of Franco, Pétain, and Mussolini, and the refusal of the Soviet Union to commit herself to a parallel attack on the British east of the Persian Gulf, convinced Hitler that he could not risk a major effort in the Middle East until he had settled with Russia.

The increased hostility of Russia towards Germany was frequently cited by Hitler as a further justification for the decision to attack Russia. But the conflicts over Finland and Rumania in the second half of 1940 were mainly the outcome of Hitler's decision to attack Russia in 1941 and the changes of policy that attended it. Thus, the deterioration of Russo-German relations was far more the result than the cause of Hitler's decision to strike in the East.

*What was the Role of the German Military Leaders in the Planning of the Russian Campaign?*

In the course of the preparations for the invasion of Russia the German military leaders conducted their usual tasks of operational and administrative planning. In addition, the OKW carried out detailed studies and plans for the economic exploitation of the Soviet Union and the OKH prepared instructions for the participation of the Army in the ideological warfare against Bolshevism. In contrast to their attitude during the planning for the campaign in the West, the Army leaders carried out their role willingly and with an optimism so great that it led to serious errors of judgement and grave flaws in the operational plan.

The attitude of most of the German military leaders towards the invasion of Russia differed little from Hitler's concept. Broadly speaking, they were anti-Bolshevist and anti-Slav. Like Hitler they saw in the establishment of an eastern empire and a row of vassal buffer states a solution to the military, economic, and political problems of Germany.

However, the majority of the senior generals had not always shown such open agreement with Hitler's *Lebensraumpolitik*. Until June 1940 their attitude had been dominated by the humiliation of the defeat they had experienced in 1918 and by the fear that Hitler's reckless foreign policy would lead only to a repetition of that calamity. Their reserve towards Hitler was heightened by their growing awareness that they had suffered at his hands a political defeat, more subtle but hardly less humiliating than their military failure in 1918. The independence in the State that their social status and political influence had given them was lost. They had become an isolated group in German society, surviving only through possession of military skills necessary to the Nazi regime. Thus there was seldom true accord between Hitler and the leaders of the Army, especially when he realized that their pessimistic assessment of the situation in the late 1930s made them unwilling to accept his grand strategic ideas for the conquest of *Lebensraum* as a serious basis for planning.

The victory over France brought about a temporary change in the attitudes of the Army leaders. They experienced an overwhelming sense of relief. Now they viewed Hitler's policy with greater optimism and saw in their contribution to its fulfilment a means of retaining some semblance of their old prestige and status. Furthermore, they acquired an inflated confidence in the invincibility of the Wehrmacht. As a result, the OKH not only began to plan the invasion of Russia early in July, but did so with a recklessness that probably surprised even Hitler since it assumed the practicability of defeating Russia in the autumn of 1940. Even though von Brauchitsch and Halder modified their views in the next ten days, they continued to believe that a decisive *Blitzkrieg* victory could be won over Russia in the course of a single campaign.

In spite of the optimism and enthusiasm for an attack on Russia that prevailed in the ranks of the German military leadership, there were no grounds for the Soviet interpretations that saw the 'fascist military clique' starting a war in the East against the wishes of Hitler. This view gave Russian historians a convenient explanation of Stalin's erroneous conviction in the spring of 1941 that he could negotiate for time with Hitler provided he avoided any action that might provoke the German generals into a hasty aggressive action. Even though there has been less need to justify Stalin's decisions since Khrushchev's famous speech before the Twentieth Party Congress in 1956 Russian historians have not accepted any radical changes on this point. By viewing Hitler as a tool of the militarists and imperialist-capitalists of the West it is easier to establish a line of continuity between the generals of the Wehrmacht and those of the Bundeswehr, NATO, and the Pentagon.

It is true that Hitler's generals were anti-Communist and some were also anti-Russian, but what made these attitudes so dangerous in 1940 and 1941 was not the power and independence of the military leaders but their isolation and narrowness. Having allowed themselves to become mere technicians, confined to purely military-strategic, operational, and tactical matters, the German generals lacked the economic knowledge and political perspective necessary for balanced judgement in the realm of grand strategy. They were left with modes of thought that were so naïve that they made an unconvincing defence at Nuremberg, and that were often paranoid in that decisions were based upon what was possible rather than what was probable. Thus, though repeatedly confronted with the evidence of a lack of aggressive intentions on the part of Russia, the Army leaders clung to the conviction that an attack upon her was fully justified. This was not merely because they felt the same vague but nagging fear of Communist Russia that haunts the Western world today. It was because they knew that their survival as a group depended upon their ability to serve the Third Reich by destroying its enemies. They had to make the gladiator's choice of killing or being killed. Even the restraint of possible defeat was reduced by the exhilaration of unexpected victories in 1940. Thus the German generals were confronted by the problems of moral responsibility, which all military leadership must face, under conditions of unusual complexity.

Even under a moral political leadership that eschews aggression, the relationship between soldiers and statesmen has caused grave problems. Under Hitler's immoral leadership the assertion of morality in a dependent institution lacking any major public support seemed not merely difficult but self-destructive. It is hardly surprising that years of training in discipline, obedience, patriotism, and narrow military specialization failed to produce men who, at the peak of their profession, were prepared to wreck their own careers and perhaps those of their colleagues by acts of insubordination over the moral issue of aggression against Russia. With the advantage of hindsight we can see that by obeying Hitler they destroyed all that they had ever worked for. But given the choice between obedience and disobedience they could hardly be sure that the consequences of the former would ultimately be worse. For the same paranoiac thinking that afflicted their judgement in grand-strategic matters also destroyed their professional perspective in military strategy, operations, and tactics. Since the war much of the blame for the defeat in the East has been placed on the convenient shoulders of Adolf Hitler. But errors committed by the Army leaders in those aspects of planning that he left in their hands go far to explain the failure of the subsequent campaign.

The claim that the General Staff's freedom of action in the planning of operations was limited by the aims and ideas imposed upon it by Hitler is not entirely true. The OKH commenced planning before Hitler made his views known. The highly inaccurate reports of its Intelligence Branch and the bold plans of its Operations Department revealed the same under-estimation of the military, economic, and political strength of the Soviet Union and over-confidence in the Wehrmacht which he later expressed. Thus the Army leaders shared Hitler's belief that the main difficulty lay not in the invasion of Russia itself, but in the creation of a situation in Europe favourable to such an invasion. Once this was achieved they convinced themselves that the Soviet state could be overthrown and most of European Russia conquered by means of a *Blitzkrieg* operation similar to those conducted in Poland and the West. They agreed, too, that the destruction of the enemy forces should be the first objective of the attack.

The subsequent objectives and lines of operation were, however, the source of disagreement between Hitler and the OKH. But the Army leaders made no attempt openly to argue their case for a direct advance on Moscow. Instead, they outwardly accepted Hitler's decision that the Baltic coast and Leningrad should first be conquered and modified the wording of their Deployment Directive to meet his requirements. Nevertheless, they neither pointed out the terrain problems that would be encountered by mobile forces in the area between Leningrad and Moscow nor did they plan details of the great turning operation toward Leningrad which Hitler had demanded. Hitler seems to have suspected that they did not really agree with his decision and repeatedly warned them that a frontal advance on Moscow would merely push back instead of enveloping the Russian Forces. The subsequent attempts of the Army leaders to develop the operations in accordance with their original plan led to a dispersal of effort and serious delays while the arguments which should have been raised before the campaign were finally settled.

Similar duplicity characterized the attitude of the OKH towards Hitler's changes in the operational plan of Army Group 'South'. The cancellation of the 12th Army's thrust from Rumania was fully endorsed by the OKH in March 1941. But this did not prevent General Halder from expressing in June belated and futile criticism of this decision.

The final phase of the operation was also the subject of further inconsistencies and omissions. Hitler's initial verbal orders demanded a single *Blitzkrieg* operation and a 'subsidiary operation' to capture the Caucasus. Later he indicated that a clear-cut end to the war was not to be expected and that almost a third of the Wehrmacht would remain in Russia to guard the eastern borders of the new Germanic empire. The OKH, however, made no adequate preparations for a long struggle extending into the winter. Even the Caucasus operation was neglected in the Army's planning. As in the case of the turning movement on Leningrad, the OKH attempted neither to reject the operation as unfeasible, nor to make provisions for its implementation.

In fact the operational plan of the OKH consisted of a *Blitzkrieg* formula based upon the experiences gained in earlier campaigns. The Army leaders assumed that the campaign would consist of a period of heavy fighting near the frontier and then a mopping-up operation and the almost unopposed occupation of the rest of the country. Their complete reliance upon such a sequence of events was made clear by their failure to provide for winter clothing and equipment and their readiness to go ahead with the campaign in spite of the warning that the available gasoline and diesel supplies would suffice only for deployment and two months of operations.

Although the Army leaders viewed the proposed operations in Russia with optimism, they were less confident when they viewed the grand-strategic situation in which Operation 'Barbarossa' was to take place. They were uneasy at the prospect of a two-front war and especially the strain it would place upon the Luftwaffe. They would have preferred to go ahead with Operation 'Sea Lion' before attacking Russia. But in expressing such a preference, they ignored the fact that the inadequate equipment of both the Luftwaffe and the Navy made a cross-Channel invasion quite unrealistic in 1940 or 1941.

In spite of their speculation in July 1940 about a campaign in the Middle East and in the Mediterranean as an alternative to 'Sea Lion', neither von Brauchitsch nor Halder expressed clear support for the complex coalition strategy in the south that Hitler attempted to develop in October 1940. It is only fair to state that Hitler did not consult them on this matter. But it is strange that they made no attempt to discuss the possibilities in the Mediterranean with the leaders of the other two services. Since they were unable to suggest any other practicable means of ending the war in the West, they were left no choice but to accept Hitler's argument that the attack on Russia would provide the solution to the problem of Britain. Thus, although the failure of the attempts to defeat Britain in 1940 was not the reason for the decision to attack Russia, it did become a major factor discouraging the German military leaders from opposing Operation 'Barbarossa'. The invasion of Russia seemed to offer them a solution to the strategic impasse in the West which would enable them to utilize the great land forces and *Blitzkrieg* methods in which they had become so confident.

The most remarkable features of the German Army leaders' role in the planning for the East was not their willingness and optimism, but their inefficiency and errors. After his impetuous and totally irresponsible proposal for an attack on Russia in the autumn of 1940, Field-Marshal von Brauchitsch played an ineffectual role as Commander-in-Chief. His contributions to the development of the operational planning were apparently negligible. His over-all concept of the campaign was grossly incomplete. He was aware of the major divergence of opinion between Hitler and the General Staff over the operational objectives but he failed to bring the question into open discussion before the campaign began. He was informed of the economic and logistic problems but left it to von Bock to discuss their implications with Hitler. He accepted Hitler's ideological policies as part of the war against Bolshevism and issued orders involving the Army in his criminal acts. In accordance with German Army tradition he left the conduct of operations to the Chief of the General Staff, but during the various conflicts with Hitler he failed to present the viewpoint of the OKH clearly or firmly. Hitler had long regarded him with contempt, and by the end of 1941 even Halder's loyalty towards him was severely strained.

The role of General Halder was, however, hardly more creditable than that of his Commander-in-Chief. He delegated the planning

for the eastern campaign to several subordinates but failed to combine their ideas and those of Hitler into a unified and realistic concept.
Halder shared with von Brauchitsch the responsibility for the omissions and deliberate evasions in the operational plan and for the
inflexibility which made Operation 'Barbarossa' a dangerous gamble.
Halder allowed himself to become too involved in detailed staff work
to retain the breadth of view and imagination necessary to foresee
the difficulties and dangers in the East. When events forced him to
face the consequences of the errors and omissions of his planning
he resorted to his original proposal for an advance towards Moscow,
dogmatically insisting, without any real justification, that this final
*Blitzkrieg* operation would prove decisive.

The attitude of the leaders of the OKW towards the Russian
campaign was at first more cautious than that of the OKH. In July
1940 when consulted on the Army's proposal for an autumn attack
Keitel and Jodl advised Hitler to postpone it until the following
spring. Keitel has claimed that he also attempted in August to persuade Hitler not to invade Russia until the war in the West was
completed. But once this advice had been rejected Keitel apparently
made no further protests and devoted his entire energies to the
furtherance of Hitler's plans. Jodl's doubts about the ability of the
German economy to support a multi-front war lasted at least until
December 1940. But he made no attempt to question or criticize
Hitler's decision to attack Russia. Late in July 1941, confronted by
the urgent need to achieve a decisive victory before winter, Jodl
supported the Army leaders' argument for an attack towards
Moscow, but as the opportunity for an envelopment at Kiev
developed, he returned to Hitler's support.

The role of the Luftwaffe leaders in the planning for the invasion
of Russia is difficult to assess. The Luftwaffe chiefs rarely took an
active part in the military conferences with Hitler. Most of the discussions of policy and strategy between Hitler and *Reichsmarschall*
Göring were conducted on a personal basis and were not recorded.
In spite of his claims to the contrary, Göring seems to have regarded
the conquest of Russia as both militarily feasible and economically
necessary. His Luftwaffe subordinates participated only in operational planning. Some of them had misgivings about the strain of a
multi-front war, but their views were rejected by the enthusiastic
young Chief of Air Staff, General Hans Jeschonnek.[1]

[1] In August 1943, overwhelmed by his responsibility for the failure of the

Due to the minor role of the German Navy in the eastern campaign the Naval Staff played little part in the planning for Operation 'Barbarossa'. Nevertheless, from its ranks came the most outspoken support and the most persistent criticism of Hitler's grand strategy. No military document independently compiled by the German service staffs in the Second World War expressed more explicit agreement with the grand-strategic, economic, and political aims of Hitler's *Lebensraumpolitik* than the Naval Staff study 'Observations on Russia', dated 28 July 1940. Furthermore, like the Army plan outlined to Hitler a week earlier, this document revealed the astonishingly optimistic belief that Russia could be defeated in the autumn of 1940. On the other hand, Admiral Raeder, from whom Hitler deliberately at first concealed his decision to strike eastward, maintained a critical attitude towards Hitler's grand strategy for several months. Unlike his fellow service chiefs, Raeder consistently advocated the alternative of a campaign in the Mediterranean and Middle East. This had the aim of first defeating Britain and so freeing the Wehrmacht for an attack on Russia from the south which would have had the advantage of commencing with the capture of the oilfields of the Caucasus. However, after Hitler's acceptance of the 'Barbarossa' plan in December 1940, Raeder, too, fell silent, and the success of Hitler's grand strategy became dependent upon the ability of the *Blitzkrieg* to defeat the Soviet Union by means of an attack from the West.

### Why did the Blitzkrieg Fail in Russia?

The *Blitzkrieg* failed in Russia because it had insufficient strength, mobility, range, and staying-power to defeat the Soviet forces and capture or destroy sufficient of the vital sources of Russia's economic strength in the course of the short campaigning season available. Furthermore, the *Blitzkrieg* as conducted in Russia had lost most of the psychological advantages that had contributed to its previous successes.

The German military leaders conceived the invasion of Russia as a *Blitzkrieg* campaign similar to those of 1939 and 1940. But even in the planning stages 'Barbarossa' lacked many of the characteristics of the *Blitzkrieg* operations in Poland and the West. The division of the Wehrmacht between the East, the West, and the Mediterranean,

Luftwaffe, Jeschonnek followed the example of the head of the Technical Directorate of the Luftwaffe, General Ernst Udet, and committed suicide.

and the size of the Soviet forces deprived the Germans of superiority or at least equality of strength they had achieved in their earlier campaigns. The decision to advance on all sectors of a wide front which became wider as they progressed prevented the Germans from achieving the same degree of concentration of force as that in Poland or the West. The main feature of *Blitzkrieg* operations, the concerted onslaught of air and armoured forces, was reduced by the lower ratio of tanks and aircraft to the distances to be covered. After the Cretan operation Hitler's decision not to employ airborne forces again deprived the *Blitzkrieg* in the East of an element that had been of great operational and psychological value. Similarly in Russia there was no attempt to use a real or even mythical 'Fifth Column' capable of undermining the confidence and unity of the enemy. On the contrary, the brutality of the Nazi racial policies soon destroyed any delusions that the Germans had come as 'liberators'. Thus the psychological impact of the entire attack was much reduced because the *Blitzkrieg* was no longer a combination of startling military novelties and skilful propaganda. The Russians had observed and, at least to some extent, prepared for it.

Furthermore, in spite of the enthusiasm and excessive optimism with which they regarded the *Blitzkrieg*, most of the German planners still lacked understanding of the technical and logistic problems of mechanized warfare. These deficiencies were of vital importance in a land almost devoid of surfaced roads and in which the railway system was useless until every yard of track had been adjusted to German gauge. As the detailed planning progressed in the early months of 1941, the conservative attitudes of some of the generals towards the employment of mobile forces began to return. The bold tactics of deep armoured thrusts which had won such successes elsewhere were overshadowed by a cautious desire to slow down the advance of the Panzer divisions and keep them in contact with the infantry on foot.

Such attitudes, combined with the difficulties of supply, the size of the theatre of operations, adverse weather and terrain, and the strength of the Soviet forces reduced the impact of the *Blitzkrieg* even in those areas where the Panzer and air forces were concentrated. On other vast sectors of the eastern front there were no elements of the *Blitzkrieg* at all. German formations were committed to fight without tank support, adequate anti-tank guns, or air cover, and with only a sporadic flow of supplies. They operated under conditions similar to those that had characterized warfare in the East in the First World War.

The Germans were not blind to the fact that the degree of surprise, concentration of force, and mobility achieved by their forces in Russia would be relatively lower than in the West. Yet they still attempted a *Blitzkrieg* campaign. They were convinced that the Soviet forces had a lower fighting value than those of the Western Allies. They believed that the Russians had lost the advantage that space had given them in combating earlier invasions because they could not abandon the industries of Western Russia. They expected that the Communist regime would be weakened and overthrown as a result of their military successes and brutal ideological warfare. The subsequent campaign proved that there were elements of truth in all these assumptions. The Soviet forces made abysmal errors and suffered defeats on a staggering scale. Many of these were sacrifices necessary to delay the loss of industrial areas. Others were the result of disloyalty or apathy towards Stalin's regime. But the very size of Russia outweighed these weaknesses. Beyond the striving claws of the German pincer movements there were always more miles of forest, marsh, and steppe, more Soviet units, more war industries, and more loyal Russians to prove that the German leaders had committed a monstrous error in believing that their *Blitzkrieg* was capable of defeating the Soviet Union.

## Hitler's Responsibility for the Failure in the East

This study of the German planning for the eastern campaign has shown that many of the errors and failures commonly attributed to Hitler were in fact those of the OKH. This does not necessitate, however, any major reappraisal of Hitler as a military leader. He displayed greater insight than most of his generals in considering the operational problems in the East and he probably understood better than they the true risks of the campaign. He had sufficient insight to recognize the possibility that the Soviet Army might elude the German attempts to envelop and destroy it, that difficulties of supply might slow down operations, and that Soviet industry might prove capable of equipping great new armies. As a result the aims of his military strategy began to shift. In December 1940 he made a partial modification of the initial aim of achieving the destruction of the Soviet Army by combining with it a second aim, that of seizing the Baltic coast as a supply base for later operations. Yet a third aim had haunted the planning of the campaign from the start, the seizure of areas of economic importance both to Germany and Russia, especially the Caucasian oilfields. But Hitler refused to accept the full implication of his own insight: that the defeat of Russia in a single *Blitzkrieg* campaign was not feasible; that a conflict of two or three campaigning seasons backed by an economy geared for total war would be required to destroy the 'vital power' of Russia. He rejected the concept of a long war in the East because he lacked the necessary time, because he was convinced that he could compensate for material deficiencies by an exercise of will, and because he was a victim of his own propaganda myths about the *Blitzkrieg* and his infallibility as a strategist.

The basic grand-strategic errors of Operation 'Barbarossa' were also of his making. They had their origin in the flaws that had marred his *Lebensraumpolitik* from the start: his misjudgement of Britain, his under-estimation of the Bolshevist regime in Russia, and his over-estimation of the aggressive capabilities of his own generals. The continued resistance of the British, who in Hitler's original concept were to have been the allies of Germany, had resulted in the division of the Wehrmacht to garrison the coasts of Europe while the conquest in the East took place. His contempt for the Slavs and the 'Jewish yoke' of their Bolshevist leadership had made him confident that Russia was 'ripe for dissolution'. He clung to the same delusion in 1941. Thus he took the risk of a two-front war confident that the bulk of the Wehrmacht could be turned to fight the British after the campaign of a few weeks in Russia. He felt no necessity to develop with Japan and his other allies a well co-ordinated coalition grand strategy against the Soviet Union, nor to win the support of the Russian people against their Bolshevik masters. He relied instead upon the military methods of the *Blitzkrieg*, combined with a campaign of political terror which staked all upon the achievement of a swift victory. But here too, he repeated an earlier error. In 1933 he had entrusted the Army leaders with the task of developing the *Blitzkrieg* instrument for the conquest of *Lebensraum*. They had disappointed him with their failure to grasp his intent and realize his wishes with imagination and enthusiasm. In 1941 they disappointed him again. But the subsequent course of the campaign in Russia was to bring not merely disappointment to its instigator but desolation to eastern Europe and death to millions of innocent victims.

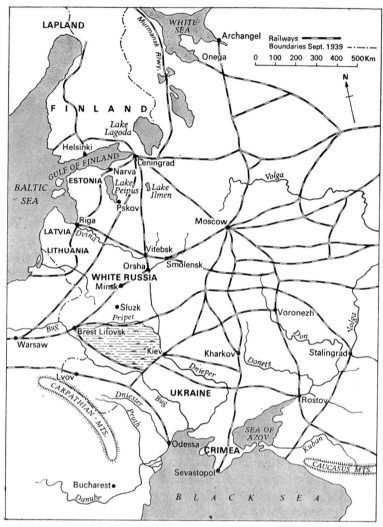

MAP 7. The Main Russian Railways, 1939

# CHARTS

### AND

# APPENDICES

# Chart I. The German High Command, 1940–1941

The Supreme Commander of the Wehrmacht: Adolf Hitler
Chief Adjutant: Col. Schmundt
Army Adjutant: Major Engel

**OKW**
Chief:
  F. M. Keitel
Chief Wfst.:
  Gen. Jodl
Dept. L.:
  Gen. Warlimont
Group 'Army':
  Col. v. Lossberg
Chief War Economy Staff:
  Gen. Thomas
*Abwehr*: Adm. Canaris

**OKH**
C.-in-C.:
  F.M. v. Brauchitsch
Chief of the General Staff:
  Gen. Halder
(Further details shown on
  Chart II)

**OKL**
C.-in-C.:
  *Reichsmarschall* Göring
Chief of the General Staff:
  Gen. Jeschonnek
Ops. Branch:
  Gen. Hoffmann v. Waldau
Intelligence:
  Col. Schmid
Q.M.G.:
  Gen. v. Seidel
Tech. Directorate:
  Gen. Udet
Air Attaché Moscow:
  Col. Aschenbrenner

**OKM**
C.-in-C.:
  Gr.-Adm. Raeder
Chief of the Naval Staff:
  Adm. Schniewind

# Chart II. The Army High Command (OKH), 1940–1941

Commander in Chief: F.M. v. Brauchitsch
G.S.O.: Lt.-Col. Siewert
Chief of the General Staff: Gen. Halder

*OQu I*: Gen. v. Stülpnagel
(till June 1940)
Gen. Paulus
(from Sept. 1940)
Ops. Branch:
Gen. v. Greiffenberg
(till Oct. 1940)
Gen. Heusinger
(from Oct. 1940)
Attached for planning East:
Gen. Marcks
(July–Aug. 1940)
Lt.-Col. Feyerabend
(July 1940)

Q.M.G.: Gen. Wagner
Chief of Army Supply Branch:
Lt.-Col. Toppe
Chief of Army Transport:
Gen. Gerke
Chief of Army Armaments:
Gen. Emil Leeb
Chief of Army Signals:
Gen. Fellgiebel

*OQu IV*: Gen. v. Tippelskirch
(till Jan. 1941)
Gen. Matzky
(from Jan. 1941)
Foreign Armies East Branch:
Col. Kinzel
Military Attaché Moscow:
Gen. Koestring
Deputy: Col. Krebs

# Chart III. The German Army in the East
## 22 June 1941

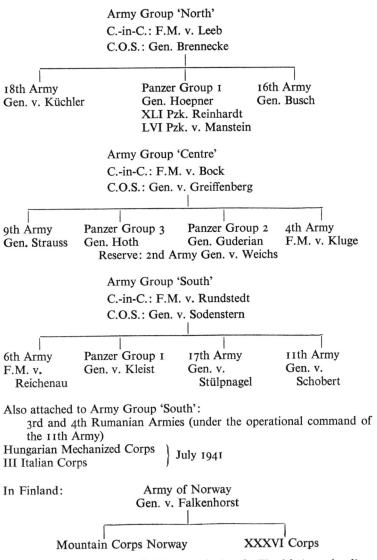

Army Group 'North'
C.-in-C.: F.M. v. Leeb
C.O.S.: Gen. Brennecke

| 18th Army | Panzer Group 1 | 16th Army |
|---|---|---|
| Gen. v. Küchler | Gen. Hoepner | Gen. Busch |
| | XLI Pzk. Reinhardt | |
| | LVI Pzk. v. Manstein | |

Army Group 'Centre'
C.-in-C.: F.M. v. Bock
C.O.S.: Gen. v. Greiffenberg

| 9th Army | Panzer Group 3 | Panzer Group 2 | 4th Army |
|---|---|---|---|
| Gen. Strauss | Gen. Hoth | Gen. Guderian | F.M. v. Kluge |

Reserve: 2nd Army Gen. v. Weichs

Army Group 'South'
C.-in-C.: F.M. v. Rundstedt
C.O.S.: Gen. v. Sodenstern

| 6th Army | Panzer Group 1 | 17th Army | 11th Army |
|---|---|---|---|
| F.M. v. | Gen. v. Kleist | Gen. v. | Gen. v. |
| Reichenau | | Stülpnagel | Schobert |

Also attached to Army Group 'South':
  3rd and 4th Rumanian Armies (under the operational command of
  the 11th Army)
Hungarian Mechanized Corps  } July 1941
III Italian Corps

In Finland:  Army of Norway
             Gen. v. Falkenhorst

| Mountain Corps Norway | XXXVI Corps |
|---|---|

Plus one German infantry division attached to the Finnish Army (13 divs.
3 bdes.)

# Chart IV. The Luftwaffe in the East
## 22 June 1941

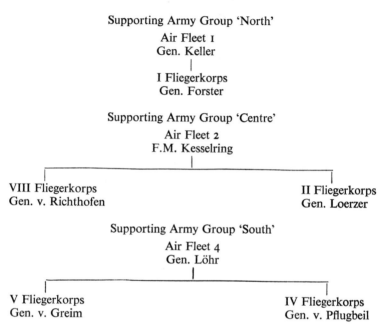

Supporting Army Group 'North'
Air Fleet I
Gen. Keller

I Fliegerkorps
Gen. Forster

Supporting Army Group 'Centre'
Air Fleet 2
F.M. Kesselring

VIII Fliegerkorps
Gen. v. Richthofen

II Fliegerkorps
Gen. Loerzer

Supporting Army Group 'South'
Air Fleet 4
Gen. Löhr

V Fliegerkorps
Gen. v. Greim

IV Fliegerkorps
Gen. v. Pflugbeil

Supporting the German-Finnish forces in Lapland
Formations from Air Fleet 5 (Norway)
Gen. Stumpff

# Chart V. General Staff of the Army Operations Branch, 1940–1941

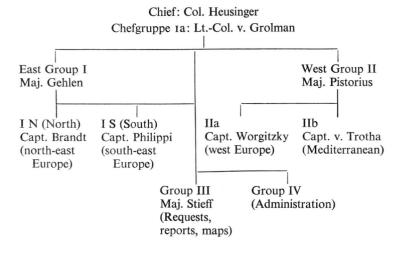

Chief: Col. Heusinger
Chefgruppe ɪa: Lt.-Col. v. Grolman

East Group I
Maj. Gehlen

West Group II
Maj. Pistorius

I N (North)
Capt. Brandt
(north-east
Europe)

I S (South)
Capt. Philippi
(south-east
Europe)

IIa
Capt. Worgitzky
(west Europe)

IIb
Capt. v. Trotha
(Mediterranean)

Group III
Maj. Stieff
(Requests,
reports, maps)

Group IV
(Administration)

# Extract: Major-General Marcks (Chief of Staff of the 18th Army)

### Draft Operational Plan East

THE purpose of the campaign is to strike the Russian Armed Forces and to make Russia incapable of entering the war as an opponent of Germany in the foreseeable future. In order to protect Germany against Russian bombers Russia must be occupied to the line lower Don–central Volga–north Dnieper. The main centres of the Russian war economy lie in the food- and raw-material-producing areas of the Ukraine and Donets Basin and the armament industries of Moscow and Leningrad. The eastern industrial regions are not yet productive enough.

Of these areas Moscow constitutes the economic, political, and spiritual centre of the USSR. Its capture would destroy the co-ordination of the Russian state.

The War Zone:

Moscow will be protected from the north and west by great forest and marsh areas which extend from the White Sea southward past Leningrad, via Vitebsk to the line Kobrin–Lutsk–Kiev. Their southern part, the Pripet Marsh, divides the frontier zone into two separate operational areas. The forest is most extensive between Leningrad and Moscow and in the Pripet Marsh. Through its narrowest and somewhat broken central region pass the main roads from Warsaw and East Prussia to Moscow via Sluzk, Minsk, and Vitebsk.

South of the Pripet Marsh lies the open country of East Galizia and the Ukraine. The terrain here is favourable for combat but mobility is limited by the lack of roads (only one main road via Kiev in an east–west direction) and by that great obstacle, the Dnieper.

The land north of the Pripet Marsh is more favourable for movement on account of its greater number of good roads, but the Ukraine is more favourable for combat. In the north battle will have to be confined mainly to the lines of the roads.

Enemy:

The Russians will not do us the favour of attacking. We must expect that the Russian Army will remain on the defensive against us and that only the Air Force and the Navy, namely the submarine arm, will attack. Russia will wage war by means of a blockade. For this purpose a Russian breakthrough into Rumania seems probable, in order to deprive us of oil. At the very least, strong air attacks on the Rumanian oilfields must be expected.

On the other hand, the Russians cannot avoid a decision as they did in 1812. Modern armed forces of 100 divisions cannot abandon their sources of supply. It is to be expected that the Russian Army will stand to do battle in a defensive position protecting greater Russia and in the eastern Ukraine. It will find a good defensive position on the line Dvina as far as Plozk–Beresina–the Pripet Marsh–Zbrutsch–Pruth or Dniester. This line is already partly fortified. A withdrawal to the Dnieper is also possible. In front of this line the Russians will probably fight delaying actions only.

Russia has at present 151 infantry divisions, 32 cavalry divisions, 38 motor-mechanized brigades. In the opinion of the 12th Section it will not be possible to increase this total appreciably by next spring. Of these forces the following are tied down:

34 infantry divs., 8 cavalry divs., 8 mot. mech. bdes. against Japan;
6 infantry divs., 1 cavalry div., against Turkey;
15 infantry divs., 2 mot. mech. bdes. against Finland
55 infantry divs., 9 cavalry divs. 10 mot. mech. bdes. in total.

This leaves against Germany: 96 infantry divs., 23 cavalry divs., 28 mot. mech. bdes.

Distribution of forces:

At present the concentrations lie on the outer wings in the Ukraine and the Baltic States. The forces are almost evenly divided south and north of the Pripet Marsh, with a reserve around Moscow. This form of distribution can also be expected in the event of a war with Germany. Whether a concentration is built up north or south depends upon political developments. The strength in the north will probably be kept greater than in the south.

The Russian Army could build up a mobile reserve of tank brigades, motorized divisions, army artillery, and cavalry divisions, which with good leadership could have significant effects. But there is so far no sign of such a force. Because the Russians no longer possess the superiority of numbers they had in the World War, it is more likely that once the long, extended line of their forces has been broken through they will be unable to concentrate or co-ordinate counter-measures. Fighting in isolated battles they will soon succumb to the superiority of the German troops and leadership.

Own Troops:

Allowing for occupation forces in Norway, Denmark, and the West the following should be available against Russia next spring: 24 Panzer divisions, 110 infantry and mountain divisions, 12 motorized divisions, 1 cavalry division. Total: 147 divisions.

Conduct of the Campaign:

Owing to the size of the combat zone and its division by the Pripet Marsh a decision will not be achieved in a single battle against the Russian Army. Initially, it will be necessary to divide and advance against the two main parts of the Russian Army separately with the object of uniting later for an operation to reach the other side of the great forest region.

Operational Intentions:

The main force of the German Army will strike that part of the Russian Army in northern Russia and will take Moscow. It will advance from the line Brest-Litovsk–Insterburg towards Rogachev–Vitebsk. South of the Pripet Marsh weaker forces will prevent the advance of the enemy southern group towards Rumania by an attack towards Kiev and the middle Dnieper. They will also prepare for subsequent co-operation with the main forces east of the Dnieper.

The attack on the Russian forces in the Ukraine is made unavoidable by the need to defend the Rumanian oilfields. If the main forces of the German Army could strike from Rumania, with support from northern Hungary, Galizia, and south-eastern Poland, they could develop the most decisive, major offensive across the Dnieper to Moscow. But neither the political situation across the Balkans nor the state of the railways and roads in Hungary and Rumania permit the concentration of large German forces in those countries before the outbreak of war. Only an attack from Galizia and south Poland towards Kiev and the middle Dnieper can be carried out with any certainty. This attack cannot be the main operation because the area is too narrow and the distance to Moscow too great. However, it should be carried out with sufficient forces to achieve the destruction of the enemy in the Ukraine and the crossing of the Dnieper. It should later be extended in close co-operation with the main operation north of the Pripet Marsh either towards Kharkov or north-eastwards. Its main concentration must be in the north; its main objective Kiev. The terrain is generally favourable there, especially for tanks. Three lines of defence will have to be overcome before Kiev.

The attack from Rumania should not, however, be abandoned even though the political situation might prevent a concentration there before the start of the campaign. An army should be made ready in the Reich to move the wheeled elements of its Panzer and motorized divisions and the necessary artillery at the start of the war through Hungary to defend Rumania during the deployment of German attacking forces there. The main attack of the Army will be directed from north Poland and East Prussia towards Moscow. There will be no other decisive operation because prior deployment in Rumania is not possible. An extension to the north would only lengthen the march and finally lead into the forest area north-west of Moscow. The main purpose of the offensive is to strike and destroy the mass of the Russian northern group before, within, and east of the forest area by means of a direct thrust towards Moscow. Then from Moscow and north Russia it will turn southwards and, in co-operation with the German southern group, conquer the Ukraine and finally reach the line Rostov–Gorki–Archangel. To cover the north flank of this operation a special force will be directed across the lower Dvina towards Pskov and Leningrad.

As in Poland and the West success must be sought by means of surprise and speed. The conduct of operations is so conceived that in all armies mobile formations in the first wave will break through the Russian troops in front of the river and forest defences and, supported by the Luftwaffe, continue the advance to seize corridors through the forests and river crossings. Following close behind some of the infantry divisions will seek to divide and destroy the out-flanked enemy, while others making use of all means of transportation will follow the mobile troops in order to secure and extend their successes. Some will also go through the Pripet Marshes making use of available roads and railways (armoured trains with Russian rail gauge!) in order to attack the enemy's rear.

The fact that the width of the combat zone will increase with the continuation of the attack necessitates the bringing up of strong army reserves which will be deployed under new corps headquarters. Part of these reserves will be immediately available to the northern army group, the rest will be allocated to areas with favourable road and rail communications so that they can reinforce both army groups.

Allocation of force: (Summary)

| | | | | |
|---|---|---|---|---|
| Army Group 'South' | — 5 Pz., | 6 mot., | 24 inf. divs. | |
| Army Group 'North'* | —15 Pz., | 2 mot., | 50 inf. | 1 cav. div. |
| Army Reserve | — 4 Pz., | 4 mot., | 36 inf. | |
| Total | —24 Pz., | 12 mot., | 110 inf. | 1 cav. div. |

 * The northernmost army—3 Pz., 12 inf. divs.

Signed: MARCKS

# APPENDIX II

# The Lossberg Study

(Operations Study 'East'
W.F.St./Op. H. 905)

Secret

Department of National Defence,                Führer H.Q., 15.9.40
Staff document
Officers only.

### Operations Study East

The aim of a campaign against Soviet Russia is to destroy the mass
of the Soviet Army in western Russia, to prevent the withdrawal of
battleworthy elements into the depth of Russia, and then, having
cut western Russia off from the seas, to advance to a line which will
place the most important part of Russia in our hands and on which
it will be easy to form a shield against Asiatic Russia. The theatre
of operations against Russia will initially be divided by the Pripet
Marshes, so that contact between the groups operating north and
south of this area will only be established in the course of the subsequent battles.

The purpose of the following Operations Plan is to set out the
basic considerations for operations in the northern and southern
areas and in particular to establish approximately where the main
thrusts will be located on each sector.

In addition to maps, notes on the Russian armed forces and war
potential are enclosed as annexures [Missing]. Reports on the
Russian fortifications are omitted as unnecessary. There are only
disconnected field fortifications on the old and new (1939) western
frontier. Reliable reports are lacking.

The map included in Annexure No. 1 [missing] gives a survey
of the expected distribution of the Russian army formations. It
should be noted that it is especially difficult in Russia to gain reasonably accurate intelligence of the enemy. Fewer assumptions about
the Russian order of battle should be based upon the present
situation as our own intentions become apparent to the enemy.
The present Russian dispositions are still the result of the recent
events in Finland, the Baltic States, and Bessarabia. However, the

following may be stressed as characteristic of all Russian deployments:

1. There does not seem to be a mobilization in the German manner in which regular divisions are brought up to full establishment and reserve divisions set up. The regular Army is now practically on a war footing. This makes it difficult to assess the degree of readiness and battleworthiness of the different formations.

2. The Russian command structure is so cumbersome and the Russian High Command's use of the railway system is probably so inadequate that any new deployment will lead to major difficulties and will require considerable time.

3. In the case of tension with Germany Russian strength will be pinned down
    (a) against Finland, here too because of German forces in Norway;
    (b) on the Rumanian border;
    (c) in the Caucasus (unreliable population, Turkey, security of the oilfields);
    (d) in the Far East.

In a war against Germany, Russia has, broadly speaking, the following three courses open:

I. In order to gain the initiative the Russians might strike at the initial stage of the German deployment.

II. The Russian armies might meet the German attack in the concentration areas near the border in order to hold their newly acquired position on both wings (i.e. on the Baltic and Black Seas).

III. The Russians might use the proved tactic of 1812, fall back into the vastness of the interior in order to impose the strain of long lines of communication and supply upon the invader, and only counter-attack at a later stage of the campaign.

These possibilities are assessed as follows:

Reference I above:

It is unlikely that the Russians will risk a major offensive against East Prussia and the north part of the General Government as long as the bulk of the German Army is not tied down for a long period on another front. Neither the leadership nor the troops are capable of this. Limited operations directed either against Finland or Rumania are more likely. An attack on Finland during a period of tension with Germany would in no way improve Russia's strategic position. On the contrary the forces committed against Finland would be in increased danger of being cut off by the attack of the German north wing along the Baltic. The circumstances arising from a Russian attack on the Rumanian oilfields would be different. Here the Russians would have an opportunity to strike at the German supply base. Under certain circumstances the employment of Russian Air Force would suffice for this purpose. In case of a ground attack the employment of the comparatively strong and apparently good Russian parachute troops seems likely. It will be the task of the future German Military Mission [in Rumania] to meet such a danger with the German 'training units' and by the organization of the Rumanian Counter-Espionage Service. The Military Mission will at the same time be regarded as the vanguard of the German south wing [for the attack on Russia].

Reference II above:

This solution seems to be the most likely, because it is improbable that so strong a military power as Russia will abandon its most valuable and in part most recently acquired territories without a fight. A vast withdrawal would also result in the early loss of the ground organization of the Soviet Air Force which, according to available intelligence, has been especially increased *west* of the Dnieper.

In the case of such a decision the Russian deployment would have a certain resemblance to the present distribution of forces, to which would be added stronger Soviet formations in the Russian-Polish area. In view of the nature of the Russian railway network the central reserve would remain in the Moscow area. Such a decision, in which the enemy commits strong formations to an early battle, would be most favourable for us, because after defeat in the battles near the frontier the Russian leadership will hardly be capable of withdrawing the whole Army in good order.

Reference III above:

The Russians might base their operations plan from the start upon the strategy of meeting the German attack with only part of their strength and concentrating the mass in depth. If so, north of the Pripet Marsh the great barrier of the Dvina and Dnieper Rivers, broken only by a gap of 70 kilometres south of Vitebsk, will facilitate this. Such a decision would be

S

unfavourable to us, but must be taken into account as a possibility. On the other hand, it is highly unlikely the Russians will give up the essential Ukraine region.

Attention is directed to the map of the German and Russian railways available for deployment and the relevant notes enclosed as Annexe No. 2 [missing]. These relate to the following proposals for our own operations. The German reports were based upon the completion of the programme 'Otto' [i.e. deployment East]. While the Russian reports are hypothetical, they assume the highest possible performance [in the use of railways for deployment].

Account should be taken of the probability that the Russian railways in the newly won Polish areas have already been changed to the Soviet gauge and that this difference in gauge can pose severe [transport] problems for us, especially after we have won large tracts of territory. It will therefore be necessary to cut off and capture sufficient Russian rolling stock, and later to relay specific Russian lines to our gauge.

In all a daily deployment rate of 7 divisions can be expected on the German side and 5 divisions on the Russian side.

Significant features of the Russian railway network are the convergence on Moscow and the inadequate north–south communications, which will make it difficult for the enemy to regroup behind the front. However all German operations must be supported in their later stages by reliable Russian railways, because in the vast spaces a transport system based only on roads will be insufficient.

### For our own Operations

. . . it is necessary to decide whether the main weight should lie north or south of the Pripet Marsh. The German superiority should leave no doubt that simultaneous operations will be conducted in both areas.

### Factors favouring the main weight in the North

include the considerably better conditions for deployment (see railway conditions); the need swiftly to destroy the Russian forces in the Baltic area; the comparatively good Russian railways which run in the direction of operations; the possibility of co-operation with Group XXI operating through Finland; the fact that Leningrad and Moscow lie within striking distance.

### Factors favouring the main weight in the South

include the [Russian] threat to Rumania; the possibility of supplying German motorized units with oil over the comparatively short distance from the Rumanian and, later, the East Galician oilfields, (however lines of communication are bad after crossing the Russian border); the significance of the Ukraine.

The course recommended is to place the main blow in the *North* and along the following operational lines:

Attack with two army groups from the general line east of Warsaw–Königsberg, main weight to be with the southerly army group, deployed in the area of Warsaw and south-east Prussia, which will have most of the Panzer and motorized formations. A supply base for this will be established in the deployment area during the winter (1940–41).

The *Southern* Army Group will launch its attack towards the gap between the Rivers Dvina and Dnieper to destroy the Russian formations in the Minsk area and to break through in the general direction of Moscow. The fact that the only completed Russian highway leads from Minsk to Moscow favours the commitment of the main weight, including strong motorized formations, in this direction.

The Northern Army Group will attack from East Prussia and across the lower Dvina River.

To achieve the basic aim (see opening sentence of study), *co-operation between the two army groups* will result in a turning of forces from the southern (main thrust) army group to the north depending upon the situation, possibly east of the Dvina, in order to cut off the Russians facing the north wing. The enormous spaces will then necessitate a *pause in operations* for supply purposes.

*Group XXI* will form a separate group in the [far] north, together with the army of the Finns, who it is anticipated will be our allies. It will have the task of striking with part of its forces from north-eastern Norway towards Murmansk. The main body of its forces will move on Swedish and Finnish railways and under Finnish protection to southern Finland, where it will pin down Russian forces and attack perhaps north of Lake Ladoga, at the latest when the German north wing (from the Baltic States) is approaching Leningrad. There is a bottleneck in the transportation route at Haparanda–Torneo. This single-tracked stretch has normal gauge in Sweden and broad gauge in Finland. The capacity on the Finnish side is estimated at 12 to 16 trains.

After setting aside a strong *reserve for the Commander-in-Chief*, one army group comprising about one-third of the entire force, including a proportionate number of mobile formations, will be available for the *operational area south of the Pripet Marsh*. This army group will have the task of destroying the enemy forces between the Pripet Marsh and the Black Sea in a double envelopment.

It will subsequently occupy the Ukraine and, after crossing the Dnieper, establish contact east of the Pripet Marsh with the German forces to the north. The strength employed in this thrust will depend upon the will to resist still shown by the Russians.

The fact that the Russians will soon have internal problems especially in the Ukraine will be of considerable advantage to the operations in the south. With encouragement from our espionage branch (*Abwehr II*), this could result in damage to the few railway links with the area. Once the Ukraine is occupied a 'Government' responsive to our wishes will probably be formed. This will ease the task of supervising the extensive occupied areas.

The heavy, partly clay, soil of the Ukraine will make the movement of motorized formations difficult in rainy periods.

The nature of later operations involving the co-operation of both main groups east of the Pripet Marsh, and the selection of the final military objective in terms of territory will depend upon whether and when Russia suffers an internal collapse as a result of the initial German successes. Even if the industrial area in the Urals . . . is taken into consideration, it seems impossible that Russia can remain capable of resistance after losing her western territories and contact with the seas. The general line Archangel–Gorki–Volga (to Stalingrad)–Don (to the Black Sea) seems feasible as the long-range objective.

. . . It should be noted that in spite of its strength the *Russian Air Force* is not capable of uniformly directed, major actions. It is more likely that it will commit its fighting formations only to limited, tactical actions. The information supplied to the Russian command by air reconnaissance will be inadequate.

The task of the Luftwaffe, once it has eliminated the Russian Air Force, will be to support the main German operational thrusts towards Minsk, and on both wings of the southern army group. Due to their importance for the [successful conduct of the German] operations the railways will be protected, especially at vulnerable places such as river crossings. . . . By their skilful employment and concentration on the most important locations (e.g. railways . . .) parachute and airborne troops will be able to land at far greater depth in Russia than was possible under the conditions prevailing in the West. [Air] attacks on Russian industry will not be possible during the main [land] operations. However upon the attainment of the final objective it will be possible to bomb the Ural region.

For *the employment of the Navy* one must consider the coastal character of the Baltic waters which rules out the employment of major surface forces against the Russian fleet and its bases. The major task of the Navy will be to secure our own coastal waters and to close the exit from the Baltic against an attempt by Russian naval forces to break out.

The transportation of iron ore through the Baltic will probably be reduced by the numerous Russian submarines and motor torpedo boats. The Russian fleet, including submarines, will cease to constitute a threat only when German army operations reach the naval bases, including Leningrad. Then the sea route can also be used for supplying the north wing. Before that lasting and secure sea communications between the Baltic States and Finland cannot be expected.

Finally it remains to be examined whether and to what extent a campaign against Russia really must be prepared during the coming autumn and winter even if England is not yet defeated. It is important that Russia must not be made aware of the threatening danger before the conquest of England and thus provoked into countermeasures (Rumania, stopping of economic deliveries). The forces available to Army Group B from the end of October (35 divisions) are fully adequate to safeguard the eastern territories and to keep Russia under sufficient military-political pressure. Should the forces in the East undergo continual further reinforcement then the Russians will feel themselves to be threatened and take countermeasures. Militarily there is no reason for us to push a further wave of the deployment to the East until the operation is almost due to begin. The poor accommodation situation in the General Government also discourages such a decision. It would be feasible to station more troops in the German eastern provinces, but this does not yield any advantage. The German railway system is superior to the Russian and so efficient, especially in the interior, that it makes no difference whether the forces earmarked for deployment are in Pomerania–Brandenburg–Silesia or in West Germany. The further we keep our forces from the real concentration area the greater the surprise we will achieve over the Russians with the comparatively swift German deployment. It is therefore important to start all preparations which serve the needs of a swift concentration at a later date (use of roads and railways—Programme 'Otto') and of supply (prior assessment, stockpiling of fuel). After a survey of buildings of cultural value on the rail and road routes thought should be given to measures for their protection, i.e. restoration, and in some cases such measures should be carried out. An increase in railway troops should be considered.

The maintenance of secrecy will require that all questions associated with a campaign in the East should be restricted to the smallest possible number of persons in the High Command and formation commands.

Annexes:

*a.* Maps
  1. Distribution of German and Russian armies (August 1940).
  2. German and Russian railways available for deployment. (Report attached).
  3. Sketch map of proposed operations.
  4. The Russian armament industry.
  5. (*a*) Range of German and Russian air forces.
     (*b*) German and Russian air forces' ground organizations and Russian distribution of forces.

*b.* General map of Baltic Sea.

[NOTE: None of the annexes is included in the version published as an appendix to Besymenski, *Sonderakte Barbarossa*, pp. 307–13. The wording of the original study may have differed from this version which appears to be translated back to German from a Russian translation of the original study.]

# OKH Deployment Directive of 31.1.41. Barbarossa

Army High Command
General Staff Ops. Branch (1)    H.Q., OKH, 31 January 1941.
No. 050/41g.K.

Deployment Directive 'Barbarossa'

1. Task

In case Russia should change her present attitude towards Germany, all preparations are to be completed, as precautionary measures, to make it possible to defeat Soviet Russia in a quick campaign even before the end of the war against England. The operations should be so conducted that the mass of the Russian army in Western Russia will be destroyed by deep armoured thrusts. The withdrawal of elements left intact into the depth of Russian space will be prevented.

2. Enemy Situation

It is assumed that the Russians will accept battle west of the Dnieper and Dvina at least with strong parts of their forces. They will make use of the partly strengthened fortifications of the new and old frontiers and of the many waterways which favour the defence. The Russian Command will therefore have to make a particular effort to commit sufficient forces to hold on as long as possible to its air and naval bases in the Baltic provinces and to the flank protection of the Black Sea. The unfavourable outcome of the battles that may be expected south and north of the Pripet Marshes will force the Russians to attempt to bring the German attack to a standstill on the Dnieper–Dvina line. The offensive commitment of stronger Russian formations employing armour is to be expected not only in countering German breakthroughs, but also in attempts to bring threatened formations back to the Dnieper–Dvina line.

3. Intention

The first intention of the OKH within the task allocated is by means of swift and deep thrusts by strong mobile formations north and south of the Pripet Marsh to tear open the front of the mass of the Russian Army which it is anticipated will be in western Russia. The enemy groups separated by these penetrations will then be destroyed. South of the Pripet Marshes *Army Group 'South',—Field-Marshall von Rundstedt*—will exploit the swift breakthrough by strong armoured forces from the Lublin area in the direction of Kiev, in order to cut the communications across the Dnieper of the enemy in Galizia and the West Ukraine. The Dnieper crossings at and below Kiev will be taken, thus ensuring the freedom for the subsequent co-operation of Army Group 'South' with the German forces operating in northern Russia or for new tasks in south Russia.

North of the Pripet Marshes *Army Group 'Centre'—Field-Marshal von Bock*—will commit strong mobile forces from the Warsaw-Sulwalki area to force a breakthrough towards Smolensk. This will permit the turning of strong formations to the north in order to co-operate with *Army Group 'North'—Field-Marshal von Leeb*, attacking from East Prussia in the general direction of Leningrad. Both army groups will destroy the enemy formations in the Baltic area, and, in co-operation with the Finnish Army and possibly German forces from Norway, finally put an end to the enemy's ability to resist in northern Russia, thus ensuring freedom of movement for further tasks—perhaps in co-operation with the German forces in southern Russia. In the event of a sudden unexpected collapse of enemy resistance in northern Russia, the abandonment of the turning movement and an immediate thrust towards Moscow could be considered.

The opening of the attack will be co-ordinated along the entire front. (B-Day, Y-hour).

*The Conduct of Operations* will be based upon the principles proved in the Polish campaign. However, it must be noted that, in spite of the clear concentration of force to be achieved at decisive points, the enemy forces on other sectors of the front must also be attacked. Only thus can powerful enemy formations be prevented from withdrawing and evading destruction west of the Dnieper–Dvina line. Furthermore, the effect of the enemy Air Force must be expected to be more strongly felt by the army, because the *full* strength of the Luftwaffe will not be available for the operation against Russia. Troops must be prepared for the use by the enemy of chemical weapons from the air.

4. Tasks of the army groups and armies

   *a. Army Group 'South'* will drive its strong left wing—with mobile forces in the lead—towards Kiev, destroy the Russian forces in

Galizia and in the West Ukraine while they are still west of the Dnieper, and achieve the early capture of the Dnieper crossings at and below Kiev for the continuation of operations both sides of the river. The operation is to be conducted so that the mobile formations from the Lublin area are concentrated for the breakthrough towards Kiev. Within the framework of this instruction Army Group 'South' headquarters will issue more detailed directives to the armies and the Panzer Group for the following tasks:

The *11th Army* will protect the area of Rumania vital to the German war economy against a breakthrough of Russian forces. As part of the attack by Army Group 'South' it will pin down the enemy forces on its sector by giving an exaggerated impression of strength, and subsequently, in co-operation with the Luftwaffe, it will prevent by means of a close pursuit the orderly withdrawal of the Russians across the Dnieper.

The first task of *Panzer Group 1* will be in co-operation with the 17th and 6th Armies to break through the enemy forces near the frontier between Rawa Ruska and Kowel, to advance via Berdishev–Zhitomir, and to reach the Dnieper as soon as possible at and below Kiev. Then, under the direction of Army Group Headquarters, it will continue the attack in a south-easterly direction along the Dnieper in order to prevent a withdrawal of the enemy in the West Ukraine across the Dnieper and to destroy him by an attack from the rear.

The *17th Army* will break through the enemy border defences north-west of Lemberg (Lvov). By means of a vigorous advance on its strong left wing, it must attempt to push the enemy back south-eastwards. In addition, the army will take advantage of the advance of the Panzer Group quickly to reach the area Vinnitsa–Berditchev so that according to the situation it can continue the attack to the south-east or east.

The *6th Army* will break through the enemy front both sides of Luck in co-operation with elements of the Panzer Group 1. While covering the north flank of the army group against interference from the Pripet Marsh area, it will follow the Panzer Group 1 to Zhitomir with all possible speed and strength. It must be ready, on the orders of Army Group 'South' headquarters, to turn south-eastwards with strong forces west of the Dnieper, in order to co-operate with Panzer Group 1 in preventing the enemy in the West Ukraine from withdrawing over the Dnieper.

*b. Army Group 'Centre'* will break up the enemy in White Russia by driving forward the strong forces on its wings. It will quickly win the area around Smolensk by uniting the mobile forces advancing north and south of Minsk and so achieve the prerequisites for co-operation between strong elements of its mobile troops and Army Group 'North' in the destruction of the enemy forces fighting in the Baltic states and the Leningrad area.

Within the framework of this instruction Army Group 'Centre' headquarters will issue more detailed directives to the Panzer groups and armies for the following tasks:

*Panzer Group 2* in co-operation with 4th Army will break through the enemy forces on the frontier at and north of Kobryn. By means of a swift advance to Slutsk and Minsk it will meet Panzer Group 3 advancing from the area north of Minsk and achieve the prerequisites for the destruction of the enemy forces between Bialystok and Minsk. In close contact with Panzer Group 3, it will quickly achieve the further tasks of winning the area around and south of Smolensk, preventing the concentration of enemy forces in the upper Dnieper region and so preserve the army group's freedom in the choice of subsequent tasks.

*Panzer Group 3* in co-operation with 9th Army will break through the enemy forces on the frontier. By means of a swift advance in the area north of Minsk, it will meet Panzer Group 2 advancing from the south-west towards Minsk and achieve the prerequisites for the destruction of the enemy forces between Bialystok and Minsk. In close contact with Panzer Group 2 it will quickly achieve the further task of reaching the area around and north of Vitebsk, preventing the concentration of enemy forces in the upper Dvina region and so preserve the army group's freedom in the choice of subsequent tasks.

*4th Army* will achieve the crossing of the Bug and thereby will open the way to Minsk for Panzer Group 2. It will advance with its main strength across the Shava River south of Slonim, and in co-operation with 9th Army it will take advantage of the advance of the Panzer Groups and destroy the enemy forces between Bialystok and Minsk. Its further tasks will be: to follow the advance of Panzer Group 2 and, protecting its south flank against [attacks from] the Pripet Marshes; to seize crossings over the Beresina between Bobruisk and Borysau; and to reach the Dnieper at and north of Mohilev.

*9th Army* in co-operation with Panzer Group 3 will break through the enemy forces west and north of Grodno. With the main weight on its north wing it will drive towards Lida–Vilna, and, taking advantage of the advance of the Panzer Groups it will establish contact with the 4th Army and destroy the enemy in the area between Bialystok and Mink. The next task of the 9th Army will be to follow Panzer Group 3 and reach the Dvina at and south-east of Polozk.

*c. Army Group 'North'* will destroy the enemy forces fighting in the Baltic area, and will deprive the Russian fleet of its bases by occupying the Baltic harbours including Leningrad and Kronstadt. At the appropriate time the OKH will order powerful mobile forces from Army Group 'Centre' advancing on Smolensk to co-operate with Army Group 'North'. Within the framework of this task Army Group 'North' will break through the enemy front with its main effort towards Dvinsk. It will drive its strong right wing with mobile troops thrusting across the Dvina as quickly as possible to reach the area north-west of Opotschka and so prevent the withdrawal of battleworthy Russian forces eastward from the Baltic region. It will also achieve the conditions for a further swift drive towards Leningrad.

*Panzer Group 4* in co-operation with 16th and 18th Armies will break through the enemy front between Wystiter Lake and the Tilsit–Schaulen highway, and will thrust to the Dvina at and below Dvinsk and establish bridgeheads across the river. Furthermore, Panzer Group 4 will be required to reach the area north-east of Opotschka in order to be able to drive on north-eastward or north-wards according to the situation.

*16th Army* in co-operation with Panzer Group 4 will break through the enemy with its main effort on both sides of the road Ebenrode–Kovno, and by rapidly advancing its strong right wing behind the Panzer corps it will reach the north bank of the Dvina at and below Dvinsk.

The next task of the army will be to follow Panzer Group 4 and to reach the Opotschka area as soon as possible.

*18th Army* will break through the enemy on its sector with its main concentration on and east of the Tilsit–Riga highway, and will cut off and destroy the enemy forces south-west of Riga by swiftly thrusting most of its forces over the Dvina at and below Stock-mannshof. It will then block the approach of Russian forces south of Lake Peipus by means of a swift advance to the line Ostrov–Pskov, and in accordance with the directive of Army Group 'North'— possibly in co-operation with mobile troops north of Lake Peipus— mop up the enemy in Estonia. Preparations are to be made so that the surprise occupation of the Baltic Islands of Oesel, Dago, and Moon can be carried out as soon as the situation permits.

5. pp. [Spare]

6. Task for the Army of Norway (directly subordinate to the OKW):
    *a.* The most important task remains to ensure the security of the entire Norwegian area not only against raids, but also against the

serious attempts at landings by the British which must be expected in the course of this summer. This task requires that:

   i. all energies and means of transport will be used to ensure that the batteries earmarked to strengthen the coastal defences will be installed by mid-May.

  ii. formations at present located in Norway will not be appreciably weakened for the achievement of tasks connect with operation 'Barbarossa'. Indeed, the sector most endangered—Kirkenes–Narvik—will be strengthened. This reinforcement is to be achieved with forces already in Norway.

  *b.* In addition to its defensive role the Army of Norway has the following tasks:

   i. advance into the *Petsamo area* at the start of the main operations, or if necessary even earlier, and, together with the Finnish forces, defend it against attacks from the land, sea, and air. Particular significance is attached to the safeguarding of the nickel mines which are important to the German war industry (Operation 'Reindeer').

  ii. Envelop, and later, when sufficient assault forces are available, capture *Murmansk* as a base for offensive action by its land, sea, and air forces (Operation 'Silver Fox'). It is to be expected that Sweden will maintain the security of her own north-east frontier with adequate forces.

### 7. OKH Reserves

At the start of the operation the reserves of the OKH will be allocated to a large group in the area Reichhof and east of Warsaw and to small groups in the Zamosc, Suwalki, and Eydtkau areas.

### 8. *Support by the Luftwaffe and Navy*

The task of the Luftwaffe is to eliminate as far as possible all interference by the Russian Air Force and to support the main operations of the Army especially those of Army Group 'Centre' and the left wing of Army Group 'South'. During the main operations the Luftwaffe will concentrate all force against the enemy Air Force and in immediate support of the Army. Attacks against the enemy industry will be carried out only after the operational objectives of the Army have been attained.

Air support is allocated as follows:

        Air Fleet 4—Army Group 'South'
        Air Fleet 2—Army Group 'Centre'
        Air Fleet 1—Army Group 'North'

In the course of conducting its main role against Britain and safe-guarding our coasts, the *Navy* will prevent enemy naval forces from breaking out of the Baltic. Until the Russian fleet has been deprived of its last Baltic base at Leningrad, major naval objectives will be avoided. After the elimination of the Russian fleet, the Navy will have the task of safeguarding sea traffic in the Baltic and the supply of the north wing of the Army.

### 9. *The Participation of other States*

The active participation of *Rumania and Finland* in a war against the Soviet Union is to be anticipated on the flanks of the operation. The form of the co-operation and of the subordination of the forces of both countries under German command will be decided upon at the appropriate time. Rumania's task will be to assist the German forces concentrated there in pinning down the enemy facing them, and also to provide assistance in the rear areas.

Finland's tasks will be to eliminate the Russian base at Hangö and to cover the concentration of the German forces in north Finland. By the time Army Group 'North' has crossed the Dvina Finland will also attack the Russian forces on her south-east front in accordance with the requirements of the OKH, concentrating either east or west of Lake Ladoga, preferably the former. She will then support Army Group 'North' in the destruction of the enemy. The active participation of Sweden is probably not to be expected. It is possible, however, that Sweden will permit the use of her railways for the concentration and supply of the German forces in North Finland.

Signed: VON BRAUCHITSCH

[SOURCE: *Halder KTB* ii. 463–9. This version is amended in accordance with the changes in the operational plan described in Chapter VI above.]

# German Intelligence Estimates of Soviet Army Strength

Total number of formations:

|  | 1940 |  | 1941 |  |  |
|---|---|---|---|---|---|
|  | 24 Jul. | 8 Aug. | 15 Jan. | 30 Jan. | 4 Apr. |
| Rifle Divisions | 151 | 151 | 150 | 150 | 171 |
| Cavalry Divisions | 32 | 32 | 32 | 32 | 36 |
| Motor Mechanized Brigades | 38 | 38 | 36 | 36 | 40 |
| Total | 221 | 221 | 218 | 218 | 247 |

Number of formations available in European Russia to meet an attack from the West:

|  | 1940 |  | 1941 |  |  |  |
|---|---|---|---|---|---|---|
|  | 24 Jul. | 8 Aug. | 15 Jan. | 30 Jan. | 3 Feb. | 21 June |
| Rifle Divisions | 90 | 96 | 100 | 121 | 121 | 154 |
| Cavalry Divisions | 23 | 23 | 25 | 25 | 25 | $25\frac{1}{2}$ |
| Motor Mechanized Brigades | 28 | 28 | 31 | 31 | 31 | 37 |
| Total | 141 | 147 | 156 | 177 | 177 | $216\frac{1}{2}$ |

Sources:  24 July 1940: Erikson, p. 557.
8 Aug. 1940: The Marcks Plan, see Appendix I.
15 Jan. 1941: USNA, Microfilm, Serial T78–335.
30 Jan. 1941: *KTB OKW* ii. 290.
3 Feb. 1941: *Halder KTB* ii. 266.
4 Apr. 1941: *Halder KTB* ii. 345.
21 June 1941: *Halder KTB* ii. 461.

# Panzer and Motorized Forces engaged in the Balkans prior to their employment in Operation 'Barbarossa'

| Formation: | Employed in Russia under: |
|---|---|
| H.Q. Panzer Group 1 | Army Group 'South' |
| H.Q. XXXXI Army Corps (Motorized) | Army Group 'North', Panzer Group 4 |
| SS Div. 'Das Reich' | Army Group 'Centre', Panzer Group 2 |
| Infantry Regiment 'Grossdeutschland' | Army Group 'Centre', Panzer Group 2 |
| H.Q. XIV Army Corps (Motorized) | Army Group 'South', Panzer Group 1 |
| 5 Panzer Division | OKH Reserve |
| 11 Panzer Division | Army Group 'South', Panzer Group 1 |
| H.Q. XXXX Army Corps (Motorized) | OKH Reserve |
| 'Leibstandarte SS Adolf Hitler' | Army Group 'South', Panzer Group 1 |
| 9 Panzer Division | Army Group 'South', Panzer Group 1 |
| 2 Panzer Division | OKH Reserve |
| 16 Panzer Division | Army Group 'South', Panzer Group 1 |

# APPENDIX VI

## Distribution of German Divisions, June 1941

| | Inf. | Security | Mtn. | Mot. (incl. SS) | Panzer | Cav. |
|---|---|---|---|---|---|---|
| **Army Group 'South'** | | | | | | |
| 11th Army | 7 | | | | | |
| 17th Army | 7 | 2 | 4 | | | |
| 6th Army/ | | | | | | |
| Pz. Gp. 1 | 11 | 1 | | 3 | 5 | |
| A. Gp. Reserve | 5 | | 2 | | | |
| | | | | | | |
| **Army Group 'Centre'** | | | | | | |
| 4th Army/ | | | | | | |
| Pz. Gp. 2 | 18 | 2 | | 4 | 5 | 1 |
| 9th Army/ | | | | | | |
| Pz. Gp. 3 | 12 | 1 | | 3 | 4 | |
| A. Gp. Reserve | 7 | | | | | |
| | | | | | | |
| **Army Group 'North'** | | | | | | |
| 16th Army | 10 | 2 | | | | |
| 18th Army | 10 | 1 | | | | |
| Pz. Gp. 4 | | | | 3 | 3 | |
| A. Gp. Reserve | 3 | | | | | |
| | | | | | | |
| OKH Reserve | 9 | | | 1 | 2 | |
| | | | | | | |
| In Finland | 2½ | | 2 | | | |
| Totals | 101½ | 9 | 8 | 14 (incl. 4 SS) | 19 | 1 |

Grand Total: 152½ divisions
plus 14 Rumanian divisions
plus 21 Finnish divisions

# Axis and Soviet Naval Strengths, 1941

In the Baltic Sea:

| | Russian | German | Finnish |
|---|---|---|---|
| Battleships | 2 | 2 (*Schleswig-Holstein* class) | — |
| Cruisers | 2 (plus 5 building) | — | 2 (coastal armoured ships) |
| Destroyers | 23 | — | — |
| Torpedo boats | 7 | — | — |
| Mine-detection boats | 14 | 50 | 7 |
| Minelayers | 7 | 11 | 4 |
| Minesweepers | 21 | 29 | 12 |
| Submarines | 59 | 5 | 5 |
| Motor boats | 79 | 40 | 7 |
| Gunboats/ patrol boats | 48 | 20 | 18 |

In the Arctic Ocean–White Sea:

| | Russian | German | Finnish |
|---|---|---|---|
| Cruisers | — | 2 (temporarily) | — |
| Destroyers | 7 | — | — |
| Torpedo boats | 3 | — | — |
| Minelayers | 4 | — | — |
| Minesweepers | 4 | — | — |
| Submarines | 21 | — | — |

In the Black Sea:

| | Russian | German | Rumanian |
|---|---|---|---|
| Battleships | 1 | — | — |
| Cruisers | 5 | — | — |
| Destroyers | 20 | — | 4 |
| Torpedo boats | 6 | — | 3 |
| Minelayers | 5 | — | 1 |
| Minesweepers | 13 | — | — |

| Black Sea (cont.) | Russian | German | Rumanian |
|---|---|---|---|
| Submarines | 42 | — | I |
| Motor boats and other light craft | several | several | 3 (escort vessels) 4 (gunboats) 3 (motor torpedo boats) |

Sources: Höhn, *Auf antisowjetischem Kriegskurs*, p. 458; Wilhelm Ernst Paulus, *Die Entwicklung der Planung des Rußlandfeldzuges*, p. 274 ff.

APPENDIX VIII

# The *Blitzkrieg* War Economy

The following statistics illustrate the effect of the *Blitzkrieg* economy on German armament production in the first two years of the war. The main characteristics are:

1. lower war production totals than those of Great Britain and the Soviet Union which adopted a total war economy;
2. increases in production to meet the requirements of specific campaigns;
3. a steady increase in tank production to meet the successive demands of *Blitzkrieg* operations in the West 1940, in the East 1941, and in the Middle East planned for 1942;
4. an inability of the aircraft industry to meet the demands placed upon it, especially in the autumn of 1940.

The low level of war production achieved by the *Blitzkrieg* economy compared with what was later achieved after the conversion to a total war economy is illustrated by the following selection of monthly production totals at the time of the German victory in the West, the attack on Russia, and the height of the battle of Normandy:

|  | June 1940 | June 1941 | July 1944 |
|---|---|---|---|
| Rifles | 106,400 | 102,280 | 249,080 |
| Machine-guns | 4,400 | 7,770 | 24,141 |
| Mortars | 1,165 | 1,073 | 2,225 |
| Artillery | 294 | 317 | 1,554 |
| Armour | 121 | 310 | 1,669 |
| Combat aircraft | 675 | 1,040 | 4,219 |

Source: *United States Strategic Bombing Survey, Economic Report*, p. 187, cited by Wilmot, p. 150.

Through adhering to the *Blitzkrieg* economy, Germany was quickly overtaken in war production by Britain, even though the latter adopted a total war economy only late in 1939.

### Output of Particular Types of Armaments in Germany and the United Kingdom, 1940–1

|  | 1940 Germany | U.K. | 1941 Germany | U.K. |
|---|---|---|---|---|
| Military Aircraft | 10,825 | 15,050 | 10,775 | 20,100 |
| Bombers | 4,000 | 3,720 | 4,350 | 4,670 |
| Fighters | 3,105 | 4,280 | 3,730 | 7,065 |
| Naval, transports, etc. | 3,720 | 7,050 | 2,695 | 8,365 |
| Armour |  |  |  |  |
| Tanks | 1,640 | 1,400 | 3,790 | 4,845 |
| Other | 500 | 6,000 | 1,300 | 10,500 |
| Trucks | 88,000 | 113,000 | 86,000 | 110,000 |
| Artillery | * | 4,700 | 11,200 | 16,700 |

* Not available

Source: Klein, p. 99.

In spite of the enormous losses of her western industries in 1941, Russia maintained a level of production in essential weapons far in excess of that of Germany. Accurate figures are not available for 1941 but the following table is indicative of the Soviet total war effort compared with that of Germany.

### German and Russian Production of Military Equipment, An Average, 1942–4

|  | Germany | Russia |
|---|---|---|
| Aircraft | 26,000 | 40,000 |
| Tanks/self-propelled guns | 12,000 | 30,000 |
| Artillery | 10,500 | 120,000 |
| Machine-guns | 516,000 | 450,000 |
| Rifles | 2,060,000 | 3,000,000 |

Source: *Statistische Schnellberichte zur Rüstungsproduktion, Februar 1945*, and Stalin's Speech, 9 Feb. 1946, *Pravda*, 10 Feb. 1946, cited by Klein, p. 210.

The periodic increases in production to meet the demands of the early German campaigns are illustrated by the following figures:

*Production of Selected Classes of Armaments*
*(1st Quarter 1940 = 100)*

| Year | Quarter | Army Weapons | Army Ammunition | Armour (total wt.) | Aircraft (total wt.) |
|------|---------|--------------|-----------------|--------------------|--------------------|
| 1939 | 4th | 94 | 96 | 85 | * |
| 1940 | 1st | 100 | 100 | 100 | 100 |
|      | 2nd | 129 | 137 | 154 | 182 |
|      | 3rd | 113 | 154 | 216 | 182 |
|      | 4th | 109 | 95 | 250 | 157 |
| 1941 | 1st | 147 | 91 | 280 | 166 |

\* Not available.

Source: Klein, p. 187

*Production of Selected Classes of Armaments, 1941*
*(1st Quarter 1941 = 100)*

| Year | Quarter | Army Weapons | Army Ammunition | Tanks | Aircraft |
|------|---------|--------------|-----------------|-------|----------|
| 1941 | 1st | 100 | 100 | 100 | 100 |
|      | 2nd | 91 | 80 | 132 | 128 |
|      | 3rd | 80 | 53 | 146 | 122 |
|      | 4th | 62 | 48 | 167 | 104 |

Source: Extracts and computation from Klein, p. 187.

The general drop in production reflects the optimistic expectation of a quick victory in the East in 1941. Tank production, however, was increased to meet the needs of the mobile operations in the Caucasus, Middle East, and North Africa planned for 1942.

# BIBLIOGRAPHY

## A. PUBLISHED DOCUMENTS

BAYNES, N. (ed.), *Hitler's Speeches*, 2 vols. (Oxford, 1942).

CIANO, COUNT GALEAZZO, *Diplomatic Papers*, edited by Malcolm Muggeridge (London, 1948).

*Documents on German Foreign Policy, 1918–1945, from the Archives of the German Foreign Ministry*, Series D, 13 vols. (Washington, 1949).

DOMARUS, MAX, *Hitler, Reden und Proklamationen, 1932–1945*. 2 vols. (Würzburg, 1962).

'Fuehrer Conferences on Naval Affairs, 1939–1945', *Brassey's Naval Annual* (London/New York, 1948), pp. 25–496.

GENOUD, FRANÇOIS (ed.), *The Testament of Adolf Hitler: the Hitler–Bormann Documents, February–April 1945*, translated by R. H. Stevens (London, 1961).

*German Order of Battle*, The War Office (London, 1944).

HILLGRUBER, ANDREAS (ed.), *Staatsmänner und Diplomaten bei Hitler* (Frankfurt a.M., 1967).

*Hitler's Secret Conversations, 1941–1944*, translated by Norman Cameron and R. H. Stevens (New York, 1953).

HOFER, WALTER, *Der Nationalsozialismus, Dokumente 1933–1945* (Frankfurt a.M., 1957).

HUBATSCH, WALTER (ed.), *Hitlers Weisungen für die Kriegführung, 1939–1945* (Munich, 1965).

JACOBSEN, HANS-ADOLF (ed.), *Dokumente zur Vorgeschichte des Westfeldzuges, 1939–1940* (Berlin/Frankfurt a.M., 1956).

—— (ed.), *Der Zweite Weltkrieg. Grundzüge der Politik und Strategie in Dokumenten* (Frankfurt a.M./Hamburg, 1965).

—— (ed.), *Kriegstagebuch des Oberkommandos der Wehrmacht (Wehrmachtführungsstab). 1 August 1940–31 Dezember 1941*, Vol. I of *Kriegstagebuch des Oberkommandos der Wehrmacht (Wehrmachtführungsstab). 1940–1945* (General editor, Percy Ernst Schramm), 4 vols. (Frankfurt a.M., 1961–5).

—— (ed.), *1939–1945. Der Zweite Weltkrieg in Chronik und Dokumenten* (Darmstadt, 1962).

KLEE, KARL (ed.), *Dokumente zum Unternehmen 'Seelöwe'. Die geplante deutsche Landung in England* (Göttingen/Berlin/Frankfurt a.M., 1959).

MENDELSSOHN, PETER DE (ed.), *The Nuremberg Documents. Some Aspects of German War Policy in 1939–34* (London, 1946).

*Nazi Conspiracy and Aggression*, 10 vols. (Washington, 1946).

Poland, Ministry of Foreign Affairs, *Official Documents Concerning Polish–German and Polish–Soviet Relations. 1933–1939* (The Polish White Book) (London, 1940).

SONTAG, RAYMOND J., and BEDDIE, JAMES S. (eds.), *Nazi–Soviet Relations 1939–41, from the Archives of the German Foreign Office* (Washington, 1948).

SZINAI, MIKLÓS, and SZÜES, LÁSZLÓ (eds.), *Horthy's Confidential Papers* (Budapest, 1965).

THOMAS, GEORG, *Geschichte der deutschen Wehr- und Rüstungswirtschaft (1918–1943/45)*, Schriften des Bundesarchivs, edited by Wolfgang Birkenfeld (Boppard am Rhein, 1966).

*Trial of the Major War Criminals before the International Military Tribunal*, 42 vols. (Nuremberg, 1947).

### B. DIARIES

CIANO, COUNT GALEAZZO, *Diary, 1939–1943*, edited by Hugh Gibson (London, 1948).

GOEBBELS, JOSEPH, *Diaries*, edited by L. P. Lochner (London, 1948).

GROSCURTH, HELMUTH, *Tagebücher eines Abwehroffiziers 1938–1940*, edited by Helmut Krausnick and Harold C. Deutsch (Stuttgart, 1970).

HALDER, FRANZ, *Generaloberst Halder: Kriegstagebuch*, edited by Hans-Adolf Jacobsen, 3 vols. (Stuttgart, 1963).

HASSELL, ULRICH VON, *The von Hassell Diaries, 1938–1944* (London, 1948),

### C. DOCUMENTS ON MICROFILM

The National Archives of the United States, The American Historical Association and General Services Administration, Microfilm Series:

*Oberkommando der Wehrmacht, Wehrmachtführungsstab* (General Jodl's files 1938–45), Roll No. T–77/775.

*Oberkommando der Wehrmacht* (File on 'War Aims East', Hitler), T–77/777.

*OKW* ('Barbarossa' File), T–77/792.

*OKH, Heeresarchiv* (Operations report, 1941), T–78/3.

*OKH, Heeresarchiv* (List of plans and policy towards Russia, 1919–1941), T–78/7.

*OKH, Heerespersonalamt* (General Schmundt—*Tätigkeitsbericht*), T–78/39.

*OKH, Generalstab des Heeres* (Concentration and plans for Operation 'Barbarossa'), T–78/335.

*OKH, Generalstab des Heeres* (Operations in Russia, Occupation policy in Russia, critiques by General Halder), T–78/336.

*Operation Abteilung III* (Feasibility study of operations in the Middle East towards Egypt via Syria), T–78/346.

*Generalstab des Heeres, Organisationsabteilung* (Operations and planning, Russia, 1942), T-78/431.
*Generalstab des Heeres/Abteilung Fremde Heere Ost/II*, (Report on Soviet Military Leadership), T-78/464.
*OKH, Abteilung IV* (Colonel Groscurth's papers), T-84/229.
*Europäischer Beitrag zur Geschichte des Weltkrieges II, 1939–45. Die deutsche Luftwaffe im Kriege gegen Rußland, 1941–45.* Institut für Zeitgeschichte, Munich, MA 54 (1).

### D. GENERAL WORKS AND MEMOIRS

ABSHAGEN, K. H., *Canaris, Patriot und Weltbürger* (Stuttgart, 1949).

ALEXANDROV, VICTOR, *The Tukhachevsky Affair* (London, 1964).

ALLEN, W. E. D., and MURSTOFF, PAUL, *The Russian Campaigns of 1941–1943* (London, 1944).

ALLMENDINGER, KARL, *Terrain Factors in the Russian Campaign*, Department of the Army Pamphlet No. 20–290 (Washington, 1951).

ANDERS, GENERAL W., *Hitler's Defeat in Russia* (Chicago, 1953).

ARMSTRONG, JOHN A., *Ukrainian Nationalism, 1939–1945* (New York, 1955).

—— *Soviet Partisans in World War II* (Madison, Wis., 1964).

ASSMANN, VICE-ADMIRAL KURT, *Deutsche Schicksalsjahre* (Wiesbaden, 1951).

BARBU, ZEVEDEI, *Democracy and Dictatorship* (London, 1956).

BARNET, CORELLI, *The Sword Bearers* (London, 1966).

BAUMBACH, WERNER, *Life and Death of the Luftwaffe* (New York, 1960).

BECK, LUDWIG, *Studien*, edited by Hans Speidel (Stuttgart, 1955).

BELOFF, MAX, *Foreign Policy of Soviet Russia, 1929–41*, 2 vols. (London, 1947–9).

BENGTSON, J. R., *Nazi War Aims, the Plans for a Thousand Year Reich* (Augustana, 1962).

BESYMENSKI, L., *Sonderakte Barbarossa*, trans. from Russian to German by Erich Einhorn (Stuttgart, 1968).

*Bilanz des Zweiten Weltkrieges* (Oldenburg/Hamburg, 1953).

BLAU, GEORGE E., *The German Campaign in Russia—Planning and Operations (1940–1942)*, Department of the Army Pamphlet No. 20–261a (Washington, 1955).

BLUMENTRITT, GÜNTHER, *Von Rundstedt. The Soldier and the Man*, translated by Cuthbert Reavely (London, 1952).

BOR, PETER, *Gespräche mit Halder* (Wiesbaden, 1950).

BRACHER, KARL-DIETRICH, SAUER, WOLFGANG, and SCHULTZ, GERHARD, *Die nationalsozialistische Machtergreifung: Studien zur Errichtung des totalitären Herrschaftssystems in Deutschland* (Cologne, 1960).

282 BIBLIOGRAPHY

BRAMSTED, ERNEST, K., *Goebbels and National Socialist Propaganda* (Michigan, 1965).

BROSZAT, MARTIN, *Nationalsozialistische Polenpolitik, 1939–1945* (Stuttgart, 1961).

BRYANT, ARTHUR, *The Turn of the Tide, 1939–1943* (London, 1957).

BUCHHEIT, GERT, *Hitler der Feldherr, Zerstörung einer Legende* (Rastatt, 1958).

BUCKLEY, CHRISTOPHER, *Norway, the Commandos, Dieppe* (London, 1951).

BULLOCK, ALAN, *Hitler, a Study in Tyranny* (London, 1962).

BURDICK, CHARLES B., *German Military Strategy in Spain in World War II* (Syracuse, 1968).

BURY, J. B., *The Ancient Greek Historians* (New York, 1958).

CARELL, PAUL, *Unternehmen Barbarossa. Der Marsch nach Rußland* (Frankfurt a.M., 1963).

CARR, E. H., *German–Soviet Relations Between the Two Wars* (Baltimore, 1951).

CARSTEN, F. L., *The Reichswehr and Politics, 1918–1933* (Oxford, 1966).

CHALES DE BEAULIEU, W., *Der Vorstoß der Panzergruppe 4 auf Leningrad* (Neckargemünd, 1961).

CLARK, ALAN, *Barbarossa: the Russian–German Conflict 1941–45* (London, 1965).

CONNELL, JOHN, *Wavell, Scholar and Soldier* (London, 1964).

CONWAY, J. S., *The Nazi Persecution of the Churches, 1933–45* (Toronto, 1969).

CRAIG, GORDON A., *The Politics of the Prussian Army* (Oxford, 1955).

—— *War, Politics and Diplomacy* (London, 1966).

—— and GILBERT, F., *The Diplomats, 1919–1939* (Princeton, 1953).

CRAIGIE, SIR ROBERT, *Behind the Japanese Mask* (London, 1946).

DALLIN, ALEXANDER, *The German Rule in Russia, 1941–45* (London, 1957).

DEICHMANN, PAUL, *German Air Force Operations in Support of the Army*, U.S.A.F. Historical Studies No. 154 (New York, 1966).

DELBRÜCK, HANS, *Krieg und Politik*, 4 vols. (Berlin, 1918–19).

DETWILER, DONALD S., *Hitler, Franco und Gibraltar: die Frage des spanischen Eintritts in den Zweiten Weltkrieg* (Wiesbaden, 1962).

DEUTSCH, HAROLD C., *The Conspiracy against Hitler in the twilight war* (Minnesota, 1968).

DIRKSEN, H. VON, *Moskau, Tokio, London, Erinnerungen und Betrachtungen zu 20 Jahren deutscher Außenpolitik, 1919–39* (Stuttgart, 1949).

DRAPER, THEODORE, *The Six Weeks War* (London, 1946).

EARLE, E. M. (ed.), *Makers of Modern Strategy* (Princeton, 1944).

ERDMANN, K. D., *Die Zeit der Weltkriege, Handbuch der deutschen Geschichte*, Band IV (Stuttgart, 1959).

EREMENKO, A., *The Arduous Beginning*, translated by Vic Schneierson (Moscow, 1966).

ERFURTH, WALDEMAR, *Geschichte des deutschen Generalstabes, 1918–1945* (Frankfurt/Göttingen/Berlin, 1960).

—— *Warfare in the Far North*, Department of the Army Pamphlet No. 20–292 (Washington, 1951).

ERICKSON, JOHN, *The Soviet High Command, A Military–Political History. 1918–1941* (London, 1962).

FABRY, P. W., *Der Hitler–Stalin Pakt, 1939–41* (Darmstadt, 1962).

FERGUSON, ALAN D., and LEVIN, ALFRED (eds.), *Essays In Russian History* (Connecticut, 1964).

FISCHER, G., *Soviet Opposition to Stalin* (Cambridge, Mass., 1952).

FITZGIBBON, CONSTANTINE, *The Shirt of Nessus* (London, 1956).

FLEMING, PETER, *Operation Sea Lion* (New York, 1957).

FOERTSCH, HERMANN, *Schuld und Verhängnis* (Munich, 1951).

—— *The Art of Modern War* (New York, 1940).

FÖRSTER, W., *Generaloberst Beck, sein Kampf gegen den Krieg* (Munich, 1953).

FULLER, MAJOR-GENERAL J. F. C., *The Second World War* (London, 1948).

—— *The Conduct of War* (London, 1961).

GAFENCU, GRIGORE, *Prelude to the Russian Campaign* (London, 1945).

GARTHOFF, RAYMOND L., *How Russia Makes War* (London, 1954).

GEMZELL, CARL AXEL, *Raeder, Hitler und Skandinavien. Der Kampf um einen maritimen Operationsplan* (Lund, 1965).

GHEORGE, JON, *Rumäniens Weg zum Satalliten-Staat* (Heidelberg, 1952).

GILBERT, G. M., *The Psychology of Dictatorship* (New York, 1950).

GORBATOV, A. V., *Years off my Life, Memoirs of a Soviet Cavalry Officer* (London, 1964).

GÖRLITZ, WALTER, *Keitel, Verbrecher oder Offizier?* (Frankfurt a.M., 1961).

—— *Paulus and Stalingrad*, translated by R. N. Stevens (London, 1963).

—— *The German General Staff, its History and Structure, 1657–1945* (London, 1953).

GOURE, LEON, *The Siege of Leningrad* (London, 1962).

GOUTARD, A., *The Battle of France, 1940*, translated by A. R. P. Burgess (New York, 1959).

GREIFFENBERG, HANS VON, *Combat in Russian Forests and Swamps*, Department of the Army Pamphlet No. 20–231 (Washington, 1951).

GREINER, HELMUTH, *Die oberste Wehrmachtführung, 1939–41* (Wiesbaden, 1951).

GUDERIAN, HEINZ, *Panzer Leader*, translated by Constantine Fitzgibbon (London, 1952).

GUILLAUME, A., *La Guerre germano-soviétique* (Paris, 1951).

GWYER, J. M. A., and BUTLER, J. R. M., *Grand Strategy, History of the Second World War*, Vol. III, Part I (London, 1964).

HALDER, FRANZ, *Hitler as Warlord*, translated by Paul Findlay (London, 1950).

HAUPT, WERNER, *Kiew, die größte Kesselschlacht der Geschichte* (Bad Neuheim, 1964).

HAUSSER, PAUL, *Waffen-SS im Einsatz* (Göttingen, 1953).

HEUSINGER, ADOLF, *Befehl im Widerstreit, Schicksalsjahre der deutschen Armee, 1923–1945* (Tübingen, 1957).

HIGGINS, TRUMBULL, *Hitler and Russia. The Third Reich in a Two Front War, 1937–1943* (New York, 1966).

HILGER, GUSTAV, and MEYER, ALFRED G., *The Incompatible Allies* (New York, 1953).

HILLGRUBER, ANDREAS, *Hitler, König Karol und Marschall Antonescu, die deutsch-rumänischen Beziehungen, 1938–1944* (Wiesbaden, 1954).

—— *Hitlers Strategie, Politik und Kriegsführung, 1940–1941* (Frankfurt a.M., 1965).

HINSLEY, F. H., *Hitler's Strategy* (Cambridge, 1951).

HITLER, ADOLF, *Mein Kampf*, translated by James Murphy (London, 1939).

—— *Hitler's Secret Book*, translated by Salvator Attanasio (New York, 1961).

HOFER, WALTER, *Die Entfesselung des Zweiten Weltkrieges* (Frankfurt a.M., 1964).

HÖHN, HANS, *et al.* (eds.). *Auf antisowjetischem Kriegskurs. Studien zur militärischen Vorbereitung des deutschen Imperialismus auf die Aggression gegen die UdSSR (1933–1941). Schriften des Deutschen Instituts für Militärgeschichte* (Berlin, 1970).

HOPTNER, J. B., *Jugoslavia in Crisis, 1934–41* (New York, 1962).

HOSSBACH, FRIEDRICH, *Zwischen Wehrmacht und Hitler* (Hannover, 1949).

HOTH, HERMANN, *Panzeroperationen. Die Panzergruppe 3 und der operative Gedanke der deutschen Führung* (Heidelberg, 1956).

HÖTTL, WILHELM, *The Secret Front*, translated by R. H. Stevens (London 1953).

HOWARD, MICHAEL (ed.), *The Theory and Practice of War* (London, 1965).

HOWELL, EDGAR W., *The Soviet Partisan Movement*, Department of the Army Pamphlet No. 20-244 (Washington, 1956).

HUBATSCH, WALTER, and SCHRAMM, PERCY E., *Die deutsche militärische Führung in der Kriegswende* (Cologne/Opladen, 1964).

ILNYTZKYJ, ROMAN, *Deutschland und die Ukraine, 1934–45* (Munich, 1958).

INGRIM, ROBERT, *Hitlers glücklichster Tag* (Stuttgart, 1962).

JACOBSEN, HANS-ADOLF, *Fall Gelb, der Kampf um den deutschen Operation-plan zur Westoffensive, 1940* (Wiesbaden, 1957).

—— and ROHWER, J. (eds.), *The Decisive Battles of World War II: the German View*, translated by Edward Fitzgerald (New York, 1965).

JONG, LOUIS DE, *The German Fifth Column in the Second World War*, translated by C. M. Geyl (Chicago, 1956).

JOST, WALTER (ed.), *Jahrbuch des deutschen Heeres, 1938* (Leipzig, 1937).

KAMENETZKY, IHOR, *Secret Nazi Plans for Eastern Europe. A Study of Lebensraumpolitik* (New York, 1961).

KENNAN, G., *Soviet Foreign Policy, 1917–1941* (New York, 1960).

KENNEDY, ROBERT M., *German Anti-Guerrilla Operations in the Balkans (1941–1944)*, Department of the Army Pamphlet No. 20–243 (Washington, 1954).

—— *The German Campaign in Poland, 1939*, Department of the Army Pamphlet No. 20–255 (Washington, 1956).

KERN, ERICH, *Dance of Death*, translated by Paul Findley (London, 1951).

KERTESZ, S. D., *Diplomacy in a Whirlpool. Hungary between Nazi Germany and Soviet Russia* (Notre Dame, Indiana, 1953).

KESSELRING, ALBERT, *Memoirs* (London, 1952).

KLEE, KARL, *Das Unternehmen 'Seelöwe'. Die geplante deutsche Landung in England, 1940* (Göttingen, 1958).

KLEIN, BURTON, H., *Germany's Economic Preparations for War* (Cambridge, Mass., 1959).

KORDT, ERICH, *Wahn und Wirklichkeit* (Stuttgart, 1947).

LEE, ASHER, *The German Air Force* (London, 1946).

LEEB, EMIL, *Aus der Rüstung des Dritten Reiches (Das Heereswaffenamt, 1938–1945)* (Frankfurt a.M./Berlin, 1958).

LEVERKUEHN, PAUL, *German Military Intelligence*, translated by R. H. Stevens and Constantine FitzGibbon (London, 1954).

LIDDELL HART, BASIL H., *Defence of the West* (London, 1950).

—— *On the Other Side of the Hill* (London, 1951).

—— *Strategy* (New York, 1954).

—— (ed.), *The Rommel Papers* (London, 1953).

—— (ed.), *The Soviet Army* (London, 1956).

—— *Thoughts on War* (London, 1944).

LOSSBERG, BERNARD VON, *Im Wehrmachtführungsstab* (Hamburg, 1949).

LUDENDORFF, ERICH, *Der totale Krieg* (Munich, 1935).

LUNDIN, CHARLES, *Finland in the Second World War* (Indiana, 1957).

MACARTNEY, C. A., 'Hungary's Declaration of War on the U.S.S.R. in 1941', *Studies in Diplomatic History and Historiography in Honour of G. P. Gooch* (London, 1961).

MANSTEIN, ERICH VON, *Aus einem Soldatenleben, 1887–1939* (Bonn, 1958).

—— *Lost Victories*, translated by Anthony G. Powell (London, 1958).

MARTIENSSEN, ANTHONY, *Hitler and his Admirals* (London, 1948).

MASER, WERNER, *Hitlers Mein Kampf. Entstehung, Aufbau, Stil, Änderungen, Quellen, Quellenwert, kommentierte Auszüge* (Munich, 1966).

MATLOFF, MAURICE, and SNELL, EDWIN M., *Strategic Planning for Coalition Warfare, 1941–1942* (Washington, 1953).

MEINCK, GERHARD, *Hitler und die deutsche Aufrüstung, 1933–1937* (Wiesbaden, 1959).

MELLENTHIN, F. W. VON, *Panzer Battles, 1939–45* (London, 1955).

MIKSCHE, F. O., *Atomic Weapons and Armies* (London, 1955).

MILWARD, ALAN S., *The German Economy at War* (London, 1965).

MOLL, OTTO E., *Die deutschen Generalfeldmarschälle, 1939–1945* (Rastatt, 1961).

MOSLEY, LEONARD, *Hirohito, Emperor of Japan* (New York, 1966).

MÜLLER-HILLEBRAND, BURKHART, *Das Heer, 1933–1945. Entwicklung des organisatorischen Aufbaus*, 2 vols. (Frankfurt a.M. 1956).

—— *German Armoured Traffic Control during the Russian Campaign*, Department of the Army Pamphlet No. 20–242 (Washington, 1952).

—— *The German Campaigns in the Balkans (Spring 1941)*, Department of the Army Pamphlet No. 20–260 (Washington, 1953).

—— *German Tank Maintenance in World War II*, Department of the Army Pamphlet No. 20–202 (Washington, 1954).

MURAWSKI, ERICH, *Der deutsche Wehrmachtsbericht, 1939–1945* (Boppard am Rhein, 1962).

NEITZEL, HASSO, *Rear Area Security in Russia*, Department of the Army Pamphlet No. 20–240 (Washington, 1951).

NEUMANN, SIGMUND, *Permanent Revolution. Totalitarianism in the Age of International Civil War* (New York, 1965).

O'NEILL, ROBERT J., *The German Army and the Nazi Party, 1933–1939* (London, 1966).

PAGET, R. T., *Manstein, his Campaigns and his Trial* (London, 1951).

PERRAULT, GILLES, *The Red Orchestra*, translated by Peter Wiles (New York, 1969).

PETROV, VLADIMIR, *June 22 1941: Soviet Historians and the German Invasion* (Columbia, S.C., 1968).

PHILIPPI, ALFRED, and HEIM, FERDINAND, *Der Feldzug gegen Sowjetrußland, 1941–45* (Stuttgart, 1962).

RAEDER, ERICH, *My Life* (U.S. Naval Institute. Annapolis, 1960).

RAUS, ERHARD, *Effects of Climate on Combat in European Russia*, Department of the Army Pamphlet No. 20–291 (Washington, 1952).

—— *Military Improvisations During the Russian Campaign*, Department of the Army Pamphlet No. 20–201 (Washington, 1951).

RAUSCHNING, HERMANN, *Hitler Speaks* (London, 1939).

REITLINGER, GERALD, *The House Built on Sand. Conflicts of German Policy in Russia, 1939–1945* (London, 1960).

—— *S.S. The Alibi of a Nation* (London, 1956).

RIBBENTROP, JOACHIM VON, *The Ribbentrop Memoirs*, translated by Oliver Watson (London 1954).

RICHARDSON, WILLIAM, and FREIDIN, SEYMOUR, *The Fatal Decisions*, translated by Constantine Fitzgibbon (London, 1956).

RIEKER, KARLHEINRICH, *Ein Mann verliert einen Weltkrieg* (Frankfurt a.M., 1955).

RITTER, GERHARD, *Die deutschen Militär-Attachés und das Auswärtige Amt* (Heidelberg, 1959).

ROBERTSON, E. M., *Hitler's Pre-War Policy and Military Plans, 1933–1939* (London, 1963).

—— (ed.), *The Origins of the Second World War* (London, 1971).

ROOS, HANS, *Polen und Europa. Studien zur polnischen Außenpolitik, 1931–1939* (Tübingen, 1957).

ROSINSKI, HERBERT, *The German Army* (New York, 1966).

RUGE, FRIEDRICH, *Der Seekrieg. The German Navy's Story, 1939–1945*, translated by M. G. Saunders (Annapolis, 1957).

SALISBURY, HARRISON E., *The 900 Days: The Siege of Leningrad* (New York, 1969).

SCHELLENBERG, WALTER, *The Schellenberg Memoirs*, translated by Louis Hagen (London, 1956).

SCHMIDT, PAUL, *Hitler's Interpreter*, edited by R. H. C. Steed (New York, 1951).

SCHMOKEL, WOLFE W., *Dream of Empire: German Colonialism 1919–1945* (Yale, 1964).

SCHRAMM-VON THADDEN, E., *Griechenland und die Großmächte im Zweiten Weltkrieg* (Wiesbaden, 1955).

SCHROEDER, PAUL W., *The Axis Alliance and Japanese–American Relations, 1941* (Cornell U.P., New York, 1958).

SEATON, ALBERT, *The Russo-German War 1941–45* (London, 1971).

SETH, ROBERT, *Operation Barbarossa, the Battle for Moscow* (London, 1965).

SHERWOOD, ROBERT E., *Roosevelt and Hopkins: An Intimate History* (New York, 1948).

SHIRER, WILLIAM L., *The Rise and Fall of the Third Reich* (New York, 1962).

SHULMAN, MILTON, *Defeat in the West* (London, 1947).

SNELL, JOHN L. (ed.), *Outbreak of the Second World War: Design or Blunder?* (Boston, 1962).

SOKOLOVSKY, V. D. (ed.), *Military Strategy, Soviet Doctrine and Concepts*, translated by Herbert C. Dinerstein, Leon Goure, Thomas W. Wolfe (London, 1963).

SOREL, GEORGES, *Reflections on Violence*, translated by T. E. Hulme (Glencoe, Illinois, 1950).

SPEER, ALBERT, *Inside the Third Reich*, translated by Richard and Clara Winston (New York, 1970).

STEETS, HANS, *Gebirgsjäger bei Uman* (Neckargemünd, 1955).

STRAWSON, JOHN, *Hitler as Military Commander* (London, 1971).

STRIK-STRIKFELD, WILFRIED, *Against Stalin and Hitler, 1941–1945*, translated by David Footman (London, 1970).

TANNER, V., *The Winter War* (New York, 1955).

TAYLOR, A. J. P., *Origins of the Second World War* (London, 1963).

TAYLOR, TELFORD, *The Breaking Wave* (New York, 1967).

—— *The March of Conquest* (New York, 1959).

—— *The Sword and the Swastika* (New York, 1952).

TELPUCHOWSKI, BORIS S., *Die sowjetische Geschichte des Großen Vaterländischen Krieges, 1941–1945*, edited by Andreas Hillgruber and Hans-Adolf Jacobsen, translated into German by Robert Frhr. von Freytag-Loringhoven *et al.* (Frankfurt a.M., 1961).

TESKE, HERMANN, *General Ernst Köstring. Der militärische Mittler zwischen dem deutschen Reich und der Sowjetunion. 1921–1941. Profile bedeutender Soldaten*, vol. I., Bundesarchiv/Militärarchiv (Frankfurt a.M., 1966).

—— *Die silbernen Spiegel: Generalstabsdienst unter der Lupe* (Heidelberg, 1952).

*The Rise and Fall of the German Air Force, 1933–1945*, Air Ministry Study (London, 1947).

TIPPELSKIRCH, KURT VON, *Geschichte des Zweiten Weltkrieges* (Bonn, 1956).

TREVOR-ROPER, HUGH R. (ed.), *Hitler's War Directives. 1939–1945* (London, 1964).

—— *The Last Days of Hitler* (London, 1947).

—— 'The Mind of Adolph Hitler'. Introduction to *Hitler's Secret Conversations, 1941–1944* (New York, 1961).

ULRICH, KARLHEINZ, UND NEUNEIER, WILLI PETER, *Sturm im Osten. Am Wege einer Panzerdivision* (Dessau, 1942).

UPTON, A. F., *Finland in Crisis, 1940–1941* (London, 1964).

VÖLKER, KARL-HEINZ, *Die Entwicklung der militärischen Luftfahrt in Deutschland 1920–1933* (Stuttgart, 1961).

*Vollmacht des Gewissens*, 2 vols, (Frankfurt a.M./Berlin, 1965).

WAGENER, CARL, *Moskau, 1941 — Der Angriff auf die russische Haupstadt* (Bad Neuheim, 1966).

WAGNER, ELIZABETH (ed.), *Der Generalquartiermeister. Briefe und Tagebuchaufzeichnungen des Generalquartiermeisters des Heeres General der Artillerie Eduard Wagner* (Munich and Vienna, 1963).

WARLIMONT, GENERAL WALTER, *Inside Hitler's Headquarters*, translated by R. H. Barry (London, 1964).

WEBER, RICHARD, AND KORBE, KARL, *Kartenskizzen zum Weltkrieg und zum großdeutschen Freiheitskampf für den Unterricht in Kriegsgeschichte* (Berlin, 1944).

WEINBERG, G. L., *Germany and the Soviet Union, 1939–1941* (Leiden, 1954).

—— *The Foreign Policy of Hitler's Germany: Diplomatic Revolution in Europe 1933–36* (Chicago and London, 1970).

WERTH, ALEXANDER, *Russia at War* (London, 1964).

WERTHEN, WOLFGANG, *Geschichte der 16. Panzerdivision, 1939–1945* (Bad Neuheim, 1958).

WHEATLEY, RONALD, *Operation Sea Lion. German Plans for the Invasion of England, 1939–1942* (Oxford, 1958).

WHEELER-BENNETT, J. W., *Nemesis of Power, the German Army in Politics, 1918–1945* (London, 1964).

—— *Brest-Litovsk: The Forgotten Peace* (London, 1938).

WILMOT, CHESTER, *The Struggle for Europe* (London, 1952).

WUORINEN, J. (ed.), *Finland and World War II, 1939–44* (New York, 1948).

ZIEMKE, KARL F., *The German Northern Theater of Operations, 1940–45*, Department of the Army Pamphlet No. 20-271 (Washington, 1959).

## E. ARTICLES AND PERIODICALS

ARETIN, KARL OTMAR FRHR. VON, 'Die deutschen Generale und Hitlers Kriegspolitik', *Politische Studien*, 10 (1959), 569–83.

ASSMANN, KURT, 'The Battle for Moscow, Turning Point of the War', *Foreign Affairs*, 28 (January 1950), 308–26.

BENZEL, ROLF, 'Die deutsche Flottenpolitik von 1933 bis 1939', Beiheft 3 der *Marine Rundschau* (Frankfurt a.M., 1958).

BROWER, DANIEL R., 'The Soviet Union and the German Invasion of 1941: A New Soviet View', *The Journal of Modern History* 41, 3 (1969), 327–34.

BUSCH, ERNST, 'Ist die schlachtentscheidende Rolle der Infantrie zu Ende?' *Jahrbuch für Wehrpolitik und Wehrwissenschaft* (Berlin, 1937-8), 11–27.

CARSTEN, F. L., 'The Reichswehr and the Red Army, 1920–1933', *Survey*, 44/45 (1962).

DALLIN, D. J., 'Die Sowjetspionage', Beilage zur Wochenzeitung *Das Parlament*, 48 (1955).

'Die amtliche militärgeschichtliche Forschung in Westdeutschland' *Zeitschrift für Geschichtswissenschaft*, 10 (1962), 1669–71.

290 BIBLIOGRAPHY

FÖRSTER, GERHARD, GROEHLER, OLAF, AND PAULUS, GÜNTHER, 'Zum Verhältnis von Kriegszielen und Kriegsplanung des faschistischen deutschen Imperialismus', *Zeitschrift für Geschichtswissenschaft*, 12 (1964), 928–48.

GATZKE, HANS W., 'Russo-German Military Collaboration during the Weimar Republic', *American Historical Review*, 63 (1958).

GEYER, HERMANN, 'Uber die Zeitdauer von Angriffgefechten', *Militärwissenschaftliche Rundschau*, 4 (1939), 649–66.

HALLGARTEN, G. W. F., 'General Hans von Seeckt and Russia, 1920–1922', *The Journal of Modern History*, 21 (1949), 28–34.

HASS, GERHARD, 'Hans-Adolf Jacobsens Konzeption einer Geschichte des Zweiten Weltkrieges', *Zeitschrift für Geschichtswissenschaft*, 13 (1965), 1148–71.

HEUSINGER, ADOLF, 'Die letzte Chance vertan', *Der Spiegel*, 16 (1966), 134.

HILL, LEONIDAS, 'Three Crises, 1938–39', *Journal of Contemporary History*, 3, 1 (1968), 113–44.

JACOBSEN, HANS-ADOLF, 'The Second World War as a Problem in Historical Research', *World Politics*, 16, 4 (1964), 620–41.

—— 'Das Halder-Tagebuch als historische Quelle', *Festschrift Percy Ernst Schramm zu seinem siebzigsten Geburtstag von Schülern und Freunden zugeeignet*, Band II (Wiesbaden 1964), 251–68.

MACARTNEY, C. A., 'Hungary's Declaration of War on the U.S.S.R. in 1941', *Studies in Diplomatic History and Historiography in Honour of G. P. Gooch* (London, 1961).

MASON, T. W., 'Some Origins of the Second World War', *Past and Present*, 29 (1964), 67–87.

MORGAN, G. A., 'Planning in Foreign Affairs: the State of the Art', *Foreign Affairs*, 34, 2 (1961), 271–8.

MOSTOVENKO, V., 'History of the T34 Tank', *Soviet Military Review*, 3 (1967), 38–9.

NIKOLAEV, P. A., 'Versuche zur Rehabilitierung des deutschen Militarismus in der modernen bürgerlichen Historiographie', *Zeitschrift für Geschichtswissenschaft*, 10 (1962).

PHILIPPI, ALFRED, 'Das Pripjet-Problem', Beiheft 2 der *Wehrwissenschaftlichen Rundschau* (Frankfurt a.M., 1956).

PRESSEISEN, E. L., 'Prelude to Barbarossa, Germany and the Balkans, 1939–41', *Journal of Modern History*, 32 (1960), 359–70.

RYABOV, V., 'Reflections on the Past War', *Soviet Military Review*, 6 (1966), 35.

SERAPHIM, HANS-GÜNTHER and HILLGRUBER, ANDREAS, 'Hitlers Entschluß zum Angriff auf Rußland', *Vierteljahreshefte für Zeitgeschichte*, 2 (1954), 239–54.

STOLFI, R. H. S., 'Equipment for Victory in France in 1940', *History*, 55 (1970), 1–20.

TERVEEN, FRITZ, 'Der Filmbericht über Hitlers 50. Geburtstag. Ein Beispiel nationalistischer Selbstdarstellung und Propaganda', *Vierteljahreshefte für Zeitgeschichte*, 8 (1959), 75–84.

TREVOR-ROPER, HUGH R., 'A. J. P. Taylor, Hitler and the War', *Encounter*, 17 (July 1961), 88–96.

—— 'Why didn't they invade?' *Sunday Times Magazine*, 16 May 1965.

UHLIG, HEINRICH, 'Das Einwirken Hitlers auf Planung und Führung des Ostfeldzuges', *Aus Politik und Zeitgeschichte*, Beilage zur Wochenzeitung *Das Parlament* 16 March 1960), 161–79, (22 March 1960), 181–98.

—— 'Der verbrecherische Befehl', *Aus Politik und Zeitgeschichte*, Beilage zur Wochenzeitung *Das Parlament* (17 July 1957).

VOGELSANG, THILO, 'Hitlers Brief an Reichenau vom 4 Dezember 1933', *Vierteljahrsheft für Zeitgeschichte*, 4 (1959).

WEINBERG, C. L., 'Der deutsche Entschluß zum Angriff auf die Sowjetunion', *Vierteljahrsheft für Zeitgeschichte*, 1 (1953), 301–18.

ZHILIN, P., 'Military History in Modern Times', *Soviet Military Review*, 10 (1966), 36–8.

ZUCKERTORT, JOHANNES, 'Der deutsche Militarismus und die Legende von Präventivkrieg Hitlerdeutschlands gegen die Sowjetunion', *Der deutsche Imperialismus und der Zweite Weltkrieg*, Materialien der Wissenschaftlichen Konferenz der Historiker der DDR und der UdSSR, 14–19 Dez. 1959 in Berlin, vol. I (Berlin, 1960), 145–54.


F. UNPUBLISHED SOURCES

'Armoured Break-through', extracts from the War Diary of Panzer Group 1, 1940–1942. Typescript translation, the War Office, London, 1948.

BOCK, FEDOR VON, 'Tagebuchnotizen', Bundesarchiv/Militärarchiv N 22/7.

CONWAY, JOHN S., 'German Foreign Policy, 1937–1939'. Unpublished Ph.D. dissertation, Cambridge University, 1956.

GEYR VON SCHWEPPENBURG, BARON, conversation with the writer, 27 June 1969.

HALDER, FRANZ, Correspondence with the writer, 1966–7. Conversation with the writer, 23 June 1969.

HEUSINGER, ADOLF, 'Dokumentenbuch Heusinger', Institut für Zeitgeschichte, Munich, 287/62, F 78.

LEYDERRY, E., 'The German Defeat in the East', Monograph, War Office, London, 1952.

MANSTEIN, ERICH VON, Conversations with the writer, 1959–60, 1969.

MÜLLER-HILLEBRAND, BURKHART, Conversations with the writer, 1960, 1965. Correspondence 1966–7.

PAULUS, WILHELM ERNST, 'Die Entwicklung der Planung des Rußland-Feldzuges', Typescript dissertation, University of Bonn, 1957.

2 U

PHILIPPI, ALFRED, Conversation with the writer, 30 May 1969.

RUNDSTEDT, GERD VON, Correspondence with the writer, 1947–9.

SIEWERT, CURT, Conversation with the writer, 8 July 1969.

WARLIMONT, WALTER, Conversation with the writer, 27 June 1969.

United States Army Historical Division Manuscripts from the Collection of the Foreign Military Studies Branch, USAREUR, Heidelberg:

BLUMENTRITT, GÜNTHER. 'Thoughts of a former Soldier on Strategy, Politics and Psychology of the 1939–45 War', MS–B647 (1947).

GUDERIAN, HEINZ, 'Interrelation of Eastern and Western Fronts', MS T–42 (1948).

HALASZYN, J. (ed.), 'German Counterintelligence Activities in Occupied Russia (1941–1944)', MS. P–122 (1953).

HALDER, FRANZ, 'Decisions Affecting the Campaign in Russia (1941–2)', MS. C–067a and b (1949).

—— 'Eastern Campaign, 1941–42 (Strategic Survey), Supplement'. MS. T–6a (1951).

—— 'The French and Russian Campaigns—8 Questions', Ms. B–802 (1947).

HEINRICI, GOTTHARD, 'Revision of MS. T–6', MS. T–6b (1954).

HEUSINGER, ADOLF, 'Eastern Campaign, 1941–2 (Strategic Survey)'. MS. T–6 (1947).

KRÜGER, WALTER, 'Conduct of Operations in the East, 1941–43', MS. C–050 (1949).

MÜLLER-HILLEBRAND, BURKHARD, 'Germany and her Allies in World War II', 2 vols. MS. P–108 (1954).

PETERSEN, WILHELM, 'Campaign Against Russia (Employment of Second Army Engineers)', MS. D–018 (1947).

RENDULIC, LOTHAR, 'A Reflection on the Causes of Defeat', MS. D–077 (1947).

'The Construction of a Strategic Defence Line in the East (A Proposal made by General Olbricht early in 1942)', MS. D–156 (1947).

TOPPE, ALFRED, et al., 'Problems of Supply in Far Reaching Operations', MS. T8 (1951).

'Transportation Problems of the 18th Army during the German Advance to Leningrad (22 June–3 September 1941)', H.Q. 18th Army, 1942, typescript translation, no date.

WARLIMONT, WALTER, 'Supplement to MS. T–6', (1947).

United States Air Force Historical Division Monographs. Aerospace Studies Institute, Air University:

PLOCHER, HERMANN, 'The German Air Force vs. Russia on the Eastern Front', AF–153–155 (1965).

# INDEX

Military formations and appointments not otherwise labelled are German. Source material and the names of towns and small formations mentioned in the appendices are not indexed.

and controversy with Bock, 115–16

and underestimation of Russian Army, 117

uncertain of Hitler's intentions, 127, 159

and logistical planning, 140

and occupation policy, 152–5

and Finnish Army operations, 186

and conduct of operations in Russia, 194–5, 198, 208, 214–17, 220.

and Russian prisoners of war, 213

resignation of, 224–5

Brennecke, General Kurt, Chief of Staff, Army Group 'North', 106

Brenner Pass, 75

Brest Litovsk, Treaty of, 11, 58, 218, 229

Briansk, 201, 222–3

British Empire, 57, 67, 71, 196–7

Brittany, 169

Brooke, General Sir Alan, 121

Bukhovina, 55, 187

Bulgaria, 127, 176

*Bundeswehr*, the, 233

Burma, 181

Bury, J. B., 63

Busch, Field-Marshal Ernst, 35, 171

Canaris, Admiral Wilhelm:

and opposition to Hitler, 33

and Balkan strategy, 43

and espionage in Russia, 91

Canary Islands, 74, 79

Cape Verde Islands, 79

Carpathian Mountains, 163–4, 188

Caucasus region:

proposed Soviet advance from, 43

as a military objective, 110, 120, 167, 193, 196–8, 214, 220, 221, 223, 225, 235, 238, 241

oilfields, 100, 120, 144–5, 146 ff., 150, 238

and political independence, 146–7

and Turkey, 189

Channel, English:

ports, 38, 42

crossing, *see* Operation 'Sea Lion'

reached by Panzer thrust, 48, 97

China, 181

Ciano, Count Galeazzo, Italian Foreign Minister, 76, 213

Clausewitz, General Carl von, 14, 47, 122, 149

Communism:

and history of World War II, 2–4

German generals and, 26, 53, 54 n., 153–4, 213, 233

Hitler wishes to destroy, 12, 48, 151–2, 156, 218, 241

ideology and Soviet State, 156

Crete, 76, 167, 239

Crimea, 196, 221–2

Cripps, Sir Stafford, British Ambassador in Moscow, 170

Croatia, 190

Czechoslovakia, 13, 18, 20, 22 n., 82, 121, 170, 228

Danube, River, 146

Danzig, 170

Dardanelles, 146–7

Dekanosov, Russian Ambassador in Berlin, 170

Denmark, 185, 190

'Directive for Handling Propaganda for Operation Barbarossa', 155

Directives, Hitler's:

preparation and issue of, 8, 31

No. 6, 9 Oct. 1939, 39

No. 16, 16 July 1940, 51

No. 18, 12 Nov. 1940, 77, 83–4

No. 21, 18 Dec. 1940, 110, 112, 114, 118, 124, 127, 166, 184, 193, 197, 214

Annexe to No. 21, 152

No. 23, 6 Feb. 1941, 131

No. 24, 5 Mar. 1941, 178

No. 32, 11 June 1941, 219

No. 33, 19 July 1941, 198

Supplement to No. 33, 23 July 1941, 198, 200, 207, 209

No. 34, 30 July 1941, 209

Division:

number of, 136

5th Light, 165

15th Panzer, 165

2nd Panzer, 166

5th Panzer, 166

*Leibstandarte SS Adolf Hitler*, 166

Panzer and motorized divisions engaged in the Balkans, 271 (Appendix V)

Distribution of, 94 n., 272 (Appendix VI)

Dnieper, River, 100-1, 114-15, 117,
139, 162-3, 193-4, 195, 201, 205,
209, 214-15
Dniester, River, 101, 163
Don Basin, 106-7, 110
Don, River, 144, 148, 198
Donets Basin, 101, 197, 208, 221-3
Dunkirk, evacuation from, 46, 48, 99
Dutch East Indies, 181
Dvina, River, 101, 108, 114-15, 117,
139, 143, 193-4, 201, 205, 216
Dvinsk, 103, 201

East Prussia, 96, 101
Economic Directives, German, 8, 51,
71, 72
Economic policy of Germany:
and autarky, 11, 62, 151, 192
and rearmament, 21
and Four Year Plan, 22
co-ordination with strategy, 30
and *Blitzkrieg*, 49, 94
after victory over France, 50
and preparations for attack on
Russia, 66, 70, 94, 133 ff., 150-1
and Mediterranean strategy, 71
Economic Staff East, 150-1
Egypt, 75
Engel, Major Gerhard, Army Adjutant
to the Führer, 127, 159
Eremenko, Alexei, Marshal of the
Soviet Union, 118
Erfurth, General Waldemar, Head
of German Liaison Staff, Finland,
186
Ethiopian War, 17
Etzdorf, Dr. Hasso von, Foreign Office
Liaison Officer to OKH, 54, 57, 73,
132

Falkenhorst, Colonel-General Niko-
laus von:
Commander, XXI Army Corps,
Norway, 45
Army of Norway, 184, 247
Far East:
communication with, 144-5, 179-
80
Fellgiebel, General of Signals Fritz, 33,
60
Feyerabend, Lieutenant-Colonel Ger-
hard, 81, 97, 100, 147
'Fifth Column', the, 239

Finland:
and German strategy, 41, 77, 79, 82,
100, 130-1, 161, 182 ff., 191, 231,
258-9, 269
as buffer state, 58, 85
Russia and, 71, 77, 132, 231, 256-7
and the Winter War, 1939-40, 86,
92, 174, 182 n., 184-5
and planning for 'Barbarossa', 176
and Eastern Karelia, 185
and volunteers for *Waffen* SS,
190
Finnish Army:
Hitler's opinion of, 162, 182
and 'Barbarossa', 184-7, 247 (Chart
III)
operations against Russia, 209, 264,
268
Finnish Navy, 237 (Appendix VII)
Flak Corps, II, 204
Florence, 76
Foertsch, General Hermann, 31
Foreign Armies East Branch of the
General Staff, *see* OKH
Four Year Plan, 22
France:
defeat of, 9, 41, 44 ff., 52, 73, 116,
125
Hitler and, 12-13, 18-19, 38 ff.,
73 ff., 228-9
Munich crisis, 18, 228
declaration of war, 20, 36, 228
Army of, 36
German campaign against, 38 ff.,
96-7, 137, 145, 228
Colonies of, 73 ff., 126, 141, 168
lacks intelligence about Soviet
Union, 91
and Operation 'Attila', 126-7, 168
under Laval, 141
German Military Administration in,
158
German occupation forces in, 168
and Anti-Comintern Pact, 176
sends volunteer formations to Russia, 190
Franco, General Francisco, 17, 74-5,
77, 231
Frederick the Great, 47
Fricke, Vice-Admiral Kurt, 29
Fritsch, Colonel-General Werner Freiherr von, Commander-in-Chief of
the Army, 1934-8, 22, 28, 32 n.

# INDEX